D1715632

current issues in animal learning

whose dissertation on the inheritance of tentacle number in hydra was done under Jennings. It is Lashley whom Watson singles out for acknowledgment of debt and appreciation in the preface in his first book, but although he also cites four other teachers and colleagues, Watson does not mention Jennings. Espousing a point of view that he had originally ridiculed must certainly have galled Watson, and it seems reasonable that he would balk at public pronouncements of debt to Jennings, a biologist, when Watson and the psychologists he wished to influence were sensitive about the independent status of psychology as a science.

In a later book, Watson comes close to acknowledging a debt to Jennings:

> Behaviorism, as I tried to develop it in my lectures at Columbia in 1912 and in my earliest writings, was an attempt to do one thing—to apply to the experimental study of man the same kind of procedure and the same language of description that many research men have found useful for so many years in the study of animals lower than man. (Watson, 1930, p. v)

In 1904 and 1907, Watson was dissatisfied with Jennings's approach; in 1908 he moved to the same institution, took courses under Jennings, and collaborated with Lashley; by 1914 he had adopted a point of view which differed little in principle from that of Jennings. For both, the theme was objective, experimental analysis of behavior. As Jennings acknowledged, this theme was not original with him but traceable to Loeb,[4] and Jennings's contribution was its careful extension to more complex situations than those consistent with Loeb's theory of tropisms and the separation of behaviorism from the reductionistic trappings of Loeb's physiochemical factors. In more modern terms, Jennings used intervening variables, whereas Loeb insisted upon hypothetical constructs.

A number of characteristics of Watsonian behaviorism are amenable to interpretation as a continuation of Jennings's views. Watson's emphasis upon objective and experimental study and his definition of psychological concepts solely in terms of behavior,

---

[4] Watson had received training under Loeb at Chicago, and this early instruction may have laid the foundation for Watson's later adoption of behavioristic views.

without reference to either phenomenology or physiology, are traceable directly to Jennings. On the other hand, Watson's environmentalism, that is, his argumentative dismissal of genetic determination of behavior, is not amenable to that interpretation but can be construed as a rejection of the field which lured Jennings away from behavioral studies. Still other characteristics of Watsonian behaviorism (i.e., the use of learning as the major explanatory concept for human behavior) appear to be independent of Watson's interaction with Jennings.

A Criticism of Experimentalism and Objectivism

Each of the characteristics of Watsonian behaviorism is subject to criticism and invites appropriate modification. Experimentalism, the view held by both Jennings and Watson that experimentation was virtually requisite for scientific status, has been attacked as inappropriate for certain topics (Deese, 1969) and impracticable in many contexts (Campbell & Stanley, 1963; Barker, 1968). It should not be forgotten that experimentation is a means to the end of obtaining unambiguous, interpretable observations which limit theory; interpretability may be improved by experimentation, but the experiment is the means and not the end. In some cases relatively unambiguous observations may be obtained without experimentation (e.g., through naturalistic observation or systematic sampling procedures) or without all the operations characteristic of experimentation (i.e., quasi-experimental designs, *ad hoc* experiments). As long as the number of reasonable, tenable hypotheses is decreased by the observations which are made, and as long as the latitude available to the theorist is decreased by observation, it matters not whether any or all of the paraphernalia of experimentation is present.

Objectivism, the restriction of scientific observation to observation of external events and the denial of scientific status to introspective or phenomenal observations, is open to modifications similar to those suggested for experimentalism. It appears likely that objective (public) and subjective (private) observations differ only slightly in character and that, under some conditions, private observations may be sufficiently unambiguous to be useful for scientific purposes. Deese (1969) provides an example in his attempt to deal with "understanding" as a psychological process.

> Understanding is the inward sign of the potential for reacting appropriately to what we see or hear. The state of understanding is simply to be contrasted with similar situations when, in reaction to linguistic segments, it does not occur. Contrast the feeling of bafflement when we listen to someone whose English we cannot comprehend, or when we read something, the words of which we know but the totality of which we cannot grasp. In the latter case, we may attend to the words (and understand them as such) or we may allow our minds to wander. In either event, we are incapable of providing a reasonable interpretation of the sequence of sentences we hear or read. (Deese, 1969, p. 516)
>
> Understanding is a psychological rather than a linguistic concept, and it receives its main force from an introspectively discovered inward sense. There are two basic facts with which to begin: one is exemplified in the interpretation of linguistic segments, and the other is the existence of a state of understanding which reveals itself as an introspectively available process. To clarify that last point, then, understanding depends upon the availability of introspection. Each human being is capable of recognizing a state of understanding. (Deese, 1969, pp. 515–516)

Deese is not alone in his renewed concern with phenomenal experience, but there is some controversy about how that experience is to be regarded—as direct knowledge of the nature of the mind or as perceptual reactions to internal rather than to external events, with all the difficulties of interpretation which accompany perceptual status. Hebb (1969) is cautionary:

> Each of us has private information about the activities within his own skin: imagery, pain from headache, hallucinations and so on. But this information—which is indeed private because it is not available to another observer—is nonetheless provided by the mechanism of perceiving the world around us.
>
> Undoubtedly you know much of what goes on in your mind and can report it. Undoubtedly you have private evidence that bears on the current activity of your mind. Thus, in important respects, your knowledge of yourself is more complete and reliable than the knowledge that others may have. Yet it is clear that this knowledge must be inferential and theoretical—at least in part. A second person may be better able than you to evaluate your present mental state and predict

your behavior. In principle self-knowledge may depend on the same kinds of inference that knowledge of another depends upon. (Hebb, 1969, p. 55)

Kendler (1969) also remarks on the relation between phenomenological and perceptual experience:

> I have already acknowledged the reality of phenomenal experience. Its raw observational character is no different from the raw observational character resulting from perceiving an event in the external environment. Consequently I must reject the common distinction between subjective and objective which implies a qualitative difference between the observational base of internally-induced phenomenal experience and the perception of external events. (Kendler, 1969, p. 7)

Interested readers are encouraged to consult the three cited papers for more detailed discussion of this matter; the conclusion here advanced is that objective and subjective evidence (public and private experience) do not differ in the logical or psychological processes involved so much as in the ease with which they may be interpreted. In the case of private experience it is difficult to rule out certain alternative explanations (lying, perceptual deficit, etc.) which can be excluded with public experience. Nevertheless, in certain cases phenomenal, private experience may be virtually the only relevant observation which is available; such observations may not be maximally interpretable, but this does not mean they must be disregarded. Just as data from experiments are generally more easily interpreted than are data gathered by naturalistic observation, so objective data are more likely to be unambiguous in interpretation than are subjective data; but the goal is unambiguous limitation of theory, and whatever observations move us toward that goal are acceptable. When patients whose brains are electrically stimulated describe their feelings and thoughts to us, we would be wise to listen; if we wish to understand psychological phenomena, be they the effects of colored lights or of drugs, it may be useful to experience those phenomena. The extent to which private, phenomenal experience is effective in restricting tenable theory depends upon the nature of that experience as well as the nature of the available hypotheses and theories, but it is clearly not a simple matter of public observations being scientifically useful and private observations being scientifically useless. As Deese (1969) states:

We have so much direct evidence as to the nature of our minds that we start with immeasurably more than does our colleague who genuinely and seriously tries to understand the mind of the dog or of the chimpanzee. (Deese, 1969, p. 517)

In summary, the behavioristic principles of experimentalism and objectivism can be subsumed under the principle of maximizing interpretable observations. The methods of preparing for observations (experimentation, survey, or naturalistic observation) and the kinds of observations (public or private) which will be more valuable depend upon the nature of the hypotheses which are still tenable; in some cases private but common observations may suffice to make certain theories untenable or unattractive.

A CRITICISM OF BEHAVIORISTIC DEFINITIONAL PROCEDURES

Behavioristic definitions of psychological concepts are normally operational. Definitions are operational when they specify, at least in principle, the procedures required to determine whether an event qualifies as an example of a concept. The operational character of behavioristic definitions is not objectionable; it is highly desirable to ensure the relevance of observations to concepts and theories (Jensen, 1961, 1967). Behavioristic definitions are normally also behavioric [5] (i.e., the operations specified include observations of overt reactions rather than of phenomenal experience, stimulus energies, physiological activity, etc.). Behavioric definitions are specifically criticized by Deese (1969) in attempting to deal with the concept of "understanding."

The important point, however, is that understanding *leads to no particular behavior*. Even when there is semantic agreement, the specific forms in which it occurs differ, and these may be of trivial importance. Thus, there is no way to link understanding or interpretation with particular behavior. There is no way, then, to tie these concepts, in the traditional sense, to dependent variables or to particular measures of behavior. Even to tie the concept to something specific that still cannot be represented behaviorally—such as paraphase—requires the introduction of an elaborate and sophisticated linguistic theory. Yet, I

[5] *Behavioric* means by behavior and contrasts with *behavioral*, pertaining to behavior. Behavioric definitions are given solely in terms of behavior.

submit that the concept is central to the theory of human thought, and any attempt to eliminate or ignore it, in the interest of making psychology conform to the reputed canons of experimental inference, is worse than misguided. (Deese, 1969, p. 516)

Even more unmanageable problems have been encountered by behavioristic treatments of sensation and perception. "Green" can be operationally defined as the wave length of monochromatic light or by the physiological response of certain kinds of cells in the lateral geniculate body, but there is no simple way to define the organismic reaction involved in behavioric terms because there is no invariant or unambiguous overt response associated with this reaction. The standard behavioristic tactic is to train an animal so that its behavior becomes contingent upon the stimulus and thereby to make the behavior of an animal unambiguous and easily interpreted as a sign of an otherwise unobservable state. Similar operations are used to ensure that verbal reports of a subject are interpretable (instructions, pretraining). It should be noted that operations intended to improve the interpretability of private phenomenal experience (i.e., replication, comparison with effects of other stimuli, etc.) are possible and appropriate, and common among psychophysicists (e.g., von Békésy, 1967), and that few significant phenomena in psychophysics have not been first identified in phenomenal experience before being demonstrated elsewhere. In the study of sensory processes, phenomenal experience has remained a major source of information for successful investigators. Despite all this, behavioristic definitions of perceptions from the time of Jennings to the present have made no use of stimulus characteristics, introspective or phenomenal aspects, or physiological mechanisms in their definitions, and have attempted to define perception as "nothing more nor less than a discriminatory response," with little regard even for the differentiation between the perception and the instrumental responding which is involved in the discriminatory response (Kanfer, 1956).

The major purpose of this paper is to present an alternative definitional procedure for psychology, one adequate for the definition of reflexes, motoric activities, sensations, motives, thoughts, and moods, and one which is free from the circumlocutions typical of behavioristic treatments of topics like perception and cognition.

The alternative definitional procedure, polythetic definition, is not restricted to behavioric characteristics.

POLYTHETICISM [6]

Polytheticism is a point of view associated with recent innovations in biological classification (i.e., in the dividing of the diversity of organisms into species, genera, and higher taxa). This point of view, which was reviewed by Sokal and Sneath in a book entitled *Principles of Numerical Taxonomy* (1963) and popularized by Sokal in *Scientific American* (1966), constitutes an approach which differs markedly from early attempts at biological classification. These early efforts were based upon Aristotelian principles and were a search for the *essence* of a taxonomic group. One or a few *key characters* were sought which expressed these essences, and membership in a group was determined by the presence of these key characters (i.e., a chordate has a notochord, an annelid has setae, a sponge has choanocytes, etc.). In contrast, the polythetic point of view holds that taxonomic concepts are not effectively defined by one or a few key characters, even though those characters may in fact serve to identify members of different groups of animals. According to this newer view, taxonomic classification divides organisms into *natural groups* on the basis of over-all similarity, and membership in such natural groups is correlated with many characters, no one of which is a priori more important than any other.

Sneath (1962) suggested that the older approach, with its reliance upon one or a few characters, be termed *monothetic*, in contrast with the newer approach, which considers many correlated characters and is termed *polythetic*. One example contrasting the approaches is the monothetic definition of man as "the biped which talks." It is possible to criticize this definition by pointing out that it would include a trained parrot in the ranks of man, but this is not the only criticism that the polythetic taxonomist would make. He would also indicate that a one-legged deaf-mute is still a man, even though he has neither of the characters in the definition. He is

<hr>

[6] This section borrows heavily from an earlier discussion of polythetic operationism (Jensen, 1967).

a man because he has hundreds of other characters (the shape of the nose, the number and kind of teeth, the human pelvis, ABO blood group, and so on) which are typically found in other men. From the polythetic point of view, no one or no small number of characters is ever either necessary or sufficient to define a class or taxon. The entire set of those characters which are typical of members of the taxon and not of members of other equivalent taxa defines the class or taxon. Polythetic and monothetic definitions differ in more than the number of characters which are used in determining classification; they differ as well in the logical relationship between characters and group membership. In monothetic classes more than one character may be relevant but all these characters *must* be present in a member of the class. In polythetic classes, group membership is determined by over-all similarity, that is, by the presence of a sizable number of the many characters typical of the group.

Although polythetic concepts are not new in science, what *is* new is the availability of sophisticated statistical techniques and electronic computational devices which make feasible the use of polythetic concepts, and much of the discussion of numerical taxonomy concerns the practical problems of exploiting the polythetic point of view with multivariate methods (cluster analysis, etc.). Our concern is not with these matters but with the conceptual advantages accruing from polythetic thinking. What are the advantages of polythetic concepts in scientific endeavors?

Sokal and Sneath (1963, p. 15) write, "The advantages of polythetic groups are that they are 'natural,' have a high content of information, and are useful for many purposes." Because of this, natural classes have the advantage of effective extrapolation or generalization. Anything which is true of one member of such a class is probably, though not necessarily, true of all other members of that natural class. In contrast, membership in a monothetically derived or "arbitrary" class may provide information only about the character defining the class; membership provides assurance only about a few characteristics and thus expresses little information.

The use of polythetic concepts and natural classes has not been restricted to taxonomic investigations but has also occurred in the study of morphology. The concept of homology, which antedated evolutionary theory, was a recognition that the "same" structure could be found repeated in one animal (serial homology) or in different animals (special homology) (Boyden, 1947). Homology can be contrasted with analogy; analogous organs have similar functions but not the mass of similar features shared by homologous organs.

Let us take a simple example: A human arm, a chimpanzee's arm, and a monkey's arm all have many characters in common; the arm of an octopus obviously has only a very few features in common with the other arms. If we define *arm* monothetically as any prehensile appendage, we classify all four arms together but abbreviate very little information. If we define the concept *arm* polythetically, we compare the four arms on the basis of a large number of characters, or features, and discover that three are very similar and that one is different from the rest. We shall therefore include only the arms of man, ape, and monkey in our scientific concept but shall thereby abbreviate much more information. Homologous organs are members of natural or polythetic classes; the arms of men, apes, and monkeys are homologous with and share an immense number of attributes with the wings of birds and bats; all these structures form a single natural group, the vertebrate forelimb. In contrast, the wings of insects and the wings of birds, even though they share certain specific characteristics appertaining chiefly to their function as aerodynamic surfaces, are not homologous, but analogous. They do not form a natural group, and the biological concept of wing, if it includes those of birds and those of bees, has little informational value. An immense amount of investigation in biology has involved the search for homologies, for natural classes which express considerable information and within which generalization or extrapolation, from one particular organ in one particular organism to other organs and other organisms, is likely to be effective.

The concepts of homology and analogy (i.e., of polythetic and monothetic classes) have been applied to behaviors as well as to organs. Behaviors are not spatial subdivisions of organisms, but subdivisions in time and space of the larger set of characters which constitute an organism. They are groups of characters which occur close together in time and space within the sequence of changing characters of an organism. Medewar's phrase is "natural behavior structures or episodes." Human walking involves a complex spatio-temporal pattern—left arm and right leg forward, and so forth. This behavior is clearly homologous to the quadripedal walking of cats, which involves similar crossed-extensor movement patterns, similar spinal mechanisms, etc. The running of a lizard and the swimming of a shark are also homologous, though less completely similar. All these behaviors involve similar patterns of torso flexion, action of reciprocally innervated muscles, equivalent neurological mechanisms, etc. In contrast, the locomotion of a planaria or a paramecium would appear to be analogous, rather than homologous, to mammalian locomotion.

The concept of homology has been implicit in the study of behavior of laboratory mammals and subsequent extrapolation to the behavior of other animals, including man. The information available about digestive behaviors of rats can usually be applied to the digestive behaviors of other mammals; the information relevant to the breathing of rabbits can usually be applied to the breathing of other mammals; a specific behavior in one mammal typically resembles that behavior in another mammal in motoric organization, internal mechanisms, and environmental controls. Much of the work of ethologists can be understood as the search for behavioral homologies, as among the various courtship ceremonies of ducks (Lorenz, 1958), the different displays of cichlid fishes (Baerends & Baerends, 1950), and the nest-building behaviors of species of lovebirds (Dilger, 1962). The differentiation between homology and analogy is frequently applied to behaviors by ethologists.

We have, so far, applied the principles of polythetic definition to organisms, organs, and behaviors. The same principles can also be applied to influences upon behavior; one can group events which influence behavior into natural classes, that is, habituation, learning, maturation, and inheritance. According to the principles of polythetic definition, these different influence processes would be expected to differ in many aspects, not simply in a particular key character or aspect. These natural classes can in turn be subdivided into natural classes. One may ask, for example, what are the polythetic, natural classes of instances of learning? This, to be sure, is not how we have usually dealt with this topic. Typically, learning has been treated monothetically, with attention to the single, minimal specification which will suffice (Jensen, 1961; Rescorla, 1967). In a controversy over whether planaria learn, several different monothetic definitions of learning were utilized: McConnell (1965) defined learning by reference to "a chemical change"; James and Halas (1964) operationally defined learning by reference to resistance to extinction; Jensen (1965) relied upon the importance of CS–US association. All three are examples of monothetic thinking and reliance upon key characters for identification of examples of concepts.

Polythetic treatment of the concept of learning was anticipated by Pantin (1965) when he wrote, "We have no guarantee that the machinery of learning, the adaptive modification of behavior through past experience, always belongs to a single class"; Jensen (1965) also anticipated this when he suggested that the problem of identifying learning was a problem of distinguishing between homology and analogy in behavioral processes. Multiple parametric characteristics have been used to define and classify instances of habituation (Thompson & Spencer, 1966). This method approximates polythetic definition, as do cases of convergent operationism (Campbell & Fiske, 1959; Garner, Hake, & Eriksen, 1956; Garner, 1954). Thompson and Spencer (1966) discuss nine common characteristics of habituation which may serve as the detailed operational definition of habituation, and then note that "the extent to which any other response decrements satisfy these characteristics will thus determine whether they can be called habituation." If not all these characteristics need be present, such a list of common characteristics would clearly constitute polythetic definition.

It must be recognized that the polythetic method requires a number of cases and a number of characters; unless an instance of a concept can be described by much more than the key character of the effect of one independent variable upon one dependent variable, the polythetic method cannot be applied. This fact has enormous consequences for the evaluation of past psychological research and for the planning of future research. It suggests that we must increase the amount and variety of information which we gather, though we presumably should do this without interfering with the increase in interpretability of data normally resulting from experimental control.

There are several techniques for increasing the information we obtain through our experimental studies. One technique, familiar to both psychologists and biologists, is the factorial experiment in which several independent variables are simultaneously manipulated. Another technique is the addition of physiological independent variables (lesions, intracranial stimulation, drug treatment, and others) and dependent variables (catecholamine levels, eosinophilia, and so forth). A third technique, typically employed by ethologists, is that of simultaneous observation and recording of many behavioral variables. One example of the use of ethological observation is the paper by Reynierse, Scavio, and Ulness which is included in this volume. Another example, from my own laboratory, is an unpublished study by Mrs. Mahmuda Khanum concerning the behavior of rats in several situations (straight runway and shock box). Seventeen distinct behaviors were distinguished and given an alphabetic designation (e, eating; a, air sniffing; d, defecating; r, resting; etc.). Every 3 seconds during an experimental trial, the rat being studied was observed, its behavior classified, and the appropriate alphabetical symbol recorded. Several groups of rats were given acquisition and extinction training with food in a straight alley; other groups were given noncontingent reinforcement training by presentation of pellets, milk, shock, or no reinforcement 30 seconds after the rat was placed in a distinctive compartment. Indicative of the potential value of polythetic data is the finding that similar behavior appeared during extinction following food-rewarded maze acquisition training and during shock training. In both cases there were decreased locomotion, increased defecation and urination, decreased sniffing, increased crouching with hair erect, and similar occurrences. Here is an example of homology in behavioral effects, a case of very different environmental events producing polythetically similar behavioral content. What Mowrer (1960) termed "disappointment" and "fear" are polythetically similar and may form a single natural class of events. To differentiate fear from disappointment solely on the basis of a difference in stimulus situations which produce these behavioral patterns would be monothetic; to combine them on the basis of many shared characteristics would be polythetic. The nature of the behavioral effect suggests very strongly that arousal of the sympathetic nervous system is prominent in fear-disappointment, since the sympathetic nervous system is responsible for defecation, urination, and hair erection. The polythetic data forced us to this view in a way that conventional data (i.e., choice and latencies) could hardly do. Collection of polythetic data seems desirable in a wide variety of behavioral situations because of the efficiency with which it determines and limits theoretical statements.

Another example of the use of polythetic principles in examining controversial phenomena involves the reports of transfer of memory by injection (e.g., Jacobson et al., 1965). One may ask the polythetic question: What is the total pattern of behavioral effects produced by training of various kinds (shock to light signal, food to light signal, and unreinforced light presentation) and by injection of RNA extracted from the animals given various kinds of training? It could be that animals injected with RNA extracted from trained donors behave in a manner polythetically similar to the behavior of the donor animals, and if this occurs, the evidence for transfer of training by injection would be very strong. It also could be possible that the behavior of recipients and donors shows very limited similarities and that there is no homology but only analogy between the behavioral effects of training and those of injection of RNA from trained animals. It is possible that RNA injections have many effects and that by using monothetic data, by restricting attention to one or a very few variables, one can make a strong case for the view that learning is transferred by injection; or by choosing other monothetic data, by attending to other variables, one can make a strong case against that proposition. One can effectively interpret the experimental results only when those results are polythetic, when the outcome is a complex of many behavioral characters rather than a single character, such as the increased speed of response.

In some cases the addition of even a single extra variable may provide a considerable increment in information which limits and determines theory. Allison (personal communication) recorded both running time and retrace time in straight alleys and found that opportunity to retrace retards extinction relative to control animals equated according to time in the goal box. This effect does not interact with effects of magnitude of reward; on these and other grounds Allison concludes that retracing does not influence the excitatory effects of reward but does reduce the inhibitory effects of nonreward. Reaching this conclusion was greatly facilitated by adding a variable (opportunity to retrace and latency of retrace) to the traditional alleyway variable (opportunity to run the alley and latency of running).

Like behaviorism before it, polytheticism originated in biology and was first applied in psychology to clarify controversies arising in the study of animal behavior. In the next section we shall see that polytheticism, like behaviorism before it, may have major consequences for general psychology.

A Polythetic Taxonomy of Psychological and Biological Processes

The principles of polythetic classification can be used to clarify the relations among major psychological and biological concepts. That these relations are none too clear is indicated by the continuation of certain controversies over many decades, despite significant empirical and theoretical advances. One such controversy involves the relationship between heredity and environment, nature and nurture, or instinct and learning (Hirsch, 1967; Lorenz, 1965). Another controversy involves the relationship between molar behaviors and intraorganismic events of other kinds (cellular and biochemical events); the reductionist would hold that behavioral events are preferably to be explained in terms of intraorganismic nonbehavioral events, but the behaviorist would hold that such reductive explanation is unnecessary for scientific psychology and that prediction from theory is all that is possible or desirable in science (Kessen & Kimble, 1952). The polythetic point of view offers a resolution to these controversies through a taxonomic analysis of events. This analysis applies the principles of polythetic taxonomy to the variety of events which scientists study.

Natural phenomena differ in spatiotemporal extension. Some are large; some are very small. Some events or phenomena are relatively permanent; these are usually called objects. Other events or phenomena are relatively brief and are termed processes or transient events; a neural impulse would be an example. Certain observational techniques (e.g., time-lapse photography) make visible the transient, changeable character of events or phenomena which are normally considered objects; the seed sprouts into a plant, grows, and finally withers. The human being proceeds from conception to birth to maturity to death. A population of organisms evolves over eons of time. Even stars age and change. Thus, although all is flux, events differ in temporal extension (time from beginning to end) as well as in spatial extension (size).

Temporal and spatial extension are not the only important characteristics of natural phenomena, but these suffice to differentiate many of the classes of natural phenomena or events. The events of biology are intermediate in extent in both space and time since organisms are moderate in size and persisting though impermanent in time. Biological events may be subdivided according to temporal extent and according to spatial extent relative to the organisms involved in them. Some biological events are phenomena of populations or groups of organisms, some of organisms, some of organs, some of tissues or cellular masses, some of cells, and some of molecules. Some phenomena at each of these levels are transient, some are persisting: a stampede is a population event which is clearly more transient than the herd which stampedes; a startle reflex, the behavior of eating, and the adolescent growth spurt are all phenomena of organisms but differ in temporal extent, the startle reflex being most transient and the growth spurt most persisting.

Different biological specialties typically focus upon different classes of biological events. Neurophysiology focuses upon transient events in neural tissue; neuroanatomy focuses upon less transient characteristics of the same tissue. Psychology, embryology, genetics, and comparative anatomy deal with organismic characteristics, with psychology focusing upon the most transient, and comparative anatomy upon the most persisting, since homologous structures may persist through geologic epochs.

While certain classes of biological events are easy to separate on the space-time continuum, some classes of biological events are not easily distinguished in terms of spatiotemporal extension. Specifically, reflexes, postures, motor activities, sensations, drives, moods, intentions, and thoughts are all organismic activities overlapping in both time and space. This suggests that all neurologically organized organismic activities (e.g., digestive reflexes, defecation, ingestion, respiration, circulation, thermoregulation, sensations, locomotion, cognitions, preferences, emotions) are members of a single natural class or taxon which differs in spatiotemporal extension from other natural classes of biological processes (e.g., phylogenesis, embryogenesis, cellular responses like neural impulses and muscular contraction, and others).

It is specifically suggested that this class of transient organismic activities, termed *biopsychological processes*, is a natural or polythetic class within which generalization and extrapolation are useful. The focal concepts of psychology (specific activities, reflexes, behaviors, and the like) fall into this group of biopsychological processes, but certain other concepts important in psychology do not. For example, learning and habituation are members of a group of longer-term organismic and histological adaptations which also includes the phsysiological adaptation to work-stress and endocrinological changes like those involved in the general adaptation syndrome of Selye. Still other psychological concepts (e.g., excitation and inhibition) refer to cellular and biochemical processes; although psychology considers these events as they influence or comprise biopsychological processes, the focus of psychology is upon biopsychological processes.

It is usually presumed that psychologists study particular biochemical events, adaptational processes, embryological changes, and genetic influences in order to predict and understand biopsychological processes. An alternative point of view is that certain of these other events are polythetic aspects of biopsychological processes and that, though various classes of events (biopsychological, embryological, phylogenetic, etc.) are polythetically different, individual events of these different classes can be combined into polythetic concepts. Certain occurrences of one type may be correlated with and causally related to events of other types; it is possible to consider these correlated events to be multiple aspects of a single polythetically conceived process. According to this usage, a polythetic biopsychological concept corresponds to the entire set of events which correlate with a particular biopsychological event; the polythetic concept of a biopsychological event would include relevant behavioric characteristics, phenomenological character, neurological activity, the stimuli which elicit it, concurrent behaviors which facilitate it, and the experiences, development, and phylogeny which are antecedent to and necessary for it.

In the space-time continuum, a polythetic biopsychological process refers to a set of correlated events; and whether an event is inside or outside the organism, or in the distant past, recent past, present, or future, is irrelevant. A polythetically conceived biopsychological process may be described as a temporally and spatially extended network of events which includes certain biopsychological events. Note that only certain, not all, events of one type will be relevant for a particular biopsychological event. The patellar reflex as a polythetic biopsychological concept includes the stimulus hammer blow to tendon but not the stimulus light to the eye, and includes neural activity in the lumbar portion of the spinal cord but not neural activity in the autonomic nervous system. A different polythetic biopsychological process, pupillary reflex, would refer to another set of correlated events that includes light to eye, activity in the autonomic nervous system, and contraction of certain smooth muscles of the iris.

The polythetic biopsychological concept is an answer to the question of what characteristics define an organismic activity. Certainly the motoric organization is relevant, but why not include the phenomenal character associated with or the neural activity producing the motoric outflow? Should the typical stimulus eliciting it not also be considered a characteristic? Should necessary conditions of training, development, and inheritance not also be included? The polythetic biopsychological concept accepts all typical characteristics of a biopsychological activity as significant portions of its definition and accepts all correlated characters as relevant. Although the core or center of the network of intercorrelations is a biopsychological event or activity, the network also includes other events, all of which are weighted according to the extent that they intercorrelate.

It should be noted that the class of biopsychological activities is broader than *behavior;* behaviors are included among the biopsychological processes, but so are a number of activities which do not qualify as overt behaviors (sensory reactions, perceptions, images, thought, moods, emotions) and some which psychologists have not typically studied (digestive reflexes, respiratory and circulatory activity). These subgroups or subspecies of biopsycholog-ical processes are polythetically defined by characteristic observable motoric and glandular components, by private phenomenal characteristics, by activity of particular classes of neurons, and by genetic differences which influence them, by influences of embryo-logical processes, and by differing effects of physiological adaptions (especially specific experiential influences through learning and habituation). Not all these characteristics need be present; for example, the biopsychological processes of sensation have few specific motoric components and the biopsychological processes of peristalsis and digestive activity normally produce no phenomenal content, but they are nevertheless members of the general class of biopsychological activities. The presence or absence of aspects as well as the character of the aspects present are all usable informa-tion for taxonomic classification of biopsychological processes into groups and subgroups (Sokal & Sneath, 1963).

The polythetic biopsychologist would hold that psychology is the science of polythetic biopsychological processes, among which generalization is reasonable. These processes may be differentiated and classified into smaller classes of greater polythetic similarity. To the polythetic biopsychologist the higher mental processes (thinking), emotions, and locomotor patterns are to be considered as different from reflexes rather than as somehow derived from them. These types of biopsychological processes have much in common but also differ substantially; they are different subcategories of the set of processes which comprise the proper subject matter of psychology.

It is difficult to estimate a priori the number of subcategories of biopsychological processes that can be usefully differentiated. The upper limit is probably the number of classes of independently functioning neurons in the central nervous system—a very great number indeed. This number can be made manageable, just as is the large number of biological species, by the use of higher taxono-mic categories.

Some psychological concepts, for example intelligence and personality, do not appear to correspond to polythetic groupings but instead appear to be monothetic groupings of polythetic biopsychological processes. Intelligence is the set of cognitive and perceptual activities which are relevant to problem solving; personality is the monothetically defined set of socially relevant biopsychological processes. Other psychological concepts, as previously mentioned for conditioning and habituation, may be members of other classes of biological processes but, although very significant to the prediction or understanding of particular biopsychological processes, are not biopsychological processes. In other words, a clear distinction can be made between biopsychological processes and the other biological processes which are determinants or aspects of many biopsychological processes. For example, learning refers to a difference in behavior dependent upon differential training. A habit, on the other hand, refers to a particular biopsychological activity or event for which training is important. Instinct can refer to either biopsychological processes or to influences upon them. Instinct, as in "the aggressive instinct," refers to a kind of behavior rather than an influence, but when opposed to learning refers to a genetic or evolutionary influence upon a biopsychological activity.

Much of the confusion regarding learning and instinct involves a failure to recognize the presence of multiple influences upon behavior (i.e., current stimulation, prior stimulation, developmental stage, genetic state) and a failure to differentiate influences upon biopsychological processes from the biopsychological activities per se. The controversies regarding nature and nurture or learning and instinct have involved differential emphasis upon different influences; the instinct theorist emphasizes the influence of evolution upon behavior, whereas the learning theorist emphasizes the effect of training on behavior. The polythetic biopsychologist would hold that any biopsychological process is certain to be the result of evolution and embryology and almost certain also to be the outcome of experiential interaction with the environment as well as of stimulation by the environment. He would hold that one must appreciate all relevant influences to predict and understand the activity being studied. Similarly the polythetic biopsychologist would take an inclusive stance in the reductionistic controversy and would maintain that the biochemical events and histologically localized processes involved in an activity are important, but that these molecular aspects are simply additional grist for the same polythetic mill and are neither more nor less important than more molar aspects of a biopsychological activity.

Psychology, according to the analysis here made, is a part of biology. Although for historical and practical reasons it will almost certainly remain separate as an academic discipline, as an intellectual discipline it is a portion of the larger field of biology because the events, processes, and phenomena it studies are subclasses of biological processes.

In one sense polythetic biopsychology is not at all a new development. More than one of my colleagues, when presented with this point of view, exclaimed that the approach was not original but was simply a description of how really thoughtful psychologists have always worked, even if their published papers do not show their concern for all aspects of the processes they study. Presumably, by naming and codifying this approach we will make it easier to teach and easier to do.

In terms of historical antecedents, polythetic biopsychology is not new. In fact, as the perceptive reader might have noted, it resembles the position which Watson expressed in 1907, before becoming a behaviorist: "Is simple reaction to a stimulus the only objective *manifestation* of the perceptual behavior in man? Certainly not! There are hundreds of others beside the overt movement. . . . It is the task of the experimental psychologist to refine upon and to add to this list of objective manifestations of the perceptual act." Let us hope that the pendulum of psychological interest, swung far to the side of introspection, phenomenal character, and sensory reactions by the structuralists and far to the side of experimental study of overt motoric behaviors by the behaviorists, will be recentered upon the study of *all aspects of all subclasses of biopsychological processes.*

Polythetic biopsychology may have an influence upon research by providing a rationale for multiplexing dependent variables and an impetus for developing standard procedures for collecting, abbreviating, and interpreting polythetic data. It may influence teaching and application by justifying a new organization of material (i.e., collection of information about all aspects of particular biopsychological processes—phenomenal character, motoric organization, neurological mechanisms, stimulus controls, interaction with other biopsychological activities, and relationship to other biological processes, including learning, maturation, and genetic determination). Polythetic biopsychology may have such effects because it represents a new style of psychological thinking. The immediate goal of psychological investigation is changed from construction and testing of complex theories which organize monothetic concepts (e.g., Kendler, 1969) to the enrichment and refinement of polythetic concepts representing particular biopsychological processes. A major goal of psychological investigation becomes the accumulation of information regarding all the aspects of all major varieties of biopsychological processes, and the development of a taxonomy of biopsychological processes which abbreviates the information accumulated, not by deduction from axioms, but by probabilistic generalization among homologues.

There are terminological and methodological differences that have divided psychologists from one another and from ethologists, neurologists, and neurophysiologists. The polythetic style of thought accepts these differences as reflecting the polythetic differences in the biopsychological processes typically studied by these groups of investigators. Polythetic biopsychology offers a means of unifying these fields of investigation by its emphasis on the fundamental similarity of all biopsychological activities and on the enlightenment that the study of one such process may provide to the study of all.

REFERENCES

Baerends, G. P., & Baerends, Jos. M. An introduction to the ethology of cichlid fishes. *Behaviour Supp.*, 1950, **1**, 1.

Barker, R. G. *Ecological psychology.* Stanford, California: Stanford University Press, 1968.

Békésy, G. von. *Sensory inhibition.* Princeton: Princeton University Press, 1967.

Boyden, A. Homology and analogy. *American Midland Naturalist,* 1947, **37**, 648.

Campbell, D. T., & Fiske, D. W. Convergent and discriminant validation by the multitrait-multimethod matrix. *Psychol. Bull.*, 1959, **56**, 81–105.

Campbell, D. T., & Stanley, J. C. Experimental and quasi-experimental designs for research on teaching. In N. L. Gage (Ed.), *Handbook of research on teaching.* Chicago: Rand McNally, 1963. Pp. 171–246.

Deese, J. Behavior and fact. *Amer. Psychologist,* 1969, **24**, 515–522.

Dilger, W. C. The behavior of lovebirds. *Scientific American,* 1962, **206**(1), 88.

Garner, W. R. Context effects and the validity of loudness scales. *J. exp. Psychol.*, 1954, **48**, 218–224.

Garner, W. R., Hake, H. W., & Eriksen, C. W. Operationism and the concept of perception. *Psychol. Rev.*, 1956, **63**, 149–159.

Hebb, D. O. The mind's eye. *Psychology Today*, 1969, **2**, 54–57, 67–68.

Hirsch, J. Behavior-genetic, or "experimental," analysis: The challenge of science versus the lure of technology. *Amer. Psychologist*, 1967, **22**, 118–130.

Jacobson, A. L., Babich, F. R., Bubash, Suzanne, & Jacobson, Ann. Differential approach tendencies produced by injection of ribonucleic acid from trained rats. *Science*, 1965, **150**, 636–637.

James, R. L., & Halas, E. S. No difference in extinction behavior in planaria following various types and amounts of training. *Psychol. Rec.*, 1964, **14**, 1.

Jennings, H. S. *Contributions to the study of the behavior of lower organisms*. Washington: Carnegie Institution, 1904.

Jennings, H. S. *Behavior of the lower organisms*. New York: Columbia University Press, 1906.

Jennings, H. S. The interpretation of the behavior of the lower organisms. *Science*, n.s., 1908, **27**, 698–709.

Jensen, D. D. Operationism and the question "Is this behavior learned or innate?" *Behaviour*, 1961, **17**, 1–8.

Jensen, D. D. Foreword to the 1962 edition. In H. S. Jennings, *Behavior of the lower organisms*. Bloomington: Indiana University Press, 1962.

Jensen, D. D. Paramecia, planaria, and pseudo-learning. *Animal Behaviour Supp.*, 1965, **1**, 9–20.

Jensen, D. D. Polythetic operationism and the phylogeny of learning. In W. Corning & S. Ratner (Eds.), *Chemistry of learning*. New York: Plenum Press, 1967.

Kanfer, F. H. Perception: Identification and instrumental activity. *Psychol. Rev.*, 1956, **63**, 317–329.

Kendler, H. H. The unity of psychology. *Newsletter of Division 1, American Psychological Association*, 1969, **8**, 1–8.

Kessen, W., & Kimble, G. A. "Dynamic systems" and theory construction. *Psychol. Rev.*, 1952, **59**, 263–267.

Lorenz, K. The evolution of behavior. *Scientific American*, 1958, **199**(6).

Lorenz, K. *Evolution and modification of behavior*. Chicago: University of Chicago Press, 1965.

McConnell, J. V. Cannibals, chemicals, and contiguity. *Animal Behaviour Supp.*, 1965, **1**, 61–66.

Mowrer, O. H. *Learning theory and personality*. New York: Wiley, 1960.

Pantin, C. F. A. Learning, world-models, and pre-adaptation. *Animal Behaviour Supp.*, 1965, **1**, 1.

Rescorla, R. A. Pavlovian conditioning and its proper control procedures. *Psychol. Rev.*, 1967, **74**, 71–80.

Sneath, P. H. A. The construction of taxonomic groups. In G. C. Ainsworth & P. H. A. Sneath (Eds.), *Microbial classification, 12th symposium of the society for general microbiology*. Cambridge, Massachusetts: Cambridge University Press, 1962. P. 289.

Sokal, R. R. Numerical taxonomy. *Scientific American*, 1966, **215**, 106.

Sokal, R. R., & Sneath, P. H. A. *Principles of numerical taxonomy.* San Francisco: W. H. Freeman, 1963.

Thompson, R. F., & Spencer, W. A. Habituation: A model phenomenon for the study of neuronal substrates of behavior. *Psychol. Rev.*, 1966, **73**, 16–43.

Watson, J. B. Animal psychology. *Psychol. Bull.*, 1905, **2**, 144–147.

Watson, J. B. The behavior of lower organisms. *Psychol. Bull.*, 1907, **4**, 288–296.

Watson, J. B. *Behavior: An introduction to comparative psychology.* New York: Holt, 1914.

Watson, J. B. *Behaviorism* (Rev. ed.). New York: Morton, 1930.

Watson, J. B. John Broadus Watson. In Murchison (Ed.), *A History of psychology in autobiography: Vol. III.* Worcester, Massachusetts: Clark University Press, 1934. Pp. 271–281.

An Ethological Analysis of Classically Conditioned Fear[1]

JAMES H. REYNIERSE, MICHAEL J. SCAVIO, Jr.,
and JAMES D. ULNESS

University of Nebraska[2]

The conventional use of observation and behavioral description by ethologists contrasts with the occasional use of these techniques within animal learning psychology. Historically, preoccupation during the 1940s and 1950s with the prevailing "drive" theories of American learning psychology, as well as the development and application of automated electronic devices for programming stimulus events and recording responses, may have encouraged recognition of the motivational and theoretical contributions of ethology and yet discouraged recognition of its methodological contributions. In this connection, Bitterman (1965), while not distinguishing between merely "watching" and the systematic observation and recording techniques of ethology, did point out in a footnote the compatibility of automated equipment and observation. Equating "watching" with systematic observation, however, would be a serious error, and although many investigators comment about observation procedures and may even rely upon casual observations as further support for behavioral interpretation, the animal learning psychologist rarely applies the same rigor to observational procedures as would normally be used in selecting an experimental design or providing control over stimulus and response contingencies.

[1] This research was supported by NIMH research grants MH 12716–01, MH 12716–02, and MH 12716–03. We are pleased to acknowledge the assistance of Dianne Burgin, Marilyn Durbon, and Kathy Ness, who cheerfully reviewed and summarized our measures of behavior from the tapes where they were recorded.

[2] Now at Hope College, Holland, Michigan; the State University of Iowa, Iowa City; and Concordia College, Moorhead, Minnesota, respectively.

Within the framework of psychological laboratory experiments, detailed observations of behavior, although infrequent, have produced fruitful results with considerable explanatory value. For example, Guthrie and Horton's (1946) detailed analyses of cats in a puzzle box revealed the stereotype and repetitiveness of cats' behavior, thereby providing support for Guthrie's contiguity position. Another classical example is Sheffield's (1948) analysis of the earlier Brogden, Lipman, and Culler (1938) experiment, which compared classical and instrumental avoidance procedures for the running response in guinea pigs and found the instrumental avoidance procedure to be superior. Sheffield replicated their study, analyzed behavior more completely, and noted that the two procedures yielded different behaviors at shock onset. Under the classical conditioning procedure, the presentation of shock frequently elicited behavior which was incompatible with running, for example, crouching, thus accounting in part for the superiority of the instrumental avoidance procedure. Most recently, Jensen (1967) pointed out the desirability of observing many behavioral variables within learning experiments and suggested that a polythetic approach which considers many correlated dependent variables is a superior strategy to the monothetic approach typical of learning experimentation which relies only upon one or a few dependent variables.

The present study applies an ethological and polythetic approach to investigate classical fear conditioning in the unrestrained albino rat.

METHODS

The subjects were 39 experimentally naïve male albino rats of the Sasco strain.[3] All rats were 100–130 days old at the beginning of the experiment.

The apparatus consisted of a plastic experimental box, 17 inches long, 4 1/2 inches wide, and 14 inches high. The front wall was constructed of clear Plexiglas, permitting unobstructed observation; the remaining three walls were opaque white plastic backed by dark blue plastic. Under the general illumination provided by a 7 1/2-watt bulb located centrally 6 inches above and 3 inches in

[3] Sasco rats were obtained from Sasco, 5309 N. 24 St., Omaha, Nebr.

front of the experimental box, the interior was white; but when the back and side walls were illuminated by several 7-watt bulbs, each mounted approximately 1 inch behind the blue plastic, the interior changed to blue. The chamber had a grid floor consisting of 1/8-inch stainless steel grids spaced 5/8 inch apart, center to center. The grids were charged through neon bulbs (NE-2) with a current of .250 ma., delivered from a constant current shock source. In this system, which replaces a scrambler, the rat is shocked when any two grids are contacted because the animals offer less resistance than the neon bulbs.[4] The ceiling was constructed of clear plastic backed by black cardboard. A Mallory Sonalert Signal, Model SC 628, was mounted on the plastic ceiling and delivered directly into the box a 2,800-cps. tone at approximately 75 db. The presentation of the conditioned stimulus (CS) and unconditioned stimulus (UCS) were programmed by appropriate relay circuitry and timing devices, which were located in an adjoining room. When the observer depressed push-button switches, each of which was associated with a specific behavior, the frequency, duration, and patterning of observed behaviors were recorded on an Esterline-Angus event recorder with a paper speed of 3 inches per minute.

Rats were assigned to seven experimental conditions, each of which was distinguished by CS and UCS presentation conditions during acquisition and extinction. The compound CS consisted of the 2,800-cps. tone plus the visual brightness cue occurring when the interior of the chamber changed from white to blue. Thus, the interior of the box was always white during the intertrial interval and changed to blue when the tone was presented. The UCS consisted of a current of .250-ma. shock delivered through the grids to the rats' feet. On Day 1 each rat was placed in the experimental chamber for 10 minutes, during which base-line behavior was observed. Following this adaptation period each animal received 10 acquisition trials, followed by 50 extinction trials. On Day 2 a 5-minute adaptation period was followed by an additional 50 extinction trials. During the delay period intervening between the two experimental sessions, each animal spent the entire time in its home cage.

The CS–UCS paired group consisted of 6 *S*s which received

[4] The shocker schematic was provided by S. P. Grossman.

ten pairings of CS and UCS during acquisition. A delayed conditioning paradigm was used in which the CS–UCS interval was 5 seconds; that is, the CS had its onset 5 seconds before the onset of the 1-second UCS, and they terminated together. During the two extinction sessions, only the CS was presented.

The remaining six groups control for characteristics of the CS–UCS paired group, but these characteristics are independent of the essential and primary pairing. The CS-only group consisted of 6 animals which were never shocked and only received the 5-second CS, 10 CS presentations during the acquisition stage, and 50 CS presentations during each of the two extinction sessions. The two UCS-only control groups consisted of 6 *S*s each and were differentiated only by their treatment during extinction. During acquisition rats in these groups were not presented with the CS and received 10 1-second shock trials. During extinction one of the two UCS-only groups received CS-only trials. In the CS–UCS paired, CS-only, and both UCS-only groups the intertrial interval was 60 seconds.

There were two pseudoconditioning control groups consisting of 6 animals each. These rats received both the CS and the UCS during acquisition, the two stimuli being presented randomly and never paired. These two groups, treated identically during extinction, were differentiated only by their treatment during acquisition. The 60-second CS–UCS unpaired group had a 60-second interstimulus interval separating the termination of any one stimulus (CS or UCS) and the onset of the next (again, since a random schedule was used, CS or UCS). Because the intertrial interval and interstimulus interval are necessarily identical in paired conditions, this control eliminates pairing, while preserving the 60-second interstimulus interval of our CS–UCS paired group. The intertrial interval, that is, time between 2 CS presentations or 2 UCS presentations, was, on the average, 120 seconds. The 30-second CS–UCS unpaired group had a 30-second interstimulus interval. Although this was shorter than the 60-second interstimulus interval of our CS–UCS paired group, this condition too eliminates pairing and maintains the rate of CS and UCS presentations in our CS–UCS paired group. During extinction, only the CS was presented at an intertrial interval of 60 seconds for both groups.

In each of the groups in which the 5-second CS was presented during extinction, 5 additional CS test trials were administered during each of the two extinction sessions. Each CS test trial consisted of the compound auditory and visual CS, was 3 minutes long, and followed each block of 10 5-second CS extinction trials.

Finally, a base-line control group consisting of 3 rats did not receive either the CS or the UCS. Their activity was recorded on two successive days for perods of time approximating the base-line, acquisition, and extinction periods of Day 1 and the base-line and extinction period of Day 2. The seven treatments are summarized graphically in Fig. 1.

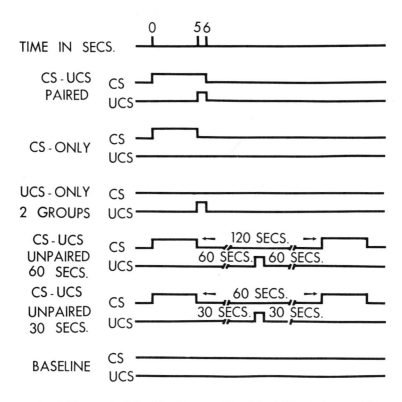

Fig. 1. Temporal relationship of the tone CS and shock UCS during acquisition procedures in each experimental and control condition.

Observation and recording procedures were carried out by two independent observers who had previously identified the salient and commonly occurring rat behaviors in our apparatus. One observer recorded the frequency and duration of ten common behaviors on an Esterline-Angus event recorder. The other observer noted specific behavioral components, idiosyncratic behavior patterns, and behavioral relationships which were not routinely recorded on the Esterline-Angus.

Behavior Classes

Preliminary observations of rats stimulated by the CS and the UCS in our apparatus permitted distinguishing ten frequently occurring behavior classes:

1. *Orienting.* A marked turning and uplifting of the head, directed toward the tone source. Usually a response to tone onset or termination, although occasionally observed at other times when the tone was not present.
2. *Crying.* A high-pitched, whinelike vocalization.
3. *General activity.* Any diffuse locomotor activity, ranging from a single step to moving about in the compartment. It consisted of all general, unoriented motor patterns and postural changes, specifically including forward movement, backward movement, turning around, and any other forepaw movement in which the forepaws were originally in contact with and movement originated from the grid floor.
4. *Grooming.* Cleaning, licking, or scratching of the body, not including the facial area.
5. *Standing.* Raising of the body on the hind legs in a vertical position and almost always accompanied by uplifting of the head.
6. *Jumping.* A momentary displacement of the rat from the grid floor so that the rat left the grid floor with all four feet, and with the possible exception of the tail, was otherwise not in contact with the grids.
7. *Face washing.* Any rubbing or cleaning of the facial area with the forepaws. This was sometimes accompanied by a licking response.

8. *Biting.* Gnawing the rods of the grid floor.
9. *Sniffing rods.* Sniffing activity directed at the grid floor, almost always accompanied by lowering of the head.
10. *Sniffing sides.* Sniffing activity directed at the walls of the compartment and usually accompanied by lateral head movements.

Other clearly differentiated behavior classes included urination, defecation, sleeping, and licking. These activities were not recorded on the event recorder but were systematically recorded by the second observer. Since these behaviors are self-explanatory, only the licking response needs further clarification. Licking consisted of both the extension and movement of the tongue and the accompanying jaw movements but occurred as an isolated response, was apparently unrelated motivationally to hunger or thirst, and appeared to be independent of face washing and other grooming behaviors.

Tone and Shock Associated Behaviors

The most conspicuous effect of the present investigation was the immediate elimination of responding in all groups receiving the aversive UCS and which was complete within 3 shock trials for every animal. During acquisition, shock elicited crying, jumping, general locomotor activity, and occasional biting. These activities were confined to the 1-second shock interval and ceased immediately with shock termination, resulting in idiosyncratic postures which were maintained through the intertrial interval until the next shock elicited new unconditioned responding and a new posture; the posture and immobility produced by termination of the last shock trial were maintained through several Day 1 extinction trials.

In general, the reduction of responding extended through the intertrial interval, CS and CS test trials during acquisition, and extinction. Only orienting responses and general activity occurred frequently during the CS period, and the frequency and duration of these two responses are summarized in Fig. 2. Orienting occurred only occasionally during the 10 acquisition trials; during extinction, orienting responses consistently occurred only within the CS–UCS paired condition. In contrast, general activity was relatively high during acquisition in all groups, reflecting the behavior occurring during the initial UCS trials. But later in acquisition and during extinction there was a significant reduction of general activity which was clearly greatest among animals in the CS–UCS paired group. These differences between CS–UCS paired and shocked control *S*s indicate that some learning was occurring within the paired group, an effect which is supported by statistical analysis. Comparing mean frequency orienting and general activity to the CS in the CS–UCS paired group with that occurring to the CS in the combined control groups receiving CS presentations during extinction indicated that the CS–UCS paired group showed significantly more orienting ($t = 2.659$, $df = 5$, $p < .05$) but less general activity ($t = 4.581$, $df = 5$, $p < .005$). Furthermore, the general activity occurring during CS periods was a consequence of shock presentations, as CS-only *S*s did not consistently show either orienting behavior or general activity to the CS. In general, similar effects occurred on CS test trials and for the regular CS-only extinction trials. Because of this similarity of effect, as well as

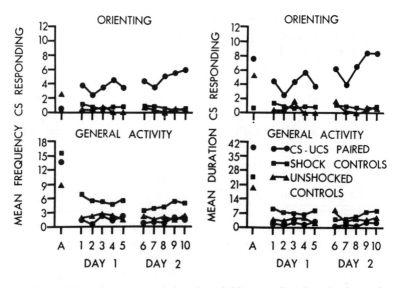

Fig. 2. Mean frequency and duration of CS responding for orienting and general activity.

because behavioral effects on CS test trials were restricted to tone onset and only an initial, brief period thereafter, CS test trials were not analyzed further and are not included here.

INTERTRIAL INTERVAL EFFECTS

Intertrial interval orienting, crying, biting, and jumping were negligible for each shocked group. General activity, high in all groups during the base-line period, was reduced during both acquisition and extinction. Except for the UCS-only no CS condition, in which only the first block of extinction trials was affected, the other shocked groups had a substantial behavioral reduction which usually lasted for the duration of the experiment.

Grooming was reduced during acquisition and extinction in all shocked groups. Recovery was slowest in the CS–UCS unpaired 60-second condition, although toward the end of the second extinction session duration of grooming was relatively long, indicating that the effects of shock were disappearing. Standing, originally a high-frequency response, was markedly reduced in all shocked groups, and recovery was incomplete and highly variable. The relatively long durations of standing indicate immobility in the upright posture and not a high incidence of active standing behaviors. Face washing was reduced in all groups and showed moderate but incomplete recovery in all groups except the CS–UCS unpaired 60-second condition. This latter group showed consistently lower levels of face washing throughout both extinction sessions. Sniffing rods occurred with a higher frequency during base line than sniffing sides. Both sniffing behaviors were considerably reduced during acquisition and extinction and generally showed little if any recovery. Only the UCS-only no CS group showed substantial recovery of the sniffing-rods behavior, while the UCS-only CS in extinction and CS–UCS unpaired 30-second conditions showed only moderate recovery. The frequency and duration of intertrial interval responding for the combined shock-control conditions are summarized in Figs. 3 and 4, respectively.

Unshocked groups only rarely exhibited intertrial interval orienting, crying, or jumping; uncommonly high frequencies of biting during the early stages of the base-line control disappeared quickly.

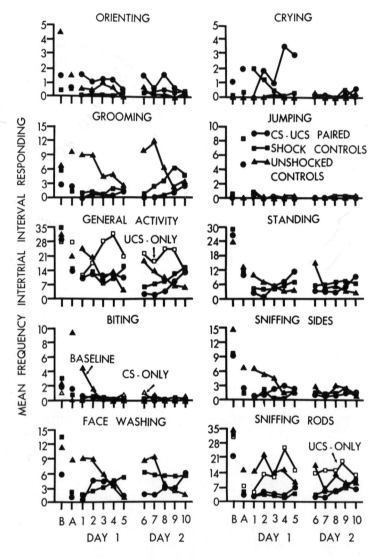

Fig. 3. Mean frequency intertrial interval responding for each of ten behavior classes. The relatively high incidence of crying in the CS–UCS paired group was the result of a single anomalous S and was not characteristic.

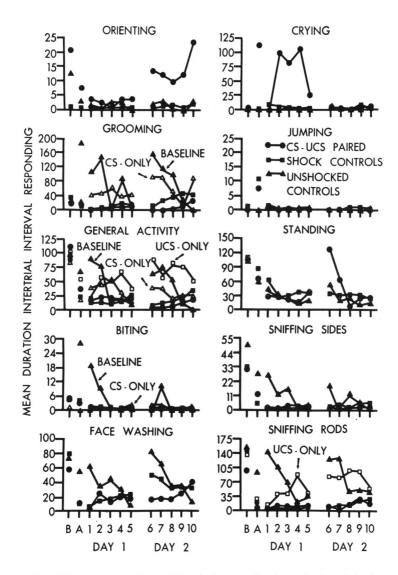

Fig. 4. Mean duration intertrial interval responding for each of ten behavior classes. The relatively high incidence of crying in the CS–UCS paired group was the result of a single anomalous S and was not characteristic.

TABLE 1

CORRELATION COEFFICIENTS FOR FREQUENCY OF INTERTRIAL
INTERVAL BEHAVIORS DURING ACQUISITION

	Orienting	Crying	General Activity	Grooming	Standing	Jumping	Face Washing	Biting	Sniffing Rods	Sniffing Sides
Orienting	1.000									
Crying	-.096	1.000								
General Activity	-.109	-.201	1.000							
Grooming	-.027	-.115	.310	1.000						
Standing	-.096	-.089	.266	.077	1.000					
Jumping	-.176	.149	.095	-.225	.086	1.000				
Face Washing	.248	-.149	-.038	.481**	-.145	-.216	1.000			
Biting	-.116	-.074	.666**	.566**	.223	.035	.107	1.000		
Sniffing Rods	.035	-.145	.384*	.548**	.548**	-.144	.296	.525**	1.000	
Sniffing Sides	-.021	-.046	.377*	.480**	.551**	-.226	.048	.571**	.761**	1.000

* p < .05
** p < .01

TABLE 2

CORRELATION COEFFICIENTS FOR FREQUENCY OF INTERTRIAL
INTERVAL BEHAVIORS DURING EXTINCTION

	Orienting	Crying	General Activity	Grooming	Standing	Jumping	Face Washing	Biting	Sniffing Rods	Sniffing Sides
Orienting	1.000									
Crying	−.099	1.000								
General Activity	−.197	−.261	1.000							
Grooming	−.185	−.319*	.407**	1.000						
Standing	−.210	−.162	.537**	.482**	1.000					
Jumping	−.006	−.074	.305	.173	.270	1.000				
Face Washing	.072	−.285	.332*	.325*	−.042	.077	1.000			
Biting	−.176	−.213	.563**	.562**	.218	.037	.288	1.000		
Sniffing Rods	−.113	−.252	.688**	.591**	.584**	.423**	.005	.486**	1.000	
Sniffing Sides	−.195	−.093	.451**	.465**	.578**	.429**	−.133	.458**	823**	1.000

* $p < .05$
** $p < .01$

Finding intertrial interval biting only in the unstimulated base-line group suggests that biting may be related to exploratory or play behavior which was inhibited by the electric shock and auditory signal in other conditions. There is partial support for such an idea since frequency of intertrial interval biting during acquisition and extinction correlated highly with several activities ordinarily considered exploratory behaviors. Correlation coefficients are summarized in Tables 1 and 2.

Reduction of general activity in the CS-only group and its early recovery indicates the inhibitory properties of the tone CS as well as habituation to it. Later decreases in responding during Sessions 1 and 2, as well as the gradual reduction in general activity for the base-line control during both sessions, probably resulted from satiation of ordinary curiosity and exploratory behaviors. Inhibitory effects of the CS were also apparent for face washing; initial CS presentations resulted in marked reduction of face washing, followed by rapid recovery after which there was a gradual decrease in responding during both extinction sessions. This latter effect also characterized the base-line control group's performance. Both the CS-only and the base-line control groups showed an increased incidence of grooming, although this did disappear late during each session for the base-line condition. Standing, sniffing sides, and sniffing rods were reduced in both unshocked groups. Although the frequency of these behaviors changed over time, reduction was gradual and there was neither the immediate nor so dramatic a change as that occurring in shocked groups. In general, by the end of Session 2, base-line control animals no longer exhibited any of the behavior classes, since all were sleeping. The frequency and duration of intertrial responding for the unshocked control conditions are summarized in Figs. 3 and 4, respectively.

MEASURES OF ADDITIONAL ACTIVITIES

Urination and defecation only rarely occurred in unshocked controls and were more frequently observed in shocked groups. Although approximately 75% of shocked animals urinated and defecated in the experimental situation, absolute incidence of these behaviors is quite low. In this connection both infrequent urination and defecation during acquisition and extinction and the uniformly nonexistent incidence of these classes of behavior during base line is somewhat artificial, since both behaviors were often observed when rats were initially handled and transported from the home cage to the experimental apparatus. Nevertheless, relative frequency of urination and defecation is striking and clearly distinguishes shocked from unshocked groups. Frequency of urination and defecation are reported in Table 3 for those groups.

TABLE 3

MEAN FREQUENCY URINATION, DEFECATION, AND MINUTES SLEEPING FOR EACH SHOCKED AND UNSHOCKED CONDITION DURING BASE LINE (B), ACQUISITION (A), AND EXTINCTION

Group	B	A	Extinction Day 1	B	Extinction Day 2	Subject Frequency
			Urination			
CS–UCS Paired	—	—	1.83	—	2.83	6.0
UCS-only CS in Ext.	—	1.17	.33	.17	.5	4.0
UCS-only No CS	—	—	.5	—	—	3.0
CS–UCS Unpaired 60 sec.	—	.5	2.17	—	.83	6.0
CS–UCS Unpaired 30 sec.	—	.17	1.0	—	—	4.0
Base Line	—	—	—	—	—	—
CS-only	—	—	.33	—	—	1.0
			Defecation			
CS–UCS Paired	—	1.33	.17	.67	1.5	5.0
UCS-only CS in Ext.	.17	.5	—	.33	.67	3.0
UCS-only No CS	—	1.67	.17	.5	1.17	4.0
CS–UCS Unpaired 60 sec.	—	2.0	.17	.5	1.33	6.0
CS–UCS Unpaired 30 sec.	—	1.0	—	.17	.33	4.0
Base Line	—	—	.33	—	—	1.0
CS-only	—	—	—	—	.17	1.0
			Sleeping			
CS–UCS Paired	—	—	—	—	—	—
UCS-only CS in Ext.	—	—	.83	—	5.33	2.0
UCS-only No CS	—	—	.83	—	—	1.0
CS–UCS Unpaired 60 sec.	—	—	—	—	—	—
CS–UCS Unpaired 30 sec.	—	—	2.5	—	3.0	2.0
Base Line	—	—	19.0	—	26.33	3.0
CS-only	—	—	18.83	—	19.33	6.0

Sleeping rarely occurred in shocked groups but was the most significant behavior pattern for each unshocked control animal. Each unshocked control rat fell asleep, and this activity filled approximately 40% of each extinction session. Time sleeping is summarized in Table 3.

Unexpectedly, during extinction several rats made licking responses that were not directed toward environmental stimuli. Tongue extension and movements did not result in contact with either other parts of the rat or environmental objects nearby. Rather, these rats licked air. In general, licking was nonexistent during base-line and acquisition stages and was low during Day 1 extinction. Licking occurred most frequently as a response to the CS during Day 2 extinction, and although intertrial licking on Day 2 was observed, its rates were much lower. The low incidence of licking in the UCS-only no CS in extinction and base-line control groups is presumably a result of the absence of the tone CS in these groups. Except for the CS–UCS paired group, high rates of licking occurred in groups receiving both tone CS and shock UCS presentations, while intermediate levels occurred in the CS-only condition. Licking rates, presented in Table 4, are conservative because they do not include rapid licking, which occurred in four shocked rats (see Table 4). Each of these animals showed frequent bursts of rapid licking, which could not be accurately recorded by our observers.

TABLE 4

MEAN FREQUENCY LICKING FOR EACH SHOCKED AND UNSHOCKED CONDITION DURING BASE LINE (B), ACQUISITION (A), AND EXTINCTION

Group	B	A	Extinction Day 1 CS	Extinction Day 1 ITI	B	Extinction Day 2 CS	Extinction Day 2 ITI	Subject Frequency
CS–UCS Paired	—	.67	.5	—	—	.83	—	4.0
UCS-only CS in Ext.	.33	—	2.33	.83	—	13.67*	2.33	5.0
UCS-only No CS	.33	—	—	.17	—	—	1.33	3.0
CS–UCS Unpaired 60 sec.	—	.17	.5*	—	—	14.83**	.33	5.0
CS–UCS Unpaired 30 sec.	—	—	1.0	.67	—	28.0	2.67	6.0
Base Line	—	—	—	.17	—	—	—	1.0
CS-only	—	1.17	6.67	2.83	—	6.0	2.83	6.0

1 animal(*) or 2 animals(**) showed additional rapid licking which could not be recorded and is not included in these means.

DISCUSSION

We have described and reported the behavioral effects during both acquisition and extinction procedures of inescapable paired and unpaired shock trials. The major findings of the present investigation were: (a) Intertrial interval behaviors disappeared almost immediately for all animals shocked during acquisition, and the immobility produced by these shock trials persisted through several extinction trials. (b) Orienting responses occurred at relatively high rates in the CS–UCS paired group, and these high rates were maintained through both extinction sessions. Compared to the low incidence of orienting in control groups, such results indicate that learning had occurred. (c) High licking rates were obtained during extinction procedures, particularly in rats stimulated by unpaired CS and UCS presentations.

The rapid elimination of intertrial responding following brief electric shock, as well as the relative permanence of shock-produced immobility, suggests that generalized nonresponding and immobility are unconditioned consequences of inescapable shock. Both the immediacy and the uniformity of the effect restricts a learning or adventitious reinforcement interpretation. Although a fixed and inescapable shock elicits unconditioned flinching, running, jumping, and prancing (Kimble, 1955; Trabasso & Thompson, 1962), we found that the termination of such a shock elicits chronic immobility and freezing. Recently, Seligman (1968) has proposed a safety-signal theory of Pavlovian fear conditioning. According to this view, when a CS predicts shock, the absence of that signal reliably predicts safety or the absence of shock. The value of this theory is evident, for it can account for the disruptive effects of unpredictable shock, that is, learned helplessness (Overmier & Seligman, 1967; Seligman & Maier, 1967) as well as the resulting conditioned suppression in the usual conditioned emotional response (CER) experiment (e.g., Kamin, Brimer, & Black, 1963). But the discrimination required to distinguish the CS from the absence of the CS may take a long time, during which the animal remains in a chronic state of fear. For example, Seligman (1968) reports that even after 15 days of predictable shock, the rate of bar pressing for food had only incompletely recovered and had not returned to its original base-line rate. Our finding that noncontingent termination of inescapable shock

produces immobility and chronic fear, although not directly supporting the safety-signal hypothesis, provides an empirical context
for both it and the disruptive effects, that is, learned helplessness
and conditioned suppression, which it predicts. Apparently these
effects are initiated and maintained, at least in part, by unconditioned immobility elicited by termination of inescapable
shock.

It is interesting to note that the behavior classes reliably elicited
by shock onset—crying, jumping, general locomotor activity, and
biting—were not conditionable. Only general activity occurred
relatively often as a response to the CS. Still, general activity
occurred more often in shocked control groups than in the paired
group, where it occurred infrequently. This is not particularly
paradoxical, however, for the immediate immobility elicited by
shock termination would doubtless mask any real classically
conditioned motor effects. Nevertheless, it is clear that our pairing
procedures produced conditioning, since animals in the CS–UCS
paired group consistently made orienting responses to the tone
CS but control group animals did not. And this conditioning,
observed increasingly as a response to the CS during extinction,
developed even though the orienting response was never elicited by
the shock UCS and only occasionally occurred as a response to the
CS during acquisition. Presumably the tone acquired significance
and "meaning" when it was consistently paired during extinction
procedures with the chronic immobility and fear that had previously
been produced by our acquisition procedures.

This is not the first time that conditioned motor activities were
not the responses elicited and strengthened during acquisition
procedures. Bindra and Palfai (1967) introduced paired presentations of a water incentive and an auditory CS to restrained thirsty
rats. Testing in another situation, they found that rats explored more
in the presence of the auditory CS than in its absence. Although
both Bindra and Palfai's (1967) and our experiment were classical
preparations in which the specific motor components that were
conditioned could not have been instrumentally reinforced or
strengthened, they differ in several respects and are not strictly
comparable. Bindra and Palfai used appetitive stimuli and tested
animals in a different situation; we used aversive stimuli, and testing

occurred in the same situation. Nevertheless, these results support the view (Bindra & Palfai, 1967; Bindra, in press) of a central motivational state which is not linked to any specific responses.

Perhaps our most significant finding was the sudden appearance, during extinction, of a licking response. Licking was apparently unrelated motivationally to those drive states, hunger or thirst, with which it is usually associated; it also appeared to be independent of face washing and other grooming activities, and was motivationally irrelevant to the chronic fear that had been produced in our experimental environment. Such irrelevant licking resembles the irrelevant behaviors, for example, preening, which may appear when two motivations are in conflict with each other and which result in ethological displacement activity (Hess, 1962; Hinde, 1966). Psychological extinction may share characteristics or properties with psychological and ethological conflict. Specifically, displacement behaviors are allochotonous, or unrelated motivationally to their own drive, and are also unrelated motivationally to either of the two conflicting drives. The licking we observed was allochotonous because it was unrelated to hunger and thirst and was an irrelevant activity for the incompatible motives (within classical fear conditioning and instrumental escape-avoidance situations) of emotionality, that is, anxiety or fear, and relaxation.

A conflict theory of extinction [5] predicts that irrelevant displacement behaviors should only occur at some point during extinction procedures where the signaling function of the CS is obscured, in other words, where its function and predictiveness are uncertain. In aversive situations displacement behaviors would not occur early during extinction, since Ss would still be fearful of the CS; similarly, late during extinction, when the CS has already lost its fear-eliciting properties, displacement would not occur because Ss would be relaxed. In both cases a single motivational state predominates and animals are not in conflict. Only when Ss are in conflict, that is, when both incompatible motivational states are approximately equal, should displacement behavior occur. Such a motivational state is achieved for the aversive case when the CS simultaneously

[5] The conflict theory of extinction which we introduce suggests the source of competing responses which interfere with continued conditioned responding. Within such a formulation ethological displacement and redirected behaviors are likely to represent the most commonly expressed responses to conflict.

elicits both fear and relaxation. That licking rates were generally high only on the second day of extinction is consistent with this prediction.

Evaluating licking during CS extinction presentations requires comparing the frequency of licking in shocked groups to that occurring in the CS-only control. Why licking should occur at all in this group is unclear. One possibility, that licking in the CS-only group was itself a displacement activity, is partially supported because the tone CS initially produced brief immobility and inhibitory effects, presumably because it was mildly aversive. Alternatively, the remote possibility that our tone CS directly elicited licking as an unconditioned response is untenable, since licking only rarely occurred as a response to the CS during acquisition. In any event, since almost all the licking that occurred during extinction was a response to the CS (intertrial interval licking was relatively negligible, and licking was almost nonexistent in control groups unstimulated by the CS), the CS-only group is the appropriate base-line comparative condition.

Compared to base-rate licking in the CS-only group, the CS–UCS paired group had a considerably reduced incidence of licking, and all shocked control groups receiving CS presentations during extinction showed high licking rates. These shocked control groups uniformly showed high rates of licking and in this qualitative sense are identical; quantitative differences distinguishing these groups (see Table 4) are not very meaningful, since the groups with the lower rates do not include several bursts of additional rapid licking which could not be recorded. The low incidence of licking in the CS–UCS paired group is not puzzling. It is clear that rats in this group have not yet extinguished. Orienting to the CS was still high, and general activity remained significantly suppressed (see Fig. 2), throughout both extinction sessions. Since the CS was still controlling behavior, these rats were not in conflict, and displacement behavior, that is, licking, would not be expected.

Since we are suggesting a conflict interpretation of extinction, the appearance of displacement licking in the shocked control groups raises an important question. These groups are controls for conventional learning (associative pairing) paradigms. Is it then permissible to emphasize a learning interpretation during extinction, as we do, for the behavior changes that occurred in our shocked control groups? The question of the appropriate controls for conditioning experiments has been discussed in detail elsewhere, most notably by Jensen (1961) and, more recently, by Rescorla (1967), and need not be introduced here. There are at least two considerations, however, which indicate that our analysis is justified. First, while the CS was not paired with shock in these control groups, other components of the environment, for example, the chamber itself, were always present during shock presentations. Because of the immediate and generalized disruptive effects of shock, as well as the fact that discriminated performance changes develop only with extended training, this factor may exert considerable influence where aversive stimuli are introduced, regardless of explicit CS and UCS pairing during acquisition. Secondly, during extinction procedures there was a perfect contingency in each shocked control group. CS presentations during extinction in both the CS–UCS paired group and shocked controls were never paired with shock and consequently perfectly predict the absence of shock. Introducing reliable contingencies is an adequate condition for learning, irrespective of earlier acquisition procedures. Finally, our analysis is based only upon the assumption that rats in the shocked control groups learned something about the CS during extinction. What was learned remains an open question, although it is quite likely that it differed from what was learned in the CS–UCS paired group, where the fact of learning is unequivocal.

REFERENCES

Bindra, D. The interrelated mechanisms of reinforcement and motivation, and the nature of their influence on response. In D. Levine (Ed.), *Nebraska symposium on motivation, 1969.* Lincoln: University of Nebraska Press. In press.

Bindra, D., & Palfai, T. Nature of positive and negative incentive-motivational effects on general activity. *J. comp. physiol. Psychol.*, 1967, **63**, 288–297.

Bitterman, M. E. Phyletic differences in learning. *Amer. Psychologist*, 1965, **20**, 396–410.

Brogden, W. J., Lipman, E. A., & Culler, E. The role of incentive in conditioning and extinction. *Amer. J. Psychol.*, 1938, **5**, 109–117.

Guthrie, E. R., & Horton, G. P. *Cats in a puzzle box.* New York: Rinehart, 1946.

Hess, E. H. Ethology. In *New directions in psychology.* New York: Holt-Rinehart-Winston, 1962. Pp. 157–266.

54   *Current Issues in Animal Learning*

Hinde, R. A. *Animal behaviour*. New York: McGraw-Hill, 1966.

Jensen, D. D. Operationism and the question "Is this behavior learned or innate?" *Behaviour*, 1961, **17**, 1–8.

Jensen, D. D. Polythetic operationism and the psychology of learning. In W. C. Corning & S. C. Ratner (Eds.), *Chemistry of learning*. New York: Plenum Press, 1967. Pp. 43–55.

Kamin, L. J., Brimer, C. J., & Black, A. H. Conditioned suppression as a monitor of fear of the CS in the course of avoidance training. *J. comp. physiol. Psychol.*, 1963, **56**, 497–501.

Kimble, G. A. Shock intensity and avoidance learning. *J. comp. physiol. Psychol.*, 1955, **48**, 281–284.

Overmier, J. B., & Seligman, M. E. P. Effects of inescapable shock on subsequent escape and avoidance responding. *J. comp. physiol. Psychol.*, 1967, **57**, 28–33.

Rescorla, R. A. Pavlovian conditioning and its proper control procedures. *Psychol. Rev.*, 1967, **74**, 71–80.

Seligman, M. E. P. Chronic fear produced by unpredictable electric shock. *J. comp. physiol. Psychol.*, 1968, **66**, 402–411.

Seligman, M. E. P., & Maier, S. F. Failure to escape traumatic shock. *J. exp. Psychol.*, 1967, **73**, 1–9.

Sheffield, F. D. Avoidance training and the contiguity principle. *J. comp. physiol. Psychol.*, 1948, **41**, 165–177.

Trabasso, T. R., & Thompson, R. W. Supplementary report: Shock intensity and unconditioned responding in a shuttlebox. *J. exp. Psychol.*, 1962, **63**, 215–216.

Habituation:
Research and Theory

STANLEY C. RATNER

Michigan State University

What happens when a stimulus repeatedly elicits a response?
In the absence of a great deal of data, the answer is simple. The
response habituates and such habituation occurs for all responses
and all organisms. But if the stimulus is very intense, does the
response still habituate? Does a response recover once it has
habituated? Do all responses habituate? More than two decades
of research involving repeated presentations of stimuli to animals,
including humans, suggests replies to these specific questions and
clearly shows that the general answer is inadequate. Attempts to
answer these and similar specific questions and the inadequacy of
the general description lead to the organization of this chapter
around three topics: (1) a review of some of the methodological
principles in the study of habituation, (2) a theoretical description
of habituation, and (3) a summary and analysis of the processes and
variables associated with habituation and this theory. For the
initial inquiry we will work with the following definition of habituation: a change, usually a reduction, in responding, associated
with repeated presentations of a stimulus.

My attention throughout this review is primarily behavioral,
so the data and theories emphasized involve intact organisms
responding to stimuli rather than physiological systems and recordings from them.

GENERAL CHARACTERISTICS AND SIGNIFICANCE OF HABITUATION

A major assumption that I make in this analysis of habituation,
and one that is shared with a number of other investigators, is that

55

habituation is profitably seen as a learning process or, more generally, as a process of behavior modification. Harris (1943), Thorpe (1963), Hinde (1960), and Thompson and Spencer (1966) also make this assumption. Although popularity of an idea is pleasing, it is not sufficient grounds for accepting that idea. What other grounds exist for assuming that habituation belongs in an analysis of learning? When the problem is put this way the answer is less self-evident. In part this is true because the problem requires a refined definition of learning that is not yet available, and in part this is true because the procedures used in studies of habituation clearly fail to include things included in most descriptions of learning. The main ingredient that habituation does not appear to contain is associations between S–R units, for example, the CS and its response and the US and its response. Rather, the typical ingredient of habituation is the reduction in responding to repetitions of a stimulus. Only one stimulus is specifically manipulated, and associations are not involved in an obvious way.

My grounds for making the assumption that habituation is a learning process are relatively indirect. If we knew exactly what process or processes characterize learning, the problem of the place of habituation would be simple. Since we do not yet know this, locating habituation in the vicinity of learning involves a statement of belief that can be assessed at some future time. Therefore I will first describe some general characteristics of habituation in order to suggest the kind of evidence that leads me to place it near learning. After the analysis of some of the data from research on habituation are presented, we will be better able to evaluate habituation and its status in relation to learning.

General Characteristics of Habituation

The principal characteristics of research with habituation are that some stimulus that the organisms can detect is repeatedly presented and the decrement in response to this stimulus is measured. For example, if an earthworm is stimulated with a pulse of light, the worm rapidly contracts one to two inches on the first trial, weakly on the twentieth trial, and not at all on the fortieth trial (Ratner & Gardner, 1968). The change in behavior from the first to the fortieth trial is conspicuous and very much like the change that occurs when a vibratory stimulus is substituted for a pulse of light (Gardner, 1968). Thus, we see that across-trials habituation involves a change in responses to a stimulus. Though the change typically involves a reduction in a response, under some conditions repeated stimulation leads to no change or to an increase. These outcomes will be discussed in later sections that deal with temporal effects and response system effects.

Thus, the habituation procedure typically leads to a modification in the response to a stimulus. Such modification constitutes one general characteristic of learning. This characteristic is described as a *change in response topography* (Ratner, 1967a) that in the earthworm takes the form of systematic disappearance of components of the response to the eliciting stimulus (Gardner, 1968). Research involving habituation typically uses measurement of a single response component, such as the GSR, or a very global component, such as amplitude of startle response. The characteristic of change in response topography therefore is difficult to evaluate from many published papers; but work in our laboratories, using subjects ranging from planaria to humans, supports the idea of a change in topography that may be subtle but occurs reliably. The change in response topography can be likened to the change that is seen in the lever-pressing response of rats during operant training.

The second characteristic of habituation that links it broadly with learning involves the generality of the finding across species. Harris (1943) and Thorpe (1963) pay particular attention to the generality of habituation by systematically reviewing evidence for habituation across all major animal groups from single-cell organisms to humans. I will also attempt to include references and data from a variety of animal species to illustrate the generality of habituation.

Generality of habituation across species does not mean that habituation is a fixed property for each individual within the species, that is, fixed in the way in which the number of eyes or the number of teeth are fixed. Rather, habituation of the response to a particular stimulus for individuals in a species or strain reveals large individual differences for subjects that are tested in identical ways. Such differences are large and relatively consistent (Koepke &

Pribram, 1966; Ratner, 1968; Askew, Leibrecht, & Ratner, 1969), much as they are in conventional learning situations. Thus, individual differences constitute the third general characteristic of habituation. The question of whether individual differences in habituation are stable across different habituation tests using the same subjects is not yet answered.

Some investigators of habituation such as Sokolov (1963) and Thompson and Spencer (1966) assume that it involves changes in the central nervous system and that it shares this characteristic with other types of learning. Though this characteristic may be valid for higher invertebrates and vertebrate species that have central nervous tissue, this view severely restricts the generality of habituation and is not assumed in the present paper. However, another idea that adheres in the assumption of the importance of the CNS is that habituation is not simply an effector or receptor change, that is, it is not a peripheral process. Concern with excluding effector or receptor changes as explanations of habituation is much like concern with the appropriate control procedures that are necessary in order to conclude that classical conditioning has occurred. In the following sections I will discuss some of the control procedures used in studies of habituation in order to test for fatigue and adaptation effects.

Another important characteristic of research on habituation concerns the properties of the eliciting stimulus. General definitions of habituation, such as the one given by Thorpe (1963, p. 58), emphasize several features: (1) the response wanes in occurrence, (2) the waning is relatively permanent, and (3) the stimulus is not followed by a reinforcing stimulus. Thorpe's definition of habituation would necessarily include the relatively permanent changes in responses to stimuli that occur from extinction of a learned response. But in practice and for good theoretical reasons extinction (when a single stimulus is repeatedly presented) is not usually regarded as an example of habituation. This is not to say that these events may not be related at some future time. *At the present time studies of habituation involve stimuli that are novel for the organism.* That is, the animal is naïve with regard to the stimulus. Thus, many studies of exploratory behavior and stimulus satiation fit into the general definitional framework of studies of habituation. However, if such studies involve specific instructions to attend to stimuli, then the inclusion of these studies is uncertain because the eliciting properties of the stimuli are confounded by the subjects' responses to instructions.

The final characteristic of habituation is that a number of variables and processes associated with multistimulus learning (e.g., conditioning) are associated with habituation. Thompson and Spencer (1966) suggest nine such areas of overlap, including variables such as stimulus duration and intensity and processes such as generalization and disinhibition (dishabituation). Although Thompson and Spencer's analysis of this overlap is uncritical in several respects, it serves to illustrate this characteristic of habituation.

In summary, then, the general defining characteristics of habituation involve: (1) modification of a response from repeated presentations of the stimulus, (2) generality of this modification across species in all phyla, (3) stable individual differences within the species when other conditions are constant, (4) a general process of behavior modification that is not explainable in terms of fatigue or adaptation effects and may involve changes in the CNS for species for which this is possible, (5) stimuli for habituation, which involve novel stimuli for an organism, and (6) many variables and processes associated with learning, which are also associated with habituation. The majority of these characteristics are also general characteristics of multistimulus learning, such as conditioning.

Significance of Habituation

Lorenz (1965, p. 50), the ethologist, discusses the adaptive significance of habituation in terms of its survival value as "the elimination of the organism's response to often recurring, biologically irrelevant stimuli without impairing its reaction to others." Lorenz suggests, as Thorpe does (1963), that habituation is probably the oldest phylogenetic process for modifying an organism's behavior. These concepts of the ethologist put the process of habituation into a broad biological perspective. The practical significance of habituation is evident from the procedure sections of virtually every report of animal learning. Specifically, some habituation procedure precedes the experimental manipulations associated with the learning procedure. Although habituation to handling and the apparatus is routine, we know very little about the process changes associated with that routine. Carlton and Vogel (1967), for example, have shown that preconditioning habituation to the stimulus affects subsequent conditioning in systematic ways, and Ratner and Stein (1965) have shown that the schedule of presentation of an unconditioned stimulus alters the frequency and latency of the unconditioned response both when the US is presented alone and during conditioning.

The use of habituation in most learning procedures and the findings regarding specific effects of habituation in relation to multistimulus learning suggest that the process of habituation is theoretically important. This is particularly true for any theory, such as Denny's (1969, and in this volume), that analyzes learning in terms of the specific responses elicited by a specific stimulus. Other examples of these theories are the ones that emphasize *stimulus control*, such as the behaviorally oriented descriptions of operant learning. Thus it appears that habituation is biologically, theoretically, and practically relevant.

STANDARD PREPARATIONS AND EXPERIMENTAL PROCEDURES

Investigators have used a remarkable number of species and stimulus-response conditions to study habituation. Table 1 shows a list of research preparations organized by animal and response that represent comparatively recent investigations dealing with the process. The list is meant to display the range of research preparations, particularly those for which two or more studies have been reported. It is not meant to be an exhaustive catalog of animals, responses, or investigators and refers to less than half the research on habituation that has appeared since the reviews by Thorpe (1956, 1963).

The preparations that are suggested in Table 1 can be further classified along a dimension that is related to Lorenz's statement about the function of habituation, namely, that habituation occurs in relation to the biological relevance of the eliciting stimulus. As described by Denny and Ratner (1970) this idea can be expressed in the language of comparative psychology in terms of the analysis

TABLE 1

SOME RESEARCH PREPARATIONS FOR THE STUDY OF HABITUATION

Animal	Response	Investigators
Hydra	contraction	Rushforth, 1967
Planaria	contraction	VanDeventer & Ratner, 1964
Polychaete (worm)	contraction	Clark, 1964
Lumbricus (worm)	contraction to light	Ratner, 1967a
	contraction to vibration	Gardner, 1968
Turtle	alarm reaction	Hayes & Saiff, 1967
Frog	wiping response	Kimble & Ray, 1965
Fish	startle (alarm)	Russell, 1967
Bird	mobbing response	Hinde, 1960
	immobility display	Ratner, 1967b
Rat	startle and heart rate	Korn & Moyer, 1966
	headshake	Askew, et al., 1969
	exploration	Denny & Leckart, 1965
Dog	rotational nystagmus	Collins & Updegraff, 1966
Cat	rotational nystagmus	Collins & Updegraff, 1966
Primate	exploration	Butler & Harlow, 1954
Infant	heart rate	Clifton, et al., 1968
	startle	Engen, et al., 1963

of stimuli and responses along a dimension from early S–R components of an orienting (appetitive) sequence to the last S–R components of a consummatory sequence. For example, a food-deprived rat moves around his environment (early orienting components), moves toward an object that looks like food (late orienting components), and bites the object (late consummatory components). A similar description can be made of courting followed by copulation.

The dimension from early orienting components to late consummatory components relates to: (1) the ease of eliciting a response and (2) the retention of habituation of the response. Specifically, the later the response in the appetitive to consummatory sequence, the more limited the stimuli that can elicit the response and the more rapid the forgetting of habituation. The data to support these generalizations about the characteristics of a research preparation are discussed in part by Denny and Ratner (1970, chapter 10) and will be examined later in this chapter. In the present section these points are important as general guides concerning the preparation for the study of habituation. That is, if a late consummatory response is to be studied, only a limited number of stimuli can be used to elicit this response. Conversely, if an early orienting response is to be studied, then many stimuli can be used. So, for example, the study of habituation of the headshake response with the rat (Askew, Leibrecht, & Ratner, 1969) involves a late component in the consummatory activities associated with care of the body surface. Only direct stimulation of the ear, for example by an insect or insect substitute, elicits this response. On the other hand, approaching an object as in exploratory behavior is typically an early response in the orienting sequence and can be elicited by many stimuli. For example, see the review by Fowler (1965).

Indexes of Habituation

As is true in investigations of learning, a large number of measures have been used to reflect the process of habituation. In general these measures show decreasing response strength with increasing numbers of habituation trials. Figure 1 shows habituation in terms of frequency of responses across blocks of trials for two aspects of the response of earthworms to vibratory stimuli. The function in Fig. 1 shows that the habituation curve derived from group data has a rapid initial decrement followed by a more gradual one. Such a curve is typical of many that are published. Among the measures that are used in studies of habituation, they can be grouped into the following familiar categories: (1) frequency of response, (2) amplitude of the response, as with the GSR and startle response, and (3) latency of response.

Although response latency is a familiar index of learning and has been used in studies of habituation, we have found in research in our laboratory that it is less desirable than other measures. This is true because of the narrow range of latencies of responses that are elicited by stimuli in studies of habituation. Since the stimuli are relatively effective elicitors, latencies are short early in habituation, increase slightly, and then become infinitely long. Ratner and Stein (1965) found this to be true for habituation of responses of worms, and Leibrecht (1969) found this for habituation of the headshake response in rats.

Other aspects of habituation that require consistent definition are rate, amount, and retention of habituation. Indexes of these various aspects of habituation are still not used consistently, as

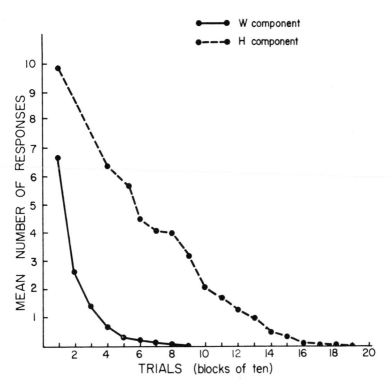

Fig. 1. Habituation of two components of the response of earthworms to vibration. (Adapted from Gardner, 1966)

noted by Askew (1969). In part this is true because of the limited theoretical demands regarding habituation; that is, theories are either very hypothetical (Thompson & Spencer, 1966) or very descriptive (Ratner, 1967a).

For future work and for purposes of this chapter, simple operational definitions of each of the aspects of habituation can be formulated. *Rate of habituation* can obviously be derived from curve fitting, but a simple operational definition that we have used (Askew, 1969) consists of determining the rate in terms of the number of trials from the initial level to the point at which the curve reaches an asymptote. This is defined as the trial on which the curve reached a level equal to or lower than the level at the end of the habituation session. So, for example, if the habituation curve reached an asymptote at the tenth trial, the rate of habituation would be calculated as ten minus one, or nine. *Amount of habituation* is indexed in a similar way but the difference between *response strengths* from the initial level to the asymptote is used. If the initial level of responding were 90% and responding dropped to 10%, the amount of habituation is 80%. However, amount of habituation can also be measured in terms of the number of *trials to reach criterion* (Gardner, 1968). *Retention of habituation* is necessarily measured by testing animals at some interval after initial habituation. The typical index of retention of habituation involves a *savings score* that is derived from a comparison of initial levels, rates, or amounts of habituation, relating the first habituation session to the following one. Later in this chapter we will discuss at length retention of habituation; this analysis will be based on savings scores, although different investigators have used different indexes to calculate savings. The statistical and theoretical properties of these various indexes, especially those that relate to retention of habituation, have not yet been examined.

Control Procedures in Studies of Habituation

In studies of habituation three, possibly four, conditions can arise that confound the results of the study and may complicate their interpretation. These conditions are associated with the effects of *base rate of responding, sensory adaptation, fatigue,* and *temporal conditioning or sensitization.*

Many responses that investigators use in studies of habituation have base rates above zero. That is, these responses occur occasionally without specific or noticeable stimulation. Common examples of such responses are the movements of invertebrates, especially planaria and earthworms; the eyeblink; and the GSR. A precise analysis of any aspect of habituation or retention of habituation requires information about the base rate of the response under study. The primary control procedure for determining the base rate of response is simple but tedious. A control group of animals is run under exactly the same conditions as the habituated groups, with the exception of the presentation of the eliciting stimulus. The response index that is used with habituated groups is utilized with the base-rate control groups, "as if the eliciting stimulus were presented." This procedure has had important consequences in studies of habituation and conditioning of earthworms, for example. Failure to run complete control groups for base rates of responding with worms led us to score forward movements as both conditioned and unconditioned responses. Later study (Ratner & Gardner, 1968) revealed that frequencies of forward movements were the same in stimulated groups as in base-rate control groups. Thus our measurement of habituation and conditioning had been confounded by this small error. Similarly, casual observation for occurrences of headshake responses suggested the rate of this response was zero, but complete testing under base-rate control conditions revealed a base rate consistently above zero (e.g., Askew, Leibrecht, & Ratner, 1969; Fig. 2).

After the investigator has a picture of the base rate of responding, control can be exercised by inserting base-rate periods into the total testing procedure. This procedure also permits evaluation of any circadian changes that may occur in conjunction with the particular testing schedule the investigator is using.

The second control procedure involves control for sensory adaptation, a condition that may also produce or interact with response decrements when we study habituation. Sensory adaptation to photic and olfactory stimuli are familiar examples of the process we are considering in relation to the question of control. However, adaptation is a general characteristic of sensory processes, so the study of habituation with most stimuli or stimulus complexes requires a control procedure to evaluate the effects of adaptation. One control procedure involves presenting the test stimulus with enough time between presentations so that recovery from sensory adaptation can occur. This procedure is only useful if long intertrial intervals are suitable in terms of the other aspects of the experiment. Another procedure involves testing the subjects a relatively short time after habituation has occurred. The time of the test is set in terms of the time required for recovery from sensory adaptation. If, for example, adaptation effects are known to recover in 30 minutes, a test is made 30 minutes after habituation occurs. Since effects of habituation are relatively permanent, that is, may last a day or more, major recovery of the response after 30 minutes would suggest that the original decrement was a result of adaptation rather than habituation. As noted above, the decrements with photic stimuli and olfactory stimuli are particularly vulnerable to adaptation effects, although these effects usually dissipate within 30 minutes. Intermediate intensities of auditory stimuli are also relatively immune to adaptation effects.

The control procedure that experimenters use to eliminate fatigue as an interpretation of a response decrement involves demonstrating that the subject can make the response after habituation to the test stimulus has occurred. To do this the experimenter uses another stimulus that elicits the same response. If the response occurs with the new stimulus, he concludes that fatigue does not explain the response decrement he found. For example, Gardner (1968) habituated the withdrawal response of earthworms to a brief vibratory stimulus, then touched the animals with tweezers and found a recovery of the withdrawal response. Hayes and Saiff (1967) controlled for fatigue by testing turtles several days after they had habituated to the original stimulus. The animals still failed to respond to this test stimulus, so the investigators concluded that fatigue should have dissipated within this time and the continued response decrement was a decrement due to habituation.

The final control procedure that is very interesting in terms of the relations between habituation and other learning procedures involves *controls for temporal conditioning or sensitization.* The total body of evidence to support the idea of temporal conditioning is relatively slim, as seen in Morgan's (1965) review of the literature. But several recent studies of habituation report increases in frequencies of response rather than decreases after hundreds of habituation trials (Franzisket, 1963; Kimble & Ray, 1965). In these studies a fixed intertrial interval, the essential requisite for temporal conditioning, was used. The results of several studies that used fixed intertrial intervals will be discussed in the section that deals with temporal variables and habituation, but the importance of this idea in this section is in terms of control for conditions that may confound effects of habituation.

The effect of temporal conditioning would be to slow the rate of habituation or reduce the amount of habituation and confound the retention in almost inestimable ways. The most common control for temporal conditioning in a conditioning study involves using a variable intertrial interval. This is also commonly done in studies of habituation. If the intertrial interval cannot readily be varied, a control session is required toward the end of the habituation session. During the control time, the animal is observed for occurrences of the response or for anticipatory components of the response that coincide with the previous schedule of stimulus presentations. According to both the review of the literature about temporal conditioning and the results of an extensive investigation with humans (Morgan, 1965), intertrial intervals of less than 30 seconds and more than 150 seconds lead to temporal conditioning. Intermediate values lead to little or no temporal conditioning. This principle can assist in selection of ITIs if fixed intervals are necessary.

An Elicitation and Interference Theory of Habituation

This theory of habituation rests on seven interrelated ideas. The first three of them are foundation ideas that are necessary in order to appreciate the later ideas that deal specifically with habituation. The foundation ideas that emphasize the comparative analysis of behavior, the theoretical style that emphasizes the eliciting value of stimuli and the effects of competing responses, are presented in work by Ratner (1956), Ratner and Denny (1964), and Denny and Ratner (1970). The ideas described as propositions, are:

1. Stimuli elicit responses in organisms, and even the absence of a familiar stimulus serves as a stimulus to elicit a response, for example, in extinction in which the absence of reinforcement elicits a response.
2. Before specific training, organisms respond to stimuli, and in general, this behavior consists of the *genetically organized* repertoire associated with consummatory activities of an organism.

3. Sequences of S–R components are involved in these consummatory activities, as discussed in the previous section. These sequences can be described in terms of at least two, sometimes three, major groups that merge into each other for the total pattern of consummatory activity. These ideas are derived in part from the usage of Konrad Lorenz following Craig (1918), who identified *orienting sequences* (which he called appetitive), *consummatory sequences* (Craig), and *postconsummatory sequences* (Denny & Ratner, 1970, chapter 5).

4. The eliciting value or association strength of a stimulus with a response depends on the nature of the stimulus and the sequence from which the S–R component comes for the particular organism or group of animals under study. For example, a biologically relevant stimulus associated with a consummatory sequence is a stronger elicitor than a biologically relevant or artificial stimulus involved in an appetitive sequence.

5. Elicitation of a response is followed by a refractory period during which the strength of the response is reduced. The refractory period arises from temporary changes in sensory, transmission, and effector processes.

6. Stimulus conditions that operate concurrently with eliciting stimuli also elicit responses that affect the originally elicited response. The concurrent stimulation may facilitate or interfere with the elicited response, depending on the stimulus and the topography of response that the concurrent stimuli elicit. Habituation involves the intrusion of competing responses that arise from the action of stronger (more dominant) eliciting stimuli during the refractory periods. The dominance of the competing response may be temporary, but if a number of such responses are elicited they may combine to equal the strength of the original response and thus cause habituation.

7. Other things equal, the amount of retention of habituation is inversely related to the strength of the association between the original eliciting stimulus and its response. In general, the closer the S–R component to the end of a consummatory sequence, the less the retention of habituation of this component. Within the interval for retention of habituation, the shorter the time after habituation the greater the retention of habituation.

DATA RELATED TO THE ELICITATION AND INTERFERENCE THEORY OF HABITUATION

Literally hundreds of published reports relating to habituation are available. Many of them, particularly those available to Harris (1943), consist of reports of demonstrations of habituation with previously uninvestigated animals or previously uninvestigated stimuli. However, a number of the reports that he used reveal some of the general characteristics of habituation. Since the first three propositions in the theory relate to a general hypothesis of the behavior of organisms, data to support them are not presented. This general theory is discussed in detail by Denny and Ratner (1970) and in summary by Ratner (1970), however. Thus, in the present section I will discuss experiments that provide evidence that concern the last four propositions, those that relate specifically to habituation. Although the propositions are interrelated to some extent, they can be classified as follows in order to treat experimental results adequately: Proposition 4, strength of the eliciting stimulus; Proposition 5, refractory effects and temporal variables; Proposition 6, facilitation and interference of habituation from concurrent stimulation; and Proposition 7, retention of habituation in relation to the strength of the original eliciting stimulus and its response.

Stimulus Effects

Proposition 4 refers to the effect of the strength of the association between the eliciting stimulus and the response. In general, the greater the strength of the association between the eliciting stimulus and the response, the less the probability of interference with the association. An index of strength of association is reflected in the initial level of response in a habituation curve, and the probability of interference is reflected in the amount of habituation that occurs during the habituation test. Data bearing on the generalization about association strength and habituation come from studies of effects of stimulus intensity, changing stimulus intensity, and stimulus duration.

The effects of *stimulus intensity* on habituation of headshake response in rats is shown in Fig. 2, which illustrates that the greater the intensity of the eliciting stimulus, the higher the initial level of responding and the greater the amount of habituation (Askew, 1969). However, Fig. 2 shows that the *final level* of responding is higher for the high-intensity stimuli. These findings are supported in detail by a study by Davis and Wagner (1968), who tested habituation of the startle response in rats by using tones of different intensity levels, 100 and 120 db.

Davis and Wagner (1968) also included a group of animals that received tone that started at low intensities and gradually

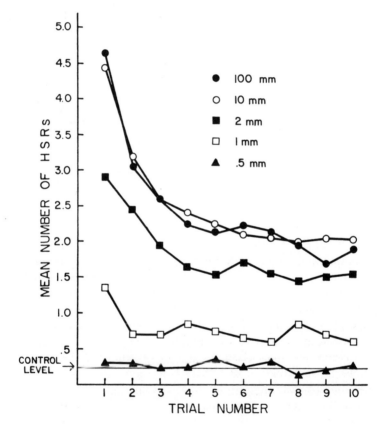

Fig. 2. Effects of stimulus intensities on habituation of the headshake response of rats to air stimulation. (Adapted from Askew, 1969)

increased across 350 or 750 trials. In this case, initial level of responding was very low, as expected from the idea that low-intensity stimuli are weak elicitors. As the intensity increased during later trials the frequency of responses increased slightly, as expected because of the belief that more intense stimuli are stronger elicitors of startle responses. By the last block of trials for the group subjected to gradually increasing intensities the stimuli were presented at the highest intensity level, 120 db. The amount of response was well below that of groups that had received all their trials at this high intensity. That is, the procedure involving *fading in of stimuli* resulted in less response at the highest intensity levels of the stimulus than a procedure of repeated presentations of the intense stimulus. (This fact seems to have been recognized by persons who break horses to saddles and riders by gradually increasing the weight on the horse until it finally includes the weight of a saddle and a rider.)

Davis and Wagner (1968) suggest that the theories of neither Sokolov (1963) nor Thompson and Spencer (1966) predict the effects of *stimulus fading* on responses to stimuli of high intensity. In the context of the present theory the joint operation of Propositions 4 and 5 are required to make this prediction. Proposition 5 refers to the refractory effects of response elicitations that are accumulated if intertrial intervals are short. Davis and Wagner massed the 350 or 750 trials using an 8-second intertrial interval. According to the present theory, the joint operation of increasing intensity and short intertrial intervals accounts for the extreme reduction in responses for the group that had the stimuli faded in during the habituation procedure.

Studies of effects of *stimulus duration* on habituation yield mixed results, although a majority of studies show no systematic effects of stimulus duration on any index of habituation. These studies are summarized by Askew, Leibrecht, and Ratner (1969), who also report no effect of stimulus duration on habituation of the headshake response in rats. This was true even if the durations of the stimuli were varied or made contingent on the occurrence of headshake responses. According to Proposition 4, stimulus duration could affect the association between the stimulus and its response, comparing very brief pulses of stimulation with durations that adequately elicit responses. In this case the differing durations would function like differing intensities, in which very brief pulses are comparable to weak elicitors and adequate durations function like higher intensity elicitors. In the study by Askew, Leibrecht, and Ratner (1969) the durations that were used were 5 seconds and 20 seconds, both of which are apparently adequate. Koepke and Pribram (1966) used similar durations and also found no differences in habituation of GSRs with humans. Keen, Chase, and Graham (1965) report effects of stimulus durations of 2 seconds versus 10 seconds on habituation of cardiac acceleration in infants to loud sounds. Their results can be interpreted in terms of the idea that duration acts like intensity. The experimenters find that the long-duration elicitor had its effects only for several trials; that is, the long-duration stimulus led to a higher initial level of responding than the short-duration stimulus. However, their procedure does not permit analysis of the effects of duration (as intensity) on amount of habituation or final level of responding. Clifton, Graham, and Hatton (1968) found similar effects for five durations (2 through 30 seconds) but found no significant effects of duration on habituation.

As noted in Proposition 4 the specific strength of the association between the stimulus and the response determines the outcomes of the stimulus presentation, so different durations may have different effects insofar as they elicit responses differentially. In addition, stimuli with very long durations may lead to the elicitation of more than one response per trial. Thus, a comparison of the effects of repeated presentations of a short duration with a very long duration stimulus may yield different habituation functions, as suggested by Clifton, Graham, and Hatton (1968).

Temporal Variables and Refractory Effects

Proposition 5 relates to the findings from physiology and ethology that the elicitation of a response is followed by a refractory period during which time the threshold for elicitation of a response is raised and the response strength is reduced. This is a key proposition for the "elicitation and interference theory of habituation" because it postulates the mechanism for "weakening" an elicited response and postulates the means by which the competing responses can intrude. The main behavioral data that relate to this proposition come from studies of effects of intertrial interval (ITI) on habituation. In general I assume that the shorter the ITI, the greater a refraction of the responses and the greater the amount of habituation. Intertrial intervals longer in duration than the hypothetical refractory period should lead to no further changes in the amount of habituation. Tentatively, this maximum effective ITI is taken to be approximately 120 seconds, although a number of consummatory responses, such as copulation, may have longer effective refractory periods even if strong eliciting stimuli are presented.

Studies by Bartoshuk (1962) concerning heart acceleration of infants, Schaub (1965) on the GSR of humans, Ratner and Stein (1965) on the contraction response of earthworms, Rushforth (1967) on the contraction response of hydra, and Askew (1969) concerning headshake of rats are among those that have investigated the effect of the ITI on habituation. The results of all the studies support the generalization of Proposition 5 that the shorter the ITI, the greater the amount of habituation. The nature of the effect for ITIs of 1, 10, and 100 seconds on frequency of the headshake response in rats is shown in Fig. 3. These results span the range of ITIs that represent the vast majority of values used in studies of this variable. However, a larger value was studied by Rushforth (1967) with hydra and Schaub (1965) with humans. In both cases the amount of habituation with ITIs longer than 100 seconds was negligible. In the language of Proposition 5 we assume that recovery from refractory effects of the previous elicitations was virtually complete and the test conditions were neutral enough so that competing responses did not become dominant.

Response sensitization or *temporal conditioning* is discussed as a control procedure in the previous section and is a reported outcome of several investigations of habituation that used fixed and short ITIs or fixed and long ITIs. This fact alone is important in view of the small amount of work concerning temporal conditioning; it is also important in relation to an analysis of habituation. Brown (1939) shocked rats at 12-second intervals for 35 trials and measured force of jumping elicited by this shock. He then shocked them at intervals of 3 to 24 seconds and found the greatest jumping force

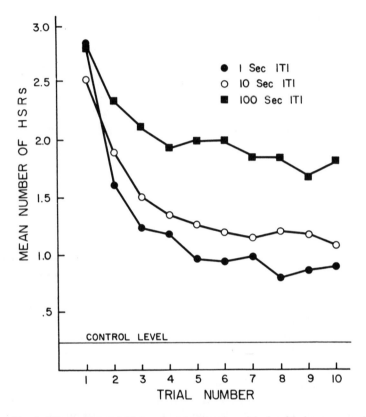

Fig. 3. Effects of intertrial intervals on habituation of the headshake response of rats to air stimulation. (Adapted from Askew, 1969)

for shocks given 12 seconds after the previous shock. The force of jumping decreased the greater the departure from the "training" delay. This is relatively indirect evidence for temporal conditioning, as compared with the results of the study of shock-avoidance learning with rats, in which case the best temporal learning occurred with ITIs of 15 seconds between shocks when no other signals were used (Bugelski & Coyer, 1959).

Other direct support for the effects of fixed and extreme ITIs on the possibility of temporal conditioning comes from a study by Franzisket (1963), who elicited the wiping response in spinal frogs by stroking their nostrils every 10 seconds. Response frequency across blocks of trials gradually increased across more than 1,000 trials. Kimble and Ray (1965) replicated this study and obtained similar results when they stimulated slightly different areas around the nostrils, but they got habituation (a response decrement) when they stimulated the same area repeatedly. They described the increase in frequency of response as "response potentiation" but do not propose the mechanism of this process. Franzisket (1963) mentions another finding from his study that further suggests temporal conditioning. He reports that the croaking response, a part of the mating sequence, that he elicited by applying pressure between the shoulders of the frogs increased in frequency just like the wiping response did when he elicited croaking. The response continued to occur on the 5-second schedule after the stimuli were discontinued. He found this true for blinded, decerebrate, and intact animals.

Table 2 shows the number of responses elicited on successive days of testing for the spinal frogs in Franzisket's study (1963) and for both groups of intact frogs in Kimble and Ray's study (1965). Table 2 gives an idea of the magnitude of increase of responsiveness after hundreds of elicitations with ITIs that would ordinarily be expected to lead to strong refractory effects and large amounts of habituation.

TABLE 2

NUMBERS OF RESPONSES OF FROGS WITH 100 TRIALS PER DAY

Group*	Day								
	1	2	3	4	5	9	10	11	12
R-increase, F	8	12	23	47	60	75	81	70	80
R-increase, K & R	33	36	38	44	47	55	58	56	62
R-decrease, K & R	35	32	33	28	22	20	17	18	17

*F refers to Franzisket; K & R refers to Kimble and Ray.
Data from Franzisket (1963) and Kimble and Ray (1965). (See the text for descriptions of each group.)

The variable of locus of stimulation investigated by Kimble and Ray (1965) obviously affects the course of response change as shown in Table 2, and Proposition 5, dealing with refractory effects, is adequate to explain habituation for the group stimulated at the same area. Difficulty arises, however, in dealing with the two reports of increases of response frequency, even if they involve stimulation of slightly different areas using fixed and short ITIs. At this time I consider the reports to be examples of temporal conditioning in which the temporal schedule provides the conditioned stimulus. In humans Schaub (1965) elicited GSRs with moderately intense auditory stimuli and found increasing amplitudes of responses when stimuli were presented with a fixed ITI of 180 seconds (temporal conditioning) and decreasing amplitudes when stimuli were presented with fixed ITIs of 30 or 60 seconds (habituation).

In summary, then, Proposition 5 is interpreted to relate to the effects of intertrial interval on amount of habituation. Data from a number of experiments show that the shorter the ITI, the greater the amount of habituation. A discontinuity occurs if ITIs are fixed and less than 30 seconds or greater than 120 seconds. In these cases responses increase in frequency (sensitization, response potentiation, or temporal conditioning). However, the discontinuity seems to be limited by the nature of the eliciting stimulus and the response system. This is seen from the studies of Kimble and Ray (1965) and Askew (1969). As shown in Fig. 2, Askew used an ITI of 1 second and found that it leads to more habituation than an ITI of 10 or 100 seconds.

Concurrent Stimulation, Including Dishabituation

Proposition 6 deals with the effects of stimulus conditions that operate concurrently with the original eliciting stimulus. According to this proposition, the concurrent stimuli also elicit responses and these may facilitate or interfere with the one originally elicited. The effect depends on the strength of these concurrent stimuli and on topography of the responses to them. Proposition 6 identifies concurrent stimulation as one of the major sources of competing responses, which are assumed to occur during the refractory periods and produce the systematic change in responding associated with the process of habituation.

As discussed by Denny and Ratner (1970, chapter 10), two types of concurrent stimulation have been studied, namely, *intermittent stimulation*, when an extra stimulus is presented occasionally around the habituated stimulus, and *constant stimulation*. Among other investigators, Ratner and VanDeventer (1965) and Brown, Dustman, and Beck (1966) using planaria, Leibrecht (1969) using rats, and Zimny and Schwabe (1966) have found that intermittent concurrent stimulation increases responses to the original habituating stimulus and leads to the loss of habituation (dishabituation), as compared with control conditions where such stimuli are not presented. Leibrecht (1969) has shown that the effect of the intermittent stimulus is actually more complex than is suggested by these other studies. The intermittent stimulus briefly increases and then briefly decreases the response to the original stimulus, but the net effect shows an increase in response (dishabituation).

Constant concurrent stimulation also has relatively complex effects on habituation, as suggested in Proposition 6. The following conclusions about effects of constant concurrent stimulation are suggested: (1) Constant concurrent stimulation that elicits responses that are similar to or compatible with the responses undergoing habituation delays habituation. For example, high water temperature that elicits thermotactic responses in planaria retards habituation of their responses to light (VanDeventer & Ratner, 1965). (2) Constant concurrent stimulation that elicits responses that compete with the responses undergoing habituation facilitates habituation. For example, a high degree of body contact that elicits cessation of movements in earthworms enhances habituation of responses of earthworms to light. Ratner and Gardner (1968) find that during habituation sessions a group of earthworms tested with a high degree of body contact made 2.33 responses to light, whereas a group with little contact made 11.00 responses. In general the effectiveness of constant concurrent stimulation arises from the fact that these stimuli can elicit responses at any time (either when the original responses become refractory or during the intertrial interval). Thus, VanDeventer and Ratner (1965) found that concurrent stimuli that elicited responses compatible with the originally elicited one increase, rather than decrease, the frequency of response to the original stimulus.

Some effects of drugs on habituation can be viewed in terms of constant concurrent stimulation. Some drugs lead to relaxation or increased activity. These responses may compete with or facilitate the originally elicited response. Spreading cortical depression in rats from potassium chloride decreases habituation of approaching responses (exploration) elicited by maze cues. Depression of the right and left cortex decreased habituation more than depression of one side of the cortex alone (Nadel, 1966). Although Hogberg (1967) found no significant effect of cortical depression on habituation of optokinetic nystagmus in turtles, he found that caffeine reduced habituation of optokinetic nystagmus. In this case we assume that caffeine increased activity in general and therefore led to a large number of interfering responses.

In summary, a number of experimental results support the idea that concurrent stimulation and its associated responses affect the strength of associations between an eliciting stimulus and its responses. In general the amount of habituation is decreased with intermittent concurrent stimulation, but this is true only if the response to the intermittent stimulus does not interfere with the response to the original stimulus. Constant concurrent stimulation can also interfere with the original response and thus facilitate habituation, or it can lead to responses that are compatible with the original response and decrease the amount of habituation.

Retention of Habituation

Proposition 7 deals with two conditions that influence retention of habituation. One is the strength of the association between the eliciting stimulus and its response, and the second is the time after habituation when the strength of the association has not fully recovered. We have already discussed the effects of the strength of association between the eliciting stimulus and its response in terms of original habituation. We used an analysis of behavior of organisms in terms of *orienting, consummatory,* and *postconsummatory sequences.* In this kind of analysis, biting food, chewing food, intromission, headshaking, and the like are examples of late consummatory components that are strongly associated with appropriate eliciting stimuli. Components such as walking toward an object and freezing to a shadow are examples of orienting components with relatively weak association between the eliciting stimuli and their responses (Denny & Ratner, 1970, chapter 5).

According to Proposition 7, other things equal, the greater the strength of the S–R association, the shorter the retention of habituation involving this association. Thus, we expect habituation of orienting components to be retained longer than habituation of consummatory components, and a number of research findings support this idea.

Retention of habituation of orienting components generally persists for more than one day. VanDeventer (1967) habituated contraction responses of planaria to a tactile stimulus and found retention of habituation for 96 hours. Gardner (1968) habituated contraction responses of earthworms to a vibratory stimulus and also found retention for more than 96 hours. Hinde (1960) found retention of habituation more than a week after eliciting orienting components of a bird's reaction to predators. Collins and Updegraff (1966) showed retention in cats and dogs of habituation of a postural response, rotational nystagmus, for more than a week. In addition, Denny and Leckart (1965) found that rats in a maze retain habituation of approach responses for at least a week. Conversely, habituation is retained for short periods if the responses are strongly associated with eliciting stimuli, namely, consummatory components. Ratner and Gardner (1968) tested earthworms for retention of habituation of contraction responses elicited by light and found full recovery of response within 24 hours. In this case, light elicits a strong and vital defensive response, as compared with vibration. Askew, Leibrecht, and Ratner (1969) found that in less than 6 hours there is full recovery from habituation of the headshake response of rats that is elicited by air directed to the ear of the animal. Black, Fowler, and Kimbrell (1964) found habituation of heart-rate increases in naïve rats that were repeatedly picked up and placed in a small box, but they also found full recovery of the increase within 24 hours. Heart-rate changes constitute one aspect of the consummatory responses involving contact with a predator, the human. Among female mice Noirot (1965) found habituation of the response of retrieving the young, but this response—a response in a consummatory sequence of care of the young—also recovered fully within 24 hours.

The findings noted above provide general support for the first part of Proposition 7, although detailed information must be obtained from a fine-grained study involving habituation and retention tests of a known set of components from orienting and consummatory sequences. One line of evidence is of this sort and supports the analysis in detail. Gardner (1968) measured habituation of two components of the worm's total response to vibration (see Fig. 1). One of these components habituated much more quickly than the other, which means it was more weakly associated with the eliciting stimulus. In the test for retention, Gardner found that habituation was kept for a shorter time for the component that was more strongly associated with the eliciting stimulus than for the other component. Specifically, the two components are withdrawal, labeled W in Fig. 1, and hooking, labeled H. This figure shows the differential rates of habituation for the two components; and from these data I predicted the results, later verified, of retention tests. That is,

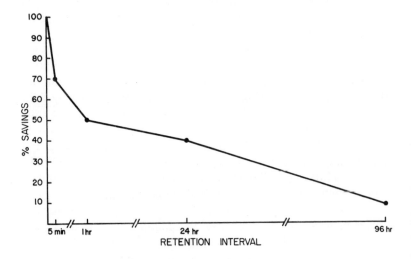

Fig. 4. Retention of habituation of responses of planaria to tactile stimulation. (Adapted from VanDeventer, 1967)

savings (reflecting retention) for the W component were greater than savings for the H component.

The final aspect of retention of habituation concerns the relations between amount of retention of habituation and time after habituation for intervals that are within the "retention time" of the response. The sort of relations that we have found in several studies, such as those by VanDeventer (1967) and Gardner (1968), are shown in Fig. 4, which also shows that the curve for retention of habituation is very similar to general forgetting curves, such as are found for forgetting of simple verbal material. That is, the major part of forgetting occurs relatively soon after the last trial, and then the curve descends more gradually to an asymptote.

SOME THEORETICAL CONCLUSIONS

Repeated stimulation of an intact organism leads to decrements in responding (habituation) under some conditions and to maintenance or increases in responding under others. In general, repeated stimulation with intertrial intervals of 150 seconds or less leads to decrements. The decrements are explained in terms of *refractory processes* occurring with the elicitation of each response and *interfering processes* associated with changes in the topography of the elicited response and interfering responses elicited by concurrent stimulation.

Repeated stimulation under three conditions leads to maintenance or increases in responding. The three conditions are: (1) fading in of stimulation from weak to intense values with brief intertrial intervals; (2) repeated stimulation with fixed and very brief or very long intertrial intervals for limited types of responses (sensitization or temporal conditioning); and (3) operation of concurrent stimulation that elicits responses that are similar to or facilitative of the responses to the original stimulus.

Duration of retention of habituation is limited by the consummatory sequence that has undergone habituation. The sequences are orienting, consummatory, and postconsummatory, with minimum duration of retention of habituation for late consummatory components, such as biting food, and increasing duration of retention for more remote components.

REFERENCES

Askew, H. R. Effects of intertrial interval and stimulus intensity on habituation of the head shake response in rats. Unpublished doctoral dissertation, Michigan State University, 1969.

Askew, H. R., Leibrecht, B. C., & Ratner, S. C. Effects of stimulus duration and repeated sessions of habituation of a head-shake response in the rat. *J. comp. physiol. Psychol.*, 1969, **67**, 497–503.

Bartoshuk, A. K. Response decrement with repeated elicitation of human neonatal cardiac acceleration to sound. *J. comp. physiol. Psychol.*, 1962, **55**, 9–13.

Black, R. W., Fowler, R. L., & Kimbrell, G. Adaptation and habituation of heart rate to handling in the rat. *J. comp. physiol. Psychol.*, 1964, **57**, 422–425.

Brown, H. M., Dustman, R. E., & Beck, E. C. Sensitization in planaria. *Physiol. and Behav.*, 1966, **1**, 305–308.

Brown, J. S. A note on a temporal gradient of reinforcement. *J. exp. Psychol.*, 1939, **25**, 221–227.

Bugelski, B. R., & Coyer, R. A. Temporal conditioning versus anxiety reduction in avoidance learning. *Amer. Psychologist*, 1950, **5**, 264.

Butler, R. A., & Harlow, H. F. Persistence of visual exploration in monkeys. *J. comp. physiol. Psychol.*, 1954, **47**, 258–263.

Carlton, P. L., & Vogel, J. R. Habituation and conditioning. *J. comp. physiol. Psychol.*, 1967, **63**, 348–351.

Clark, R. B. The learning ability of nereid polychaetes and the role of the supra-aesophageal ganglion. *Animal Behaviour Supp. 1*, 1964, 89–99.

Clifton, R. K., Graham, F. K., & Hatton, H. M. Newborn heart-rate response and response habituation as a function of stimulus duration. *J. exp. child Psychol.*, 1968, **6**, 265–278.

Collins, W. E., & Updegraff, B. P. A comparison of nystagmus habituation in the cat and dog. *Acta oto-laryng.*, 1966, **62**, 19–26.

Craig, W. Appetites and aversions as constituents of instincts. *Biol. Bull.*, 1918, **34**, 91–107.

Davis, M., & Wagner, A. R. Startle responsiveness after habituation to different intensities of tone. *Psychon. Sci.*, 1968, **12**, 337–338.

Denny, M. R. Relaxation theory and experiments. In F. R. Brush (Ed.), *Aversive conditioning and learning*. New York: Academic Press, 1969. Chap. 10.

Denny, M. R., & Leckart, B. T. Alternation behavior: Learning and extinction one trial per day. *J. comp. physiol. Psychol.*, 1965, **60**, 229–232.

Denny, M. R., & Ratner, S. C. *Comparative psychology* (Rev. ed.). Homewood, Illinois: Dorsey, 1970.

Engen, T., Lipsitt, L. P., & Kaye, H. Olfactory responses and adaptation in the human neonate. *J. comp. physiol. Psychol.*, 1963, **56**, 73–77.

Fowler, H. *Curiosity and exploratory behavior*. New York: Macmillan, 1965.

Franzisket, L. Characteristics of instinctive behavior and learning in reflex activity of the frog. *Animal Behaviour*, 1963, **11**, 318–324.

Gardner, L. E. Habituation in the earthworm: Retention and overhabituation. Unpublished doctoral dissertation, Michigan State University, 1966.

Gardner, L. E. Retention and overhabituation of a dual-component response in *Lumbricus terrestris. J. comp. physiol. Psychol.*, 1968, **66**, 315–318.

Harris, J. D. Habituatory response decrement in the intact organism. *Psychol., Bull.*, 1943, **40**, 385–423.

Hayes, W. N., & Saiff, E. I. Visual alarm reactions in turtles. *Animal Behaviour*, 1967, **15**, 102–106.

Hinde, R. A. Factors governing the changes in the strength of a partially inborn response, as shown by the mobbing behavior of the chaffinch. III. *Proc. Roy. Soc. B.*, 1960, **153**, 398–420.

Hogberg, D. K. The effects of cortical spreading depression, tectal and cortical lesions, and caffeine on opto-kinetic nystagmus habituation and reflex rebound in the painted turtle. Unpublished doctoral dissertation, State University of New York, at Buffalo, 1967.

Keen, Rachel E., Chase, Helen H., & Graham, Frances K. Twenty-four hour retention by neonates of an habituated heart rate response. *Psychon. Sci.*, 1965, **2**, 265–266.

Kimble, D. P., & Ray, Roberta S. Reflex habituation and potentiation in *Rana pipiens. Animal Behaviour*, 1965, **13**, 530–533.

Koepke, J. E., & Pribram, K. H. Habituation of GSR as a function of stimulus duration and spontaneous activity. *J. comp. physiol. Psychol.*, 1966, **61**, 442–448.

Korn, J. H., & Moyer, K. E. Habituation of the startle response and of heart rate in the rat. *Canad. J. Psychol.*, 1966, **20**, 183–190.

Leibrecht, B. C. Dishabituation of the head-shake response in the rat. Unpublished doctoral dissertation, Michigan State University, 1969.

Lorenz, K. *Evolution and modification of behavior.* Chicago: University of Chicago Press, 1965.

Morgan, R. F. Temporal conditioning in humans as a function of intertrial interval and stimulus intensity. Unpublished doctoral dissertation, Michigan State University, 1965.

Nadel, L. Cortical spreading depression and habituation. *Psychon. Sci.*, 1966, **5**, 119–120.

Noirot, Elaine. Changes in responsiveness to young in the adult mouse. III. The effect of immediately preceding experience. *Behaviour*, 1965, **24**, 318–325.

Ratner, S. C. Effect of extinction of dipper approaching on subsequent extinction of bar pressing and dipper approaching. *J. comp. physiol. Psychol.*, 1956, **49**, 576–581.

Ratner, S. C. Annelid learning: A critical review. In W. C. Corning & S. C. Ratner (Eds.), *Chemistry of learning.* New York: Plenum Press, 1967a, 391–406.

Ratner, S. C. Comparative aspects of hypnosis. In J. Gordon (Ed.), *Handbook of clinical and experimental hypnosis.* New York: Macmillan, 1967b, 550–587.

Ratner, S. C. Reliability of indexes of worm learning. *Psychol. Rep.*, 1968, **22**, 130.

Ratner, S. C. Comparative psychology. In A. Gilgen (Ed.), *Scientific Psychology: Perspectives*. New York: Academic Press, 1970.

Ratner, S. C., & Denny, M. R. *Comparative psychology*. Homewood, Illinois: Dorsey, 1964.

Ratner, S. C., & Gardner, L. E. Variables affecting responses of earthworms to light. *J. comp. physiol. Psychol.*, 1968, **66**, 239–243.

Ratner, S. C., & Stein, D. G. Responses of worms to light as a function of intertrial interval and ganglion removal. *J. comp. physiol. Psychol.*, 1965, **59**, 301–305.

Ratner, S. C., & VanDeventer, J. M. Effects of water current on responses of planaria to light. *J. comp. physiol. Psychol.*, 1965, **60**, 138–139.

Rushforth, N. B. Chemical and physical factors affecting behavior in hydra: Interactions among factors affecting behavior in hydra. In W. C. Corning & S. C. Ratner (Eds.), *Chemistry of learning*. New York: Plenum Press, 1967. Pp. 369–390.

Russell, E. M. Changes in the behaviour of *Leibistes reticulatus* upon a repeated shadow stimulus. *Animal Behaviour*, 1967, **15**, 574–585.

Schaub, R. E. The effect of interstimulus interval on GSR adaptation. *Psychon. Sci.*, 1965, **2**, 361–362.

Sokolov, Ye. N. *Perception and the conditioned reflex*. New York: Macmillan, 1963.

Thompson, R. F., & Spencer, W. A. Habituation: A model phenomenon for the study of neuronal substrates of behavior. *Psychol. Rev.*, 1966, **73**, 16–43.

Thorpe, W. T. *Learning and instinct in animals*. London: Methuen, 1956.

Thorpe, W. T. *Learning and instinct in animals*. London: Methuen, 1963.

VanDeventer, J. M. Responses to repeated tactile stimulation in the planarian, *Dugesia tigrina*. Unpublished doctoral dissertation, Michigan State University, 1967.

VanDeventer, J. M., & Ratner, S. C. Variables affecting frequencies of responses of planaria to light. *J. comp. physiol. Psychol.*, 1964, **57**, 407–411.

Zimny, G. H., & Schwabe, L. W. Stimulus change and habituation of the orienting reflex. *Psychophysiology*, 1966, **2**, 103–115.

Determinants of Heart Rate Classical Conditioning[1]

NEIL SCHNEIDERMAN

University of Miami

During the past several years much of the research in my laboratory has focused upon the behavioral and physiological determinants of heart rate (HR) classical conditioning. Basically, we have used three research strategies to examine these determinants. First, we have compared the HR response with various somatic responses. Second, we have examined HR as an autonomic response and have compared it with other autonomic responses. Third, we have begun to examine the central nervous system determinants of HR conditioning. The purpose of this chapter is to review some of our recent findings and to relate them to the results of other experiments which have studied cardiovascular regulation and conditioning. Before turning to an examination of the determinants of HR conditioning, however, let us briefly review some of the basic variables involved in cardiovascular regulation and conditioning.

Response Measures of Cardiovascular Regulation

The quantity and distribution of blood flowing through different vascular networks of the body changes in response to the demands of various tissues and organs. During physical exertion, for example, blood flow through the skeletal muscles is increased. In contrast, when food is being digested there is an increase in blood flow through the mesenteric vessels. Blood flow through the skin is also subject

[1] The research from my laboratory described in this chapter was primarily supported by National Science Foundation research grants GB–5307 and GB–7944 as well as by NIH HD training grant 00187 in quantitative organismic biology to the Laboratory for Quantitative Biology.

to change and is influenced by external temperatures, emotional factors, and other variables. Although some of the demands of the body can be met by simply changing the relative distribution of blood flow from one vascular bed to another, most of these needs are met by changing the total blood flow throughout the systemic circulation.

The total blood flow throughout the circulation is referred to as the cardiac output. Cardiac output is defined as the quantity of blood ejected each minute by one of the ventricles. This quantity is a function of the number of cardiac strokes per minute (HR) multiplied by the cardiac output stroke volume. The stroke volume in turn represents the volume of blood in the ventricle at the end of diastole (filling stage) minus the ventricular volume at the end of systole (ejection stage). Cardiac output can thus be modified by changes in HR, diastolic volume, or systolic volume, as well as by some combination of these. Consequently, consideration of only one of these variables to the exclusion of the others can be quite deceptive. Moreover, a complete knowledge of all three can still be misleading if we have inadequate information about the distribution of blood flow throughout the different vascular beds.

The blood forced into the aorta during systole exerts considerable pressure. This pressure, however, falls rapidly as the blood passes from the larger arteries to the smaller arteries and arterioles. The fall in pressure occurs because the small vessels offer greater resistance to flow. Blood pressure (BP) in the cardiovascular system is thus a function of cardiac output (HR × stroke volume) and peripheral resistance. The relationship between flow, pressure, and resistance may be expressed:

$$\text{Resistance} = \frac{\text{Pressure}}{\text{Flow}}$$

During each cardiac cycle, the peak BP value reached is referred to as the systolic pressure; the minimum value is referred to as the diastolic pressure. This relationship is expressed as the systolic pressure over the diastolic pressure measured in millimeters of mercury (e.g., 120/70 mm. Hg). In man the difference between the systolic and diastolic pressure is typically about 50 mm. Hg. Mean BP, which refers to the average pressure throughout the cardiac cycle, is determined by integrating the area under the pressure curve.

Peripheral Neural Regulatory Mechanisms

Although cardiac tissue is intrinsically rhythmic, its activity is modulated bilaterally by neural inputs from the sympathetic and parasympathetic divisions of the autonomic nervous system. Basically, the cardiac branch of each vagus nerve provides a cholinergic (acetylcholine secreting) parasympethetic input which is responsible for decreasing HR. In contrast, the cardiac accelerator nerves provide adrenergic (norepinephrine secreting) sympathetic inputs which can accelerate HR and increase the force of cardiac muscle contraction.

Ordinarily, at rest there is little tonic discharge in the cardiac sympathetic nerves, so that cutting them has relatively little effect upon resting HR. In contrast, if the vagus nerves are cut bilaterally or the S is given an appropriate parasympathetic blocking agent such as atropine, a pronounced increase in HR will occur. Although the neural inputs to the heart ordinarily play a large role in normal cardiovascular regulation, these inputs must be severed during heart transplants. In this case, cardiovascular function immediately after transplant is governed by humoral influences as well as by neural control of blood vessels.

Virtually all blood vessels except capillaries contain smooth muscles which receive their innervation from the sympathetic nervous system. In general, these fibers tend to be adrenergic and vasoconstrictor in function. The most conspicuous exceptions are: (a) cerebral vessels, which receive little neural innervation, (b) adrenergic fibers to the coronary vessels, which exert a vasodilator effect, and (c) cholinergic sympathetic vasodilators, which travel with the sympathetic nerves to skeletal muscle.

BP is importantly regulated by sensory stretch receptors in the walls of the heart and blood vessels. Best known of these pressures or baroreceptors are the carotid sinus and aortic receptors. The carotid pressoreceptors are located in the bifurcation of the carotid artery in the neck; the aortic receptors are found mostly in the vicinity of the aortic arch. Basically, the pressoreceptors increase their firing as arterial BP increases and send this message to the cardioinhibitory center in the medulla. Under certain conditions the message initiates a reflex decrease in HR, primarily by means of the vagal input to the heart. A schematic representation of the baroreceptor-initiated vagal compensatory reflex circuit is shown in Fig. 1.

Recording Methods

The most useful measures for studying cardiovascular conditioning have been HR, BP, and blood volume. Significant additional information could be obtained by concurrently measuring blood flow.

HR is usually determined from the electrocardiogram (EKG), which is a record of potential fluctuations occurring during each cardiac cycle. These potentials can be recorded from the body because its fluids make it an excellent volume conductor. In our experiments recordings are easily obtained between subdermal pins inserted into an upper and a lower extremity.

BP can be measured either indirectly or directly. The indirect method is usually based upon using an inflatable arm cuff and a microphone. This permits detections of pulsations distal from the cuff. By gradually deflating the cuff the investigator can detect the pressures at which the first systolic sounds appear and also when the diastolic sounds disappear. In contrast to this indirect measure, we use a direct measure in which one end of a silicone rubber (Silastic) or polyvinyl chloride tube is inserted into an arterial lumen, and the other end of the tube is connected to an unbonded strain gauge transducer.

Although blood flow can be measured in a variety of ways, ultrasonic and electromagnetic flow meters are favored because they can record from individual vessels without having to penetrate them. Basically, the ultrasonic flowmeter uses crystals on one side of a vessel to generate sound waves, which are recorded across the diameter of the vessel. Changes of flow in the vessel alter the sound frequency at the receiver, and this is then translated into an electrical signal. In the case of the electromagnetic flowmeter a magnetic field is set up perpendicular to the direction of flow in the vessel.

VAGAL COMPENSATORY REFLEX

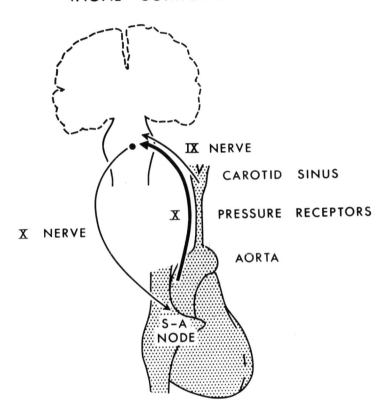

Fig. 1. Schematic representation of the vagal compensatory reflex circuit. Pressoreceptors in the carotid sinus send afferents to the medulla by means of the nerve of Hering, which joins the glossopharyngeal (IXth) nerve. Likewise, afferents from the aortic arch receptors transmit impulses by means of the vagus (Xth) nerve. When increases in pressure stimulate the pressoreceptors, activity decreases in the sympathetic input to the heart (not shown) but increases in the vagal efferents to the sino-atrial (S–A) node. Note that the vagus is a mixed nerve containing afferent and efferent fibers.

Recording electrodes, perpendicular to the flow and the field, detect currents generated by the flow of blood through the field.

Blood volume in a limb or a tissue segment can be measured by a variety of methods commonly referred to as plethysmography. In general the most useful methods for measuring blood volume or content use electrical impedance or photoelectrical transduction. These methods, however, are limited by the fact that they provide only relative measures of change. Nevertheless, when several of them are used together they can reflect changes taking place in different vascular beds. In our experiments monitoring blood content we use cadmium sulfide cells to detect variations of light intensity passing through tissue as a function of changes in blood volume.

BEHAVIORAL ANALYSES

Directionality of Heart Rate Responses

The nature of HR changes accompanying exercise, orienting responses, reaction-time anticipation, and conditioning have been extensively investigated. These experiments have established that the direction and magnitude of HR changes are importantly influenced by the species involved and the nature of the experimental task. An example of species involvement can be seen in the fact that rats increase their HR to the same electric-shock stimulus which elicits a decrease in the rabbit. Concerning tasks, HR increases and decreases are related to the general energy requirements of the organism.

During tasks involving muscular exertion, increases occur in both HR (Gasser & Meek, 1914; Krogh & Lindhard, 1913) and strength of cardiac contraction (Sarnoff, 1955). The increase in rate appears to be the result of a decrease in vagal firing accompanied by an increase in sympathetic activity (Warner, 1960). Besides the autonomic effects upon the heart itself, the increase in sympathetic activity raises BP by means of peripheral vasoconstriction (Herrick et al., 1940).

Correlative analyses of HR and general somatic activity have been conducted in a wide variety of experimental situations. In general, these studies have supported the notion of a strong positive relationship between HR and general somatic motor activity. In one experiment, for example, Webb and Obrist (1967) made food reinforcement in dogs contingent upon an increase followed by a decrease in somatic activity. They observed that HR accelerated when somatic activity increased, and decelerated below base line during somatic inhibition. Similar findings have been observed in the case of aversive classical conditioning by Obrist (1965); Obrist and Webb (1967); Obrist, Webb, and Sutterer (in press); Obrist, Wood, and Perez-Reyes (1965); and Wood and Obrist (1964).

Although the HR changes during conditioning are intimately related to gross motor activity and the energy requirements of the organism, several experiments have indicated that HR conditioning is not mediated by gross motor responding. Thus, Black (1965); Black, Carlson, and Solomon (1962); and Black and Lang (1964) have demonstrated that the HR CR in dogs is qualitatively the same whether the *S*s are run under a paralyzing drug or in the normal state. The results have been further confirmed in rabbits by Yehle, Dauth, and Schneiderman (1967).

A recent experiment by DiCara and Miller (1969) suggests that although the central commands for HR and somatic activity may be closely related, they are not identical. Basically, DiCara and Miller observed that when separate groups of rats learned to either increase or decrease their HR to escape and/or avoid electric shock, the initial differences between groups in breathing and somatic activity decreased with continued training.

Although the cardiac-somatic linkage undoubtably plays an important role in determining the form of the HR response, numerous instances have been recorded in which particular kinds of somatic activity have not been related to HR changes. Thus, for example, the acquisition rate of HR conditioned responses (CRs) appears to be unrelated to the acquisition rate of bar-press suppression in rats and monkeys (e.g., DeToledo & Black, 1966; Goldberg, in press; Parrish, 1967), nictitating membrane (NM) and breathing-rate (BR) responses in rabbits (e.g., Elliott & Schneiderman, 1968; VanDercar & Schneiderman, 1967), or leg-flexion responses in dogs and cats (e.g., Jaworska, Kowalska, & Soltysik, 1962; Bruner, 1969).

In many experimental situations both HR and gross motor activity decrease in the interval preceding the unconditioned stimulus (US). One possibility to consider is that the HR decreases provide a mechanism for maintaining adaptive circulatory homeostasis. According to this notion, sympathetic responses to the conditioned stimulus (CS), excluding HR, prepare the organism for a rapid expenditure of energy. Meanwhile, the HR decrease acts as a disengaged clutch until rapid, increased perfusion is needed in the large muscles.

The HR decreases which occur in anticipation of motor responses have also been interpreted as part of an attentional process. This viewpoint is in large part derived from Sokolov's (1963) theory of perception and maintains that the HR decrease is an orienting response. Support has come from Lacey and his collaborators (Coquery & Lacey, 1966; Lacey & Lacey, 1964, 1966) in reaction-time experiments which indicate that HR decelerates in the interval between the "ready" and "go" signals.

In a rather ingenious experiment, Chase, Graham, and Graham (1968) examined the relationship between attention and exercise in a reaction-time task. Basically, they examined whether HR would accelerate during the 4-second ready-go interval if the reaction involved a greater expenditure of energy than is usually involved in reaction-time experiments. Consequently, responses preceding a leg-lift exercise task were compared with responses preceding the usual button-push reaction.

Chase, Graham, and Graham (1968) examined the HR response topography of the ready-go interval in considerable detail and succeeded in identifying three components of the HR response. Immediately after the onset of the ready signal, they observed a decrease in rate, which they interpreted as an orienting response. The second component consisted of a rate decrease in the button-push but a rate increase in the leg-lift condition. Finally, a decrease in HR immediately preceded the go signal under both experimental conditions. On the basis of their findings, Chase, Graham, and Graham concluded that both stimulus reception and the energy requirements of the organism determine the nature of anticipatory cardiac responses.

Comparisons of Heart Rate with Somatic Motor Activity

One of the research strategies we have used to examine the behavioral characteristics of HR conditioning has been to contrast it with performance concomitantly elicited from other response systems. Thus, in a series of studies conducted upon rabbits in our laboratory we documented differences in performance between HR and specific somatic responses. These differences occurred in rate of CR acquisition, extinction rate, maintenance of responding over sessions, discrimination capability, reactivity to drugs, responsiveness to stimulus uncertainty and stress, shape of the interstimulus interval (ISI) function, and performance under delay versus trace conditioning. A description of these differences and a discussion of their theoretical significance has recently been provided by Schneiderman (in press).

Acquisition Rate. An experiment conducted in my laboratory by Yehle (1966, 1968) is typical of our studies comparing HR with specific somatic responses. In this experiment differences in performance among rabbit response systems were compared during classical conditioning of a discrimination among three tones differing in frequency. The response measures were HR, NM, and BR.

Basically, four groups of eight Ss received one day of adaptation to the three tones, eight days of classical discrimination conditioning, and three days of extinction. Three different frequency tones (350, 1,650, and 2,950 Hz.) were employed as CSs in a design which had either one or two of the three tones in each group paired with the shock US. This pairing occurred in either a unidirectional or a bidirectional manner.

Responses to the reinforced (CS+) and nonreinforced (CS−) tones for each of the three response systems are shown for combined groups in Fig. 2. It can be seen that: (a) HR conditioning occurred before NM conditioning, (b) HR conditioning but not discrimination decreased, whereas NM conditioning increased over sessions, and (c) differentiation was greater in the NM and HR than in the BR system.

The early and consistent discrimination (within 10 CS–US

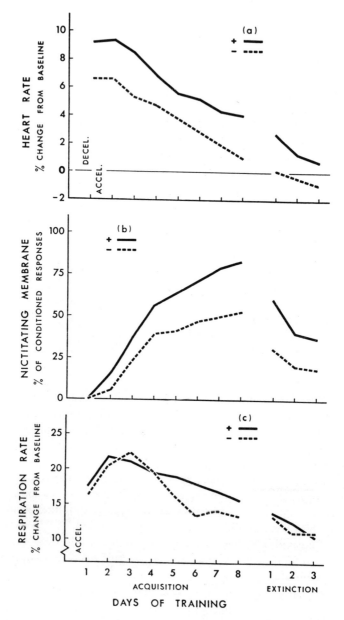

FIG. 2. Combined responses to the reinforced (+) and nonreinforced (−) tones for each of the three response systems. (Yehle, 1968)

pairings) in the HR response system indicated that the Ss had in effect associated the CS + with shock and the CS − with no shock soon after acquisition commenced. Thus, the gradual acquisition and discrimination formation evidenced in the NM system must have reflected something in addition to an S merely learning that a US follows the CS or that a US follows the CS + but not the CS −. This was most dramatically illustrated in the + − + group in which the high and low, but not the middle frequency, tones were paired with shock. In this group a reliable HR discrimination was demonstrated very early in training, but none of the Ss revealed any evidence of NM discrimination.

In general, the data in the Yehle (1968) experiment were consistent with Mowrer's (1950, 1960) proposition that conditioned anxiety (in this case manifested by HR conditioning) occurs early in training and that the performance of instrumental responses (e.g., NM CRs) helps to reduce the anxiety (as indicated by a decrease in the magnitude of HR CRs).

An alternative to the proposition that the decreased HR responding results from an increase in NM responses, however, is readily available. In this case we need only assume that: (a) the initial pairings of the CS and the US lead to conditioned freezing, and (b) the primary reason that NM responses do not occur is that they are incompatible with behavioral freezing. According to Obrist (1965), Obrist and Webb (1967), Obrist, Wood, and Perez-Reyes (1965), and Wood and Obrist (1964), conditioned HR decelerations are consistent with an inhibition of somatic motor responses.

If the added assumption is made that conditioned fear or freezing diminishes as a function of time in the experimental situation and/or repeated presentations of the US, NM frequency could be expected to increase as behavioral freezing and HR response magnitude diminish. A recent experiment by Schneiderman, VanDercar, Yehle, Manning, Golden, and Schneiderman (1969) supports this assumption. In one experiment in this study electric shocks were repeatedly presented at an intertrial interval of 3 minutes. The basic findings indicated that the magnitude of HR unconditioned responses (URs) decreased over trials.

Another experiment in my laboratory (Dauth, 1969; Dauth, Schneiderman, & Lordahl, in preparation) casts further doubt upon the notion that NM CRs are directly responsible for the reduction of HR responses. In this experiment, analysis of the data from individual *S*s indicated that HR CRs frequently began to diminish in amplitude before *S*s began making their first NM CRs.

Further evidence elucidating the relationship between behavioral freezing and specific somatic conditioning has been provided by Bruner (1969). Basically, Bruner recorded body tremor, HR, and leg flexion in cats during aversive classical conditioning. Bruner's *S*s were randomly divided into two groups. In one group *S*s received USs of 3–4 mA. Bruner found that in the threshold group neither leg-flexion tremor decreases nor HR responses became conditioned. In contrast, in the 3–4 mA. shock groups, conditioned HR decelerations and tremor decreases became apparent after as few as two trials, but leg flexions conditioned much later in training.

The comparisons between HR and specific somatic responses suggest that in contrast to Mowrer's (1950, 1960) formulation both systems may be reflecting the same process throughout acquisition, but that the specific somatic CR occurs later, because it is incompatible with behavioral freezing.

In contrast to the delayed acquisition of specific somatic responses, decreases of general somatic activity appear to condition extremely rapidly. Bruner (1969), for example, observed that tremor decreased within two trials. In experiments comparing acquisition rates of bar-press suppression and HR in rats (DeToledo & Black, 1966; Parrish, 1967) and monkeys (Goldberg, in press), bar-press suppression conditioned more rapidly than the HR responses. Thus, conditioned HR and bar-press suppression do not appear to be measuring the same thing.

Interstimulus interval functions. Besides the important differences which occur among HR and other response systems in rates of CR acquisition and discrimination formation, major differences occur among these systems as a function of ISI.

In our first experiment investigating this problem VanDercar and Schneiderman (1967) classically conditioned NM and HR discriminations in four groups of 8 rabbits at ISIs of .25, .75, 2.25, and 6.75 seconds. The major results of the experiment included findings that: (a) percentages of NM CRs were inversely related to

ISI, and (b) maximum magnitude of HR conditioning occurred at 2.25 seconds. Although reliable HR conditioning and discrimination occurred at 6.75 seconds, NM conditioning failed to occur at that interval. Finally, an examination of the HR response topographies during test trials (VanDercar, 1967) indicated that the maximum HR changes centered around the temporal point at which the US was presented.

In a second ISI experiment comparing NM and HR peformance, Meredith and Schneiderman (1967) studied these variables as a function of delay versus trace procedures. Basically, one dimension of a 2 × 2 factorial design, numbering eight rabbits per cell, consisted of .35-second or 1.00-second ISIs; the other dimension consisted of a .25-second trace procedure, or a delay procedure in which the CS and US offset simultaneously. The chief findings of the experiment were that HR performance was directly related and NM performance inversely related to ISI. It was also found that the trace procedure debilitated NM performance at the 1.00-second interval.

In a third ISI experiment Manning, Schneiderman, and Lordahl (1969) studied delay versus trace HR conditioning at ISIs of 7, 14, and 21 seconds. Under the delay procedure CS and US offset simultaneously; under the trace procedure a 5-second CS duration was employed. The chief findings of the study were that: (a) level of conditioning and discrimination formation varied inversely with ISI, and (b) at each interval delay was superior to trace conditioning.

At present, the most parsimonious explanation to account for the findings of the three experiments is to relate them to differences among response systems in terms of their CR and/or UR durations. Ebel and Prokasy (1963), for example, have proposed that kinesthetic feedback from the CR–US (reinforcement) relationship may influence the course of conditioning. Basically, they suggested that, by means of response shaping, Ss learn to make time discriminations which facilitate CR–US overlap. Relating their hypothesis to ISI, Ebel and Prokasy further suggested that the ISI functions reflect the efficiency with which S is able to maximize the CR–US reinforcement contingency. At short intervals the efficacy of the CR–US relationship may be restricted by S's inability to fully execute a CR, and at extended intervals by an incapacity to make successful time discriminations.

In the HR response system the UR duration to shock is approximately 4 seconds, and the CR has its maximum response amplitude when elicited at an ISI of about 2 seconds. Using our usual classical conditioning procedures, HR CRs can extend in time for approximately 20 seconds, but this is accomplished at the cost of diminished response amplitude. In the NM response system both the CR and the UR duration are typically less than 1 second. Because the HR CR has a longer duration than the NM CR, the HR response seems able to maximize the CR–US reinforcement contingency at longer ISIs. Thus HR conditioning in rabbits occurs at ISIs as long as 21 seconds, whereas NM conditioning fails to occur at an ISI of 7 seconds.

In the VanDercar and Schneiderman (1967) and Meredith and Schneiderman (1967) experiments, HR, but not NM conditioning, was less than optimum at ISIs less than 1 second. According to the Ebel and Prokasy (1963) hypothesis this occurred because the US truncated the long-duration HR response at short intervals, thus interfering with S's learning to time its discrimination.

The differences between delay versus trace conditioning as a function of ISI were consistent with the same hypothesis. According to this notion, when the peak CR occurs at an interval no longer than the ISI, S needs only to respond as rapidly as possible in order for CR–US overlap to occur; at longer ISIs, S must rely upon cues from the CS in order to make a successful time discrimination. Presumably, a gap between the CS and US disrupts the timing operations. In the Meredith and Schneiderman (1967) experiment NM conditioning was not debilitated at a .35-second ISI, nor was HR conditioning disrupted at a 1.00-second interval under the trace procedure. In contrast, at intervals longer than the ISI at which peak CRs were elicited in the particular system, Meredith and Schneiderman found debilitated NM conditioning, and Manning, Lordahl, and Schneiderman (1969) observed disrupted HR conditioning.

Although the Ebel and Prokasy (1963) hypothesis adequately handles the available data, Schneiderman and Gormezano (1964) have alternatively invoked Hull's (1943, 1952) stimulus trace formulation to account for ISI functions. According to this formulation, conditioning occurs to the intensity of the trace at US occurrence and generalizes to greater (and lesser) trace intensities. Presumably, the differences in ISI functions among response systems in this formulation would result from differences in the ubiquitousness of the responses involved. In any event, the empirical findings of our experiments indicate that HR can be classically conditioned at much longer intervals than those described for specific somatic responses.

PHYSIOLOGICAL ANALYSES

Heart Rate as an Autonomic Response

In our initial HR classical conditioning experiment in rabbits (Schneiderman, Smith, Smith, & Gormezano, 1964, 1966) we determined that the HR CR to tone paired with shock was a decrease in rate. This decelerative response was uncontaminated by pseudo-conditioning or sensitization. Since Obrist and his collaborators (Obrist, 1965; Obrist, Wood, & Perez-Reyes, 1965; Wood & Obrist, 1964) indicated that accelerative but not decelerative HR responses were related to changes in respiration and increases in gross bodily movement, the rabbit seemed to be a good candidate for the study of autonomic conditioning.

The finding in our first experiment that the HR CR was a decrease in rate, however, presented us with something of a paradox. Since we were using a presumably noxious electric shock as the US we might expect to obtain responses related to the activity of the sympathetic nervous system. In contrast, the HR decreases we obtained were not characteristic of sympathetic activity. Consequently, we set out to determine whether the HR decreases were results of (a) an artifact of somatic responding, (b) an inhibition of sympathetic activity, (c) an increase in general parasympathetic activity, or (d) a more localized parasympathetic response, perhaps related to the baroreceptor-initiated vagal compensatory reflex.

Our investigation of the problem began with a 2 × 2 factorial design using 32 rabbits (Yehle, Dauth, & Schneiderman, 1967). One dimension was comprised of paired or unpaired presentations of tone and electric shock; the other dimension consisted of injections of saline or gallamine triethiodide (Flaxedil). Flaxedil, of course, is a curarizing agent that paralyzes the *S* by competing for receptor sites at the end plates of skeletal muscle. In the doses we use, it blocks gross muscular activity, including movement of the diaphragm. For this reason, the *S*s must be artificially ventilated. Depth of curarization is continually monitored by means of electromyographic recordings. In our experiments adequacy of ventilation in the curarized preparation has been assessed by examining the stability of the HR base line and/or by monitoring PCO_2.

The Yehle, Dauth, & Schneiderman (1967) experiment differed from our more behavioral studies in two respects. First, it was an acute rather than a chronic experiment, since we performed a tracheotomy, cannulated a carotid artery, implanted intracranial recording electrodes, and ran our *S*s on the same day. Second, we employed a 20-mA. electric shock as the US. In most of our other work we used shock intensities ranging from 3 to 5 mA.

Figure 3 shows that rabbits immobilized by Flaxedil, or run in the normal state, revealed reliable HR decreases when the CS was paired with shock. In the explicitly unpaired control group, however, no evidence of nonassociative HR responding was obtained. The conditioned HR decreases were accompanied by conditioned BP elevations and neocortical desynchronization. In nonimmobilized rabbits receiving paired CS–US presentations, conditioned BR increases were also elicited. Although the URs of the different response systems occurred jointly and simultaneously, the CRs occasionally occurred independently of one another.

The pattern of URs obtained in the experiment was consistent with the hypothesis that the shocks elicited generalized sympathetic activation. The unconditioned HR decrease appeared largely to reflect a compensatory adjustment to increased arterial BP, which was transmitted to the heart by means of the vagus nerve. Recall from our earlier discussion that baroreceptors in the carotid sinus and aortic arch are known to provide such a mechanism for restoring BP to prestimulus levels.

Yehle, Dauth, and Schneiderman (1967) observed that conditioned HR responses were sometimes elicited in the absence of BP CRs. In a subsequent classical conditioning experiment

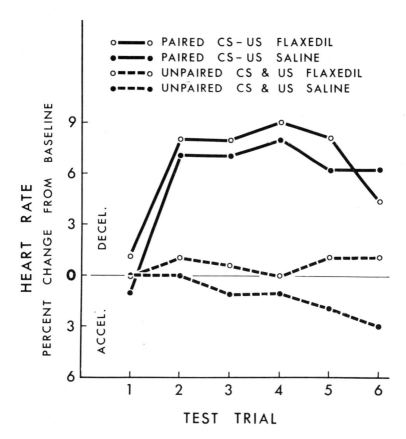

FIG. 3. Percent heart rate changes following successive blocks of 10 trials. Test trial 1 followed 10 CS-alone adaptation trials; test trial 2 followed 10 CS–US paired or 10 CS and 10 US presentations given unpaired.

Schneiderman et al. (1969) selected a lower US shock intensity, with the expectation that this would further increase the frequency of trials during which HR CRs would be elicited without concomitant conditioned BP responses. In addition, the study was designed to examine the role played by the vagal compensatory adjustment in the development of decelerative HR conditioning.

To the extent that the vagal compensatory adjustment plays a role in the development of HR conditioning, the development should be impeded by either (a) pharmacological (e.g., atropine) or surgical (bilateral cervical vagotomy) blocking of the vagal innervation of the heart, or (b) central dampening of the BP response to shock through the use of an alpha-adrenergic blocking agent such as Hydergine.

In the case of the vagal innervation of the heart, the chemical transmitter is acetylcholine (ACh). Unlike the action of curariform drugs such as Flaxedil and d-tubocurarine chloride, which block ACh transmission at the junction between motor neurons and striated muscle, atropine blocks the action of ACh upon cardiac and smooth muscle. The difference in drug effect is a result of the nature of the receptor sites present in each type of muscle.

In contrast to the cholinergic blocking agents such as atropine and Flaxedil, adrenergic blocking agents are drugs which oppose the effects of sympathetic stimulation. Ahlquist (1948) has pointed out that there appear to be two types of adrenergic receptors, which he called alpha and beta. The alpha receptors are primarily concerned with excitatory adrenergic responses except cardioacceleration and myocardial augmentation. Beta receptors, on the other hand, are the sites of inhibitory sympathetic activities and cardioacceleration. Cohen and Pitts (1968), for example, were able to abolish most conditioned HR increases in the pigeon by using a beta-adrenergic blockade, although there was some vagal contribution to the response.

While the beta-adrenergic blockade prevents HR increases by directly abolishing the sympathetic input to the heart, alpha-adrenergic blockades have little direct influence upon the heart. In contrast, they block HR decreases only to the extent that they diminish BP increases, which in turn reduce baroreceptor firing.

In the Schneiderman et al. (1969) study two sets of experiments were conducted in order to explore the relationship of the vagal compensatory reflex to the development of conditioned HR decreases. In the first experiment we examined the effects of adrenergic and cholinergic blockades upon unconditioned cardiovascular responses, and in the second experiment we examined the consequences of these effects upon classical discrimination conditioning.

Basically, the first experiment consisted of a 2 × 5 factorial design, with 6 rabbits in each cell. One dimension of the design consisted of 33 presentations of 3- or 20-mA. intensity electric shocks, which were presented alone every 3 minutes. The other dimension consisted of control, bilateral cervical vagotomy, atropine sulfate, Hydergine (alpha-adrenergic blockade), and Flaxedil treatments. Chief findings of the first experiment were that: (a) atropine and bilateral cervical vagotomy eliminated the HR decrease without influencing BP, (b) Hydergine diminished BP responses and HR decreases, and (c) HR decreases sometimes occurred in the absence of BP responses.

In the second experiment of the Schneiderman et al. (1969) study, six groups of 9 rabbits were given classical discrimination conditioning training. One group served as the control; the others were subjected to unilateral or bilateral cervical vagotomy, or were injected with Flaxedil, Hydergine, or atropine sulfate. The major finding of the experiment was that although all groups revealed unconditioned BP responses, virtually no conditioned BP responses were recorded in any group. Both atropine and bilateral cervical vagotomy abolished HR conditioning, and Hydergine diminished both BP and HR responses.

The data in the shock-alone experiment were consistent with the hypothesis that BP increases contributed to HR decelerations. However, the finding that HR changes sometimes occurred in the absence of BP responses indicates that other mechanisms were also operating. Although the classical discrimination conditioning experiment also indicated that HR CRs can occur in the absence of BP conditioning, the discovery that HR conditioning was debilitated in the Hydergine group suggests that the compensatory vagal reflex contributes to the development, if not the elaboration, of HR CRs.

Central Nervous System Determinants of Heart Rate Conditioning

In our studies of autonomic conditioning we determined that conditioned HR decelerations could be elicited in the absence of BP responses. DiCara and Miller (1968) have further reported that differential vasomotor changes between the two ears can be instrumentally conditioned in curarized rats. Since such findings cannot be easily accounted for in terms of simple vasomotor regulation in the medulla, the data suggest that HR CRs may in large part be integrated at supermedullary levels of the brain.

Kaada (1960), in his chapter in the *Handbook of Physiology*, cites numerous studies in cats, dogs, and monkeys documenting changes in BP as a result of stimulating various cortical areas. Green and Hoff (1937), for example, reported that the area anterior to the precentral motor cortex showed cardiovascular responses to electrical stimulation of the brain (ESB). Further study of the orbital surface of the cat and the monkey brain has suggested that it contains a sensory-motor representation of the vagus nerve. According to Bailey and Bremer (1938) and Dell (1952), excitation of the vagus nerve influences this area, and ESB delivered to this cortical region elicits responses that are highly similar to those obtained by vagal stimulation alone. Kaada (1951, 1960) has suggested that afferent impulses in the vagi and descending impulses from the cortical vagus motor field apparently act upon the same brain-stem mechanism, producing similar visceromotor and somatomotor responses.

To examine the effects of HR conditioning in the absence of cortical influence, several investigators have shown that HR conditioning proceeds normally after neodecortication (e.g., Bloch & Lagarrigue, 1968; Bloch-Rojas, Toro, & Pinto-Hamuy, 1964). In contrast to the decortication studies, Hendrickson and Pinto-Hamuy (1967) failed to obtain HR classical conditioning under bilateral spreading depression (SD). This finding is understandable, however, when one considers Weiss and Fifkova's (1961) report that unilateral SD influences important ipsilateral subcortical as well as cortical mechanisms.

In our laboratory we have examined the effects of unilateral versus bilateral SD[2] upon HR classical discrimination conditioning, using a procedure developed by Swadlow, Schneiderman, and

[2] The term *behavioral depression* should probably be substituted for *spreading depression* in most conditioning studies which have induced depression pharmacologically. In the present study, as well as in several other conditioning experiments, at least some Ss failed to reveal all the symptoms typically associated with the spreading depression of Leao (1944). Although the present study demonstrated that behavioral base lines were recoverable after KCl application, histological analyses revealed the presence of extensive cortical lesions similar to those described by Hamburg, Best, and Cholewiak (1968).

Schneiderman (1968). Basically, a discrimination was classically conditioned in 12 rabbits by pairing electrical stimulation of one lateral geniculate, but not the other, with peripheral electric shock. Following seven days of discrimination training, 9 Ss revealing asymptotic NM performance and exceeding 90% CRs to the CS + were used to assess the effects of unilateral and bilateral KCl upon the conditioned discrimination. Base-line data were obtained by applying isotonic saline to the dura bilaterally on Day 8 and unilaterally on Days 10 and 12. Wetted crystals of potassium chloride (KCl) were applied on Days 9, 11, and 13. The order of KCl applications above the CS + and CS − hemispheres was randomized over Ss.

The efficacy of the HR discrimination can be seen in Fig. 4. This figure also shows that on saline days the Ss recaptured their behavioral base lines, whereas KCl debilitated HR conditioning

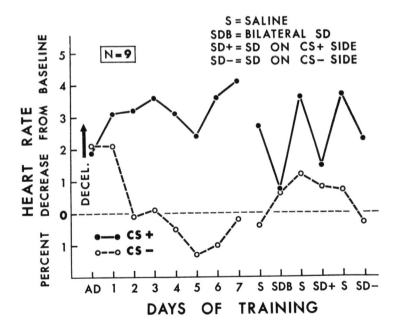

Fig. 4. Percent heart rate changes to the CS + and the CS − during adaptation, acquisition, saline base line, and spreading depression (SD) sessions.

under all treatment procedures. The greatest HR debilitation occurred after application of bilateral KCl; the least HR debilitation occurred when the KCl was applied above the CS− hemisphere. In contrast to HR, NM conditioning and discrimination was totally abolished after KCl application.

In the Swadlow, Schneiderman, and Schneiderman (1968) experiment ESB was used as both the CS+ and the CS−. In other brain stimulation conditioning experiments in my laboratory ESB has been used as both the CSs and the US. Before these experiments, Lico, Hoffman, and Covian (1968), Malmo (1965), and Shinoda and Ban (1961) conditioned various cardiovascular responses using subcortical ESB as the US. Thus, Malmo found that HR decelerations elicited by septal stimulation as the US (a) became conditioned to a tone, (b) were uncorrelated with BR, and (c) were not a result of pseudoconditioning or sensitization. In the second part of Malmo's study the same Ss learned to press a bar for septal stimulation delivered through the US electrode. Subsequently, Lico, Hoffman, and Covian classically conditioned BP decreases to septal stimulation in the anesthetized rabbit.

Ban and Shinoda (1956, 1960) conditioned pupillary changes, BR, and gastromotility in rabbits, using tone as the CS and hypothalamic stimulation as the US. Basically, sympathetic-like changes occurred when stimulation of the ventromedial hypothalamus served as the US, whereas parasympathetic-like changes were elicited when US stimulation consisted of lateral hypothalamic stimulation. In a subsequent experiment, Shinoda and Ban (1961) found conditioned increases in blood sugar level and leukocyte counts to ventromedial stimulation, but observed conditioned decreases in these measures when lateral hypothalamic stimulation was used as the US.

In my own laboratory Dr. D. A. Powell and other coworkers examined HR and BP URs to septal region, preoptic, hypothalamic subthalamic, and midbrain stimulation. Although we have not yet completed our studies involving pharmacological blockades of these responses, our findings have thus far supported Ban's (1966) contention that there is an organized septo-preoptico-hypothalamic system involved in autonomic regulation. According to this formulation, most of the medial structures in the hypothalamus, with the exception of the periventricular stratum and the medial mam-millary nuclei, have essentially sympathetic functions, whereas most of the septal, lateral preoptic, and lateral hypothalamic areas have parasympathetic functions. At this time, however, the complete system has not been worked out. Thus, within the sympathetic zone, for example, some structures provide BP increases accom-panied by HR decreases, whereas other structures elicit both HR and BP increases.

In our initial classical discrimination conditioning experiment using ESB as both CSs and US we examined HR responses in 20 rabbits during two days of adaptation and four days of acquisition training (Elster, VanDercar, & Schneiderman, in press). Basically, stimulation of one geniculate (CS +) was paired with diencephalic (posterior hypothalamus, subthalamus) or midbrain (reticular formation, central gray) stimulation. Stimulation of the contra-lateral geniculate (CS −) was presented alone. In some *S*s the discrimination was between dorsal lateral geniculates, and in other *S*s it was between medial geniculates.

The major finding of the study was that discriminations could be classically conditioned in the rabbit when both CSs and the US consisted of subcortical ESB. It was also found that: (a) both lateral and medial geniculate placements provided adequate CSs, (b) reliable HR discriminations were conditioned to both midbrain and diencephalic USs, (c) using identical stimulus parameters, reliably greater HR discriminations occurred when the US con-sisted of diencephalic stimulation than when midbrain stimulation was employed, (d) directionality of HR responses was firmly linked to gross motor activity, and (e) in both the diencephalon and the midbrain some US locations led to accelerative and some to decelerative HR responding to the CS +.

In a subsequent experiment VanDercar, Elster, Sideroff, and I have been examining HR, BP, and plethysmographic responses to medial and lateral septal region and anterior hypo-thalamic stimulation. In this experiment the *S*s receive one day of US-alone trials, two days of CS-alone adaptation trials, and six days of classical discrimination conditioning at an ISI of 2 seconds. As in the previous studies in this series the discrimination con-ditioned is between lateral geniculates. Basically, the CSs consist of 2-second trains of 15-Hz., 0.5-msec. duration monophasic rectangular pulses presented at a current intensity of .20 mA. The US consists of a 1-second train of 200-Hz., 0.25-msec. duration monophasic rectangular pulses. Although the unconditioned BP responses have differed with location, the HR CRs have been consistently decelerative. Interestingly, in some locations conditioned HR decreases and plethysmographic responses have been elicited in the absence of BP CRs.

Figure 5 shows the HR response topography of an *S* receiving .5-mA. septal stimulation as the US. It can be seen that little HR responding occurred during adaptation but that marked conditioning and discrimination occurred during the first acquisition session. On nontest trials the US typically occurred at about the eighth beat. That most of the conditioned HR deceleration occurred in the second and third blocks of five beats (beats 6 through 15) is seen in Fig. 5.

For the *S* shown in Fig. 5, the HR response threshold occurred at .3 mA. At .5 mA., which was later used as the US for conditioning, the HR response was a marked deceleration without pronounced bodily movement. The BP UR was originally biphasic and consisted of a decrease followed by an increase in mean pressure. The initial BP decrease was related to immediate suppression of a single R wave in the electrocardiogram. During the first acquisition session the BP UR was a decrease in pressure, and this form of the response remained until after conditioning and discrimination formation began. Toward the end of the first acquisition session, however, the BP UR again became biphasic and the latency of the BP increase gradually moved toward US onset. Finally, by the end of the second acquisition session the BP UR was a monophasic increase. The BP conditioning which subsequently developed also consisted of an increase in mean and systolic BP. Examination of changes in the forms of URs, and in the developing relationships of BP and HR CRs and URs to one another, have become a prime concern in our laboratory.

In addition to ESB experiments, subcortical influences upon HR conditioning have been investigated, using lesioning techniques. Thus Durkovic and Cohen (1969a and 1969b) recently have paired light and shock in pigeons, and investigated the effects of rostral

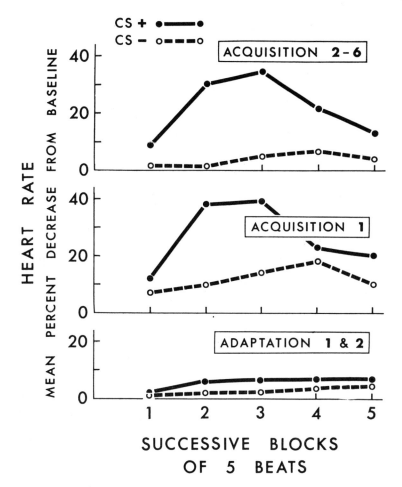

Fig. 5. Mean test trial heart rate decreases from base line to the CS+ and the CS− during each successive five-beat block following CS onset.

and caudal midbrain lesions on conditioning of HR accelerations and BR responses. Basically, Durkovic and Cohen have found that although their lesions did not abolish unconditioned HR responding, lesions of the ventromedial tegmentum at the level of the red nucleus produced striking deficits in conditioned HR and BR responding. In contrast, they found that: (a) injury of the dorsolateral

tegmentum at the level of the oculomotor nucleus produced a
severe deficit in conditioned HR but not BR responses, and (b)
lesions of the ventromedial tegmentum at the level of the caudal
interpeduncular nucleus significantly enhanced the magnitude of
HR CRs without influencing BR conditioning. The ESB and
lesioning experiments have thus begun to elucidate the nature of
some of the descending supramedullary pathways and possible
integrative structures involved in HR conditioning.

SUMMARY AND CONCLUSIONS

The purpose of this chapter was to describe some of the behavioral
and physiological determinants of HR conditioning. Obrist and
his collaborators have emphasized the existence of a cardiac-
somatic linkage during conditioning. Although HR changes are
usually related to the energy requirements of the organism, Black
and his coworkers have demonstrated that HR conditioning is
not mediated by gross motor responding. Recent experiments from
Miller's and other laboratories have further suggested that the
central commands for HR and somatic activity are closely related
but not identical.

In my own and other laboratories differences have been documented in performance between HR and various somatic responses.
These differences occurred in rates of CR acquisition, extinction
rate, maintenance of responding over sessions, discrimination
capability, reactivity to drugs, responsiveness to stimulus uncertainty and stress, shape of the ISI function, and performance
under delay versus trace conditioning. Comparisons which have
been made between specific somatic and HR response systems
suggest that both may be reflecting the same process throughout
acquisition but that specific somatic CRs may occur later because
they are incompatible with the initial conditioning of behavioral
freezing. Evidence was also presented that HR becomes classically
conditioned at longer ISIs than specific somatic responses, because
the CRs and/or the URs have a longer duration.

In some species, such as the pigeon, the predominant HR CR
is an increase in rate. This acceleration seems to be mediated
primarily by an increase in sympathetic activity mediated by the

cardiac accelerator nerves; the vagus nerves, however, also contribute toward the response. Blockade of the sympathetic input to the heart by a beta-adrenergic blocking agent seriously debilitates the accelerative CR.

In contrast to the cardioacceleration of the pigeon, the usual HR response in the rabbit is a decrease in rate. In this species either appropriate doses of atropine or bilateral cervical vagotomy abolish HR URs and CRs, indicating that the HR decrease is mediated by the vagus nerves. Since alpha-adrenergic blockades, having little direct effect upon the heart, diminish BP and HR URs and CRs, it appears that the compensatory vagal reflex contributes to the development of conditioning. However, the finding that HR CRs can occur in the absence of BP conditioning indicates that although the compensatory vagal reflex contributes to the development of conditioning, it does not contribute to the elaboration of the HR CR.

Miller's group, in an exciting series of experiments, has emphasized the specificity of autonomic responses during instrumental autonomic conditioning. Thus, for example, DiCara and Miller (1968) have reported that differential vasomotor changes between the two ears can be instrumentally conditioned in curarized rats. Since such findings cannot easily be accounted for in terms of simple vasomotor regulation in the medulla, the data suggest that HR CRs may in large part be integrated in locations anterior to the vasomotor center in the medulla.

Several studies have indicated that HR conditioning proceeds normally after neodecortication, but the role of cortical involvement needs to be investigated more fully. Important questions remain unanswered concerning the normal role of the cortex in HR conditioning and the extent to which the cortex is essential for discrimination conditioning.

Attention has also focused upon the role of subcortical mechanisms in HR conditioning. Experiments using ESB have established that either accelerative or decelerative HR classical discrimination conditioning can be elicited from different subcortical locations. Some excellent lesion studies have also located different subcortical locations where BR conditioning is not influenced but where injury selectively enhances or abolishes HR conditioning.

112   *Current Issues in Animal Learning*

Most of the major findings concerning the determinants of HR conditioning have been made during the past decade. Much of the progress seems related to the increased attention which has been paid to relevant physiological as well as behavioral issues. As investigators in the area of cardiovascular conditioning become increasingly familiar with the technology and considerations of physiology as well as psychology, research progress in this area should accelerate during the next decade.

REFERENCES

Ahlquist, R. A study of the adrenotropic receptors. *Amer. J. Psychol.*, 1948, **153**, 586–600.

Bailey, P., & Bremer, F. A sensory cortical representation of the vagus nerve. With a note on the effects of low blood pressure on the cortical electrogram. *Neurophysiol.*, 1938, **1**, 405–412.

Ban, T. The septo-preoptico-hypothalamic system and its autonomic function. In T. Tokizane & J. P. Schade (Eds.), *Progress in Brain Research*, 1966, **21A**, 1–43.

Ban, T., & Shinoda, H. Experimental studies on the relation between the hypothalamus and conditioned reflex. *Medical Journal of Osaka University*, 1956, **7**, 643–676.

Ban, T., & Shinoda, H. Experimental studies on the relation between the hypothalamus and conditioned reflex II. On the conditioned response in EEG and gastric motility. *Medical Journal of Osaka University*, 1960, **11**, 85–93.

Black, A. H. Cardiac conditioning in curarized dogs: The relationship between heart rate and skeletal behavior. In W. F. Prokasy (Ed.), *Classical conditioning*. New York: Appleton-Century-Crofts, 1965. Pp. 20–47.

Black, A. H., Carlson, N. J., & Solomon, R. L. Exploratory studies of the conditioning of autonomic responses in curarized dogs. *Psychol. Monographs*, 1962, **76**, No. 29 (Whole No. 548).

Black, A. H., & Lang, W. H. Cardiac conditioning and skeletal responding in curarized dogs. *Psychol. Rev.*, 1964, **71**, 80–85.

Bloch, S., & Lagarrigue, I. Cardiac and simple avoidance learning in neodecorticate rats. *Physiol. & Behav.*, 1968, **3**, 305–308.

Bloch-Rojas, S., Toro, A., & Pinto-Hamuy, T. Cardiac vs. somatic-motor conditioned responses in neodecorticated rats. *J. comp. physiol. Psychol.*, 1964, **58**, 233–236.

Bruner, A. Reinforcement strength in classical conditioning of leg flexion, freezing, and heart rate in cats. *Conditional Reflex*, 1969, 24–31.

Chase, W. G., Graham, F. H., & Graham, D. T. Components of HR response in anticipation of reaction time and exercise tasks. *J. exp. Psychol.*, 1968, **76**, 642–648.

Cohen, D. H., & Pitts, L. H. Vagal and sympathetic components of conditioned cardioacceleration in the pigeon. *Brain Research*, 1968, **9**, 15–31.

Coquery, J. M., & Lacey, J. I. The effects of foreperiod duration on the components of the cardiac response during the foreperiod of a reaction-time experiment. Paper presented at Society for Psychophysiological Research meeting, Denver, 1966.

Dauth, G. W. The effects of variable versus fixed interstimulus intervals on classical aversive conditioning in the albino rabbit. Unpublished masters thesis, University of Miami, 1969.

Dell, P. Corrélations entre le système végétatif et le système de la vie de relation. Mesencéphale, diencéphale et cortex cérébral. *J. Physiologie (Paris)*, 1952, **44**, 471–557.

DeToledo, L., & Black, A. H. Heart rate: Changes during conditioned suppression in rats. *Science*, 1966, **152**, 1404–1406.

DiCara, L. V., & Miller, N. E. Instrumental learning of vasomotor responses by rats: Learning to respond differentially in the two ears. *Science*, 1968, **159**, 1485–1486.

DiCara, L. V., & Miller, N. E. Transfer of instrumentally learned heart rate changes from curarized to noncurarized state: Implications for a mediational hypothesis. *J. comp. physiol. Psychol.*, 1969, **68**, 159–162.

Durkovic, R. G., & Cohen, D. H. Effects of caudal midbrain lesions on conditioning of heart and respiratory rate responses in the pigeon. *J. comp. physiol. Psychol.*, 1969a, **69**, 329–338.

Durkovic, R. G., & Cohen, D. H. Effects of rostral midbrain lesions on conditioning of heart and respiratory rate responses in the pigeon. *J. comp. physiol. Psychol.*, 1969b, **68**, 184–192.

Ebel, H. C., & Prokasy, W. F. Classical eyelid conditioning as a function of sustained and shifted interstimulus intervals. *J. exp. Psychol.*, 1963, **65**, 52–58.

Elliott, R., & Schneiderman, N. Pentylenetetrazol: Facilitation of classical discrimination conditioning in rabbits. *Psychopharmacologia* (Berlin), 1968, **12**, 133–141.

Elster, A., Van Dercar, D., & Schneiderman, N. Classical conditioning of heart rate discriminations in rabbits using subcortical stimulation as conditioned and unconditioned stimuli. *Physiol. and Behav.* In press.

Gasser, H. S., & Meek, W. J. A study of the mechanism by which muscular exercise produces acceleration of the heart. *Amer. J. Physiol.*, 1914, **34**, 48–72.

Goldberg, S., Schuster, C., & Woods, J. Nalorphine: Conditioning of drug effects on operant performance. In G. T. Heistad, T. Thompson, & R. Pickens, *Stimulus properties of drugs*. New York: Appleton-Century-Crofts. In press.

Green, N. D., & Hoff, E. C. Effects of faradic stimulation of the cerebral cortex on limb and renal volumes in the cat and monkey. *Amer. J. Physiol.*, 1937, **118**, 641–658.

Hamburg, M. D., Best, P. J., & Cholewiak, R. W. Cortical lesions resulting from chemically induced spreading depression. *J. comp. physiol. Psychol.*, 1968, **66**, 492–494.

Hendrickson, C. W., & Pinto-Hamuy, T. Nonretention of a visual conditioned heart-rate response under neocortical spreading depression. *J. comp. physiol. Psychol.*, 1967, **64**, 510–513.

Herrick, J. F., Grindlay, J. H., Baldes, E. J., & Mann, F. C. Effect of exercise on the blood flow in the superior mesenteric, renal and common iliac arteries. *Amer. J. Physiol.*, 1940, **128**, 338–344.

Hull, C. L. Principles of behavior. New York: Appleton-Century, 1943.

Hull, C. L. A behavior system. New Haven: Yale University Press, 1952.

Jaworska, K., Kowalska, M., & Soltysik, S. Studies on the aversive classical conditioning I. Acquisition and differentiation of motor and cardiac conditioned classical defensive reflexes in dog. *Acta Biologiae Experimentalis*, 1962, **22**, 23–24.

Kaada, B. R. Somato-motor, autonomic and electrocorticographic responses to electrical stimulation of "rhinencephalic" and other forebrain structures in primates, cat and dog. *Acta Physiologica Scandinavia*, 1951, **24**, supp. 83, 1–285.

Kaada, B. R. Cingulate, posterior, orbital, anterior insular and temporal pole cortex. In J. Field, H. W. Magovn, & W. E. Hall (Eds.), *Handbook of physiology*. Vol. 2. Baltimore: Williams & Wilkins, 1960.

Krogh, A., & Lindhard, J. The regulation of respiration and circulation during the initial stages of muscular work. *J. Physiol.*, 1913, **47**, 112–136.

Lacey, B. C., & Lacey, J. I. Cardiac deceleration and simple visual reaction time in a fixed foreperiod experiment. Paper presented at Society for Psychophysiological Research meeting, Washington, 1964.

Lacey, B. C., & Lacey, J. I. Changes in cardiac response and reaction time as a function of motivation. Paper presented at Society for Psychophysiological Research meeting, Denver, 1966.

Leao, A. A. P. Spreading depression of activity in the cerebral cortex. *J. Neurophysiol.*, 1944, **7**, 359–390.

Lico, M. C., Hoffmann, A., & Covian, M. R. Autonomic conditioning in the anesthetized rabbit. *Physiol. and Behav.*, 1968, **3**, 673–675.

Malmo, R. B. Classical and instrumental conditioning with septal stimulation as reinforcement. *J. comp. physiol. Psychol.*, 1965, **60**, 1–8.

Manning, A. A., Schneiderman, N., & Lordahl, D. S. Delay vs. trace heart rate classical discrimination conditioning in rabbits as a function of ISI. *J. exp. Psychol.*, 1969, **80**, 225–230.

Meredith, A. L., & Schneiderman, N. Heart rate and nictitating membrane classical discrimination conditioning in rabbits under delay vs. trace procedures. *Psychon. Sci.*, 1967, **9**, 139–140.

Mowrer, O. H. *Learning theory and personality dynamics*. New York: Ronald Press, 1950.

Mowrer, O. H. *Learning theory and behavior*. New York: John Wiley & Sons, Inc., 1960.

Obrist, P. A. Heart rate during conditioning in dogs: Relationship to respiration and gross bodily movements. *Proceedings of the 73rd Annual Convention of the American Psychological Association*, 1965, 165–166.

Obrist, P. A., & Webb, R. A. Heart rate during conditioning in dogs: relationship to somatic-motor activity. *Psychophysiology*, 1967, **4**, 7–34.

Obrist, P. A., Webb, R. A., & Sutterer, J. R. Heart rate and somatic changes during aversive conditioning and a simple reaction time task. *Psychophysiology*, 1969, **5**, 696–723.

Obrist, P. A., Wood, D. M., & Perez-Reyes, M. Heart rate during conditioning in humans: Effects of UCS intensity, vagal blockade, and adrenergic block of vasomotor activity. *J. exp. Psychol.*, 1965, **70**, 32–42.

Parrish, J. Classical discrimination conditioning of heart rate and bar-press suppression in the rat. *Psychon. Sci.*, 1967, **9**, 267–268.

Sarnoff, S. J. Myocardial contractility as described by ventricular function curves. *Physiolog. Rev.*, 1955, **35**, 107–122.

Schneiderman, N. Response system divergences in aversive classical conditioning. In A. H. Black & W. F. Prokasy (Eds.), *Classical conditioning.* II. Appleton-Century-Crofts, in press.

Schneiderman, N., & Gormezano, I. Conditioning of the nictitating membrane of the rabbit as a function of CS–US interval. *J. comp. physiol. Psychol.*, 1964, **57**, 188–195.

Schneiderman, N., Smith, M. C., Smith, A. C., & Gormezano, I. Heart rate classical conditioning in rabbits. Paper presented at Midwestern Psychological Association meetings, Chicago, 1964.

Schneiderman, N., Smith, M. C., Smith, A. C., & Gormezano, I. Heart rate classical conditioning in rabbits. *Psychon. Sci.*, 1966, **6**, 241–242.

Schneiderman, N., VanDercar, D. H., Yehle, A. L., Manning, A. A., Golden, T., & Schneiderman, E. Vagal compensatory adjustment: relationship to heart rate classical conditioning in rabbits. *J. comp. physiol. Psychol.*, 1969, **68**, 175–183·

Shinoda, H., & Ban, T. Experimental studies on the relation between the hypothalamus and conditioned reflex III. Conditioned response in the variation of the leucocyte count and the blood sugar level. *Medical Journal of Osaka University*, 1961, **11**, 439–453.

Sokolov, E. N. *Perception and the conditioned reflex.* New York: Macmillan, 1963.

Swadlow, H., Schneiderman, E., and Schneiderman, N. Classical conditioning of a discrimination between electrically stimulated lateral geniculate bodies in the rabbit. *Proceedings of the 76th Annual Convention of the American Psychological Association*, 1968, **3**, 313–314.

VanDercar, D. H. Influences of response systems upon the interstimulus interval function of the rabbit in classical discrimination training. Unpublished masters thesis, University of Miami, 1967.

VanDercar, D. H. & Schneiderman, N. Interstimulus interval functions in different response systems during classical discrimination conditioning of rabbits. *Psychon. Sci.*, 1967, **9**, 9–10.

Warner, H. R. The control of heart rate by sympathetic efferent information. *Physiologist*, 1960, **3**, 173.

Webb, R. A., & Obrist, P. A. Heart-rate change during complex operant performance in the dog. *Proceedings of the 75th Annual Convention of the American Psychological Association*, 1967, 137–138.

Weiss, T., & Fifkova, E. Bioelectric activity in the thalamus and the hypothalamus of rats during cortical spreading EEG depression. *J. EEG clin. Neurophysiol.*, 1961, **13**, 734–744.

Wood, D. M., & Obrist, P. A. Effects of controlled and uncontrolled respiration on the conditioned heart rate response in humans. *J. exp. Psychol.*, 1964, **65**, 221–229.

Yehle, A. L. Divergent characteristics of response systems in the rabbit as a function of a three-tone classical discrimination situation. Unpublished doctoral dissertation, University of Miami, 1966.

Yehle, A. L. Divergences among rabbit response systems during three-tone classical discrimination conditioning. *J. exp. Psychol.*, 1968, **77**, 468–473.

Yehle, A., Dauth, G., & Schneiderman, N. Correlates of heart-rate classical conditioning in curarized rabbits. *J. comp. physiol. psychol.*, 1967, **64**, 98–104.

Influences of Appetitive Pavlovian Conditioning upon Avoidance Behavior[1]

J. BRUCE OVERMIER and JOHN. A. BULL, III

University of Minnesota

THE PROBLEM

American learning psychologists historically have been primarily concerned with the study of simple instrumental motor learning. Their analyses focused upon the manipulation of behavior through the direct manipulation of instrumental response-reinforcement contingencies; this emphasis on the study of response contingent reinforcement is reflected in the laws of behavior which have been developed. However, current psychological theories about the mechanism(s) through which response-contingent reinforcements exert their influence typically invoke a Pavlovian conditioning process (e.g., Logan & Wagner's $_sIN_r$ and $_sNI_r$, 1965; Mowrer's fear, hope, etc., 1960; and Spence's r_g–s_g mechanism, 1956). That is, the acquisition and performance of instrumental behaviors are thought to be mediated (at least partially) through Pavlovian conditioning. These theoretical efforts have been somewhat less than fully successful because so very little is known in general about how Pavlovian conditioning effects or influences instrumental behavior. Indeed, there is one possible kind of Pavlovian conditioning $\rightarrow$ instrumental response interactive influence about which we have essentially no information at all.

[1] This research was supported primarily by NIMH grant MH 13558 to Overmier and in part by grants to the Center for Research in Human Learning, University of Minnesota, from the National Institute of Child Health and Human Development and National Science Foundation, and the University of Minnesota. Bull was a U.S. PHS predoctoral fellow during the conduct of this research. The assistance of Ralph J. Payne, Karl Schwarzkopf, Richard Knutson, Kenneth Pack, and Mary Conroy is acknowledged.

The research to be reviewed and discussed here is concerned with the details of a variety of Pavlovian → instrumental interactions. Therefore, discussion will be facilitated if certain distinctions and terminology are developed at the outset.[2]

First, we distinguish between two classes of instrumental behaviors and their training operations. Instrumental *reward* behavior or responding refers to skeletal-motor responses which are established by making the occurrence of the reinforcer (usually food or water) contingent upon the prior occurrence of the response.[3] Similarly, instrumental *avoidance* behavior or responding refers to skeletal-motor responses which are established by making the omission of an aversive event (typically shock) contingent upon the prior occurrence of the specified response. A stimulus indicating when performance of the given response will be reinforced is called an S^D.

Second, we distinguish between two classes of Pavlovian conditioning operations. *Appetitive* Pavlovian conditioning operations refer to the presentation of neutral stimuli either positively correlated, negatively correlated, or uncorrelated with alimentary events such as food or water (UCS) under conditions over which the subject has no control; that is, there exists no contingency between behavior and the occurrence of the UCS. *Defensive* Pavlovian conditioning operations refer to the presentation of neutral stimuli either positively correlated, negatively correlated, or uncorrelated with aversive events (typically shock) under conditions over which the subject has no control. The stimulus which signals an impending alimentary or aversive event (i.e., positive correlation) is called a CS +, while a stimulus which signals a period in which the alimentary or aversive event will not be presented (i.e., negative correlation) is called a CS −. A stimulus with no signal value (i.e.,

---

[2] Because we have distinguished between Pavlovian and instrumental operations here does not necessarily mean a commitment to the view that the two sets of operations effect learning through different mechanisms. Indeed, we are considerably impressed by Perkins's (1968) argument and therefore wish to leave the multiple learning mechanism question an open one.

[3] The use of the adjective *skeletal-motor* is not intended to imply any biases about the trainability of autonomic or smooth muscle responses. The term simply reflects that all the instrumental indicator responses which will be discussed are skeletal-motor acts.

UCS uncorrelated) is called a CS⁰. The CS + in aversive Pavlovian conditioning has been termed a conditioned "fear" signal because it elicits behavioral and physiological responses indicative of anticipation of the aversive event. Similarly, we could refer to the CS + in appetitive Pavlovian conditioning as a conditioned "hope" signal (Mowrer, 1960) because it elicits responses indicative of anticipation of the alimentary event.

A number of experimental reports have appeared in the psychological literature over the last 20 years which leave little doubt that at least some Pavlovian conditioned stimuli can strongly influence the performance of instrumental motor acts.[4] For example, defensive Pavlovian conditioned stimuli have been shown to exert striking control over the occurrence of both instrumental reward and instrumental avoidance responding. Presentations of conditioned fear signals (CS +) result in a marked decrease in the rate of ongoing instrumental reward responding (Brady & Hunt, 1955; Estes & Skinner, 1941); this is the well-documented conditioned suppression (or CER) phenomenon. Furthermore, experiments by Ray and Stein (1959) and Hammond (1966) suggest that a stimulus contrasted with the presentation of shock, a defensive Pavlovian CS−, can in some circumstances enhance the rate of ongoing instrumental reward responding. In contrast, conditioned fear signals result in a marked increase in the ongoing rate of instrumental avoidance responding (Rescorla & LoLordo, 1965) and will also elicit avoidance responses previously trained to another S^D (Solomon & Turner, 1962). Interestingly, Rescorla and LoLordo (1965) also showed that a defensive Pavlovian CS− can suppress ongoing avoidance responding.

Because conditioned fear signals exert strong control over both instrumental reward and avoidance responding, it seemed logical to inquire experimentally if conditioned hope signals also exert influences over instrumental reward responding. Moreover, because conditioned fear signals and conditioned hope signals are based

---

[4] The influences upon instrumental responding must, at some level, be caused by facilitating or interfering mediating responses (or their feedback) elicited by the conditioned stimuli as a result of prior Pavlovian conditioning operations. However, because these responses are unspecified, and perhaps unspecifiable, the discussion will emphasize the functional properties of the stimuli with respect to instrumental responding rather than the interaction of two classes of responses.

upon antipodean events during conditioning, one might suppose that the changes in behavior produced by these two kinds of conditioned stimuli would be opposite. Indeed, a number of experiments suggest that this is the case. An appetitive Pavlovian CS + does, for example, result in a slight increase in amount of instrumental reward responding during extinction (Walker, 1942; Estes, 1943, 1948). More recent studies have shown that prior discriminative appetitive Pavlovian conditioning subsequently markedly facilitates the acquisition and generalization of discriminated instrumental reward responding when the Pavlovian CS + is used as the S^D in instrumental reward training (Bower & Grusec, 1964; Trapold & Fairlie, 1965; Trapold & Winokur, 1967). Furthermore, Trapold et al. (1968) have demonstrated that the acquisition of an instrumental reward discrimination is also facilitated if the S^Δ had been previously established as an appetitive Pavlovian CS −.

These studies investigating the effects of conditioned hope signals upon instrumental reward responding have clearly demonstrated that appetitive Pavlovian conditioning operations endow the conditioned stimuli with certain functional properties with respect to instrumental reward responding. In general, the effects of an appetitive Pavlovian CS + or CS − upon instrumental reward responding have been demonstrated to be opposite those of a defensive Pavlovian CS + or CS −, respectively.

Given that defensive Pavlovian CSs influence both reward and avoidance responding and that appetitive Pavlovian CSs influence reward responding, we were led to ask: Do appetitively based CSs have any effects upon instrumental avoidance responding? Few studies in the literature have explored this interactive influence.[5]

Coulson and Walsh (1968) carried out an experiment which was essentially the inverse of the typical CER experiment. They superimposed a tone (CS +) followed noncontingently by food upon an unsignaled instrumental avoidance base line of behavior. They found that the CS + produced a slight increase in rats' rate of bar-press avoidance responding. In contrast, Grossen, Kostansek, and Bolles (1968) have reported the opposite finding. Here, groups of rats were first trained to avoid a periodic unsignaled shock. Second,

[5] Indeed, when we began the experiments reported here, no studies had reported on it.

they received one of three kinds of Pavlovian conditioning: (a) a CS + paired with food, (b) a CS − contrasted with food presentations, and (c) a CS^0 presented randomly with respect to food. These groups were then tested by presenting the CS while performing the avoidance response. They reported that the appetitive CS + depressed avoidance responding, while the CS − facilitated avoidance responding relative to the CS^0 group.

Our information about this class of interaction, then, is scanty and inconsistent. Resolution of these experimental differences must be achieved if we are ever to develop viable theories concerning if and how Pavlovian operations influence instrumental behavior.

There are two theories of major importance concerning how different Pavlovian conditioned mediational states interact to determine instrumental responding. One (cf. Sheffield, 1966) attributes general motivational effects to all types of mediators. This general motivation or excitation combines additively when mediators interact and "energizes" all responding. The second (cf. Mowrer, 1960) suggests that mediating motivational states based on aversive events are inherently incompatible with those based on appetitive events. Thus when the two types of mediators interact they do so subtractively, possibly through some sort of motivational "reflex interrelation" (Rescorla & Solomon, 1967).

We feel that it is important to have as complete a knowledge as possible about *all* possible Pavlovian → instrumental interactions because of the importance which currently popular psychological theories of learning give to Pavlovian conditioned responses in the determination and control of specific instrumental-motor acts. Knowledge about these kinds of response interactions are even important to the evaluation of Estes's (1969) new stimulus-sampling theory of punishment, in which no learning-process distinctions are made.

With this body of data and correlated theoretical discussion forming a background, we set ourselves the task of experimentally investigating the interaction between appetitive Pavlovian conditioned stimuli and instrumental avoidance behavior. We entered upon these researches specifically believing we would find evidence for such interactions and that the qualitative nature of the effects of an appetitive CS+, a hope signal, upon instrumental avoidance responding would be the opposite of the effects of a defensive CS+, a fear signal. We also held similar expectations with regard to the CS− effects.

There were two bases for our a priori beliefs. First, each of the other interactive effects between Pavlovian conditioning and instrumental responding (reviewed above), taken by itself, might lead us to expect that appetitive Pavlovian CSs might influence instrumental avoidance responding. Taken as a group, these almost demand that we expect appetitive CSs to influence avoidance. Further, our qualitative expectations about the influences of appetitive CSs upon avoidance responding were, in part, based upon the observations that: (a) appetitive and defensive CS+'s have opposite effects upon reward responding, and (b) defensive CS+'s have opposite effects upon reward and avoidance responding. If the effects of appetitive and defensive CS+'s are in general opposite, and given that defensive CS+'s facilitate avoidance responding, then our appetitive CS+'s should suppress avoidance. A similar line of reasoning can be applied to the CS−'s.

Second, counterconditioning experiments provide a basis for our intuitions. By counterconditioning we mean the reduction or elimination of defensive reactions to an originally aversive stimulus as a result of association of the aversive stimulus with some pleasurable experience (usually alimentary). Pavlov (1927, p. 29) demonstrated that the defensive reactions of a dog to painful electric shock diminished if the shock was consistently paired with food. More recently, Williams and Barry (1966, p. 154) found that the "effectiveness of shock in reducing lever pressing rate was reduced when food and shock were always presented together, rather than always separately." Furthermore, to the extent that unconditioned startle reactions can be considered as aversively motivated responses analogous to the defensive reactions elicited by shock, we find additional support for our belief. Armus and Sniadowski-Dolinsky (1966) have reported that presentation of a signal, previously paired with food in Pavlovian conditioning, produces a decrement in the magnitude of a startle reaction. These experiments show that food presentations do influence aversively motivated instrumental behaviors.

RESEARCH

Several different experimental paradigms have been used to demonstrate the interaction effects reviewed, and each has had its own impact upon theories of learning. But, in our opinion, the most powerful and theoretically important demonstrations have used what is generically called a transfer of control paradigm. The rationale for the transfer of control experiment is derived directly from the tenets of two-process theory (cf. Rescorla & Solomon, 1967). The prototypical experiments involve three phases: (a) a Pavlovian conditioning phase in which a stimulus is established as a signal for a motivationally relevant event, (b) an instrumental training phase in which a specific motor response is learned, and (c) a transfer of control test phase in which the signal is tested for its power to evoke the instrumental response. The common results of these are that the signal, in the presence of which our subject has never before performed the specific instrumental response, immediately assumes some control over the instrumental response as a result of the Pavlovian operations.

We chose to use the transfer of control experiment as our basic investigatory tool. However, we did incorporate one basic modification: the conditioning and instrumental phases were conducted in different apparatus units (transsituational). True, the transsituational technique probably reduces the effectiveness of the Pavlovian stimuli through stimulus-generalization decrements. However, there are subtle benefits. This modification reduces the possibility that any feeder-approachlike behaviors acquired in the Pavlovian conditioning phase will impinge on the instrumental behavior we are measuring during the test phase. Thus, it eliminates the need for special measures (e.g., curarization) to prevent the occurrence of the instrumental response during the Pavlovian phase. Hence, *ad hoc* explanations of the observed transfer effects in terms of learned overt motor responses are made difficult.

The two apparatus units were: (1) a movement-restricting stand and harness, located inside a sound-insulated booth, and (2) a two-way shuttlebox, a rectangular box which is divided into two compartments by a low barrier; each section has an electrifiable grid floor.

Experiment One

We begin our researches in perhaps the simplest possible way—
a way which only now we are beginning to learn was doomed to
failure at the outset. Although our primary interest was in the
effect of an appetitive Pavlovian CS + upon avoidance behavior, we
also were interested in the effects of an appetitive CS −, a stimulus
contrasted with presentations of the appetitive event. Therefore, in
the first experiment we began by carrying out discriminative
Pavlovian conditioning in the booth with two tones; one tone
reliably signaled the occurrence of food pellets, and the other always
signaled a period without food. The second phase consisted of
establishing avoidance behavior in the shuttle box. The base-line
avoidance behavior chosen, upon which the tone signals were later
to be superimposed, was temporally paced, unsignaled avoidance
(Sidman avoidance). Such behavior is very easy to establish in
dogs, shows little variance, and is extremely resistant to extinction.
The final phase, or test phase, consisted of simply presenting noncontingently the tone CSs in the shuttle box for fixed durations while
the dogs were performing avoidance responses. If these Pavlovian
CSs were to influence Sidman avoidance behavior, differences in the
rates of responding between the pre-CS periods and the CS periods
should be noted. To our surprise, no such differences were consistently observed. In some *S*s, CS + produced a small decrement in
response rate and CS − had no effect; in other *S*s both CSs produced decrements; and in still others both tones failed to have any
effects.[6]

Two conclusions were open to us: (a) appetitive Pavlovian CSs,
as such, do not influence instrumental avoidance behavior, or (b)
appetitive Pavlovian stimuli may well influence avoidance behavior,
but our technique was unsatisfactory for demonstrating this influence. Given our knowledge about the existence of Pavlovian to
instrumental transfer effects of other kinds, we opted for the second
conclusion. In doing so, we recognized that the only way to establish
the possible validity of the first alternative conclusion (i.e., no

[6] Here and throughout this paper the statement that some operation has an
effect or that a difference exists implies statistical significance of *at least* $p < .05$.

interaction effects) was to seek to demonstrate the effects of appetitive Pavlovian CSs upon avoidance behavior using a variety of techniques, and to fail every time.

Experiment Two

When one reflects upon the first experiment, one recognizes that the finding of a transfer interaction is dependent upon the CSs signaling to the dog something about the availability of food. Were our CSs functional? One way to know that the CSs meet our requirements would be to observe whether or not differential salivation occurred to the two tones. This technique, however, required surgical, measurement, and instrumentational capabilities not immediately available. Alternatively, one could take advantage of the fact that every discrete-trial, discriminative instrumental training situation has embedded in it all the elements for discriminative Pavlovian conditioning. That is, using two tones the researcher could train in the booth a discriminative pedal-pressing response for food. When clear discriminative behavior was manifested, he would know that the tones had signal value for the dog. Of course, if a "transfer interaction effect" were observed after having established a pedal-pressing response in the "Pavlovian" phase, the researcher would be in doubt about the source of the interaction effect, wondering whether it was because of the influences of the concomitantly established Pavlovian processes, as we would wish to infer, or a result of incompatibility between the two instrumental responses. We felt that if a transfer effect were observed we could later control for the incompatibility argument with special techniques.

This was exactly our procedure. We replicated Experiment One, except that in phase one we trained a discriminative pedal-press response for food in our booth using two tones as signals. Second, we established Sidman avoidance base-line behavior in the shuttle box. Third, during avoidance extinction we presented the appetitive "Pavlovian CSs" for 5-second periods. The rates of jumping during each CS presentation were compared to the rates of jumping during the pre- and post-CS periods. No consistent pattern of change in responding during the CSs was observed in our dogs.

Once again we were faced with the choice between the two alternative conclusions presented above and once again we chose to attempt to refine our techniques.

Experiment Three

Due to a wide variety of pilot manipulations which followed our first two experiments, and discussions with colleagues who had failed to find effects of appetitive Pavlovian CS + 's upon unsignaled reward responding, we concluded that the unsignaled avoidance base-line of behavior was too stable to be sensitive to the effects (if any) of food-paired stimuli which are presumably relatively weak. However, a *signaled* avoidance base-line performance might be more sensitive. Thus, we developed a new discrete-trial, discriminated avoidance technique in which responses are ineffective for periods of time following trial S^D onset. In the terminal conditions of this procedure, a trial consisted of two periods: (a) an initial variable delay or hold period (0, 6, or 18 seconds) during which responses were not effective in terminating the S^D or avoiding the shock; (b) this was followed by a period (5 seconds) during which a response was effective in terminating the S^D and preventing shock. If no response occurred in this second period, an intense, brief shock was given. This schedule of avoidance resulted in a stable rate of hurdle jumping, controlled by a discrete trial stimulus, and is in many ways analogous to a discriminative appetitive VI schedule, which is reportedly very sensitive to motivational shifts.

Assuming that this schedule was going to be sensitive to our appetitive stimuli, we recognized that we would want to compare the effects of our appetitive stimuli on this base-line behavior to the effects of aversive stimuli. Therefore, as basic groundwork to further progress and understanding, we replicated earlier "classic" experiments which reported the effects of tones paired and contrasted with shock presentations upon unsignaled avoidance behavior. Our unsystematic replication involved explicit compounding of CSs with the S^D in the test for transfer of control. We found that a CS + which has signaled shock during Pavlovian conditioning increased avoidance responding when it was compounded with an S^D for avoidance, while a CS − which had signaled a period free from shock had the opposite effect when compounded with the S^D for avoidance. Evidence was derived from (a) comparisons of responding during the compounds to responding during avoidance S^D alone, and (b) comparisions of the experimental group's responding during the compounds to the responding during CS^0 plus S^D compounds by a control group for whom there had been no CS — shock contingency during Pavlovian conditioning (random control).

Avoidance behavior established using our new technique was influenced by "fear" signals in ways identical to avoidance behavior developed under other schedules of training. This is shown in Fig. 1. Thus, results we might obtain using our new schedule and superimposed appetitive Pavlovian CSs should be noncontroversial from a technical standpoint.

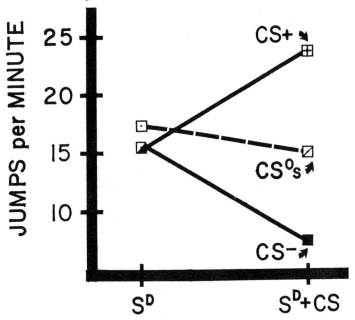

FIG. 1. Mean rate of avoidance responding by the experimental (solid-line) and control (dashed-line) groups in the presence of the S^D and in the presence of the defensive Pavlovian CSs when compounded with the S^D. Means averaged over three days.

Experiment Four

Having developed and validated this new, hopefully more sensitive, technique for assessing the effects of Pavlovian stimuli, we began again to investigate whether a tone which had signaled food in the booth could later influence avoidance behavior trained and tested in the shuttle box. However, avoidance training on the VI-hold schedule is required for several days to establish stable behavior. Therefore, to eliminate a long delay between Pavlovian conditioning and transfer testing, the order in which we carried out the first two phases of the transfer of control experiment was reversed from the order used in the first two experiments. Overmier and Leaf (1965) have shown that the order of these two phases is not critical to the qualitative outcome obtained.

First, dogs were avoidance trained in the shuttle box. We used the discriminated VI-hold avoidance procedure with a visual S^D until their behavior was stable. Then, the dogs were divided into three groups and exposed in the booth to Pavlovian operations with a tone CS and a food UCS. For one group (CS +) the tone and food were always paired; for one group (CS −) the tone explicitly signaled a period (≥ 40 seconds) in which no food would be presented; and for one group (CS⁰) the tone and food were scheduled independently of one another (random control). Last, after one day of retraining on the avoidance task, transfer of control tests were carried out in the shuttle box. There were two types of trials: (a) presentations of the avoidance S^D alone, and (b) presentations of a compound composed of the appetitively based CS and the avoidance S^D. We found that compounding of either the CS⁰ or the CS − with the S^D had very little effect upon the rate of avoidance. In contrast, compounding the CS + for food with the S^D markedly reduced the rate of avoidance responding. The results are presented in Fig. 2.

Here, then, we have a clear demonstration that a stimulus which has served as a signal for food in one place can and does influence the rate of discriminated avoidance responding in a different place. This influence is of an interference type; a hope CS appears to inhibit fear-motivated avoidance behavior.

However, before we can conclude that this interference effect is based upon a motivational reflex interaction, we must eliminate one

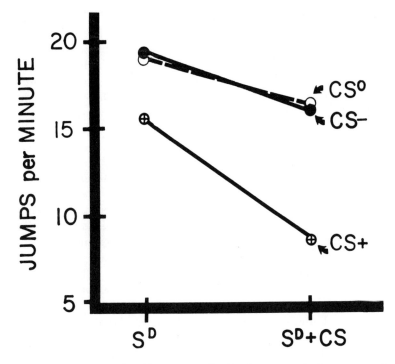

Fig. 2. Mean rate of avoidance responding for three groups in the presence of the S^D and in the presence of appetitive Pavlovian CSs when compounded with the S^D. Means averaged over three days.

possible alternative explanation. This is a simple "operant" explanation. In spite of our transsituational design, it is conceivable that our dogs inadvertently learned some instrumental behavior during the Pavlovian phase. This behavior, controlled by the CS+, may be evoked later in the transfer test and prove to be incompatible with the hurdle-jumping response. Therefore, we undertook an experiment to eliminate this alternative explanation.

Experiment Five

This experiment makes use of the fact that, on net account, a given instrumental response cannot simultaneously be both facilitative of and interfering with a second instrumental response. In addition, we did not want to leave to chance the question of whether or not the dogs acquired "instrumental" responses in the Pavlovian stage. We made sure such a response was established and that it was the same for all groups by explicitly training a discriminative pedal-press response in our "Pavlovian" phase. The pedal-press training constituted the Pavlovian conditioning phase because the Pavlovian paradigm is embedded in every discriminative instrumental task.

First, three groups of dogs received pedal-press training until they were reliably and discriminatively responding. One group (ApCS+) was trained to press a pedal in the booth to obtain food on discrete trials. A tone signaled the availability of food. A second group (AvCS+) was trained to press the same pedal in order to avoid shock. Again, a discrete-trial technique was used and the tone signaled the trial and impending shock. A supplemental special control dog was trained to press the pedal to obtain food on a VI schedule (S^R density equated with group ApCS+). This dog also received tone (ApCS⁰) presentations scheduled randomly, that is, the tone had no signal value.

Second, the dogs were trained to avoid shock in the shuttle box discriminatively, using the VI-hold technique with visual S^D. Last, they were given transfer of control tests with the S^D and the CS plus S^D compound. The results are presented in Fig. 3.

We see that, in agreement with our last experiment, ApCS+, the tone which had signaled the availability of food, *reduced* the rate of avoidance responding when compounded with the S^D. This effect could be attributed to a mechanical incompatibility between pedal pressing and hurdle jumping. Conversely, AvCS+, the tone which had signaled impending shock and also controlled pedal-press avoidance responding, *increased* the rate of shuttle-box avoidance responding when compounded with the S^D. This second effect argues against the possibility that any evoked pedal-pressing tendency is mechanically incompatible with hurdle jumping. And, nicely enough, we found that ApCS⁰, a tone with no signal-or response-controlling properties, had little effect upon avoidance responding.

We feel that the results of this experiment make it unlikely that the transfer of control effects observed in Experiment Four and in the

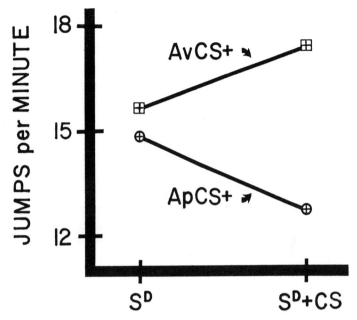

FIG. 3. Mean rate of avoidance responding for two groups—one having received defensive conditioning and one having received appetitive conditioning—in the presence of the S^D and in the presence of Pavlovian CSs when compounded with the S^D. Means averaged over three days.

present experiment results from interaction of instrumental responses. An adequate explanation of the phenomenon must lie elsewhere. One possibility suggested by the preceding results is that conditioned anticipatory states based upon food and shock interact subtractively. This is consonant with the reflex interaction of motivational states hypothesis proposed by Rescorla and Solomon (1967) and described earlier.

Given the results of our experiments, the results of Grossen, Kostansek, and Bolles (1968), and the symmetrical fit of data in the pattern of results obtained with the other classes of transfer inter-actions, we had great confidence that hope and fear were incom-patible conditioned motivational states. Therefore, we set ourselves the task of demonstrating this incompatibility with other experi-mental techniques. For example, if an appetitive CS+ elicits a state which is incompatible with "fear," then it should be more difficult to establish a stimulus as an S^D for avoidance if it has previously served as a CS+ for food. We tested this proactive interference hypothesis.

Experiment Six

In contrast to earlier experiments in which control of performance was at question, this experiment inquired whether appetitive Pavlovian conditioning subsequently influences the *acquisition* of an instrumental avoidance response when the same stimulus is used in both operations. For example, we wondered whether acquisition of an avoidance response would be slower to an appetitive CS+ than to a control stimulus.

First, dogs were trained to jump the hurdle in the shuttle box in order to escape shock. No signals were used. The purpose of this pretraining was to reduce or eliminate the extreme variability of dog escape behavior one normally encounters when carrying out instrumental avoidance training by the method of emergence. This training was carried out until each dog escaped shock reliably and with short latency. This ensured that when avoidance training was begun in stage three all earned shocks would be of approximately the same duration.

Second, three groups received Pavlovian conditioning in the booth with a tone and food. One group (CS+) had the tone paired with food, one group (CS⁰) had the tone and food presented on independent schedules; and for the third group (CS−) the tone signaled a period in which no food would be presented.

Last, the dogs were given instrumental avoidance training in the shuttle box, using the CSs established in the Pavlovian phase as the signal for avoidance. Several measures of acquisition were used and all revealed the same relationships.

The groups did not learn the avoidance task equally well. The group for which the CS+ had initially signaled food and was used to signal impending shock learned most rapidly. The CS− group was slowest to learn. These differences appear on early trials and persist throughout acquisition, though significance is lost as we approach criterion levels of performance. These results are presented in Table 1 and Fig. 4.

TABLE 1

AVOIDANCE ACQUISITION INDEXES FOR APPETITIVELY BASED PAVLOVIAN CSs

Groups	Trials to 1st Avoidance	Trials to 5 Consecutive Avoidances	% Shocks to 5 in row	% Shocks to Criteria	Mean No. Avoid on Trials 1–10
CS+	2.5	11.5	30.1	19.0	6.7
CS⁰	3.0	18.0	39.6	29.6	4.7
CS−	4.5	18.5	52.4	40.4	3.8

It should be made very clear that this is *not* the result we had anticipated. Indeed, it is exactly opposite what we had expected, based upon our earlier experiments and the motivational reflex-interaction hypothesis. Quite honestly, we did not know what to make of this outcome.

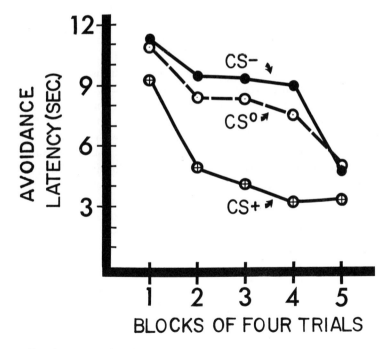

FIG. 4. Mean median latency of avoidance response by three groups during acquisition of avoidance using as the Sᴰ a stimulus which had previously been used in appetitive Pavlovian conditioning.

Half hopeful, half fearful that the failure to find proactive interference to the CS + was an artifact of our technique, we tested the same hypothesis, again using a transfer of control design but this time modified to include two Pavlovian conditioning phases.

Experiment Seven

A group of dogs was initially given discriminative appetitive Pavlovian conditioning in the booth with two tones and food. One tone (CS +) always signaled food presentations; the other tone (CS −) signaled a period in which no food would be delivered. Then the second Pavlovian phase was begun, and both tone CSs were paired with electric shock in the booth. Next, we trained the dogs in the shuttle box on a temporally paced instrumental avoidance schedule. Finally, they received transfer of control test trials with both CSs. If hope elicited by CS + is incompatible with fear, then fear should be established to the CS + more slowly and weakly than to a stimulus which signaled the absence of food (i.e., CS −). The CS which elicits the most fear should produce the greatest rate of avoidance responding during transfer of control tests. The results are presented in Fig. 5.

Once again, counter to our expectation, we see that the previous CS + for food results in a higher rate of avoidance than the CS −. Prior pairing of a CS with food does *not* interfere with its subsequent establishment as a fear CS relative to a CS − control stimulus. Indeed, it appears as if the prior appetitive Pavlovian conditioning makes it *easier* to establish the stimulus as a signal for shock. Alternatively, the CS − might be showing something akin to latent inhibition (Lubow & Moore, 1959). While the present experiment does not allow for their separation, reference to Experiment Six and Fig. 4 suggests both enhanced fear acquisition to CS + and interference to CS −. We feel that this result and that from Experiment Six are not in accord with reasonable expectations based upon the motivational reflex-interaction hypothesis.

How do we understand this data? We believe the answer is not to be found in a motivational analysis. It looks as if once a stimulus is established as a cue for some reinforcement event, it is later easier to make that same stimulus a cue for a different reinforcer—

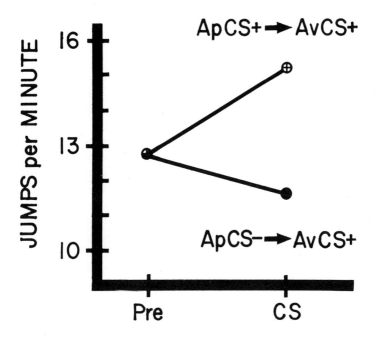

Fɪɢ. 5. Mean rate of avoidance responding during each of two CSs superimposed on a Sidman avoidance base line compared to the base-line rate (Pre). Before this the group had received discriminative appetitive Pavlovian conditioning to the CSs followed by defensive Pavlovian conditioning wherein both CSs were paired with shock. Means averaged over three days.

even if they are based upon qualitatively opposite reinforcers. This resembles a learning-to-learn phenomena and suggests that Pavlovian conditioning not only endows a stimulus with motivation- and expectation-eliciting powers but also endows it with *general* cue properties. Furthermore, the latter are apparently sometimes more persistent than the former. This view is further supported by the incidental observation that the CS − in Experiment Six proved quite difficult to establish as a signal for avoidance (cf. Table 1 and Fig. 4) relative to a random control. We are not the first to believe that we have found evidence for a primacy or learning-to-learn process in Pavlovian conditioning; indeed, Konorski and Szwejkowska (1952), Lubow and Moore (1959), and more recently

Maier, Seligman, and Solomon (1969) have discussed data and phenomena which could reflect such a process(es).

This hypothesis is suggestive of two lines of research: (a) it suggests that we explore Pavlovian conditioning → Pavlovian conditioning "transfer of training" designs, and (b) it suggests that, though we have been studying the motivational functions of Pavlovian conditioned mediators, we have been ignoring their possible cue functions and properties. If mediators have strong cue properties, do these cue properties get hooked up to responses? (Remember the "s_g" in Spence's $r_g - s_g$!) This line of reasoning led us to design an experiment in which we pitted the reflex interactions of the motivational properties of Pavlovian conditioned mediators against their possible cue properties.

Experiment Eight

We reasoned that if, for example, an instrumental response were first established to a specific stimulus using an appetitive reinforcer, and then the same response to a second stimulus, using an aversive reinforcer, were established, test presentations of a compound of the two stimuli would achieve an assessment of the relative contributions of motivational and response-cuing mechanisms of the mediators elicited by the two stimuli. Integrating our Experiment Four and the hypothesis of reflex interactions of conditioned motivations based upon antipodean reinforcers, we would expect the rate of responding to be *less* during the compound than during either of the individual stimulus conditions. On the other hand, both stimuli would cue the same response; expectations based upon the cue function of the elicited mediational states and a review of similarly designed experiments using appetitive rewards in both stages lead us to expect the rate of responding to be *greater* during the compound than during either of the individual stimulus conditions. Or perhaps the two functions will offset each other.

The following two-group experiment, using hurdle jumping in the shuttle box as the training and indicator response, tested these conflicting expectations. One group (ApCS on AvBase) initially was trained to hurdle jump discriminatively on a VR-3 to obtain food. Only jumps in the presence of CS+ (a tone) were reinforced, while jumps in the presence of CS − (a contrasting tone) or during the intertrial interval (i.e., in the presence of general apparatus stimuli alone) were never reinforced. After the dogs had reached the criterion of stability and discrimination, they were shifted to training on a temporal avoidance schedule (R–S = 30 seconds), presumably under the partial control of general apparatus stimuli; tones were never presented during avoidance training. Finally, test trials were conducted by superimposing the tones on the avoidance behavior base line (i.e., compounding the appetitive stimuli with the aversive general apparatus stimulus conditions).

The other group was treated similarly except that the roles of the reinforcers were switched. This group (AvCS on ApBase) initially was trained to hurdle jump discriminatively on a VR–3 in order to avoid shock. The CS + tone warned of shock, but the CS − tone was never followed by shock. After the avoidance

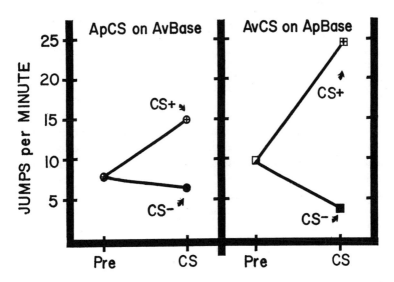

FIG. 6. Mean rates of responding by two groups during each of two CSs tested on a base-line schedule (Pre). One group (ApCS on AvBase) had discriminative appetitive signals superimposed on a Sidman avoidance base line; the other group (AvCS on ApBase) had discriminative defensive signals superimposed on a VI–15 seconds food base line. Means averaged over five blocks of seven trials each.

discrimination was well established, the dogs were shifted to appetitive training on a VI–15 seconds in the presence of the general apparatus stimuli alone; tones were never presented during this appetitive training. Finally, test trials were conducted by superimposing the tones on the ongoing appetitive behavior base line (i.e., compounding the aversive stimuli with the appetitive general apparatus stimulus conditions).

The data from both groups can be summarized together because the effects of the test presentations were the same. The results are presented in Fig. 6. During the CS + the rate of responding was markedly greater than that observed in the presence of the general apparatus stimuli alone. The addition of the CS + did *not* reduce the rate of responding as if it were eliciting a mediational state which had incompatible motivational properties, despite its prior association with an event whose hedonic properties were the opposite of those of the event supporting the base-line behavior. The addition of the CS + facilitated responding as if there were more response-controlling stimuli present. This strongly implicates the response-cuing functions of conditioned mediators.

CONCLUDING COMMENTS

The questions with which we began these projects are still not answered and are in need of additional research. However, we do now know that there are several phenomena worth exploring. In addition, we have found indications that there are a number of complex, confounding factors that must be taken into account in any future research. One of the basic factors is the experimental paradigm used. Our work suggests that different paradigms are differentially sensitive to the processes which underlie the transfer interactions. For example, we found a discriminated avoidance to be more sensitive than nondiscriminated, temporally paced avoidance to the presentations of appetitive Pavlovian CS +'s. Also, other of our experiments (not reported here) have indicated that the effect of an appetitive Pavlovian CS − upon discriminated avoidance behavior depends upon how the CS − is established, that is, upon whether the CS − is simply contrasted with food presentations in a between-*S*s design, as in Experiment Four, or whether it is contrasted with both a CS + and food in a within-*S*s design, as in Experiment Eight. The latter procedure seems to make the CS— a powerful general inhibitor in later transfer tests. Although one would not be surprised to find quantitative differences between procedures (Grice & Hunter, 1964), the qualitative differences observed distress us. Understanding why these paradigm differences occur surely will be important to an adequate theory of conditioned mediation.

Furthermore, our data suggest that more than just conditioned motivational states affect the transfer phenomena. In particular, cuing functions of these conditioned mediators have been implicated; our experiments suggested that there are cases where they even outweigh the motivational functions. It seems to us that inadequate attention has been paid to cuing functions as a basis for the kinds of transfer effects heretofore observed; a well-formulated stimulus-associative model may be able to handle most, if not all, of the available transfer data.

A second possible influential process implicated in this series of experiments is a Pavlovian level, learning-sets process. Though learning-set phenomena resulting in proactive facilitation (Harlow, 1949) are known with respect to instrumental responses, this kind of process on the Pavlovian level has not been explored. There may be strong primacy effects of establishing CS+ and CS— functions, regardless of the hedonic nature of the UCS. Since the outcomes and interpretations of some tests of hypotheses about transfer interactions would be influenced by whether or not Pavlovian learning sets do exist, research along these lines is clearly indicated.

Although our research has not yet provided clear answers to any questions, it has (a) indicated that more than simple motivational interactions underlie transfer of control phenomena, (b) revealed that we need to explore the possibility of response-cuing functions of mediators, and (c) suggested that *new* learning phenomena and behavioral processes are lurking around, waiting to be discovered.

REFERENCES

Armus, H. L., & Sniadowsky-Dolinsky, D. Startle decrement and secondary reinforcement stimulation. *Psychon. Sci.*, 1966, **4**, 175–176.

Bower, F., & Grusec, J. Effect of prior Pavlovian discrimination training upon learning an operant discrimination. *J. exp. anal. Behav.*, 1964, **7**, 401–404.

Brady, J. V., & Hunt, H. F. An experimental approach to the analysis of emotional behavior. *J. Psychol.*, 1955, **40**, 313–324.

Coulson, G., & Walsh, M. Facilitation of avoidance responding in white rats during a stimulus preceding food. *Psychol. Rep.*, 1968, **22**, 1277–1284.

Estes, W. K. Discrimination conditioning. I. A discriminative property of conditioned anticipation. *J. exp. Psychol.*, 1943, **32**, 150–155.

Estes, W. K. Discriminative conditioning. II. Effects of a Pavlovian conditioned stimulus upon a subsequently established operant response. *J. exp. Psychol.*, 1948, **38**, 173–177.

Estes, W. K. Outline of a theory of punishment. In R. M. Church, and B. A. Campbell, (Eds.), *Punishment and aversive behavior.* New York: Appleton-Century-Crofts, 1969.

Estes, W. K., & Skinner, B. F. Some quantitative properties of anxiety. *J. exp. Psychol.*, 1941, **29**, 390–400.

Grice, R. G., & Hunter, J. J. Stimulus intensity effects depend upon the type of experimental design. *Psychol. Rev.*, 1964, **71**, 247–256.

Grossen, N. E., Kostansek, D., & Bolles, R. C. Effects of appetitive discriminative stimuli upon avoidance behavior. Paper presented at Psychonomic Society meeting, St. Louis, 1968.

Hammond, L. J. Increased responding to CS– in differential CER. *Psychon. Sci.*, 1966, **5**, 337–338.

Harlow, H. F. The formation of learning sets. *Psychol. Rev.*, 1949, **56**, 51–65.

Konorski, J., & Szwejkowska, G. Chronic extinction and restoration of conditioned reflexes. IV. The dependence of the course of extinction and restoration of conditioned reflexes on the "history" of the conditioned stimulus (the principle of the primacy of first training). *Acta Biologiae Experimentalis* (Warsaw), 1952, **16**, 95–113.

Logan, F. A., & Wagner, A. R. *Reward and punishment.* Boston: Allyn & Bacon, 1965.

Lubow, R. E., & Moore, A. U. Latent inhibition: The effect of nonreinforced pre-exposure to the conditioned stimulus. *J. comp. physiol. Psychol.*, 1959, **59**, 415–419.

Maier, S. F., Seligman, M. E. P., & Solomon, R. L. Pavlovian fear conditioning and learned helplessness: Effects on escape and avoidance behavior of (a) the CS–US contingency and (b) the independence of the US and voluntary responding. In B. A. Campbell, and R. M. Church (Eds.), *Punishment.* New York: Appleton-Century-Crofts, 1969.

Mowrer, O. H. *Learning theory and behavior.* New York: Wiley, 1960.

Overmier, J. B., & Leaf, R. C. Effects of discriminative Pavlovian fear conditioning on previously or subsequently acquired avoidance responding. *J. comp. physiol. Psychol.*, 1965, **60**, 213–217.

Pavlov, I. P. *Conditioned reflexes.* Trans. by G. V. Anrep. London: Oxford University Press, 1927.

Perkins, C. C. An analysis of the concept of reinforcement. *Psychol. Rev.*, 1968, **75**, 155–172.

Ray, O. S., & Stein, L. Generalization of conditioned suppression. *J. exp. anal. Behav.*, 1959, **2**, 357–361.

Rescorla, R. A., & LoLordo, V. M. Inhibition of avoidance behavior. *J. comp. physiol. Psychol.*, 1965, **59**, 406–412.

Rescorla, R. A., & Solomon, R. L. Two-process learning theory: Relationships between Pavlovian conditioning and instrumental learning. *Psychol. Rev.*, 1967, **74**, 151–182.

Sheffield, F. D. New evidence on the drive-induction theory of reinforcement. In R. N. Haber (Ed.), *Current research on motivation*. New York: Holt, Rinehart & Winston, 1966. Pp. 111–122.

Solomon, R. L., & Turner, Lucille H. Discriminative classical conditioning in dogs paralyzed by curare can later control discriminative avoidance responses in the normal state. *Psychol. Rev.*, 1962, **69**, 202–219.

Spence, K. *Behavior theory and conditioning*. New Haven: Yale University Press, 1956.

Trapold, M. A., & Fairlie, J. Transfer of discrimination learning based upon contingent and noncontingent training procedures. *Psychol. Rep.*, 1965, **17**, 239–246.

Trapold, M. A., Lawton, G. W., Dick, R. A., & Gross, D. M. Transfer of training from differential classical to differential instrumental conditioning. *J. exp. Psychol.*, 1968, **76**, 568–573.

Trapold, M. A., & Winokur, S. Transfer from classical conditioning and extinction to acquisition, extinction, and stimulus generalization of a positively reinforced instrumental response. *J. exp. Psychol.*, 1967, **73**, 517–525.

Walker, K. C. Effect of a discriminative stimulus transferred to a previously unassociated response. *J. exp. Psychol.*, 1942, **31**, 312–321.

Williams, D. R., & Barry, H., III. Counterconditioning in an operant conflict situation. *J. comp. physiol. Psychol.*, 1966, **61**, 154–155.

The Noncontingent Manipulation of Incentive Motivation[1]

ROBERT C. BOLLES and NEAL E. GROSSEN

University of Washington

The ordinary operant or instrumental learning procedure is a *contingent* procedure in the sense that the availability of reinforcement is made contingent upon the occurrence of the response. Using a contingent procedure it is easy to show that the strength of the response is a function of the conditions of reinforcement, that is, the amount, quality, and schedule of reinforcement.

There are a number of reasons for supposing that the variations in response strength which correspond to variations in the conditions of reinforcement are motivational in character. Consider, for example, that rats run faster for food if they are given more of it. This finding alone does not indicate a motivational effect; what does suggest a motivational interpretation is that while the asymptotic performance level depends upon the amount of reinforcement, the rate of approaching the asymptote does not. Furthermore, when the amount of reinforcement is suddenly shifted there is a corresponding shift in performance which occurs quite quickly—much more quickly than the response was originally acquired. There is a mass of evidence (Bolles, 1967; Hall, 1966) which is not only consistent with an incentive motivational interpretation of these kinds of effects but which seems virtually to demand such an interpretation.

Granting for the time being the viability of some kind of incentive motivation theory, we are confronted with three sets of questions.

[1] This research was supported by National Science Foundation grant GB–8035.

143

1. Is the reinforcement contingency necessary, that is, do the conditions of reinforcement produce incentive motivation only when reinforcement is contingent upon the motivated response? There are both theoretical and empirical grounds for believing that contingency is not required and that comparable motivation effects can be obtained with *noncontingent* procedures. The question is whether incentive motivation can be manipulated independently of instrumental behavior.

2. If comparable effects can be obtained with noncontingent procedures, are they as durable and as large, and can they be obtained over the same range of learning parameters (e.g., the same number of acquisition trials) as those obtained using the more customary contingent procedures? In other words, if noncontingent procedures can produce the same kinds of effects as contingent procedures, are they quantitatively the same?

3. If the same kinds of incentive effects can be found, and if they are quantitatively similar, then are they the same thing? Are they based on the same mechanisms, or are there really two kinds of mechanisms to be found, one of which merely mimics the effects of the other?

In what follows, a little of the theory and much of the research bearing on these questions will be discussed. There will be no firm answer to any of the three main questions. Although appropriate noncontingent effects will be described, it will not be obvious that they are motivational or that they are durable, large, or easily obtained. And as attractive as the idea might be from a theoretical standpoint, it will appear doubtful that noncontingent procedures involve the same mechanisms as the more common and powerful contingent procedures.

SOME THEORETICAL BACKGROUND

The chief proposal for a theoretical mechanism to account for incentive motivation was made many years ago by Hull (1930). He proposed that when the consummatory response (eating) occurs in the goal box, it tends to become conditioned to apparatus cues; extramaze cues which are similar to those existing at the goal box will also tend to elicit the consummatory response. Although eating is not allowed to occur in the start box, a certain hypothetical fraction of the eating response (salivation and such) can occur there, and Hull proposed the occurrence of this fractional anticipatory response (r_G) helps maintain S's running. Initially, Hull (1930) viewed r_G merely as a source of stimuli; its feedback was merely part of the total start-box stimulus configuration to which running ultimately becomes conditioned, but it was a critical part of the total stimulus pattern because it was the feedback from r_G which, in effect, signaled the nature of the goal object and enabled S to appear to anticipate it. Later, Hull (1952) gave r_G a motivational interpretation: in addition to being a source of important controlling stimuli, it was also assumed to make a contribution to the animal's total motivation. The vigor of r_G was hypothesized to determine the magnitude of K which multiplied whatever habits were operative in the situation. The greater K was in a given situation, the greater the animal's motivation was in that situation.

One further feature of Hull's analysis is vitally important: he hypothesized that r_G became established through classical conditioning. Thus, though the instrumental response itself requires contingent reinforcement if it is to be acquired, r_G, K, and incentive motivation do not. They are acquired merely by the consummatory response occurring in the presence of certain stimuli.

Although not all theorists have endorsed all of the features of Hull's analysis, there does seem to have been wide acceptance of the general idea that something special and important happens in the goal box besides the reinforcement of the instrumental response. Sometimes the goal box is said to have acquired secondary reinforcing properties, sometimes it is said to have become a discriminative stimulus in the presence of which reinforcement can occur, sometimes it is said to elicit hunger, or appetite, or incentive motivation. Moreover, it is nearly always assumed that this something special that happens in the goal box occurs purely by contiguity, that is, it is not supposed to matter how S got into the box, or what S does there.[2] It ought to be possible to produce incentive motivation (or whatever it is that is produced by S's eating in the goal box) by passively placing S there. Following passive placement, an increment in incentive motivation ought to be evident if S is subsequently tested under circumstances where, for example, it has to run into the box; it should run faster. Curiously, no one seems to have used such a simple design. But Seward (1949) obtained the indicated results using a somewhat more complicated noncontingent procedure. Rats were permitted to explore a T-maze and were then passively placed in one goal box and fed there. On a subsequent test trial a significant proportion of the group went to the appropriate side, the side where they had eaten. Other experimenters have not always gotten positive results (Denny & Davis, 1951; Seward, Datel, & Levy, 1952), and as interest in the "latent learning" problem has waned, so has the use of this kind of noncontingent procedure.

LATENT EXTINCTION

Seward and Levy (1949) were the first to use another procedure, which has continued to enjoy more success. They asked: If incentive motivation can be built up by noncontingent reinforcement (or even if it cannot), is it possible to *reduce* previously established incentive motivation by noncontingent *withdrawal* of reinforcement? They first trained a running response on an elevated runway and then passively placed Ss at the goal without food; these Ss subsequently extinguished running more quickly than controls that lacked the preextinction or "latent extinction" experience. They argued that, in effect, the tendency for goal cues to elicit r_G had been at least partially extinguished by this experience and that, therefore, incentive motivation had been weakened. We may note

[2] It is obvious, however, that S has to eat in the goal box or there is no point in being there. A few theorists (e.g., Mowrer, 1960; Spence, 1956) have noted this singular fact and suggested that the reinforcement operation, drive reduction or whatever it may be, can, should, and must operate under such circumstances. Thus, incentive learning almost has to be learning by reinforcement. Curiously, however, most theorists appear to be quite happy with the totally unsupported idea that the special thing that happens in the goal box happens because of classical conditioning.

that the latent extinction effect was much more dramatic and durable than the latent learning effects Seward and his students had been able to report. There was something peculiarly prophetic about this asymmetry, and perhaps someone should have noted it at the time but no one did. That both effects could be found at all was seen as support for an r_G-based incentive theory of motivation.

The hypothetical r_G mechanism is supposed to be involved not only in incentive (i.e., acquired) motivation but in secondary (i.e., acquired) reinforcement as well. It ought to be possible, therefore, to observe the effects of latent extinction not only in the loss of incentive motivation, as in Seward and Levy's experiment, but in a corresponding failure of secondary reinforcement. Moltz and Maddi (1956) reported such an effect. Rats were first trained to run in a runway. Two goal boxes were used; on some trials they ran to one box and received food, while on other trials they ran to a distinctively different box and received no food. When subsequently tested in a T-maze, Ss showed a preference for the previously positive box, although neither box contained food at the time of testing. This is a standard secondary reinforcement procedure. One group of Ss had a brief preextinction or latent extinction session interposed between runway training and T-maze testing; food was withdrawn from the positive box at that time. These Ss showed no preference for the previously positive box.

In 1957, Moltz reviewed the latent extinction literature to that time and was able to defend several conclusions, all based upon r_G theory. He proposed that the latent extinction effect depends upon the unreinforced evocation of r_G. Thus, all factors which affect the strength of r_G should also affect the strength of the effect. For example, the higher the deprivation level, the more pronounced the latent extinction effect should be. Moltz and Maddi had previously found that this was the case; experience with the withdrawal of food had produced no effect when Ss were not hungry. Moltz (1957) suggested that all the variables that influence instrumental performance may do so through the r_G–s_G mechanism.

However, things were to turn out to be a little more complicated than Moltz supposed. Hughes, Davis, and Grice (1960) deduced from Moltz's analysis that if the latent extinction effect was mediated by the r_G–s_G mechanism, then the effect should be greater if the alley is more like the goal box. They used two goal boxes, one distinct from and the other quite similar to the alley. They found that latent extinction experience affected running speed in the predicted way but did not affect the number of responses to extinction. In fact, this measure came out in the wrong direction. In a replication of the Hughes, Davis, and Grice (1960) experiment, Koppman and Grice also found no effect of the noncontingent extinction experience on choice behavior on the T-maze. Moreover, the results with the running-speed measure, the one response measure which showed a latent extinction effect, did not depend upon which goal box was used. These authors therefore concluded that the r_G mechanism, as it had been generally understood, did not adequately explain the phenomenon. Similar failures to support r_G theory have been reported by DiLollo (1964), Gonzalez and Diamond (1960), and Stein (1957).

Young, Mangum, and Capaldi (1960) found a latent extinction effect and found that its size was directly related to the amount of preextinction goal-box exposure. These authors also reported that the intertrial interval interacted with the duration of goal confinement. Dyal (1962) systematically investigated both the duration parameter and the number of direct placements. He ran his rats in a Y-maze with either 1, 5, or 10 direct placements and with durations of either 30, 60 or 300 seconds. The latent extinction effect was greatest on the first test trial and then rapidly disappeared. Effects were found for the goal measure (speed) and the number of errors. Dyal also found that what latent extinction effects appeared depended on the response measure used and the particular experimental conditions. It seems that at least three of the variables influencing latent extinction interact.

Clifford (1964) introduced another dimension into these studies. He investigated the effects of different numbers of prior reinforcements. He used five different amounts of training—24, 48, 84, 132, or 192 trials—and either extinction or control placements. Clifford found that all preextinction groups subsequently extinguished faster than their controls. However, contrary to the theoretical comments of other investigators, Clifford suggests that these noncontingent procedures may involve frustration in addition to incentive motivation. The withdrawal of food is, after all, the way to produce frustration.

Amsel (1958, 1962) has proposed that in addition to the r_G-s_G mechanism there is a similar but antagonistic mechanism, r_F-s_F, which is based upon frustration. Frustration is defined by Amsel as the absence of reward following reward, and he considers r_F-s_F to be acquired in a manner similar to r_G-s_G. That is, if r_G has become conditioned to goal stimuli and then reinforcement, primary frustration and its anticipatory factional component, r_F, will be conditioned to these stimuli. Presumably S can learn a new response which avoids this predicament, such as withdrawing from the empty goal box. With frustration, as with incentive, there are supposed to be two distinct processes involved in the performance of instrumental behavior. First, S learns a kind of negative incentive— certain stimuli now predict withdrawal of reinforcement—and, secondly, S learns an instrumental response which minimizes the negative incentive—the termination of this aversive state should reinforce any effective avoidance behavior.

A study by Trapold and Doren (1966) is relevant at this point since it seems to indicate that r_F-s_F may be involved in the direct placement procedure in the same way it is in partial reinforcement (see Amsel, 1962, for a frustration theory analysis of partial rein- forcement). Trapold and Doren ran groups under two kinds of noncontingent conditions: under one, S was required to run 8 inches to the food cup on direct placement trials; under the other condition, S was placed with its nose in the empty food cup. It was found that Ss which ran 8 inches were more resistant to extinction on the instrumental running response than Ss which did not run at all. In spite of the expectation that running would have been par- tially extinguished for these Ss, it evidently was not. It could be argued that the cues of anticipatory frustration (r_F) had become associated with approach stimuli by allowing Ss to locomote 8 inches in the goal area. That is, running was conditioned to r_G and in addition, in the group which locomoted 8 inches, r_F was also conditioned to running. Thus, r_F was associated with the same cues as approach, giving rise to increased resistance to extinction. However, for the nonlocomotion group, r_F was not associated with approach cues and consequently this group did not show any increased resistance to extinction. It could be inferred that the latent extinction procedure results in a buildup of r_F to the pre- viously rewarded goal cues and subsequently facilitates extinction.

This analysis could also account for the results of Hughes, Davis, and Grice (1960). The Trapold and Doren (1966) results were replicated by Trapold and Holden (1966), who added a control which had reinforced direct-placement trials. Again it was found that the running direct-placement Ss showed prolonged extinction. The two experiments taken together provide rather firm evidence that frustration is involved in the latent extinction effect.

Recent latent extinction studies have been done mainly within the context of frustration theory. For example, Jones, Narver, and Bridges (1967) found that rats trained on a FR schedule in the runway and then given one nonreinforced direct placement would decrease their running speed on the very next trial, although they showed greater speed on later trials. Again, their data are consistent with frustration theory, since r_F is presumably conditioned to approach cues in the partial reward situation.

Daly (1969) gave Ss either 60 reinforced placements followed by 12 nonreinforced placements accompanied by a light stimulus, or placements with no reward and no stimulus. She found in subsequent hurdle-jump tests that Ss which were frustrated in the presence of the light cue would jump a hurdle in order to escape this cue associated with nonreward. This experiment clearly indicates that r_F-s_F can be conditioned independently of S's instrumental behavior and that this type of incentive-motivational system is of an aversive nature. We are left with the very serious question of whether withdrawal of food in noncontingent situations weakens r_G, produces r_F, or both. How can these two intimately related hypothetical mechanisms be experimentally separated?

THE CONTINUING SEARCH FOR r_G

A few experimenters have tried to eliminate peripheral correlates of r_G with drugs in the hope that this would permit a direct manipulation of r_G. These studies have either eliminated the salivary component of the consummatory response or partially reduced oral stimulation.

Three studies by Lewis and his students will serve to illustrate the general procedure. Lewis, Butler, and Diamond (1958) used a T-maze apparatus and activity as their dependent variable. The experimental manipulation was the injection of drugs known to decrease the salivary response. There was no conclusive evidence that the drugs affected activity under these conditions, but the authors admitted that under the conditions they used, negative results were also consistent with r_G theory. Lewis and McIntire (1959) essentially replicated the previous study except that they used an activity wheel for the apparatus. They injected pilocarpine or benzocaine and looked for a subsequent decrease in activity. They found none. A third study, by Lewis and Kent (1961), was a further replication using slightly different groups in a T-maze. Again it was found that blocking salivation or oral stimulation by the use of drugs had little effect on activity level. At this point the authors wondered if there was such a thing as r_G. They did not entertain any alternative to the old idea that r_G has to be located in the mouth.

There have been a number of studies in which the presumed peripheral components of r_G (e.g., salivation) have been measured rather than eliminated, and these measurements correlated with instrumental behavior. Shapiro (1962) reported one of the first such studies. He trained dogs to bar press for food on a DRL schedule. Salivation increased during the time-out interval, and the dogs often salivated following a lever press, but not nearly so much as they did immediately preceding a lever press. In a similar experiment, Kintsch and Witte (1962) had dogs bar pressing on one of three schedules—CRF, FI, or FR. They found that bar pressing and salivation tended to occur together, but salivation also occurred more or less independently under some reinforcement schedules. A further study by Shapiro, Miller, and Bresnahan (1966) involved dogs that had been trained on a DRL schedule for food (bar pressing). Three kinds of test trials were used. The first type was a dummy on which just salivation was measured, a second type of trial consisted of presenting a novel stimulus, and the third type of trial introduced a stimulus which had been established in Pavlovian situations as a food signal $(S+)$. The $S+$ elicited salivation, the occurrence of which was highly correlated with instrumental behavior, but in the other two types of trials there was less salivation and it bore no relationship to instrumental behavior.

The elusive r_G has also resisted efforts at measurement where tongue licking was measured. The first such study was by Miller and DeBold (1965). They conditioned drinking and then measured anticipatory licking in an incompletely learned discrimination problem. Licking was found both to precede and to follow the response (bar pressing), but its occurrence was highly correlated with bar pressing. In 93% of the trials, tongue licking occurred in the 5 seconds immediately before a bar press, while tongue licking occurred in only 53% of control intervals of the same duration. In general, then, few bar presses occurred without licks, although licks often occurred without bar pressing. DeBold, Miller, and Jensen (1965) found that conditioned tongue licking would take place only if the animal was deprived.

Patten and Deaux (1966) trained rats in a classical conditioning situation in which a tone CS preceded water by 3 seconds. The control was a group for which the tone occurred randomly in time. The tongue-licking response could be classically conditioned in about 70 trials but it showed very little resistance to extinction. The authors suggested that this rapid extinction suggests the operation of some process other than classical conditioning and that, therefore, the "conditioned" licking may not be a correlate of r_G, since r_G is supposed to be classically conditioned.

The evidence for the existence of a peripheral correlate of r_G is not abundant. However, the evidence is suggestive that salivation may be an antecedent of instrumental behavior, even though reinforcement is in no way contingent upon its occurrence. Perhaps what happens in the noncontingent situation is that the salivary response becomes conditioned to the food cue, and then when this cue is introduced in the instrumental situation it elicits salivation, which constitutes r_G, which motivates or provides stimulus support for the previously acquired instrumental behavior. We have seen that some of the data are consistent with such an analysis. But it also seems clear that r_G theory has reached an impasse. We can hardly distinguish between the reciprocal effects of incentive and frustration. The attempts to anchor r_G operationally, though admirable in their scope and persistence, no longer engender our enthusiasm. We really know little more today about what r_G is or how it works than Hull did in 1952. It is fortunate that the behaviorist can proceed with his principal task, which is to find rules for predicting behavior, without first finding out how r_G works.

The rule which enables us to predict behavior on the basis of the conditions of reinforcement turns out to be this: an S+ stimulus which has been paired with or which predicts reinforcement will facilitate behavior leading to that reinforcer. There is a corollary: an S− stimulus which has been paired with the withdrawal of reinforcement or which predicts the withdrawal of reinforcement will suppress behavior related to that reinforcer. Such a summary statement is intended to be theoretically neutral, and that is evidently the way many writers today prefer to have it. To be sure, we need to sharpen the rule, to be able to specify what facilitation and suppression mean, for example. Are they motivational or purely associative? We need to know what relationships have to obtain between the index response and the reinforcer. Must there be a contingency relationship, or are the facilitation and suppression effects general across response classes? We need to know whether prediction of reinforcement, or mere contiguity, is the critical element in producing these effects. These are some of the questions to which we now turn. We will leave behind r_G theory and Hull's particular incentive model and try to deal with alternative and theoretically more neutral models.

DISCRIMINATED OPERANTS

The noncontingent manipulation of motivation was first demonstrated in a remarkable set of studies some years ago at Minnesota. The first of these (Estes & Skinner, 1941) showed that a stimulus which had preceded unavoidable shock in one situation would suppress ongoing behavior in another situation, just as presenting shock there would. Other studies (Walker, 1942; Estes, 1943) showed that a stimulus which was a noncontingent discriminative stimulus for food would strengthen a response, just as food reinforcement would, even though that particular S–R association had never been reinforced with food. At that time Estes called this a classically conditioned anticipation effect.

Estes's basic procedure involved giving rats in a Skinner box occasional free food signaled by a stimulus, S+. The S− was merely the absence of S+, when there was no food. S+ was then introduced as a probe while *S* was pressing the bar. The effects of

S + can be demonstrated either before bar-press training, that is, its effect can be observed upon the operant rate, or during extinction if the response had been previously acquired. (The effect upon extinction was evidently more dramatic and durable.) The procedure gives the effect of a discriminative stimulus from a noncontingent situation upon presumably unrelated operant performance.

Recent interest in the discriminated noncontingent procedure has followed the discovery of Bower and Grusec (1964) that S − and S + effects could transfer to an instrumental discrimination learning task. The new discrimination was more rapidly acquired and better performed by Ss for which S − and S + were consistent with S^Δ and S^D than by Ss for which they were reversed.[3] Such transfer had been shown before (Walker, 1942; Morse & Skinner, 1958; Bower & Kaufman, 1963) during the extinction of the index response, but Bower and Grusec were the first to demonstrate the discriminative functions of S − and S + in acquisition. It was not acquisition of a new response, however, but the establishment of discriminative control. We cannot keep from wondering to what extent discrimination learning involves extinction (of responding to S^Δ), or frustration, or some other kind of inhibition process.

One other feature of the procedure should disturb us, not because it was unique to the Bower and Grusec study, but because it is actually characteristic of the genre. This is that a great number of noncontingent presentations of S − and S +—300 of each—were given. Recall that, by contrast, Gilchrist (1952) had found that in the latent extinction situation, the latent extinction effects were nearly at full strength after just one noncontingent experience in the goal box (see also Dyal, 1962). Recall too that in the case of a shift in the amount of reinforcement, the corresponding shifts in performance occur in only a few trials. We cannot keep from wondering if Bower and Grusec have discovered a new method for manipulating incentive motivation or something else quite different which has a slight effect upon behavior but acts in the same direction.

---

[3] The terminology is awkward. I will use S + and S − as the signals for food and no food, respectively, in the noncontingent situation. These stimuli may be the same as S^D and S^Δ, which set the occasion for reinforcement and no reinforcement in the contingent situation, or they may be different, as they were in the Bower and Grusec study.

One final question should be borne in mind as we proceed. Although it was apparent that Bower and Grusec's Ss responded more to $S+$ and less to $S-$, it is not so obvious that both $S+$ and $S-$ effects are genuine; it is possible that, for example, only the $S-$ effect is real, that is, that $S-$ actively inhibits behavior, and that the $S+$ effect is a result of contrast or induction from $S-$. We need the results of a separate-groups design in which some Ss receive a noncontingent $S+$ and others a noncontingent $S-$.

The recent work with this type of discriminated operant procedure has been largely dominated by Trapold and his students. Initially, Trapold and Odom (1965) and Trapold and Fairlie (1965) investigated the transfer of $S+$ and $S-$ effects across different operants. When one response, R_1, was brought under discriminative control by S^D and S^Δ, the control was found to transfer almost immediately to a second response, R_2. Although the two responses would appear to be quite similar (pressing one bar vertically and pressing another horizontally), Trapold argued that the transfer of discriminative control could not be just response generalization because there had been no transfer or savings in the initial acquisition of the two responses (i.e., before discrimination training). Trapold favored the interpretation given many years before at Minnesota, namely, that the prior discrimination training had given $S+$ and $S-$ rather general powers to control a wide class of responses. This class might be assumed to include all responses reinforced the same way, but Hyde and Trapold (1967) have shown, as Estes (1949) had before, transfer of $S+$ and $S-$ from hunger to thirst, that is, from food-reinforced to water-reinforced behaviors. Presumably, $S+$ and $S-$ effects have considerable generality. The question is how much and what defines it. Hunger and thirst are not unrelated physiologically.

Trapold (1966) reported that when a bar press had been brought under discriminative control, it could be rapidly reversed by interposing a series of sessions with reversed discriminative training in a noncontingent situation, that is, when the old S^Δ was made a noncontingent cue to food, and the old S^D was made a cue to no food, these Ss acquired the reversed discrimination much faster than controls without noncontingent reversal experience. Trapold, Carlsen, and Myers (1965) investigated the discriminative control (presumably temporal) involved in establishing the FI scallop. Rats were trained on an FI-2 schedule after some had received 300 noncontingent reinforcements on a fixed 2-minute schedule and others had received 300 noncontingent reinforcements on a variable 2-minute schedule. The former developed the FI scallop much more quickly than the latter. One might suppose that during noncontingent sessions postreinforcement times less than, say, 1 minute had acquired S − values, whereas postreinforcement times longer than 1 minute had acquired S + value, and that these values transferred directly to the FI training task. This simple and elegant interpretation is clouded somewhat, however, by the fact that both groups showed depressed rates of responding at all postreinforcement intervals when compared with control *S*s that had received no noncontingent experience! It appears that what had been thought of as an S + effect may have been an S − effect that was somewhat weaker than that produced by the S − itself.

None of the discrimination transfer studies to this point had demonstrated unequivocal S + and S − effects; the situation was analogous to what Black (1968) has called a nonspecific contrast effect. Part of the difficulty resulted from the failure to establish a true base line against which facilatory and inhibitory effects could be individually compared. Trapold and Winokur (1967) attempted to overcome this difficulty by training rats to respond discrimina- tively to a tone and then giving them a series of sessions in which other stimuli, a clicker or a light, had different S + and S − values for different groups. All *S*s were then run in generalization tests with the three stimuli. The S + effect appeared to predominate, but this tendency was obscured by the generalization among stimuli and the interaction of generalization by S + and S − conditions. On the other hand, Trapold, Lawton, Dick, and Gross (1968) seem to have found transfer of S − to be the main factor in another situation. They trained rats in a discriminated bar-press task after one group had received consistent noncontingent training while another group had received reversed noncontingent training. Differential latencies (this was a discrete-trial procedure) were found to the new S^Δ but not to the new S^D. More recently, Trapold, Gross, and Lawton (1969) reversed a bar-press discrimination after the experimental group had received noncontingent reversal training. Again, the latency to respond to S^D appeared to show less transfer, compared with controls which had no interpolated experience, than the tendency not to respond to S^Δ. One possibility is that the response to S^D, which is reinforced, leads to a rapid build-up of incentive motivation, which masks differences in transfer when the trials are treated by blocks. Perhaps the inhibitory effects of $S-$ can be rapidly disinhibited by a few reinforcements, whereas the facilatory effects of $S+$ require a large number of nonreinforcements before it extinguishes. It should be possible to investigate these possibilities by investigating discrimination reversal on a shorter time scale.

Perhaps the most fundamental question in this area is whether the $S+$ and $S-$ effects that have been reported by Trapold and others reflect the same kinds of processes that are involved in the more conventional response-contingent manipulations of incentive motivation. In short, does the noncontingent procedure produce the same kind of incentive motivation as conventional contingent procedures, or does it produce effects which merely mimic incentive motivation? Trapold and Fairlie (1965) found that a bar-press discrimination was reversed no more rapidly by *S*s with prior instrumental discrimination reversal experience than by yoked control *S*s in which all the contingencies between stimuli and reinforcement were independent of behavior. This finding is rather remarkable and suggests that noncontingent experience leads to no decrement relative to a comparable contingent experience. However, we should recall that the initial instrumental response was different from the final index response and that there was, in fact, no generalization between the two. Thus, the conclusion must be limited to the statement that the contingent procedure did not produce a larger effect on an unrelated response than the noncontingent procedure. On the other hand, when the conditions of reinforcement pertain to the index response itself, for example, in an amount of reinforcement study, shifts in these conditions can lead to corresponding changes in behavior in just a few trials, whereas the noncontingent transfer effects that have been reported have involved 120 or more stimulus pairings. Are this many pairings really necessary, or does the use of such extended training mask the real effectiveness of the noncontingent technique? There are no data from a direct comparison, although the data of Trapold et al. (1968) suggest that 240 noncontingent pairings may be about as effective as 25 response-contingent reinforcements in establishing an S^D.

Another important theoretical problem is whether $S+$ and $S-$ effects are motivational in any strict sense, or whether they merely demonstrate the transfer of some kind of generalized discriminative function? Is the $S+$ effect the same kind of mechanism as is produced by giving S a large amount of reinforcement? Is the $S-$ effect anything like the mechanism that is involved when S is given a reduced amount of reinforcement or a zero amount? Some evidence concerning this question comes from a study by Hyde, Trapold, and Gross (1969). They found that although the latency of a bar-press response was a function of the amount of reinforcement it produced (1 versus 10 pellets), latency did not vary when stimuli correlated with 1 or 10 pellets in a noncontingent situation were introduced as cues. If it is true that $S-$ and $S+$ can effectively signal absence and presence of food, but not differential quantities of food, then they would appear to operate through some mechanism other than incentive motivation.

Recently published results of Campbell, Fixen, and Phillips (1969) may alter this picture somewhat. Using a fixed amount of reinforcement, they trained rats on a runway and then extinguished the running response. Following extinction, different groups of rats were given direct placements in the goal box with different amounts of food. On a subsequent running test, all groups showed more recovery of running than spontaneous recovery controls, and the amount of recovery was nicely graded in terms of the amount of reinforcement received in the noncontingent period. Perhaps the "latent reacquisition" situation involves different mechanisms than those involved in Trapold's bar-press situation. Perhaps, for some reason which we do not yet understand, the latent reacquisition procedure allows for the demonstration of motivational effects, while the discriminated operant procedure does not.

A final problem in this work is that one cannot guarantee that during the noncontingent discrimination training S will not acquire superstitious behavior, and that the transfer effects are mediated by instrumental behaviors that have been differentially, albeit adventitiously, reinforced in the noncontingent situation. There is no easy solution to this problem. One could use a response contingency, as Trapold and Fairlie did, provided that it was established that there was no response generalization to the subsequent individual test situation. Alternatively, it would be possible to introduce different response requirements, as Grossen, Bolles, and Kostansek (1969) did, in order to be able to assess the effects of response compatibility. It is also possible to bypass the instrumental chain, even the approach to the food cup, by direct injection of food into the mouth (Gross, Trapold, & Hyde, 1968), but this trick only guarantees noncontingency; it does not guarantee that S will not superstitiously emit some behavior which is then reinforced.

SOME OTHER NONCONTINGENT TECHNIQUES

Discriminated operant techniques have a number of virtues, including that they are easy to instrument, but they do not lend themselves too readily to the elucidation of the mechanisms of learning. Although they provide an automatic index of the extent to which the discriminative stimulus has gained control over the response, this control is invariably gained slowly, and we are left wondering what stimulus the animal was responding to during the first several hundred trials. Can the results of such studies shed any light on the mechanisms involved in incentive shift effects, for example, the Crespi effect (1942), which become evident in a mere handful of trials? Is it safe to assume that the same mechanisms are responsible for noncontingent discrimination reversal and latent extinction just because the formal properties of the situations are the same, for example, the absence of a reinforcement contingency? We need to know what happens in simpler situations.

There have been a few reports with other procedures. Bindra and Palfai (1967) studied $S+$ and $S-$ effects on completely noncontingent behavior; their Ss were merely observed in a standardized arena. They found that the $S+$ for water increased the incidence of locomotion and exploration. In other words, it had a rather generalized motivation effect. There was also evidently an increase in behavior addressed specifically to the water-delivery mechanism.

Presentation of the S— had the opposite effect; it suppressed exploratory and locomotive behavior. Comparable results were obtained by Zamble (1967), using an electrical general-activity sensing device. One feature of Bindra's study is worth special note, namely, that the effects were obtained with as few as 50 noncontingent pairings.

Trapold has suggested that S+ and S— effects are not motivational (Hyde, Trapold, & Gross, 1969). This interpretation is based in part upon his earlier finding that an S+ failed to facilitate the startle reflex (Trapold, 1962). Although this result seems to be readily replicable (e.g., Armus et al., 1964), the argument seems to be a little too strong. Thus, there is little indication that drive (i.e., deprivation) facilitates the startle reflex (Bolles, 1967), and we must begin to wonder if in order to be a motivation effect it must be possible to demonstrate the facilitation of any and all behavior in *S*'s repertoire. Is it not sufficient to find a facilitation of some limited class of behaviors, perhaps those related in some way to the reinforcer? Could we not call an effect motivational even if it applied only to the reinforced operant?

One study using the much (and mysteriously) neglected runway has been reported. Marx and Murphy (1961) trained rats to run and gave them a cue in the goal box whenever food was presented. The cue was not a discriminative stimulus for food, but was merely paired with food. Two groups of *S*s were then extinguished, and those *S*s which had the food cue presented *in the start box* showed greater resistance to extinction than controls which did not receive the cue. The cue appears to motivate running during extinction.

A recent experiment from our own laboratory replicates and extends this finding but raises an interesting question. Hargrave, Grossen, and Bolles (1969) trained three groups of rats in a runway, then moved *S*s into a separate noncontingent conditioning chamber where they received a series of 5-second tones. For the S+ group the tone immediately preceded food presentation, for the S— group the tone never occurred closer than 30 seconds before food, and for the control group the tones were scheduled randomly with respect to the presentation of food. In extinction it was found that S+ facilitated performance (Marx and Murphy's results), and that S— depressed performance with respect to the control *S*s. In the acquisition of the running response, however, there were no differences among groups, either in latencies or in running speeds. Previous studies had suggested that S+ and S− effects are more demonstrable on extinction than on acquisition, but the total absence of effects except on extinction rather startled us. We are forced to conclude that the S+ and S− effects may be extinction phenomena and may have little to do with incentive motivation as it is ordinarily conceived.

THE AVERSIVE CASE

Noncontingent procedures using aversive stimuli have been studied rather extensively since 1941, when Estes and Skinner first described such a procedure. They found that a stimulus which predicted shock, that is, a stimulus which consistently preceded shock regardless of S's behavior, would dramatically suppress operant behavior. This procedure has become known as the CER (conditioned emotional reaction), or conditioned suppression procedure (the latter name is preferable and is the one we will use here). Though the data leave some room for doubt that a cue for food facilitates a hunger-motivated response, there can be no doubt that a cue for shock suppresses such behavior; the effect is rapidly acquired, frequently involves 100% suppression, and is quite resistant to extinction. It is a very impressive effect. We will not be so concerned with the conditioned suppression effect here, however, as with the complementary effect, which might be called the conditioned facilitation effect. Just as we may consider as a danger signal (DS) the cue which predicts shock, so we may think of a cue which predicts no shock, that is, a cue which is consistently followed by the absence of shock, as a safety signal (SS). And we may ask whether a safety signal, established in a noncontingent situation, has a motivational effect which is in any way comparable to the appetitive S+.

Hammond (1966) used a standard operant situation in which rats were lever pressing for water on a VI schedule. Two types of noncontingent trials, signaled by two kinds of cues, were superimposed on the schedule. One cue, the DS, was followed by shock, while on the other type of trial the other cue, the SS, was presented and was never closely followed by shock. Hammond found, as had previous investigators, that the DS suppressed instrumental responding. The SS, however, resulted in enhancement of lever pressing back nearly to its pretraining level. (The response rate in conditioned suppression is usually considerably reduced as compared with the rate before the introduction of shock; the usual reason given for this is that fear becomes conditioned to apparatus cues, so that some generalized suppression occurs in the absence of the specific DS signal.) Subsequently, Hammond (1967) reported a study that was similar to the first except that a random control procedure was incorporated. Rats were trained to lever press for water. The experimental group received a DS which was followed on some trials by shock but which was followed on other trials by another stimulus, the SS, instead (this is Pavlov's "contrast procedure" for establishing inhibition). Control Ss received the same stimuli but they were presented randomly with respect to shock. After 20 days of training, the experimental group was suppressing to the DS but not to the SS when these stimuli were introduced as probes and when performance was compared with that of the controls. These differences held up during extinction. Hammond's results indicate that there is an SS effect, and he suggested that both the DS and the SS effects represent separate active processes which are relatively long lasting.

A study by Hendry (1967) replicated Hammond's result but included a further stage of training in which Ss could *produce* the SS at any time by pressing the lever. This behavior was acquired, suggesting that the SS acquires positive reinforcing powers. It should be pointed out, however, that Ss were making the same response in the same situation where shock had been previously presented, so the test for reinforcement is rather weak. There were, no doubt, sufficient apparatus cues for the elicitation of fear, and the lever pressing may have reflected the production of fear inhibition, that is, negative reinforcement rather than positive reinforcement. A basic question which will probably be with us for some time is whether in this type of situation the SS acts as (1) a reinforcer, (2) an incentive motivator, or (3) an inhibitor of fear.

The fear-inhibition hypothesis has been vigorously defended by Solomon and his coworkers at Pennsylvania, and they have produced a mass of experimental evidence for it. Let us consider some of this evidence. Solomon and Turner (1962) paralyzed dogs with a curare-type drug (which is certainly one way to eliminate the response-reinforcement contingency) and paired a DS with shock. Later the DS was found to facilitate a previously established panel-pushing avoidance response. At this time certain assumptions were made which have subsequently become a permanent part of these investigators' position (e.g., Rescorla & Solomon, 1967). It is assumed that avoidance behavior is motivated, that it is motivated by fear, and that the more fear S has, the better its avoidance performance will be. For experimental purposes the predictions are conveniently just the opposite of those one would make for the conditioned suppression situation. While the DS suppresses appetitive behavior, it facilitates avoidance; and while the SS reconstitutes the suppressed appetitive response, it washes out the avoidance response. We soon will see that there are some problems for these assumptions, but for the moment let us see what the Pennsylvania investigators, particularly Rescorla, have done with them.

Rescorla and LoLordo (1965) reported three related studies using dogs in a barrier-jump free-operant (i.e., Sidman) avoidance task. In the first experiment a cue, CS_1, was turned on and followed in a few seconds either by shock or by a second cue, CS_2, and no shock. Ninety such trials were given noncontingently. Following this conditioning the two stimuli were presented as probes while Ss were performing a previously learned free-operant avoidance response. The CS_1 (DS) facilitated avoidance responding, while CS_2 (SS) produced a decrement in it. A second type of conditioning employed by these authors was the standard delay-conditioning procedure in which CS_1 was followed by shock. For an SS they used a procedure in which CS_2 was never followed closely by shock (a form of backward conditioning). The results were the same as in the first experiment. The third experiment was confined to the SS effect; again the investigators found that SS inhibited avoidance responding. From these three studies the authors concluded, among other things, that the conditioning of fear follows the laws of Pavlovain conditioning, that in the case of aversive conditioning there are conditioned inhibitors and facilitators which operate in much the same way as S + and S − do in the appetitive case, and that the appetitive and aversive cases are really quite parallel. Rescorla (1967) has also suggested that the frequently used "pseudo-conditioning" type of procedure is an inappropriate control in avoidance studies because it results in an SS effect and indicates a base line that is too low. The first study to use the appropriate control was one by Rescorla (1966). After dogs had been trained in a free-operant avoidance task, a DS and an SS were established in different groups in a noncontingent situation. His control was a group in which the stimulus and the shock occurred purely randomly with respect to one another. The stimulus was then presented as a probe while Ss were performing on the avoidance schedule; it had no effect upon the group for which it had been randomly associated with shock, but it facilitated avoidance responding for the DS group and inhibited the response for the SS group.

Rescorla's random procedure provides a control for the possibility that Ss may acquire a safety-signal effect, but it raises the possibility that Ss may acquire a helplessness effect during the unpredictable series of events that occur in the noncontingent situation. It also fails to provide a control for pseudoconditioning effects and other phenomena the experimenter may be interested in. It is likely that there is no single, over-all control procedure that provides a true base line, good for all purposes. Grossen and Bolles (1968) have shown that as far as the rat is concerned, the choice of control procedure is relatively unimportant. We used a separate-groups design in which the DS Ss received a noncontingent cue to shock; the SS Ss received the same cue, but it followed shock, thereby predicting a period of safety. When subsequently tested on a previously learned avoidance task the DS group showed an increased rate of responding when the cue was introduced as probe, but the SS group showed a lowered rate. In the absence of the cue, all Ss performed at the same level—the level that all Ss had shown before the noncontingent sessions, and the same level shown by both random controls and sensitization controls throughout testing. In other words, the rat's rate of responding on the Sidman schedule in a shuttle box was extremely stable, was not affected by the administration of noncontingent shock in another situation, and showed no long-term effect of presenting various kinds of stimuli. On this stable base line it was easy to demonstrate highly reliable DS and SS effects.

Having established the reality of the SS effect in the Sidman shuttle-box situation, we are confronted with a rather serious dilemma because, so far, no one seems to have succeeded in demonstrating comparable effects in other kinds of avoidance situations. Certainly one should expect the speed and the probability of the avoidance response in a discrete-trial situation to be increased by a DS and decreased by an SS. Such effects have not been reported, however, and in our own laboratory the attempts to find these effects in the runway, the shuttle box, and lever-press apparatus have been notably unsuccessful. They simply are not there when we use a discrete-trial procedure. Is it possible that for some reason the DS and SS effects are restricted to the shuttle box? Is the demonstration of these effects dependent upon the use of a free-operant (Sidman) procedure? If so, why? Weisman and Litner (1969) have shed a little light on the subject; they found large, consistent, and durable SS effects using a manual wheel-turning response. Thus, the effect does not seem to be tied to locomotion in the shuttle box. These experimenters did not use a Sidman schedule, but they used a rather unusual schedule which did result in their *S*s' generating a number of responses on each trial, so that their *S*s were, in effect, on an operant schedule. The implication is that, for some reason which still eludes us, the DS and SS effects only appear if the base-line avoidance behavior is free operant and the rate of responding is used to measure its strength. It is not clear to us whether this is really the case, or why it might be the case. It should be clear, though, that if there is this kind of restriction upon the conditions under which SS and DS effects can be demonstrated, our current theoretical statements about these matters will require some extensive revision.

One problem which arose in connection with the appetitive case arises again when we consider the aversive case, namely, that while some noncontingent effects are very rapidly established and are extremely persistent once they are established, others are fragile and only slowly acquired. Can the same learning processes be responsible for conditioned suppression, which can be readily demonstrated after one or two noncontingent trials, and Rescorla's SS effect, which appears to require 100 or more pairings of the cue with the absence of shock?

Some Theoretical Conclusions

Putting aside some difficult questions for the moment, it is possible to see some very elegant parallels between the effects of the DS and SS in avoidance situations and the effects of S+ and S− in appetitive situations. In the past, behavior theory has been sadly negligent about constructing parallel accounts of aversive and appetitive motivation. Rescorla and Solomon (1967) can be commended for their provocative attempt to bring these two realms together and to put noncontingent procedure on an equal footing with the more familiar contingent procedures. Their paper emphasizes the formal similarities between the aversive and appetitive cases and stresses that contingent and noncontingent techniques can produce the same behavioral effects. In brief they propose that whether by response-contingent or by noncontingent procedures, a factor something like incentive is established and motivates instrumental behavior. These factors may be positive, like hunger (or the excitement that is correlated with hunger), or negative, like fear. In either case, Pavlov is supposed to have found the mechanism as well as the procedure for governing these states: they are classically conditioned. Fear, conditioned to the DS, motivates avoidance behavior and interferes with appetitive behavior. The safety signal is a Pavlovian inhibitor of fear, and it unmotivates avoidance and allows for the renewed vigor of appetitive behavior that has been suppressed (Hammond, 1966). The extremely attractive theoretical package Rescorla and Solomon have put together is based upon a neat realignment of familiar themes and is esthetically pleasing in many respects. But like many of our other theories, it is more of a program for research to be done than a summary of what has already been accomplished; it is admitted to be supported by minimal data at many points. We will close this chapter by merely mentioning some of the main points of weakness because they constitute the main theoretical and empirical problem now confronting us.

One problem with Rescorla and Solomon's account is that it tends to confuse the *processes* assumed to underlie classical conditioning with the *procedures* used in studying it. Classical conditioning differs in a number of respects from operant conditioning: a different response system is involved, there is no reinforcement operation, the critical temporal intervals are shorter, the response is weakened by inhibition instead of response competition, there is no reinforcement contingency, and so on. It seems gratuitous at this point to lump all these properties together with the assumption that motivation is acquired in animals in just the way that Pavlov proposed for all learning. We believe that some of these distinguishing or defining characteristics are more important than others for an understanding of motivation, and we propose that noncontingency is the key element in the noncontingent procedure studies of, for example, Trapold and Rescorla and LoLordo. Hence the title of the present chapter, which we could not comfortably call "The Classical Conditioning of Motivation," although until recently we did feel comfortable with a similar title (Grossen & Bolles, 1968). It remains to be seen whether the lack of the response-reinforcement contingency is the key to what happens in Pavlovian conditioning or whether it merely defines a separate class of experimental procedures.

A second difficult point is that the DS effect can be demonstrated very easily in some situations, for example, conditioned suppression, but the SS effect apparently requires many noncontingent pairings, the use of certain procedures and response measures, and a fair amount of luck besides. Can Pavlov help us understand this discrepancy? More importantly, can we subsume both effects under any common set of explanatory principles? We have noted above that there is an analogous discrepancy in the appetitive case where latent extinction is a robust effect, as are many of the response-contingent manipulations of incentive motivation, but the noncontingent increase in incentive is not. Can these different effects and the various disparities among them all be subsumed under a common set of explanatory principles? Much of the research we have reviewed here points menacingly to a trap which might be called the Quantitative Fallacy. If a theorist is looking for effect A to come out in the same direction as effect B, and it does, he is then tempted to assume that A and B reflect the same basic process (the one implicated by his theory). The fact that he always gets effect B in a trial or two whereas he can get effect A only after several hundred trials has to be ignored if he is going to treat them alike. We suspect that the various noncontingent motivational effects differ sufficiently in quantitative dimensions that they cannot reasonably be treated alike.

A third problem in Rescorla and Solomon's treatment is that, like Mowrer's (1960) somewhat similar one before it, it appears to involve a peculiar redundancy of explanatory motivational mechanisms. Intuitively, the S + is a "good" thing, and so is the SS. Again, both the S − and the DS are "bad." What a coup it would be to reduce the four incentive-inducing cues to two, a good one and a bad one. Some suggestion that this might be possible comes from the finding that the DS suppresses appetitive behavior. We ordinarily assume that conditioned suppression results either from motivational competition (the animal is too frightened to be hungry), or from response competition (the animal is too busy freezing to press the bar for food). But the case may be simpler than that; to put it into operational terms, a DS which predicts shock may simply reduce incentive motivation for food. We attempted to test this type of hypothesis by determining if an S + or an S − for food would affect rats which were performing a previously learned avoidance response (Grossen, Kostansek, & Bolles, 1969). We found that a cue for food, established in a different noncontingent situation, suppressed avoidance behavior when it was introduced as a probe. The S − signaling no food facilitated avoidance responding. We are still somewhat at a loss to explain these results; it seems hardly plausible to suppose that they are a result of either motivational competition (the animal is suddenly too hungry to be frightened) or response competition (the animal is too busy salivating, or something, to move in the shuttle box). The opposite effects with S − are no more reasonable in terms of a competition model, and we are left with little more than the data themselves: transfer of incentive motivation is possible across motivational systems.

One further combination of factors remains to be studied, namely, the effect of a safety signal upon appetitive behavior: it should produce a facilitation if the SS is equivalent to the S+. We are currently working on this problem, and the results appear to indicate that the facilitation effect, originally described by Hammond (1966), does occur but that it is severely limited in one respect. Hammond found that an SS returned the suppressed appetitive response nearly to the base line; it did not push the level of performance beyond the original base line. We have found the same thing. Grossen's Ph.D. dissertation study, now in progress, seems to indicate that in order for there to be any kind of facilitation there must be some generalized suppression of the base line, perhaps a result of conditioning fear to background cues or apparatus cues. In other words, the data suggest that the role of the SS is to inhibit fear (Rescorla and LoLordo's hypothesis), not to increase positive incentive motivation, and to depress avoidance behavior by that route. In short, we do not seem to be able to get by with just two motivating factors; it looks as if there are at least three.

We have one further comment on the Rescorla and Solomon paper. They presume at the outset that avoidance behavior is motivated. They do not doubt that the greater the animal's fear is, the stronger its avoidance behavior will be. There is very little support for such an assumption either from direct monitoring of the autonomic nervous system or by inference from animals' overt behavior. In some situations avoidance behavior deteriorates with increasing shock intensity (e.g., Bolles & Warren, 1965), and in other situations there is no effect of shock intensity. One could argue that high shock intensity introduces competing behavior which may effectively interfere with a more highly motivated avoidance response. Whereas this may well be true, however, such an interpretation does nothing to support the Rescorla and Solomon interpretation. In our lab we have been unable to show that shock intensity has any effect either upon the rate of acquisition of Sidman avoidance or upon the level of performance obtained once it is acquired. Nor have we been able to show that cues to differential shock intensity affect ongoing avoidance when they are introduced as probes. That is, when we introduce a "serious" DS it has no more effect upon the base-line avoidance performance than an "inconsequential" DS. Both facilitate the rate of responding on a Sidman schedule. How can it be, then, that an increase in rate of responding in the presence of a DS results from the elicitation of more fear?

There is a fascinating complementarity between motivation and reinforcement. Thus, we may explain some behavior by citing how it is motivated, but we may also be able to explain it by references to how it is reinforced. Without necessarily denying the validity or usefulness of a motivational interpretation of the DS and SS effects, we may note that an alternative, and complementary, reinforcement interpretation may be possible. Does the DS punish ongoing operant behavior, and does it, in particular, suppress behavior upon which its occurrence is made contingent? There seem to be no data about this question, but there is some evidence to support the other aspect of the reinforcement idea, namely, that an SS can reinforce instrumental behavior. Such results have been recently reported by Bolles and Grossen (1969), Rescorla (1968), and Weisman and Litner (1969). After the SS is established, its occurrence is made contingent upon some new response or upon some characteristic of the old response, such as a low rate, and its reinforcing effect upon that behavior is determined. The SS does seem to reinforce. There are, however, a number of questions (they should be familiar by now), such as whether the apparent reinforcement effects are limited to particular response classes or kinds of schedule, and whether they are as durable as the contingencies which ordinarily reinforce avoidance behavior—whatever they might be. Is fear a necessary background for such a reinforcement effect? We do not know. Is it possible to reinforce avoidance behavior only in this manner? Again we do not know, but like most of the other questions we have mentioned here, it should be relatively easy to obtain an empirical answer.

Motivation theory is accustomed to its comfortable old clothes, but the drive concept is embarrasingly worn and has to be replaced. Fear as an acquired drive is in disarray, and the incentive concept, which never did match very well, is not so stylish as it was. Now we can see a bright new fabric, a fabric sturdily woven of both contingent and noncontingent threads, a fabric from which we may be able to fashion matching appetitive and aversive garments. Our concern should now be whether our attractive new garments will fit.

REFERENCES

Amsel, A. The role of frustrative nonreward in noncontinuous situations. *Psychol. Bull.*, 1958, **55**, 102–199.

Amsel, A. Frustrative nonreward in partial reinforcement and discrimination learning: Some recent history and a theoretical extension. *Psychol. Rev.*, 1962, **69**, 306–328.

Armus, H. L., Carlson, K. R., Guinan, J. F., & Crowell, R. A. Effect of a secondary reinforcement stimulus on the auditory startle response. *Psychol. Rep.*, 1964, **14**, 535–540.

Bindra, D., & Palfai, T. Nature of positive and negative incentive-motivational effects on general activity. *J. comp. physiol. Psychol.*, 1967, **63**, 288–297.

Black, R. W. Shifts in magnitude of reward and contrast effects in instrumental learning: A reinterpretation. *Psychol. Rev.*, 1968, **75**, 114–126.

Bolles, R. C. *Theory of motivation.* New York: Harper & Row, 1967.

Bolles, R. C., & Grossen, N. E. Effects of an informational stimulus on the acquisition of avoidance behavior in the rat. *J. comp. physiol. Psychol.*, 1969, **68**, 90–99.

Bolles, R. C., & Warren, J. A. The acquisition of bar press avoidance as a function of shock intensity. *Psychon. Sci.*, 1965, **3**, 297–298.

Bower, G., & Grusec, T. Effect of prior Pavlovian discrimination training upon learning an operant discrimination. *J. exp. anal. Behav.*, 1964, **7**, 401–408.

Bower, G., & Kaufman, R. Transfer across drives of the discriminative effect of the Pavlovian conditioned stimulus. *J. exp. anal. Behav.*, 1963, **6**, 445–448.

Campbell, P. E., Fixen, D. L., & Phillips, E. The reinstatement effect: Amount of noncontingent reward in the runway. *Psychon. Sci.*, 1969, **14**, 228–229.

Clifford, T. Extinction following continuous reward and latent extinction. *J. exp. Psychol.*, 1964, **68**, 456–465.

Crespi, L. P. Quantitative variation of incentive and performance in the white rat. *Amer. J. Psychol.*, 1942, **55**, 467–517.

Daly, H. B. Is instrumental responding necessary for nonreward following reward to be frustrating? *J. exp. Psychol.*, 1969, **80**, 186–187.

DeBold, R. C., Miller, N. E., & Jensen, D. D. Effect of strength of drive determined by a new technique for appetitive classical conditioning of rats. *J. comp. physiol. Psychol.*, 1965, **59**, 102–108.

Denny, M. R., & Davis, R. H. A test of latent learning for a nongoal significant. *J. comp. physiol. Psychol.*, 1951, **44**, 590–595.

DiLollo, V. Runway performance in relation to runway-goal-box similarity and changes in incentive amount. *J. comp. physiol. Psychol.*, 1964, **58**, 327–329.

172   *Current Issues in Animal Learning*

Dyal, J. A. Latent extinction as a function of number and duration of pre-extinction exposures. *J. exp. Psychol.*, 1962, **63**, 98–104.

Estes, W. K. Discriminative conditioning. I. A discriminative functional property of conditioned anticipation. *J. exp. Psychol.*, 1943, **32**, 150–155.

Estes, W. K. Generalization of secondary reinforcement from the primary drive. *J. comp. physiol. Psychol.*, 1949, **42**, 286–295.

Estes, W. K., & Skinner, B. F. Some quantitative properties of anxiety. *J. exp. Psychol.*, 1941, **29**, 390–400.

Gilchrist, J. C. Characteristics of latent and reinforcement learning as a function of time. *J. comp. physiol. Psychol.*, 1952, **45**, 198–203.

Gonzalez, R. C., & Diamond, L. A. test of Spence's theory of incentive motivation. *Amer. J. Psychol.*, 1960, **73**, 396–403.

Gross, D. M., Trapold, M. A., & Hyde, T. S. A simple technique for delivering liquids directly to the mouth of an unrestrained rat. *J. exp. anal. Behav.*, 1968, 11, 191–195.

Grossen, N. E., & Bolles, R. C. Effects of a classically conditioned "fear signal" and "safety signal" on nondiscriminated avoidance behavior. *Psychon. Sci.*, 1968, **11**, 321–322.

Grossen, N. E., Kostansek, D. J. & Bolles, R. C. Effects of appetitive discriminative stimuli on avoidance behavior. *J. exp. Psychol.*, 1969, **81**, 340–343.

Hall, J. F. *The psychology of learning.* New York: Lippincott, 1966.

Hammond, J. L. Increased responding to CS– in differential CER. *Psychon. Sci.*, 1966, **5**, 337–338.

Hammond, J. L. A traditional demonstration of the active properties of Pavlovian inhibition using differential CER. *Psychon. Sci.*, 1967, **9**, 65–66.

Hargrave, G. E., Grossen, N. E., & Bolles, R. C. Effects of conditioned appetitive stimuli on the acquisition and extinction of a runway response. Paper presented at Western Psychological Association meeting, San Francisco, 1969.

Hendry, D. P. Conditioned inhibition of conditioned suppression. *Psychon. Sci.*, 1967, **9**, 261–262.

Hughes, D., Davis, J. D., & Grice, B. R. Goal box and alley similarity as a factor in latent extinction. *J. comp. physiol. Psychol.*, 1960, **53**, 612–614.

Hull, C. L. Simple trial-and-error learning. *Psychol. Rev.*, 1930, **37**, 241–256.

Hull, C. L. *A behavior system.* New Haven: Yale University Press, 1952.

Hyde, T., & Trapold, M. A. Enhanced stimulus generalization of a food reinforced response to a CS for water. *Psychon. Sci.*, 1967, **9**, 513–514.

Hyde, T. S., Trapold, M. A., & Gross, D. M. Facilitative effect of a CS for reinforcement magnitude: A test of incentive motivation theory. *J. exp. Psychol.*, 1969, **78**, 423–428.

Jones, E. C., Narver, R. L., & Bridges, C. C. A facilitating effect of latent extinction in a partial reinforcement situation. *Psychon. Sci.*, 1967, **7**, 23–24.

Kintsch, W., & Witte, R. S. Concurrent conditioning of bar press and salivation responses. *J. comp. physiol. Psychol.*, 1962, **55**, 963–968.

Koppman, J. W., & Grice, G. R. Goal-box and alley similarity in latent extinction. *J. exp. Psychol.*, 1963, **66**, 611–612.

Lewis, D. J., Butler, D., & Diamond, A. L. Direct manipulation of the fractional anticipatory goal response. *Psychol. Rep.*, 1958, **4**, 575–576.

Lewis, D. J., & Kent, N. D. Attempted direct activation and deactivation of the fractional anticipatory goal response. *Psychol. Rep.*, 1961, **8**, 107–110.

Lewis, D. J., & McIntire, R. A control for direct manipulation of the fractional anticipatory goal response. *Psychol. Rep.*, 1959, **5**, 753–756.

Marx, M. H., & Murphy, W. W. Resistance to extinction as a function of the presentation of a motivating cue in the start box. *J. comp. physiol. Psychol.*, 1961, **54**, 207–210.

Miller, N. E., & Debold, R. C. Classically conditioned tongue-licking and operant bar pressing recorded simultaneously in the rat. *J. comp. physiol. Psychol.*, 1965, **59**, 109–111.

Moltz, H. Latent extinction and the fractional anticipatory response system. *Psychol. Rev.*, 1957, **64**, 229–241.

Moltz, H., & Maddi, S. R. Reduction of secondary reward value as a function of drive strength during latent extinction. *J. exp. Psychol.*, 1956, **52**, 71–76.

Morse, W. H., & Skinner, B. F. Some factors in the stimulus control of operant behavior. *J. exp. anal. Behav.*, 1958, **1**, 103–107.

Mowrer, O. H. *Learning theory and behavior.* New York: Wiley, 1960.

Patten, R. L., & Deaux, E. B. Classical conditioning and extinction of the licking response in rats. *Psychon. Sci.*, 1966, **4**, 21–22.

Rescorla, R. A. Predictability and number of pairings in Pavlovian fear conditioning. *Psychon. Sci.*, 1966, **4**, 383–384.

Rescorla, R. A. Pavlovian conditioning and its proper control procedures. *Psychol. Rev.*, 1967, **74**, 71–80.

Rescorla, R. A. Pavlovian conditioned fear in Sidman avoidance learning. *J. comp. physiol. Psychol.*, 1968, **65**, 55–60.

Rescorla, R. A. & LoLordo, V. M. Inhibition of avoidance behavior. *J. comp. physiol. Psychol.*, 1965, **59**, 406–412.

Rescorla, R. A., & Solomon, R. L. Two-process learning theory: Relationships between Pavlovian conditioning and instrumental learning. *Psychol. Rev.*, 1967, **74**, 151–182.

Seward, J. P. An experimental analysis of latent learning. *J. exp. Psychol.*, 1949, **39**, 177–186.

Seward, J. P., Datel, W. E., & Levy, N. Tests of two hypotheses of latent learning. *J. exp. Psychol.*, 1952, **43**, 274–280.

Seward, J. P., & Levy, N. Sign learning as a factor in extinction. *J. exp. Psychol.*, 1949, **39**, 660–668.

Shapiro, M. M. Temporal relationship between salivation and lever pressing with differential reinforcement of low rates. *J. comp. physiol. Psychol.*, 1962, **55**, 567–571.

Shapiro, M. M., Miller, J. M., & Bresnahan, J. L. Dummy trials, novel stimuli, and Pavlovian-trained stimuli: Their effect upon instrumental and consumatory response relationships. *J. comp. physiol. Psychol.*, 1966, **61**, 480–483.

Solomon, R. L., & Turner, L. H. Discriminative classical conditioning in dogs paralyzed by curare can later control discriminative avoidance responses in the normal state. *Psychol. Rev.*, 1962, **69**, 202–219.

Spence, K. W. *Behavior theory and conditioning.* New Haven: Yale University Press, 1956.

Stein, L. The classical conditioning of the consumatory response as a determinant of instrumental performance. *J. comp. physiol. Psychol.*, 1957, **50**, 269–278.

Trapold, M. A. The effect of incentive motivation on an unrelated reflex response. *J. comp. physiol. Psychol.*, 1962, **55**, 1034–1039.

Trapold, M. A. Reversal of an operant discrimination by noncontingent discrimination reversal training. *Psychon. Sci.*, 1966, **4**, 247–248.

Trapold, M. A., Carlsen, J. G., & Myers, W. A. The effect of noncontingent fixed- and variable-interval reinforcement upon subsequent acquisition of the fixed-interval scallop. *Psychon. Sci.*, 1965, **2**, 261–262.

Trapold, M. A., & Doren, D. G. Effect of noncontingent partial reinforcement on resistance to extinction of a runway response. *J. exp. Psychol.*, 1966, **71**, 429–431.

Trapold, M. A., & Fairlie, J. Transfer of discrimination learning based upon contingent and noncontingent training procedures. *Psychol. Rep.*, 1965, **17**, 239–246.

Trapold, M. A., Gross, D. M., & Lawton, G. W. Reversal of an instrumental discrimination by classical discrimination conditioning. *J. exp. Psychol.*, 1969, **78**, 686–689.

Trapold, M. A., & Holden, D. Noncontingent partial reinforcement of running: A replication. *Psychon. Sci.*, 1966, **5**, 449–450.

Trapold, M. A., Lawton, G. W., Dick, R. A., & Gross, D. M. Transfer of training from differential classical to differential instrumental conditioning. *J. exp. Psychol.*, 1968, **76**, 568–573.

Trapold, M. A., & Odom, P. B. Transfer of an operant discrimination and a discrimination reversal between two manipulandum-defined responses. *Psychol. Rep.*, 1965, **16**, 1213–1221.

Trapold, M. A., & Winokur, S. Transfer from classical conditioning and extinction to acquisition, extinction, and stimulus generalization of a positively reinforced instrumental response. *J. exp. Psychol.*, 1967, **73**, 517–525.

Walker, K. C. Effects of a discriminative stimulus transferred to a previously unassociated response. *J. exp. Psychol.*, 1942, **31**, 312–321.

Weisman, R. G., & Litner, J. S. Positive conditioned reinforcement of Sidman avoidance behavior in rats. *J. comp. physiol. Psychol.*, 1969, **68**, 597–603.

Young, R. K., Mangum, W. P., Jr., & Capaldi, E. J. Temporal factors associated with nonresponse extinction. *J. comp. physiol. Psychol.*, 1960, **53**, 435–438.

Zamble, E. Classical conditioning of excitement anticipatory to food reward. *J. comp. physiol. Psychol.*, 1967, **63**, 526–529.

Elicitation Theory Applied to an Analysis of the Overlearning Reversal Effect

M. RAY DENNY

Michigan State University

The overlearning, or overtraining, reversal effect (ORE) has been a puzzling and somewhat paradoxical phenomenon ever since its discovery by Reid (1953). This discovery has led to more than 50 experimental reports and several theoretical analyses (Lovejoy, 1966, 1968; Mackintosh, 1965a, 1969; Paul, 1965; and Sperling, 1965a, 1965b). The reviews of the ORE literature have clarified some of the questions raised by the diverse results, but a substantial part of the puzzle remains unsolved. This paper is an attempt to explain from the orientation of elicitation theory all the results so far reported (Denny, 1966, 1967, 1970; Denny & Adelman, 1955; Maatsch, 1954).

DEFINITION OF ORE

ORE can be defined as the facilitation of reversal learning as the result of overtraining. The effect is typically studied in rats in a two-group experiment. Both groups are trained on a discrimination task to criterion, to 18 correct out of 20 consecutive responses, for example. The experimental group is then given from 100 to 300% overtraining on the original task and then reversed (overtraining is often designated in absolute number of trials rather than by percentage). The control group is reversed immediately after it has reached criterion on the original discrimination.

This procedure has yielded three kinds of experimental results: (a) the experimental group learns to reverse faster than the control

175

group, ORE or positive ORE, (b) there is no significant difference between the two groups, no ORE, and (c) the control group reverses faster than the experimental group, reverse or negative ORE. Thus any satisfactory explanation of ORE must also explain its variants.

ORE is studied either in a visual discrimination task (brightness or pattern discrimination) in which values of the positive and negative cues are reversed or in a spatial discrimination task (T-maze or Y-maze) in which direction of turn is reversed. When a large incentive has been used in the experiment or its use can be inferred, ORE occurs about equally often in both visual and spatial discriminations (see Table 1); but a reverse ORE only occurs in spatial discriminations.

Another important aspect of ORE is that it is a robust phenomenon. If it occurs the effect is clearly apparent and statistically significant with a relatively small N. This means that the data-digesters' task is to unravel the procedural differences among experiments in order to identify the variables that account for the diversity of results.

THE ELICITATION POSITION

Elicitation theory originated at Michigan State University in the early 1950s. At that time it was an attempt to integrate the neobehavioristic theories of Hull, Guthrie, Skinner, and Tolman, plus the older ideas of Pavlov. The position represents a synthesis of the main points that each of these theorists was promulgating, with a few new twists added. As such, it is a monistic position in which all learning is viewed in a contiguity framework in which classical conditioning principles are exploited.

The theory states that learning depends upon consistently eliciting the to-be-learned response in close temporal contiguity with a particular stimulus situation. This in turn means minimizing the elicitation of alternative responses to the same or a similar stimulus situation. In this way, the response that is being learned wins out over other possible responses. Guthrie made the same kind of point, but he did not exploit incentives or reinforcers as the important elicitors in the learning situation—stimuli which elicit a characteristic response over and over again and thereby minimize the occurrence of competing responses.

Learning presumably occurs when a response is consistently elicited in any manner, that is, by a CS or S^D as well as by a US, but for infrahuman organisms there are probably a US and its UR somewhere in the learned sequence. In operant, or instrumental, learning situations, several responses are being learned together or in sequence. As a result, the critical UR that elicitation theory holds is present may not be discerned. Perhaps for this reason, at least in part, many theorists distinguish instrumental learning from classical conditioning on more than operational grounds.

Elicitation theory, on the other hand, states that the UR of approaching the goal object (food, water, or whatever) is always present in an instrumental learning situation and that this UR mediates the learning of the entire instrumental chain. For example, when a rat is learning to press the bar in a Skinner box, the first thing the rat learns is to make a clear-cut approach response to the food tray or water dipper. With the strengthening of this approach response, *S* learns to be a goal sticker, making strong approaches to the food tray (dipper) without first pressing the bar. But such behavior means that *S* is not being reinforced. At this point another characteristic response presumably gets elicited. According to the theory, the absence of the incentive in the tray (dipper) is itself a US which elicits antagonistic responses—responses that take the animal directly away from the tray (such frustration-instigation, because of its dependence on prior learning, is called *secondary* elicitation in the theory). The antagonistic responses can involve aggressive or tangential responses that include "banging away" at the bar, so that the rat typically finds food in the tray at the next visit. A type of discrimination learning then proceeds in which the rat learns to press the bar *before* visiting the food tray. That is, the rat learns to inhibit direct approaches to the food tray and to approach it by way of the detour route of first going to the bar, pressing it, and then going to the tray.

Theoretically this chain is constructed in the following order. The cues attendant upon bar pressing, which usually include the "click" of the reward mechanism, are conditioned to the response of approaching the incentive (before *S* can eat or drink it must first approach the goal object). With further conditioning (back-chaining) the stimuli produced by the response of approaching the bar become conditioned to pressing the bar; and finally the response-produced cues of ingesting the food (water) become the main CS (S^D) for approaching the bar. The chain is complete.

This theoretical approach to learning grew out of data first obtained in extinction experiments (Maatsch, 1951). In 1950, I was a confirmed Hullian, though greatly dissatisfied with prevailing theories of inhibition or extinction, and the data of Maatsch's M.A. thesis were hardly sufficient to cause scrapping one paradigm and replacing it with another. Even so, Maatsch suggested that we accept the implications of the data rather than attempting to rationalize them into the established system (he was already disenchanted with journal articles in which inconsistent data, as he saw it, were rationalized into prevailing theories). I soon went along with this, and we interpreted his thesis results accordingly.

Maatsch's study involved a number of runway experiments with rats, in which, for the same S, some trials were spaced, some massed, some reinforced, and some nonreinforced. His unpublished results suggested the following conclusions:

1. When a set of two trials is massed, rats run just as fast on the second trial as when the set of two trials is spaced. There is no detectable increment in inhibition that comes strictly from an immediately prior response.
2. After a nonreinforced trial the immediately following running response is just as fast as any spaced trial or as fast as a trial which is immediately preceded by a reinforced trial.
3. Inhibition (increased running time) only builds up gradually on that trial that is consistently nonreinforced each day and then only when there is a cue present at the beginning of that trial.

Massing a trial with respect to the previous trial was found to be a sufficient cue to mediate the learning of inhibition (an increase in running time from about 1 second to about 30 seconds). What was critical here was independent of whether the *previous* trial was reinforced or nonreinforced. Inhibition only developed in Maatsch's study if the trial that immediately followed another trial was consistently nonreinforced. Such a finding simply reflected the presence of a discrimination-learning paradigm, which we promptly recognized. But the important point was that the results, literally interpreted, contradicted prevailing two-factor theories of inhibition. Interfering responses (increased running times) were readily learned without there being the slightest evidence in measurable behavior of the existence of a negative drive state (I_R or frustration drive) which, when subsequently reduced, was supposed to mediate the learning of the interfering response (e.g., S^IR). The intrinsic, or negative-drive, component of two-factor inhibition theory appeared to be excess baggage.

What we observed in the animal's behavior immediately upon its being nonreinforced was the same as I had observed earlier (Denny, 1946), namely, vigorous escape and withdrawal responses that were antagonistic to the original approach response. This characteristic class of competing responses (R_c) had the character of a good UR and was so designated. Thus R_c was assumed to be classically conditioned to the concurrent stimuli, solely on the basis of contiguity considerations. Extinction resulted because R_c was pitted directly against the original response tendency (R_0) and effectively competed with it.

The logic behind the analysis of Maatsch's data is very similar to the logic one can apply to discrimination-learning experiments in which trials are highly spaced. Inhibition ordinarily develops to the negative cue, even though the degree of spacing used would seem to preclude the presence of intrinsic inhibition. At the time, however, only our own data had much of an impact on our own theorizing. The next step was to assume that if this is how extinction-producing responses are learned then perhaps all learning proceeds in the same way. Such were the beginnings of elicitation theory.

COMMENTS ON THE DATA OF ORE EXPERIMENTS

When a small incentive, one or two 45-mg. Noyes pellets, is used to study ORE, the results are uniformly negative. There is either no significant difference between the overlearning group and the control on reversal, or the control reverses significantly faster than the overtrained group (Clayton, 1963b). In studies in which the size of the incentive has not been specified, ORE may occur (e.g., Brookshire, Warren, & Ball, 1961). The inference is that the incentive size in such studies was *not* small. In the present analysis, studies which have used a small incentive have typically been ignored. The exceptions are two experiments by Clayton (1963b) and some of the current research by Tortora and myself. The present focus is on understanding the diversity of results that occurs when the incentive is known to be large or on any result in which an ORE occurs. That is, I have assumed that any interpretation that can handle data involving a large incentive should also cover situations in which the incentive size is unknown but is assumed to be large because an ORE was obtained. Frustration is a central concept in the present analysis, and since the degree of frustration effect tends to vary directly with magnitude of original incentive (Amsel, 1962, 1967; Bower, 1962), the failure to find an ORE with a small incentive appears to be the expected result and not one that requires special theoretical concern.

Mackintosh's Theory of ORE

If, however, frustration is missing from one's interpretation of ORE, then it is incumbent on the theorist to incorporate the size of incentive variable into his analysis, as has Mackintosh (1969) in the context of a mathematical model. For Mackintosh, the occurrence of ORE depends on the joint satisfaction of two conditions, a difficult discrimination and a large incentive. As a leading proponent of the application of a two-stage attentional model to the explanation of ORE (Lovejoy, 1966), Mackintosh assumes that ORE occurs only when the probability of attending to the relevant dimension (+ versus − cues) is not very high at the outset of training. Another way of saying this is that the ORE will only occur when rats are trained in a relatively difficult discrimination. In such a situation, overtraining increases the probability of attending to the relevant dimension and decreases the probability of attending to the irrelevant dimension(s). Thus, overlearning facilitates reversal learning. When the discrimination is easy the relevant dimension is strong from the outset and no benefit is supposed to accrue from overtraining.

Mackintosh introduces size of incentive into this theory by means of values assigned the "reward" operators in the Bush and Mosteller stochastic model of learning. When Mackintosh ran "stat-rats" in a "Monte Carlo" procedure, the fit between obtained experimental data and the model was fairly acceptable but contained a number of discrepancies. In this analysis the psychological meaning of incentive size seems to be left hanging.

The studies listed in Table 1 are perhaps more representative than exhaustive and include only those using simple, two-choice procedures for which reports were readily available. Table 1 indicates the results in the literature that conform to Mackintosh's position and those that do not. The present analysis is most concerned with those that do not. The results in (A) under Visual Discrimination (Reid, Pubols, Hooper, and Mandler) are definitely at odds with Mackintosh's views because ORE occurs in an easy black-white discrimination. The results in the top half of (A) under Spatial Discrimination disagree with Mackintosh because ORE occurs when all cues are relevant and the discrimination is easy. The results in (C) under Spatial Discrimination tend not to agree with Mackintosh's position because a definite trend toward a reverse ORE occurs in a difficult discrimination with a large incentive and obvious irrelevant cues. (That the discrimination in Tortora's experiment was difficult is supported by the fact that these *S*s required more than double the trials to learn, when compared to groups in which the orientation of the stem was held constant and all other factors were the same.)

The data in (C) under Spatial Discrimination were unavailable to Mackintosh; and the studies by Clayton (B), though by most measures they yielded a reverse ORE in a difficult discrimination with obvious irrelevant cues, employed only a small incentive. In other words, the studies and results under Spatial Discrimination that are listed in (A) are considered by Mackintosh to be the more damaging to his views; accordingly, he has discussed some of them in his recent monograph (Mackintosh, 1969). There he accepts the difficulty posed by Capaldi's data (1963) but minimizes the results of Theios and Blosser (1965) because of an alleged lack of control of motivation level during reversal training in the overtrained group (lower level than controls).

Mackintosh's argument against Theios and Blosser is not in agreement with our current research findings. Tortora (1970) controlled the amount eaten per day by *S*s in the experimental and control groups in five different spatial discrimination experiments.

The only time a positive ORE was obtained was when conventional T-maze training (all cues relevant) and a large incentive were used, that is, under the same conditions as in the Theios and Blosser study except that Tortora used a noncorrection procedure. In this positive case, both original learning and reversal learning for all Ss were extremely rapid, and the superiority of the overlearning group ($N = 6$) in terms of mean trial of last reversal error before the criterion run was statistically significant ($M = 4.1$ versus 11.1, $p < .02$). It would seem that studies using a conventional T- or Y-maze procedure, a low or nonstringent acquisition criterion, and a large incentive yield quite valid ORE results; there are no data in the literature that specifically contradict them. (The importance of the acquisition criterion used will be discussed later.)

The upshot of this discussion is that Mackintosh's analysis falls short of a comprehensive explanation of the ORE data. The present attempt to effect an explanation began with a perusal of procedures in the literature, and finally the picture as presented in Table 1 began to emerge, with the elicitation position guiding the detective work.

Elicitation Theory Applied to Visual Discrimination Experiments

The elicitation framework stresses that the extinction of the original response is essential and automatic in reversal learning. Extinction *is* the result of pitting one response tendency against another, and without competition from an alternative response the original response will never be replaced. Thus extinction of the original response is going on throughout reversal learning. According to the theory (Denny & Adelman, 1955), the extinction of R_0 in reversal learning is a specific result of the elicitation of withdrawal responses by the omission of food from the food tray. Once a behavioral sequence has been established for a particular incentive, the removal of that incentive serves as an unconditioned stimulus, consistently eliciting a characteristic class of responses that are typically antagonistic to the original response (e.g., approach to food). Such consistently elicited antagonistic responses are conditioned to contiguous stimuli and through backchaining become conditioned to earlier stimuli in the chain. Eventually these antagonistic responses compete effectively with the incipient stages of the

TABLE 1

ANALYSIS OF OVERLEARNING REVERSAL EFFECT (ORE) IN RATS

Type of Learning Situation (Large Incentive except Where Noted)	Finding	Investigators
Visual Discrimination		
A. Black vs. white—only cues are a black or white door in an alley a foot or so in front of the goal region, in Y-maze or Grice box. End boxes following + and − cues are identical.	Positive ORE (against Mackintosh)	Reid, 1953 Pubols, 1956 Hooper, 1967—more ORE with correction procedure Mandler, 1968
B. Black vs. white or lighted vs. unlighted alleys. The cues fill the whole alley and are continuous with the goal region, or a Lashley jumping stand is used.	No ORE (for Mackintosh) Slightly positive ORE when both food dishes were unpainted, or when the aversive, brightly lit alley was positive, or when trained against preference.	Mackintosh, 1969 Lukaszewska, 1968 Erlebacher, 1963 D'Amato & Schiff, 1965. — Mackintosh, 1969 Brookshire, Warren, & Ball, 1961 Birnbaum, 1967
C. As in (B) above except the discrimination is more difficult: light gray vs. dark gray or black and white stripes vs. checkerboard.	Positive ORE (for Mackintosh)	Mackintosh, 1969 Sperling, 1968
Spatial Discrimination		
A. Typical T-maze learning—many cues relevant and redundant, including intramaze and extramaze visual cues.	Positive ORE (against Mackintosh) All used low acquisition criterion —	Capaldi, 1963 Ison & Birch, 1961 Tortora & Denny, current research Theios & Blosser, 1965—good ORE with correction procedure Kendler & Kimm, 1967 (ORE not significant but size of food was visually large rather than large in amount eaten)
B. Intramaze cues, extramaze cues, or both are made irrelevant, with direction of turn being the main, but not only, relevant cue.	No ORE (for Mackintosh) Used high acquisition criterion Positive ORE (for Mackintosh) — Reverse or negative ORE (indeterminate)	Clayton, 1963a Pubols, 1956 Brookshire, Warren, & Ball, 1961
C. Pure spatial—T-maze with the stem randomly alternated 180° so that only spatial cues are relevant; all other cues are irrelevant.	Reverse ORE with small incentive. Nonsignificant reverse ORE with large incentive (against Mackintosh).	Clayton, 1963b (2)—only 2 45 mg. pellets used. Tortora & Denny (both large and small incentive; Ss randomly assigned for direction of turn)—most like Clayton in (B) above, current research.

original instrumental response (R_0). In reversal learning this means that R_c must chain to the choice point area before it affects the choice response. But before R_c can do this it must be conditioned to the relevant stimuli that are most closely associated in time with the empty food tray—those stimuli that were consistently and closely associated with food during original learning (this aspect of the theory provided an important orientation for examining the procedural variations of the published overlearning reversal studies, and there is nothing here that implies that an enhanced extinction effect from overlearning should manifest itself immediately after reversal training has begun, as implied by Mackintosh [1965a, 1969]).

At this point the reader's looking and reading behavior is directed toward the puzzling visual discrimination studies in the upper half of Table 1, with special reference to the studies in (B) in which the relevant cues fill the whole alley and the goal area. Here, theoretically, the R_c that is elicited in reversal learning is directly conditioned to the cue that was originally positive (new negative). R_c then generalizes to the same cue at the choice point, and reversal learning should be relatively fast. Speed of reversal learning, irrespective of original acquisition level, is not critical to the present analysis of ORE, however. What is important in regard to explaining the results of overlearning reversal experiments is how much R_c will generalize to the *new* positive cue. If generalization is minimal, that is, if a strong R_c is discrete to the new negative cue without the benefit of overtraining, then overtraining will not produce an ORE. Such an analysis explains the failure to find an ORE in a black-white discrimination in which the cues of the choice point are continuous with the goal area. Black and white are naturally distinctive and traditionally used to effect stimulus differentiations. Thus R_c to the new negative cue during black-white reversal learning is no more discrete after overtraining than at the end of acquisition.

Such a state of affairs is not the case in a more difficult discrimination, for instance with dark gray versus light gray ([C] under Visual Discrimination). At criterion in such a discrimination task, the degree of discrimination that permits 18 correct out of 20 responses very probably has not been perfected. Overlearning

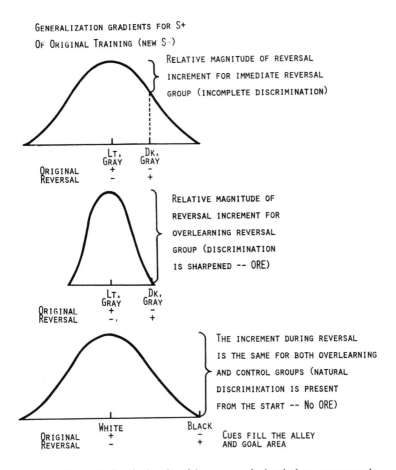

GENERALIZATION GRADIENTS FOR S+
OF ORIGINAL TRAINING (NEW S-)

RELATIVE MAGNITUDE OF REVERSAL
INCREMENT FOR IMMEDIATE REVERSAL
GROUP (INCOMPLETE DISCRIMINATION)

	LT. GRAY	DK. GRAY
ORIGINAL	+	-
REVERSAL	-	+

RELATIVE MAGNITUDE OF
REVERSAL INCREMENT FOR
OVERLEARNING REVERSAL
GROUP (DISCRIMINATION
IS SHARPENED -- ORE)

	LT. GRAY	DK. GRAY
ORIGINAL	+	-
REVERSAL	- ,	+

THE INCREMENT DURING REVERSAL
IS THE SAME FOR BOTH OVERLEARNING
AND CONTROL GROUPS (NATURAL
DISCRIMINATION IS PRESENT
FROM THE START -- NO ORE)

	WHITE	BLACK	
ORIGINAL	+	-	CUES FILL THE ALLEY
REVERSAL	-	+	AND GOAL AREA

FIG. 1. Theoretically, the bracketed increments depicted above represent the difference between the amount of R_c in reversal training that is conditioned to the new S− and the new S+. The bigger the increment, the more specific R_c is to the new S−.

trials should yield a finer discrimination or narrowing of the positive stimulus generalization gradient. This means that R_c in the over-learning group does not generalize to the new positive cue as much as in the control group, and thus reversal learning is facilitated. The ORE occurs (see Fig. 1).

It so happens that Sperling (1968) has collected excellent data in support of the argument that the discrimination continues to improve after the acquisition criterion of a difficult discrimination (black and white stripes versus black and white checkerboard) has been reached. She has latency data at the choice point for both the responses to the negative cue and the positive cue. Postcriterion in the overlearning groups, the latency of the occasional response to the negative cue steadily continues to increase, while the latency of the response to the positive cue continues to decrease. In other words, just as Mackintosh claims, but for different reasons, it makes sense that the ORE occurs in a difficult visual discrimination and not in an easy one. Lukaszewska (1968) failed to find an ORE when a more difficult discrimination was used, but in her experiment difficulty was increased by adding an irrelevant dimension to the relevant cues on the Lashley jumping-stand card, not by decreasing the discriminability of $S+$ and $S-$. Thus this failure to find an ORE bothered Mackintosh (1969) but seems consistent with the present interpretation.

The analysis is by no means complete, however; ORE also occurs in a black-white discrimination in which the cues are attached only to one-way valve doors that are located a foot or so from identical, say, gray end boxes (A). Here in reversal learning, R_c is elicited in direct contiguity with many irrelevant intra- and extramaze cues. The only relevant or consistent cue present is the perseverative trace of the previously positive cue that the rat passed as it went through the one-way door. Now, as seems quite well established, the traces of stimuli are not particularly discriminable or undergo more cross generalization than prevailing stimuli. This is probably best represented for the rat in that the traces of black and white stimuli after a 5-second interval are not sufficiently discriminable to mediate appreciable simultaneous or successive discrimination learning (Grice, 1948; Smith, 1951). In other words, when the visual trace of a black or white cue is all that is present when a frustration-instigated R_c occurs, the situation is very much like more difficult discriminations in which $S+$ and $S-$ are quite similar. Thus overtraining presumably produces a finer discrimination between the trace of black and the trace of white and thereby permits the conditioning of R_c specifically to the new negative cue. This results in an ORE. In Fig. 1, substitute perseverative traces of black and white for dark gray and light gray to get a schematic representation of the effect. The present analysis would also predict an ORE when perseverative traces of stimuli that are less distinctive than black and white are present in the goal regions. Results of an unpublished study by Spanier (1968) in which the doorway stimuli were horizontal and vertical stripes directly support this hypothesis.

It should be pointed out that Amsel's theory of extinction (Amsel, 1962), which in this regard has considerable similarity to the elicitation position, is capable of making the same sort of analysis. In Amsel's framework, however, the emphasis on the motivational and cue effects of frustration and the restriction that any classical conditioning of R_c that goes on, as Hull and Spence contended, is limited to fractional components of R_f (symbolized r_f) might not be quite as conducive to the present kind of analysis of ORE as the elicitation framework.

The pattern so far outlined explains (a) ORE when $S+$ and $S-$ in the "goal" region are preseverative traces of preceding cues, (b) ORE when cues at the choice point and respective goal areas are the same, and $S+$ and $S-$ are fairly similar to each other (dark gray and light gray), and (c) the absence of ORE when distinctive relevant cues such as black and white are present in the goal area, as is the case in many Y-maze and Grice box studies and in the Lashley jumping stand when S knocks down the door (new negative cue) so that it is face up on top of the empty food platform. There are data, as can be seen in the upper half of Table 1 (B), that do not completely fit this pattern; but such data, when carefully examined, seem to support the most general form of the present analysis rather than detract from it.

Mackintosh (1969) found marginal ORE with solid black and white alleys, but, as already discussed, this does not agree with his most recent analysis. He only found this marginal ORE in an experiment in which both food cups were similar and unpainted, that is, when a very short visual trace of the new negative cue (black or white) may have been operative for the rat on reversal trials when it peered into and withdrew from the empty food cup.

In the study by Birnbaum (1967) the discriminative stimuli consisted of a lighted alley and a darkened alley. In the subgroup in which the nonpreferred or aversive lighted alley was the positive cue, learning was slow and only in this subgroup was there evidence of an ORE. That is, reversal learning benefited from overtraining because, in this instance, frustration or nonreinforcement is maximally effective in yielding an inhibitory effect only when the response being inhibited is relatively strong. As shown by Denny and Dunham (1951), nonreinforcement of an incorrect, *nonpreferred* response has little if any effect on the learning of the correct response, whereas nonreinforcement of an incorrect, *preferred* response clearly facilitates the learning of the correct (nonpreferred) response. Presumably, overtraining in the Birnbaum study for the subgroup that was trained against preference results in the strengthening of the approach value of the original positive cue to the point where frustration can elicit a vigorous R_c and thus facilitate reversal learning. (One implication here is that the criterion in original learning for this subgroup may have been reached primarily through nonreinforcement of the preferred incorrect response.)

In the Birnbaum study and the Brookshire, Warren, and Ball study (1961), the steepness of the stimulus-generalization gradients or their relative separation is not being invoked as an explanatory principle; but the same general notion for interpreting ORE is being exploited, namely, that whenever overtraining enhances the consistent elicitation of R_c specifically to the new negative cue an ORE occurs.

There is some additional support for the present analysis in the finding that the correction technique produces a greater ORE than the noncorrection procedure (Hooper, 1967). In the correction procedure, R_c, when elicited, is *directly* incompatible with the R_0 of original learning; on incorrect reversal trials S withdraws from the new negative cue and approaches the new positive cue.

ORE In Spatial Discrimination

Several reviewers and investigators of ORE have concluded, perhaps uncautiously, that ORE is limited to visual discrimination tasks. But, in fact, when a large incentive is employed in spatial discrimination tasks the box score for ORE is possibly better than it is in the visual discrimination situation (Table 1). The procedural variations that have been used in T- and Y-mazes, if anything, exceed those found in visual discrimination tasks, and the results obtained (ORE, no ORE, or reverse ORE) seem to depend quite directly on the type of procedure employed.

In research barely completed, Tortora and Denny have succeeded in obtaining all three effects ($+$, $-$, and no ORE) in the very same T-maze (in certain experiments the length of the stem was varied, but that was all). Negative ORE was best obtained with a small incentive, though a nonsignificant but definite trend toward a negative or reverse ORE was found with a large incentive. No ORE occurred with both small and large incentives, while a positive ORE was obtained only with a large incentive. The procedure that produced a negative ORE with a small incentive and a tendency in that direction with a large incentive was very similar to the one used by Clayton (1963b). The particular procedure that we used made all cues irrelevant except direction of turn, right versus left. On a quasi-random schedule the direction of the stem was continually changed in orientation by 180° so that intra- and extramaze cues were irrelevant, leaving mainly kinesthetic cues as the critical cues to mediate learning (Clayton varied the cues in the choice point area and switched the arms around but did not scramble extramaze cues either by using a double-stemmed crossmaze or by switching the orientation of the stem). From the point of view of Mackintosh, the presence of many salient irrelevant cues and a concomitant difficult discrimination should be conducive to the occurrence of an ORE. As just indicated, the opposite tends to occur, however.

Since this procedure puts all the stimulus control on cues at the choice point or even before (kinesthesis attendant upon centrifugal swing in the stem of the T-maze), it follows that R_c is not going to be readily conditioned to the new negative cue during reversal training. Only a perseverative trace of kinesthesis is present when R_c is elicited. The effect of overtraining seems to be twofold: (a) through backchaining, the critical kinesthetic cue is pushed back down the stem, further away in time and space from the locus of the frustration A elicitation of R_c during reversal training, producing a reverse ORE, and (b) the perseverative traces of left turn and right turn, as in the parallel black-white discrimination, do become more discriminable with additional practice, partially compensating for the backchaining effect and yielding a smaller, nonsignificant reverse ORE when the role of frustration is enhanced by the use of a large incentive. (In our experiments the reverse ORE with a large incentive would presumably be significant if the N in each group were about 20 instead of 6.)

Such an analysis of reverse ORE is consistent with a description of T-maze learning in elicitation terms (Denny, 1967, 1970) and with results obtained by Mackintosh (1965b) which show that when all cues are relevant, kinesthesis (direction of turn) acquires an increasing proportion of stimulus control as the number of trials is increased. The apparent exceptions to this analysis (Pubols, 1956, and Brookshire, Warren & Ball, 1961, in [B] of Spatial Discrimination, Table 1), studies in which an ORE occurred, seem to be amenable to reclassification in Table 1. The only irrelevant cues in the Pubols study were the black and white doors (same as used in his visual discrimination study) set part-way down each gray arm of a Y-maze. All other cues were relevant, including the consistent extramaze cues that S would be able to perceive from both the goal area and the choice point. This makes Pubols's experiment most similar to the spatial discrimination studies classified under (A), in which all cues are relevant and in which an ORE typically occurs.

The Brookshire, Warren, and Ball experiment is more complicated and handled somewhat more speculatively, but when reclassified it goes either in (A) or in (C) of Visual Discrimination. Like Pubols, these investigators used the same apparatus for studying ORE in a spatial discrimination as for studying it in a visual discrimination. The apparatus was a cross maze in which trials in a random alternation began equally often in each stem or start box (both gray). One arm was consistently white and the other consistently black. This arrangement meant that the rat could actually learn a conditional discrimination during 120 overlearning trials, namely, to approach, for example, black when leaving start box 1 and to approach white when leaving start box 2. (It is assumed that the two start boxes were discriminably different to the rat in a variety of unspecified ways, even though both were painted gray.) That is, an overtrained S on reversal trials could enter the new negative side contiguous with a compound stimulus that included the perseverative trace of the start box it had just left plus either black or white. The learning of such a discrimination means that the compound cue will probably supplant any learning based earlier on kinesthesis and that a relevant cue in the behavioral chain (black or white) will be contiguous with frustration during reversal trials. Obviously, overtraining will help perfect this discrimination and thereby facilitate reversal learning.

Indirect support for this interpretation includes the following: (a) the initially irrelevant black and white cues were quite salient or ready to be used, for the original learning was slow, requiring over 110 trials on the average; (b) the total of 230 trials or more that preceded reversal training for most overtrained Ss was not out of line with the finding that a rat can learn a form-brightness conditional discrimination in approximately 300 trials (Eimas & Doan, 1966); and (c) chickens were also run by Brookshire, Warren, and Ball, and the overtrained group showed no ORE (since conditional discriminations require many more trials at lower phyletic levels [Denny & Ratner, 1970], it follows that 120 extra trials may have produced an ORE in rats but not in chickens).

Finally, for Table 1, we need to explain the positive ORE results in (A) of Spatial Discrimination, plus the one exception to them. The most critical aspect of this interpretation is that the acquisition criterion for all studies in which an ORE occurs was low enough so that the total number of trials in original learning typically did not exceed 32 and was frequently much less. Since, with a noncorrection procedure, even fewer trials were reinforced, it follows that an ORE can be traditionally explained here as being a result of the general enhancement of the frustration effect by strengthening the expectation of the reward or incentive (Amsel, 1962; Birch, 1961). In the theory, this means a more consistent elicitation of a more vigorous R_c. Several studies indicate that the frustration effect increases with number of original reinforcements (Adelman, 1954; Marzocco, 1951; Yelen, 1969) and requires at least 35 to 40 reinforcements to reach asymptote (Amsel, 1967).

When all cues are relevant, as in the studies of (A), learning is fast and can be terminated before the expectation has been maximized. Many of these cues are also contiguous with the frustration event that occurs on incorrect reversal trials, so that R_c is directly conditioned to them and can readily yield an ORE following overtraining. The study by Clayton (1963a) with a large incentive which failed to find an ORE required S to reach an acquisition criterion of 18 or more correct responses on two consecutive days. The mean trials to criterion, in this case, was 41 and the mean errors 9.7. Therefore each S had an average of 31 reinforcements before reversal training, reducing to a minimum any benefit that might be gained from overtraining.

A clear implication here is that, because visual discrimination experiments typically require 60 or more trials for criterion to be reached, an ORE in visual discrimination tasks cannot be explained by the presumption that overtraining increases the frustration effect through building up the expectation of the incentive. The present analysis handles this point as well as the diversity of results in the overlearning reversal area. At critical points the analysis is also quite amenable to direct experimental test, and some of this research is underway.

REFERENCES

Adelman, H. M. Resistance to extinction as a function of type of response elicited by frustration stimulation and level of reinforcement. Unpublished portion of doctoral dissertation, Michigan State University, 1954.

Amsel, A. Frustrative nonreward in partial reinforcement and discrimination learning: Some recent history and a theoretical extension. *Psychol. Rev.*, 1962, **69**, 306–328.

Amsel, A. Partial reinforcement effects on vigor and persistence: Advances in frustration theory derived from a variety of within-subjects experiments. In K. W. Spence & Janet T. Spence (Eds.), *The psychology of learning and motivation.* Vol. I. New York: Academic Press, 1967.

Birch, D. A motivational interpretation of extinction. In M. R. Jones (Ed.), *Nebraska symposium on motivation, 1961.* Lincoln: University of Nebraska Press, 1961. Pp. 179–202.

Birnbaum, I. M. Discrimination reversal, extinction, and acquisition after different amounts of overtraining. *Amer. J. Psychol.*, 1967, **80**, 363–369.

Bower, G. H. The influence of graded reductions in reward and prior frustrating events upon the magnitude of the frustration effect. *J. comp. physiol. Psychol.*, 1962, **55**, 582–587.

Brookshire, K. H., Warren, J. M., & Ball, G. G. Reversal and transfer learning following overtraining in rat and chicken. *J. comp. physiol. Psychol.*, 1961, **54**, 98–102.

Capaldi, E. J. Overlearning reversal effect in a spatial discrimination by rats. *Percept. mot. Skills*, 1963, **16**, 335–336.

Clayton, K. N. Overlearning and reversal of a spatial discrimination by rats. *Percept. mot. Skills*, 1963a, **17**, 83–85.

Clayton, K. N. Reversal performance by rats following overlearning with and without irrelevant stimuli. *J. exp. Psychol.*, 1963b, **66**, 255–259.

D'Amato, M. R., & Schiff, D. Overlearning and brightness discrimination reversal. *J. exp. Psychol.*, 1965, **69**, 375–381.

Denny, M. R. The role of secondary reinforcement in a partial reinforcement learning situation. *J. exp. Psychol.*, 1946, **36**, 373–389.

Denny, M. R. A theoretical analysis and its application to training the mentally retarded. In N. R. Ellis (Ed.), *International review of research in mental retardation.* Vol. 2. New York: Academic Press, 1966.

Denny, M. R. A learning model. In W. C. Corning & S. C. Ratner (Eds.), *The chemistry of learning.* New York: Plenum Press, 1967.

Denny, M. R. Relaxation theory and experiments. In F. R. Brush (Ed.), *Aversive conditioning and learning.* New York: Academic Press, 1970.

Denny, M. R., & Adelman, H. M. Elicitation theory. I. An analysis of two typical learning situations. *Psychol. Rev.*, 1955, **62**, 291–296.

Denny, M. R., & Dunham, M. D. The effect of differential nonreinforcement of the incorrect response on the learning of the correct response in the simple T-maze. *J. exp. Psychol.*, 1951, **41**, 382–389.

Denny, M. R., & Ratner, S. C. *Comparative psychology.* Homewood, Illinois: Dorsey Press, 1970.

Eimas, P. D., & Doan, Helen. Conditional discrimination learning in rats. *Psychon. Sci.*, 1966, **4**, 109–110.

Erlebacher, A. Reversal learning in rats as a function of learning. *J. exp. Psychol.*, 1963, **66**, 84–90.

Grice, G. R. The relation of secondary reinforcement to delayed reward in visual discrimination learning. *J. exp. Psychol.*, 1948, **38**, 1–16.

Hooper, R. Variables controlling the overlearning reversal effect (ORE). *J. exp. Psychol.*, 1967, **73**, 612–619.

Kendler, H. H., & Kimm, J. Reversal learning as a function of the size of reward during acquisition and reversal. *J. exp. Psychol.*, 1967, **73**, 66–71.

Lovejoy, E. Analysis of the overlearning reversal effect. *Psychol. Rev.*, 1966, **73**, 87–103.

Lovejoy, E. *Attention and discrimination learning.* San Francisco: Holden-Day, 1968.

Lukaszewska, Irena. Some further failures to find the visual overlearning reversal effect in rats. *J. comp. physiol. Psychol.*, 1968, **65**, 359–361.

Maatsch, J. L. An exploratory study of the possible differential inhibitory effects of frustration and work inhibition. Unpublished M.A. thesis, Michigan State College, 1951.

Maatsch, J. L. Reinforcement and extinction phenomena. *Psychol. Rev.*, 1954, **61**, 111–118.

Mackintosh, N. J. Selective attention in animal discrimination learning. *Psychol. Bull.*, 1965a, **64**, 124–150.

Mackintosh, N. J. Overlearning, transfer to proprioceptive control and position reversal. *Quart. J. exp. Psychol.*, 1965b, **17**, 26–36.

Mackintosh, N. J. Further analysis of the overtraining reversal effect. *J. comp. physiol. Psychol. Monograph*, 1969, **67**, No. 2, Pt. 2.

Mandler, Jean M. The effect of overtraining on the use of positive and negative stimuli in reversal and transfer. *J. comp. physiol. Psychol.*, 1968, **66**, 110–115.

Marzocco, F. M. Frustration effect as a function of drive level, habit strength and distribution trials during extinction. Unpublished doctoral dissertation, State University of Iowa, 1951.

Paul, C. Effects of overlearning upon single habit reversal in rats. *Psychol. Bull.*, 1965, **63**, 65–72.

Pubols, B. H., Jr. The facilitation of visual and spatial discrimination reversal by overlearning. *J. comp. physiol. Psychol.*, 1956, **49**, 243–248.

Reid, L. S. The development of noncontinuity behavior through continuity learning. *J. exp. Psychol.*, 1953, **46**, 107–112.

Smith, M. P. The stimulus trace gradient in visual discrimination learning. *J. comp. physiol. Psychol.*, 1951, **44**, 154–161.

Spanier, D. A. Overtraining reversal effect as a function of incorrect response consequences. Unpublished doctoral thesis, University of Nebraska, 1968.

Sperling, Sally E. Reversal learning and resistance to extinction: A review of the rat literature. *Psychol. Bull.*, 1965a, **63**, 281–297.

Sperling, Sally E. Reversal learning and resistance to extinction: A supplementary report. *Psychol. Bull.*, 1965b, **64**, 310–312.

Sperling, Sally E. Position responding and visual discrimination learning. Paper presented at Western Psychological Association meeting, San Diego, 1968.

Theios, J., & Blosser, D. The overlearning reversal effect and magnitude of reward. *J. comp. physiol. Psychol.*, 1965, **59**, 252–256.

Tortora, D. F. Overlearning reversal effects in spatial discrimination. Unpublished M.A. thesis, Michigan State University, 1970.

Yelen, Delphine. Magnitude of the frustration effect and number of training trials. *Psychon. Sci.*, 1969, **15**, 137–138.

Response-Correlated Stimulus Functioning in Homogeneous Behavior Chains[1]

JOHN R. PLATT AND PETER C. SENKOWSKI

University of Iowa

Properties of homogeneous behavior sequences (HBS) have frequently been of interest to behavior theorists. Ideally a HBS may be defined as a series of substantially identical S–R units followed by some terminal reinforcing event (S^R). This idealization must of course be immediately tempered to take into account that the occurrence of prior responses may substantially modify subsequent stimulation, even though situational stimuli under E's control are held constant. It may thus be proposed that by HBS is meant a terminally reinforced series of S–R units which differ only in respect to response-correlated stimuli (RCS).

Under this definition a straight-alley runway approximates a HBS to the extent that exteroceptive stimulation is constant throughout the runway, and inertial properties of the locomotor response are disregarded. A somewhat better approximation is probably obtained with free-operant or discrete-trials ratio schedules in operant chambers where possible heterogeneity should be limited to the first response of a sequence. Both the runway situation and fixed-ratio (FR) schedules in operant chambers have typically been designed in such a way that a perfect negative correlation exists between the time an organism spends executing the response

[1] The research reported in this chapter was supported by United States Public Health Service grant MH–15380, John R. Platt, principal investigator. Computer time was provided by the graduate college of the University of Iowa. Appreciation is expressed to Stephen Bitgood, David Johnson, and Robert Mann, all of whom assisted in the execution of the research.

requirement and the immediacy with which S^R is obtained. Although this particular correlation is by no means the only possible one (Logan, 1960), it will be the only one of concern in this paper.

Quantitative theoretical treatment of the problem of behavioral chaining appears to have begun with Hull's (1932) postulation of a logarithmically decreasing gradient of response strength as a function of the distance of a particular choice point from the goal of a multiple maze. In an attempt to obtain more direct measures of response strength in theoretically simpler situations, Hull (1934) soon extended his goal-gradient hypothesis to speed-of-locomotion gradients from segmented, straight-alley runways. The speed-of-locomotion gradients reported by Hull were not positively accelerated, decreasing functions of distance from the goal as might have been expected on the basis of the goal-gradient hypothesis, but rather were of an inverted U-shape. Studies since that time have reported similarly shaped speed gradients for both the runway (Crespi, 1942; Deaux, 1967; DiLollo & Walker, 1964; Drew, 1939; Weiss, 1960; Wist, 1962) and for discrete-trials lever pressing (Weiss, 1961). However, both monotonically increasing (Crespi, 1942) and monotonically decreasing gradients (Collier, Knarr, & Marx, 1961; Knarr & Collier, 1962) have occasionally been reported for the runway.

Hull (1934) attempted to resolve the disparity between a positively accelerated goal gradient and an inverted-U-shaped speed-of-locomotion gradient by making two additional assumptions. The negatively accelerated, increasing side of the speed gradient was said to reflect the joint action of the positively accelerated goal gradient and a negatively accelerated relationship between response strength and speed of locomotion. The decrease in speed near the end of the runway was attributed to anticipatory stopping. The first of these assumptions has the disadvantage of contradicting what Spence (1954) has shown to be implicit in Hull's (1943) assumptions concerning oscillatory inhibition and reaction threshold, namely, a linear relationship between response speed and excitatory potential. The assumption concerning anticipatory stopping is interesting but lacks any suggestion of a quantitative specification of the spread of this anticipation over the behavior chain or its combination with the strength of the locomotion tendency. In addition, it is not at all clear how one would ever obtain independent measures of the strengths of running and stopping in order to verify that these are actually two different responses rather than the latter simply being the absence of the former.

As a result of the work of Perin (1943), Hull (1943) was led to elaborate the goal-gradient hypothesis in terms of two delay of reinforcement gradients. The first of these was called the gradient of reinforcement and represented a positively accelerated, decreasing effectiveness of primary or unconditioned reinforcement (S^R) as the temporal interval by which it followed the learned response increased. The second gradient, which was assumed to be similar in shape to the first, represented the acquisition of secondary or conditioned reinforcement (S^r) properties by stimuli as a decreasing function of their temporal precedence of S^R. Not only did this theoretical extension considerably complicate the theoretical treatment of behavior chains, but it also appears to have had the effect of directing interest away from the internal properties of chains to the study of what Hull (1952, p. 127) later called non-chaining delay of reinforcement—a procedure which involves delaying S^R for some period after an organism completes a required response or sequence of responses.

Spence (1947) rejected Hull's notion that the learning of responses temporally separated from S^R involves a temporal spread of effect. Rather, learning in such situations was assumed to be solely the result of S^r which takes place immediately upon occurrence of the response. It was further assumed that any stimulus would serve as a S^r to the extent that stimulus generalization occurred between it and the stimulus pattern immediately preceding S^R. This formulation thus paralleled Hull's original one in that effects of separating a response from its S^R were to be accounted for by means of a single process or gradient. However, the effective variable in such separations became stimulus dissimilarity rather than time per se. In spite of this shift away from time as the dependent variable of the goal gradient, the empirical emphasis of Spence's treatment remained on nonchaining cases of delay of reinforcement.

Spence (1956, pp. 148–154) later adopted a contiguity position for instrumental reward learning, thus rejecting the S^r account of delay of reinforcement just outlined. In this later theory Spence assigned the effects of within-chain delay of reinforcement to incentive motivation by way of its underlying fractional anticipatory goal-response mechanism r_g-s_g. The dependent variable for the goal gradient, however, remained stimulus dissimilarity. At the same time, Spence assigned the effects of nonchaining delay of reinforcement to the conditioning of competing behaviors occurring during the delay period in order to offer the clear suggestion that the extensive literature on nonchaining delay was irrelevant to the understanding of behavior within homogeneous chains. In spite of these theoretical modifications, very little research indicative of a renewed interest in the properties of HBSs has been forthcoming from within the Hull-Spence framework.

On the other hand, Skinner (1938) and his followers (e.g., Kelleher, 1966; Keller & Schoenfeld, 1950) have displayed a continued interest in the properties of HBSs. This operant literature has been extensively reviewed by Kelleher (1966) and requires only selective mention here. Early operant analyses of HBSs were largely dictated by Skinner's (1938) statement of the behavioral chaining hypothesis. According to this hypothesis, each response in a sequence gives rise to distinctive stimulus consequences which function both as S^r for the response just executed and as a discriminative stimulus (S^D) for the next response in the sequence. Most of the research generated within this tradition has had the nonquantitative goal of simply supporting the assumed existence and functions of RCSs in behavioral sequences.

More recently the distaste of operant investigators for the admittedly hypothetical RCS has led to an emphasis on the study of exteroceptive stimuli which are introduced into a behavior sequence under the control of E. This research tradition may be traced to such procedures as Ferster and Skinner's (1957, pp. 89–116) use of "added counters," whereby progress through a FR response requirement is displayed to S by way of a graded exteroceptive stimulus. The function of RCSs is then inferred from the effects of this added counter on S's gradient of response rate over the ratio. Another commonly used operant procedure for the study of chaining phenomena is the so-called chain schedule (Ferster & Skinner, 1957). In essence this procedure requires S to respond in the presence of one S^D in order to obtain another S^D in which responding produces food. Presentation of the second S^D is considered to constitute S^r as a result of its contiguity with food, so responding in the first S^D may be used to analyze the behavior-maintaining properties of S^r.

Although both of the procedures just mentioned are admirable in respect to the degree of control which E may have over the stimuli of interest, they cannot ultimately solve the problems of identification and quantification of the stimulus dimensions actually involved in HBSs. Such procedures can perhaps modify these dimensions or provide facsimiles of their operation, but one must eventually face the task of measurement and control of the actual stimuli involved in a minimal HBS. The research to be reported in this chapter is part of a continuing program of such measurement and control which has been initiated in the authors' laboratories.

A GENERAL MODEL

In order to begin an experimental analysis of any collection of behavioral processes, such as those represented by the HBS, it is desirable to formulate a working model of those processes. Such a model provides both a framework for the formulation of experimental questions and a modifiable and expandable structure within which to summarize results. It is ultimately desirable that such a model be as explicit and quantified as possible, but a premature implementation of these goals is likely to be both narrowing and frustrating. The model from which the present research was generated was thus formulated with a minimum of detail being given to the quantitative properties of the processes assumed. Indeed, the research to be reported should be viewed as an attempt to begin amassing the kind of systematic data which would allow such quantification.

The particular model chosen was built around Skinner's (1938) treatment of behavioral chaining. It was felt that of the available alternatives this formulation had received the most systematic development and documentation. Nevertheless, several initial additions to the model were necessary. In the first place, no explicit suggestions seem to have been made by Skinner or his followers concerning how the S^r strength of the RCSs might be distributed over a HBS. Since the function of these stimuli as S^D's would presumably follow a stimulus-generalization gradient from the stimuli immediately preceding the last response in a HBS, it was decided to assume a similar gradient for their S^r function (Spence, 1947). In addition, it was felt that previous analyses of HBSs had not given sufficient attention to the nonhomogeneous terminal behaviors characteristic of such sequences. Hull (1934) gave ad hoc recognition to the role of such behaviors when he attributed the terminal decrement in response speed gradients to an anticipatory form of the stopping necessary for eating in his runway. Kelleher (1966) has treated, as a special case, HBSs in which the terminal behavior is different from the earlier responses in the chain. The present model assumes that essentially all HBSs involve terminal behaviors necessary for obtaining and consuming S^R. To the extent that such behaviors are usually different from the homogeneous response, it will be assumed that their anticipatory occurrence interferes with the homogeneous response, although highly compatible terminal behaviors might actually be facility to the HBS, as suggested by Spence's (1956) treatment of the fractional anticipatory goal response. Finally, a mechanism for anticipatory occurrence of such terminal behaviors will be proposed in such a way as to be conducive to eventual quantification.

A schematic representation of a four-unit HBS is shown in Fig. 1. The response components are represented along the bottom of the figure. Any orienting behaviors necessary to bring the organism into position to initiate the chain are represented by R_0. The four homogeneous responses in the chain are indicated by R_1 through R_4, and those behaviors required for the organism to obtain S^R following completion of the last homogeneous response are represented by R_T.

Along the top of Fig. 1 are shown the hypothetical stimulus and reinforcement components of the chain. Broken lines are used to denote learned S–R connections, and solid lines represent relationships between a response and its consequences. Starting with the posterior end of the chain, the accumulated stimulus feedback of four homogeneous responses (s_4), together with any exteroceptive stimuli (S_T) occasioned by completion of the homogeneous portion

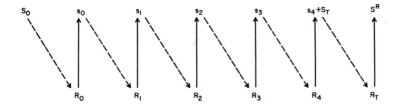

FIG. 1. Schematic representation of a hypothetical 4-unit response chain. See text for a complete explanation.

of the chain, are conditioned to R_T by S^R. Now s_4 and S_T stand in a relationship to S^R so that they take on a S^r function and thus may support the conditioning of R_4 to the accumulated stimulus feedback (s_3) of three homogeneous responses. Similarly, s_0 through s_2 may provide S^r for the responses preceding them in the chain, to the extent that stimulus generalization occurs from $s_4 + S_T$ to the stimulus in question.

The existence of a stimulus-generalization gradient over the successive RCSs of a behavioral chain not only provides S^r for the homogeneous responses but also gives rise to the mechanism by which R_T becomes anticipatory to $s_4 + S_T$. Early in the development of a HBS the generalization of R_T to stimuli earlier in the chain would be expected to follow the same function as the S^r properties of the RCSs. If such a state of affairs were to persist, little would be expected to develop in the way of a response-velocity gradient, since any increases in S^r for the homogeneous responses would be offset by a corresponding increase in generalized intrusions of R_T. However, it is to be noted immediately that R_T is undergoing discrimination training, since it is followed by S^R only in the presence of $s_4 + S_T$, and its anticipatory occurrence does nothing to increase the similarity of the accumulated RCSs to s_4 in order to provide S^r. Further, since R_T is maintained by S^R, its nonreinforced anticipatory occurrence may be actively frustrated (Amsel, 1958). At the very least such anticipatory intrusions of R_T decrease the immediacy of S^R. Any or all of these factors should lead to a steepening of the gradient of intrusions of R_T into the homogeneous portion of the chain. Such extensive discrimination of the S^r gradient for the RCSs of homogeneous responding would not be expected, since these responses receive *only* S^r and this is received with perfect consistency.

At this point a general picture of the assumed development of a HBS may be presented. Figure 2 shows the strength of the homogeneous responses (solid line) and R$_T$ (broken line) as a function of increasing dissimilarity of stimuli from those immediately preceding S^R. Frame A of the figure represents an early stage of training, and Frame B corresponds to a later stage. The point on the abscissa labeled *O* represents the stimuli coincident with S^R, and *X* corresponds to the stimuli immediately preceding the last homogeneous response of the chain. For simplicity it is assumed that the maximum possible number of homogeneous responses is equal to the minimum number required for reinforcement. Such a state of affairs would hold true for most currently used discrete-trials situations. The strength of R$_T$ at *O* is shown as larger than that of the homogeneous response at *X*, since the former is conditioned by S^R while the latter relies on S^r derived from that S^R. Also, the continuity represented in the function for R$_T$ over the point *X* would only hold for the

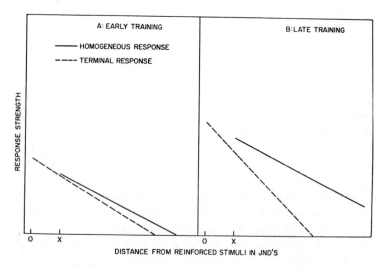

Fig. 2. Hypothetical gradients of response strength for a homogeneous response sequence and its nonhomogeneous terminal behavior, early and late in training.

idealized case in which no distinctive exteroceptive stimulus change was occasioned by completion of the homogeneous portion of the chain.

In going from Frame A to Frame B of Fig. 2, the increasing strength of both responses as a result of increasing numbers of S^R's, as well as the above described increase in steepness of the generalization gradient for R_T, are indicated. It is to be emphasized that the linear form of the strength gradients shown here is assumed to hold only when the abscissa is scaled in equal-appearing behavioral units. It can thus be seen that, within the context of that model, a major research issue is the determination of stimulus generalization and discrimination gradients for number of responses as a stimulus. It would only be in the light of adequate behavioral scaling of discriminability along such a dimension that extensive quantification of the model would be possible. Indeed, the research to be reported below had as its major goal the determination of differential responding along this stimulus dimension.

RESPONSE VELOCITY GRADIENTS IN HOMOGENEOUS CHAINS

Many different paradigms might be used to investigate either an organism's localization of position within a HBS or discrimination of numbers of homogeneous responses as stimuli. Two such general paradigms have been employed in the present research. The one to be considered in this section involves measurement of response-velocity gradients over the course of HBSs. As was mentioned earlier, such gradients have usually been found to be of an inverted U-shape in both the straight-alley runway and with ratio schedules in discrete-trials, lever-pressing situations. According to the present model, the increasing side of these gradients reflects the rising strength of S^r for the homogeneous response as its accumulated RCSs become more and more similar to those at the end of the sequence. The terminal decrease in the velocity gradient is presumably a result of interference generated by the relatively steep gradient relating R_T to successive RCSs in the homogeneous sequence. Furthermore, as training proceeds on a particular HBS the response-velocity gradient would be expected not only to heighten but also to move its peak toward the end of the gradient as a result of steepening of the R_T gradient with additional discrimination training. Rarely observed instances of monotonically increasing or decreasing gradients would be assumed to result from very favorable or very unfavorable conditions, respectively, for the discrimination of the R_T gradient.

This particular analysis of response-velocity gradients in HBSs carries considerable significance for the problem of investigating RCS functions, since according to it the difference between the position of the peak of such a gradient and its total length may be considered as a sort of differential threshold for number of responses as a stimulus. That is, the peak represents a point beyond which the accumulated RCSs are sufficiently indiscriminable from those at the end of the sequence to bring the gradient of generalized R_T above threshold. The position of the peaks of response-velocity gradients in HBSs of different lengths, thus, might be used to investigate the discriminability of adjacent points on the stimulus dimension of numbers of responses as a function of position on that dimension. Similarly, the discriminability of numbers of responses might be compared for different response systems. However, it should be emphasized that such differential thresholds would not in any way represent sensory absolutes, since the position of the peak of a response-velocity gradient would also be expected to be affected by such variables as the effortfulness of the homogeneous response, relative to that of R_T, as well as the rewards and punishments for each. The effect of such nonsensory factors would, however, be minimal if consideration were limited to the *relative* position of the peak among velocity gradients involving common response systems and common rewards and punishments.

Unfortunately, very few investigations of response-velocity gradients as a function of length of HBS have been reported. Hull (1934) compared velocity gradients of 20-foot and 40-foot segmented, straight-alley runways. He reported that the gradient for the shorter runway simply resembled a foreshortening of the longer gradient; that is, both gradients peaked at the same absolute distance from the beginning of their respective runways. This was of course just the opposite of what Hull had expected on the basis of the goal-gradient hypothesis. Since distance from S^R was assumed by his hypothesis to be the effective variable determining the velocity gradient, gradients of different lengths were expected to be congruent in their terminal, rather than their initial, segments.

Within the context of the present model, since the accumulated RCSs at equal distances into either runway would presumably be identical and since peaking of the two gradients at the same absolute position would indicate equal discriminability of this position from the respective terminal stimuli of the two runways, Hull's result might be taken to indicate that the RCSs at the end of the 40-foot runway were not discriminably different from those at the end of the 20-foot one. This conclusion hardly seems justified, however, for two reasons. In the first place, the extremely small amount of training (35 trials) given Hull's Ss introduces the possibility that their velocity gradients had not obtained final form. More importantly, localization of position within Hull's runways was probably based as much on extramaze, spatial cues as on accumulated RCSs. Indeed, Knarr and Collier (1962) have shown that monotonically decreasing velocity gradients are likely to result when such extramaze cues are minimized. Within the context of the present model, such a trend to very early peaking indicates an impoverishment of stimuli differentiating the S^R and pre-S^R periods. Thus, if Hull's Ss chiefly utilized such spatial cues for localization of position within the runway, his results have little relevance for the dimension of number of responses as a stimulus.

At least one study (Weiss, 1961) has been reported which investigated response-velocity gradients as a function of chain length within a discrete-trials, lever-pressing situation which has the advantage of not confounding accumulated RCSs with spatial cues. Similar to Hull's result, Weiss found that the velocity gradient for a four-press chain peaked at the same absolute ordinal response position as that of an eight-press chain. However, in the case of Weiss's data there was a marked trend toward both a sharper rise and a sharper fall in the gradient of the shorter chain, thus offering some indication for the discriminability of the accumulated RCSs of four lever presses from those of eight. Like Hull, Weiss used a very small amount of training (96 trials) on his response chains. Data will be presented shortly to show that much more training is necessary to obtain response-velocity gradients in their final form with discrete-trials lever pressing.

Further information about the effects of length of HBS on response-velocity gradients is available in the nature of cumulative records of free-operant behavior under various FR requirements (e.g., Ferster & Skinner, 1957). For several reasons such data are not well suited for present purposes. In the first place, the rather gross graphical manner in which such data are collected is not conducive to quantitative analysis or to the averaging of gradients across individual trials for smoothing purposes. In addition, the cumulative format of such data make identification of the position of maximum response velocity within the gradient extremely difficult. Indeed, Ferster and Skinner reported on the basis of cumulative records that moderate FR requirements did not produce a visible velocity gradient, only an initial pause followed by an apparently constant rate of responding.

Experiment One

In light of the paucity and difficulties of available data, the present authors set out to investigate the effects of length of HBS on response-velocity gradients under conditions of extended training. In order to avoid complications owing to spatial cues, a discrete-trials, lever-pressing situation was employed. In the first experiment to be reported here, 36 food-deprived (11 grams per day) rats were employed to determine the effects of size of a discrete-trials FR requirement on response-rate gradients across the ratio, as well as the degree to which relationships between these gradients were independent of Ss' general motivational level. One-third of the Ss were trained on a 4-response sequence, another third on an 8-press requirement, and the remaining third received S^R for 12 responses. Half the Ss in each chain-length condition always received their entire supplemental food ration (8.3 grams) 1 hour before being run, while the remaining Ss received it 20 minutes after leaving the experimental chamber. All Ss were conditioned as rapidly as possible to their appropriate chain length and then withheld from the experimental apparatus until Ss with longer chains were brought up to their appropriate values. Group 8 thus received one more pretraining session than Group 4, and Group 12 received yet one more session. All Ss were then given 24 sessions of

20 trials each under their assigned conditions. During this time all trials terminated with presentation of three 45-milligram food pellets and successive trials were initiated at the rate of 1 per minute. Between trials the lever was retracted and house lights were dimmed. The latency of each chain and the interresponse time (IRT) of all other lever presses were recorded to the nearest 0.1 second on punched paper tape. Results were converted to a rate index of response velocity by computing the reciprocal of each S's mean response times.

As training proceeded, all gradients became both higher in over-all rate and increasingly inverted U-shaped, with peaks which occurred later and later in the chain. This pattern of results offers at least qualitative support for the proposed model of HBSs. The response-rate gradients for the three chain-length conditions over the last 8 training sessions (17–24) are shown in Fig. 3. As can be seen, all three gradients were of an inverted U-shape with peaks of approximately the same height. The three gradients did not peak at the same absolute ordinal response position as did Hull's and Weiss's, although examination of the results indicated that such a conclusion might have been reached in the present case if only the first 100 or 200 trials had been examined.

Although the velocity gradients in Fig. 3 clearly indicate the mutual discriminability of RCSs of 4, 8, and 12 lever presses, at a more quantitative level one can consider what the relationship between these gradients implies in respect to a discriminability function for number of responses as a stimulus. In order to examine this question, it is useful to consider an ideal case. Suppose that Weber's law were to hold for this stimulus dimension. Under this hypothesis, the differential threshold represented by the difference between the total length of the HBS and the ordinal response position of the peak of its velocity gradient would be expected to be some constant proportion of the chain length. That is

$$\Delta I = KI$$

where ΔI is the prescribed difference threshold, I is chain length, and K is Weber's fraction for this particular stimulus dimension. If the present results were to display this relationship, then all three velocity gradients would have peaked at the same relative proportion

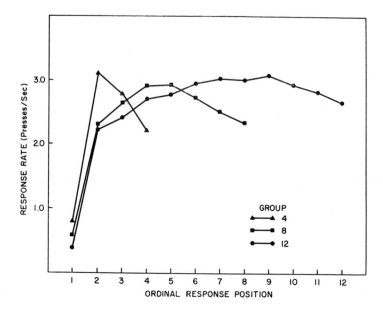

Fig. 3. Response-rate gradients for 3 chain-length conditions in the last 8 sessions of Experiment One.

of their respective lengths. In actuality, however, the longer gradients peaked proportionally later in the response chain than did the shorter ones. Such a progressive increase over the degree of discriminability predicted by Weber's law as chain length increases would indeed be interesting, but several considerations suggest that such a conclusion is not justified.

In the first place, the fact that number of responses is an integer variable places some limitation on the degree of resolution of the placement of the peak of the response-velocity gradient, particularly with very short chains. This factor alone could not, however, completely explain the deviation just noted. Somewhat more important is the observation that the particular formulation of Weber's law given above is seldom found to be applicable in practice. This formulation implies that discriminability becomes unlimited as stimulus magnitude approaches 0. Such an absurdity is usually avoided by taking into account the existence of a detection threshold for the stimulus dimension in question. Under these circumstances the expression for Weber's law becomes

$$\Delta I = C + KI$$

where C is the first discriminable step above the detection threshold. In the case of an integer dimension like number of responses, the minimum possible value for C would be 1. If C is set to 1 and K to 1/4, the peaks shown in Fig. 3 at the second, fifth, and ninth ordinal response positions would be in perfect agreement with this formulation of Weber's law. Although the beauty of such a conclusion is very compelling, a considerable amount of caution should be exercised. In the first place, very little comfort is to be taken in the fitting of what amounts to 3 data points by the estimation of 2 parameters. More importantly, an examination of Fig. 3 reveals that the longer gradients not only peaked proportionally later in the chain but also showed less severe terminal decrements in response rate. Extrapolating this phenomenon to longer chain lengths would lead to the expectation that the velocity gradient for a chain of 20 or more responses might well be monotonically increasing, while the above application of Weber's law would predict a peak at the fourteenth position for a chain of length 20. Indeed, Donahoe, Schulte, and Moulton (1968) have reported monotonically increasing rate gradients with free-operant FRs of 20 and 40. This flattening of the gradient is undoubtedly caused in part by an averaging artifact resulting from an increase in both between- and within-*S*s variability in placement of the peak as chain length increases. Unfortunately, this same variability precludes the possibility of not averaging to avoid the artifact. It is thus clear that a definitive statement of a discriminability function for number of responses as a stimulus, based on velocity-gradient data, will require both the investigation of more different chain lengths and a technique which produces smaller individual differences. Velocity gradients, nevertheless, still pose a viable testing ground for the present model of behavioral chaining to HBSs.

Turning to the question of motivational effects in the data just reported, although there was a trend for postfed *S*s to respond at higher over-all rates than prefed *S*s, this effect only obtained statistical significance at the first ordinal response position. Not even a trend was present for the motivational variable to affect placement of the peak of the velocity gradient, thus supporting a sensory interpretation of this dependent variable. The effects of the prefeeding manipulation on response rate at the first ordinal response position is shown in Fig. 4 for the last 8 sessions of training. As can be seen, starting rate was positively related to both motivational level and shortness of the chain, with the motivational effect being most pronounced at the shorter chain lengths. This interaction would certainly be in line with a Hullian treatment in terms of the motivational variable combining multiplicatively with an associative vari-

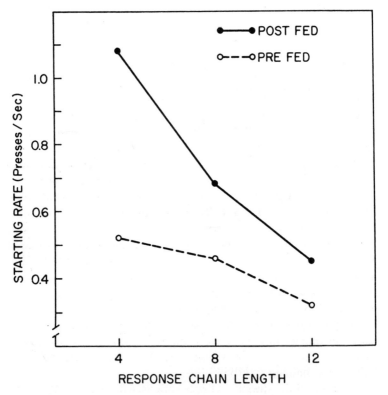

FIG. 4. Rate of initiation of response chains in the last 8 sessions of Experiment One as a function of chain-length and deprivation time.

able determined by delay of reinforcement. Such an account would not, however, do justice to the lack of control by these variables throughout the remainder of the velocity gradient. The present results would probably best be taken as suggesting a difference in process between the initiation of a HBS and the completion of it, once it has been initiated. Any such difference might have been enhanced in the present situation by use of a retractable lever with rather slow extension times (0.4 seconds), which meant that a response topology appropriate to striking a moving object was likely for the first response of the chain. In any case, the first response of a lever-pressing sequence certainly involves orientation components not required for further responses. It is, thus, not unreasonable to suggest that once the chain has been initiated, it is run off under the control of the successive RCSs and a "preset" collection of parameter values, provided *S*s have not been trained to expect further discriminative stimuli (Platt, Senkowski, & Mann, in press).

Experiment Two

As has already been alluded to, one of the chief difficulties with the data just presented was the high degree of individual differences in placement of the peaks of the velocity gradients. In order to avoid the averaging artifacts which resulted from this variability, it was deemed desirable to obtain relationships between chain length and peak placement within individual organisms. Eight food-deprived (12 grams per day) rat *S*s were trained for 44 sessions in the manner of the postfed group of the previous experiment, except that a random half of their trials involved a chain length of 6, while 12 responses were required for the remaining trials. All chains terminated with the presentation of one 45-milligram food pellet. Since no differential exteroceptive stimuli were correlated with chain length during this period, the condition resembled what Ferster and Skinner (1957) have called a "mixed schedule" and is here referred to simply as *uncued*. Following this training, an additional 36 sessions were administered in which 4- and 10-KHz. pure tones were used to differentiate 6-response trials from those of

12 responses. This latter condition of course resembles Ferster and Skinner's "multiple schedule" and is referred to here as *cued*. It was hoped that the uncued condition would provide a nondifferentiated base line against which discriminated velocity gradients appropriate to the two lengths of chains could be displayed in the cued phase. Some indication of the relationship between chain length and peak position could then be obtained for each *S*, and further studies could fill in this function by examining more different chain lengths.

The velocity transform used for this experiment was slightly different from that of the previous one in that individual IRTs were reciprocalized before any averaging took place. This represents the measure of response speed, as opposed to rate, and is perhaps more familiar to discrete-trials investigators. No systematically differential effects of these two transforms have been found in our data, except for the higher over-all velocities given by the speed measure as a result of its weighting of very short IRTs. The speed transform has the advantage, as will be seen in the next experiment, of allowing nonarbitrary values to be assigned to responses which do not occur as a result of the elapsing of an experimenter-defined time limit.

The upper frame of Fig. 5 shows the response-speed gradients for 6- and 12-response trials, separately, over the last 8 sessions (37–44) of the uncued phase of the experiment. There is clearly no differentiation of the two gradients. The 6-response gradient closely resembled what the last experiment suggests such a gradient would be like in *S*s exposed only to this chain length. The 12-response gradient simply continued to decrease beyond the sixth response position. This early peaking with an uncued mixture of chain lengths is quite in line with the present model for HBSs, since the frequent reinforcement of R_T in the presence of the accumulated RCSs of 6 responses would presumably prevent extinction of the R_T gradient beyond that position allowed by simple exposure to a 6-response chain.

The lower frame of Fig. 5 shows the response-speed gradients for the 2 chain lengths during the last 8 sessions (73–80) of the cued phase. As can be seen, there was essentially no evidence for the differentiation of these two gradients, which in turn closely resembled the corresponding gradients from the uncued phase. Since the very

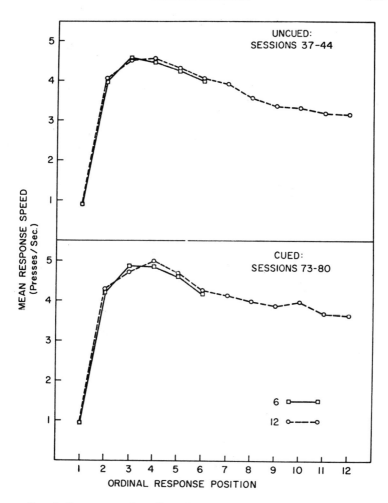

Fig. 5. Response-speed gradients for cued and uncued mixtures of 6- and 12-response chains in Experiment Two.

same tones used in this experiment have been shown to support rapid and substantial differential conditioning (Platt, Senkowski, & Mann, in press), the lack of differential gradients in the cued phase deserves some attention. A rethinking of the logic of the present procedure suggests that it was incredibly naïve because differentiation of the two gradients was not being differentially reinforced in any of the usual senses.[2] A S which responded with no regard for the tones, thus placing its R_T appropriately to the 6-response chain, continued to receive substantial partial reinforcement of these responses. If the degree of this partial reinforcement was not sufficiently low to produce any apparent shift in the peaks of the uncued gradients toward that appropriate to a 12-response chain, then there would certainly be no reason to expect differential extinction of R_T in the early response positions of the 12-response chain simply because a unique stimulus was present.

Ferster and Skinner (1957, pp. 531, 591–594) have reported differential responding in multiple FR reinforcement schedules, but only with much greater discrepancies between the lengths of the 2 chains. Even in these cases differential responding appeared to be most pronounced in respect to the speed of initiation of the chain, an effect which, not unreasonably, has been attributed to the possible aversiveness of stimuli associated with the beginning of an extremely large FR. In any case the present technique does not appear to be adequate to the purpose of obtaining within-Ss estimates of the function relating ordinal position of the peak of a response-velocity gradient to length of the HBS. Another alternative would of course be sequentially to obtain from S gradients of the various lengths desired. In view of the extensive amounts of training which appear to be needed to stabilize such velocity gradients, such a procedure would be very costly and would assume a degree of long-term stability that does not appear to typify such gradients.

Experiment Three

In search of more promising techniques for scaling number of responses as a stimulus, several alternatives were considered. Rilling (1967) and Rilling and McDiarmid (1965) have investigated the discrimination of FRs of two different lengths by requiring S to make a choice response based on the length of a FR it has just completed. Although this technique appears to produce sensitive quantification of such discriminations, it is not clearly relevant to the present problem, since considerable operational disparity

[2] The authors acknowledge the aid of Judson S. Brown, who first suggested this point to us.

exists between Rilling's task of discriminating which of several FRs has been completed and the present concern with localization of position within a HBS.

Ferster and Skinner (1957) proposed two other techniques which are relevant to the present problem. The first of these techniques (pp. 580–590) involved exposing Ss to an uncued mixture of two FR requirements, much as was done in the first phase of Experiment Two above. They found that if the two FRs were sufficiently different in length, and the larger was sufficiently long, pauses characteristic of the initiation of long FRs would occur at some point beyond completion of the number of responses appropriate to the smaller FR. The variance in the placement of such pauses might of course be taken as indicative of S's discrimination of the accumulated RCS associated with completion of the smaller FR from those spread throughout the larger FR. The disadvantage of this technique lies in the requirement that the larger FR be long, both absolutely and in relation to the smaller. As reference to Fig. 5 suggests, this pausing phenomenon simply does not occur in the range of RCSs currently being investigated.

A second technique proposed by Ferster and Skinner (1957, pp. 616–619) involved the interspersion of timed blocks of extinction into a FR schedule, with no correlated exteroceptive stimulus change. It was found that in such extinction periods Ss would come to emit somewhat more than the number of responses required for reinforcement on the FR, and then abruptly stop responding. On the assumption that this stopping was controlled by the accumulation of RCSs to a point of first discriminability from those present at the end of the FR, a difference threshold could obviously be calculated.

In order to investigate the applicability of a variate of this latter technique in the present situation, seven Ss from the last experiment were again exposed to a random, uncued mixture of half 6-response chains and half 12-response chains. The procedure was identical to that in the uncued phase of the last experiment, except that S^R was always omitted from one or the other chain length. Three Ss were trained to stability with the 12-response chain nonreinforced (12NR) and then retrained with the 6-response chain nonreinforced (6NR). The other four Ss received the treatments in the opposite order, and no effects of order were observed

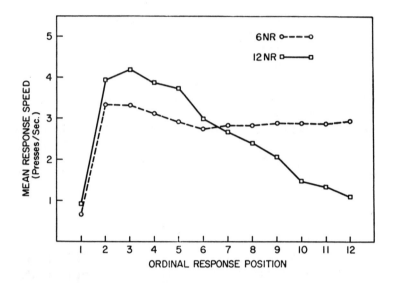

Fig. 6. Response-speed gradients for uncued mixtures of 6- and 12-response chains in Experiment Three, when one or the other chain length was consistently nonreinforced.

in the stabilized behavior. Any chain not completed within 27 seconds was terminated without S^R.

In Fig. 6 the mean response-speed gradients for all Ss on the 12-response chains over the last 8 sessions on each condition are shown separately. A decrease in over-all response speed from that shown in Fig. 5 is apparent. More importantly, the 12NR gradient showed a markedly increasing decrement in response speed from about the sixth response on, while the 6NR gradient simply yielded a mild over-all depression centered around the sixth response position. For the first time in the data thus far presented, the mean gradients shown in Fig. 6 provided a faithful representation of all the individual Ss. Although the over-all response speeds and the exact point of the crossing of the 6NR and 12NR gradients varied somewhat from S to S, the interaction indicated between these two gradients was exhibited by every S. Nevertheless, one aspect of the 12NR gradient does reflect an averaging artifact. The apparently gradual decrease in response speed after the fifth position was largely a result of an increasing probability of cessation of lever pressing as the trial proceeded.

The results of this experiment clearly indicate the applicability of Ferster and Skinner's technique to the present situation. It would appear that while the accumulated RCSs at the point of S^R had positive reinforcement properties, the terminal RCSs of the non-reinforced chain were actually aversive. This was made most apparent by the central depression of the 6NR gradient, in spite of the delay of S^R which this depression produced. In any case, the difference between the ordinal response position at which S ceases to respond and the length of a shorter, reinforced chain should provide a differential threshold measure for number of responses which does not depend on the earlier assumptions concerning the role of R_T. Even more ideally, a relative frequency distribution of the ordinal position of the last response could be obtained, and the standard deviation of this distribution could be used as an index of the differential threshold. This latter alternative would presumably have the advantage of being less affected by such nonsensory factors as the length of the longer, nonreinforced chain and the effortfulness of the response. Although parametric determinations of a discriminability function for number of responses as a stimulus, using the method just described, are planned, no results are as yet available from the authors' laboratories.

MEASUREMENT OF TERMINAL RESPONSES IN HOMOGENEOUS CHAINS

The techniques thus far discussed for obtaining a discriminability function for number of responses as a stimulus all involved use of the response-velocity gradient or, in the case of the last technique, simply the probability of occurrence of the homogeneous response at each ordinal response position. Within the context of the present model for HBSs, another set of possibilities exists on the basis of direct measurement of anticipatory R_T's. Perhaps the most direct evidence available concerning the role of R_T in HBSs comes from a study by Denny, Wells, and Maatsch (1957). These investigators used a modified operant chamber consisting of a 2-foot alley with a lever at one end and a food tray at the other. Trips to the food tray between lever presses were objectively recorded by means of a treadle-switch arrangement. In a free-operant procedure rats which had executed 40 continuously reinforced lever presses were then allowed to obtain 80 additional reinforcements under a FR schedule which required 5 presses per S^R. Over the 80 FR reinforcements, the mean number of tray approaches per S^R reduced from 5 to less than 3. Further, this reduction was most pronounced at the earlier ordinal response positions, so there eventually emerged a very steep gradient relating tray approaches to ordinal position within the FR, much as has been described for the present model of HBSs.

If this technique were to prove reliable, one could obviously attempt to scale number of responses as a stimulus in terms of the asymptotic variability of placement of these tray-approach responses within the HBS. Preliminary investigations of this technique were executed in the authors' laboratories, using a standard operant chamber in which a Gerbrand's food tray was mounted directly above and behind the retractable lever. A photobeam across the mouth of this food tray was used to detect anticipatory R_T's. It was hoped that this more standard arrangement of lever and food tray would yield R_T data more directly relevant to the velocity gradients already reported.

Results of these preliminary investigations were in essential agreement with those of Denny, Wells, and Maatsch, but with more extended training it was found that essentially all anticipatory food-tray entries were eliminated from the behavior of most of the *S*s. Use of this technique thus appeared to necessitate either the use of preasymptotic data or the selection of only about one-quarter of the *S*s. Since neither of these alternatives was acceptable, this technique was abandoned for the time being.

Experiment Four

The results of the preliminary investigations just reviewed bring into some question the role assigned to R_T by the present model of HBSs. Although considerable individual variability was present in the degree to which asymptotic response-velocity gradients displayed a terminal decrement, almost all *S*s showed such a decrement, even though only about one-fourth of the *S*s showed any sustained anticipatory R_T's as measured by food-tray entries. It would thus appear either that the role of R_T's has been incorrectly conceived in the present model, or that actual entry into the food tray is a relatively insensitive measurement of these anticipatory R_T's. The latter alternative is certainly not unlikely in view of the fact that considerable interference with the HBS could occur as a result of fractional anticipatory components of R_T, without these ever becoming sufficiently overt or complete to be recorded as actual food-tray entries.

Before developing any further techniques involving the measurement of R_T, additional evidence that it does possess the role assigned to it by the present model would seem to be in order. Since R_T is presumably given rise to at the end of a HBS by presentation of S^R, elimination of this S^R, while maintaining lever pressing, might be expected to greatly attenuate the terminal decrements in response-velocity gradients. In order to investigate this possibility, 16 food-deprived (12 grams per day) rats were trained for 48 sessions on a sequence of 2, 8-response chains. A trial began with an increase in illumination, extension of the lever, and presentation of a 4-KHz. tone. After 8 lever presses, the lever was retracted for 10 seconds. Upon reextension of the lever, the tone changed to 10 KHz. and an additional 8 responses retracted the lever, terminated the tone, dimmed illumination, and generated a variable intertrial interval with a mean value of about 40 seconds. Ten such trials were run each session. For one-half the Ss (Group 0), only the second chain of 8 responses terminated with presentation of three 45-milligram food pellets. The remaining Ss (Group 100) served as a control group with both response chains terminating in presentation of three food pellets.

Mean response rate gradients for both groups in the first and second chains of the sequence are shown for the last 8 sessions (41–48) in Fig. 7. The first-chain gradient for Group 0 was essentially monotonic, while that for Group 100 showed a characteristic terminal decrement. In the second chain, the gradients for the two groups were similarly shaped, but that for Group 0 was somewhat higher in a positive behavioral contrast. The fact that these second-chain gradients did not show so drastic a terminal decrement as might have been expected may have been related to the very short interval separating the 2 chains in the sequence. In any case, the results of this experiment would certainly appear to support the assumed role of R_T in HBSs. These results further indicated that R_T in such cases does represent a response to food presentation, as opposed to other events at the end of the HBS, such as lever retraction or a period during which S^R is unavailable. This latter conclusion rests on the fact that all the end-of-chain events except for the presentation of food at the end of the first chain, were identical for the two groups in the present experiment.

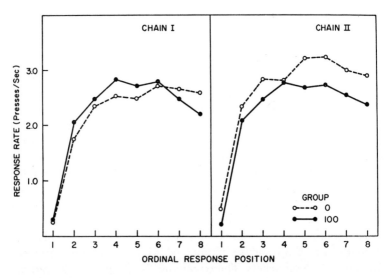

Fig. 7. Response-rate gradients in the two successive 8-response chains of Experiment Four, with and without reinforcement at the end of the first chain.

Several cautions should be appended here in respect to the generality of the attenuation of terminal decrements in response-velocity gradients obtained in the present experiment. In the first place, this effect appears to result only if the first chain has not had a history of S^R. When food was later eliminated from the first chain for Group 100, no attentuation of the terminal decrement was observed. Similarly, when Group 0 was later given experience with food at the end of the first chain, and then again had it omitted, the usual terminal decrement persisted. These results are in general agreement with those of Experiment Three in suggesting that local decrements in response-velocity gradients may be based on anticipatory avoidance of RCSs associated with *frustrative* non reinforcement (Amsel, 1958), or the omission of S^R in the presence of strong S^r.

A similar limitation worth mentioning here relates to an attempt to eliminate the terminal decrement in response-velocity gradients by introducing a 5-second delay between lever retraction and presentation of food in Ss which had been extensively trained on a 6-response chain without delay. Such a disappearance of the terminal decrement did emerge after about 4 sessions with the delay, but then gradually returned over the next 8 sessions. In addition to the possible aversive effects of the delay period after extensive experience with nondelayed S^R, there is a chance that competing behaviors occurring during the delay period eventually became anticipatory to the end of the HBS (Spence, 1956). Further consideration of this delay technique for eliminating terminal decrements in response-velocity gradients will have to await its use in naïve Ss, with attempts being made to control or measure the occurrence of competing behaviors during the delay period.

Experiment Five

With some reassurance concerning the importance of R_T in HBSs, attention may be returned to the search, using measurement of R_T, for a discriminability function for number of responses as a stimulus. The technique finally adopted for this purpose was initially suggested by the work of Mechner (1958a; 1958b; Mechner & Guevrekian, 1962). With Mechner's technique, rats are trained in a two-lever operant chamber, with S^R being delivered either upon the completion of N consecutive responses on lever A or else upon the completion of a minimum of N consecutive responses on lever A, followed by an additional response on lever B. If S switches to lever B before completing N responses on lever A, the entire sequence must be repeated.

Using this technique Mechner (1958a) was able to show that the median run length on lever A varied in approximately a direct proportion with variations in N through a range of at least 4 to 16. More precisely, the median number of lever-A responses, preceding a response on lever B, was always slightly more than the minimum number (N) required for S^R. In addition, the effects of increasing the probability (P) that N consecutive lever-A responses would be reinforced without a shift to lever B were qualitatively similar to the effects of increasing N. In a later study (Mechner & Guevrekian, 1962) it was shown that these results were insensitive to Ss' general motivational level as manipulated by deprivation.

It is clear from the data just reviewed that median length of lever-A runs would not provide a reasonable datum for scaling, since it was so sensitive to manipulation of the nonsensory variable P. However, it might be hoped that the variability of the frequency distribution of run lengths on lever A might provide a suitable psychophysical index. Unfortunately, Mechner (1958a) did not report values for such a variability measure in those cases where N or P was manipulated. It was reported, however, that the variability in lengths of lever-A runs increased with increases in either N or P, both of which effectively increased the median run length.

In order to adapt the Mechner technique to the context of the present investigations, several modifications were made. Although Mechner had contrived a terminal response by use of the second lever, the current model explicitly identifies R_T in an operant chamber with food-tray approach. Thus, the experiments to be reported here replaced Mechner's second lever with the breaking of a photobeam inside the food tray, as described in the introduction to this section. This modification should make results more comparable to the HBSs involved in the studies already reported here. In addition, Mechner's technique was modified to obtain discrete trials, again to achieve comparability to data which had already been obtained in the authors' laboratories.[3]

In the first experiment using this modification of Mechner's procedure, 8 mildly food-deprived (14 grams per day) rats were pretrained on a free-operant FR 20 with reinforcements of two

[3] Subsequent to the preparation of this report it was found that H. M. B. Hurwitz (1962, pp. 167–173) had reported use of food-tray responses in place of Mechner's second lever in a free-operant situation. Unfortunately, Hurwitz did not report variability values for lengths of lever-press runs either.

45-milligram food pellets. They were then all exposed to 4 sessions in which 16 or more lever presses, followed by food-tray entry, produced two food pellets and a 10-second lever retraction and blackout. Entry into the food tray before 16 lever presses had all the same consequences except no food was presented. Throughout the experiment, each session consisted of 100 food-tray entries, and daily food rations were corrected for amount of food obtained in the experimental apparatus. Following this preliminary training, *S*s were successively exposed to lever-press requirements (N) of 4, 8, 12, and 16, with the orders of exposure being assigned across *S*s according to a Latin square. Each value was in effect for 14 sessions before the next value was introduced, and a total of 6 such exposures were given so that each *S* was on two of the four values of N twice.

The upper frame of Fig. 8 shows the mean numbers of lever presses per trial, as a function of N, for all *S*s over the last 4 sessions of their last exposure to each value of N. Points were plotted separately on the basis of whether the previous trial had terminated in S^R. The liberty was taken of fitting straight lines to these data points by the method of least squares. As can be seen, these fits were very good and made clear that both functions displayed a slope of approximately 1.0, with the after-nonreinforcement function overshooting the minimum response requirement by slightly more than the after-reinforcement function. It should also be added that these fits to the mean data points provided good fits to all the individual *S*s, although there was a small degree of between-*S* variability in the Y-intercept of the individual functions. These results were in general agreement with those of Mechner (1958a) and offered evidence for the effectiveness of the present manipulation of N as a way of controlling the value of a standard RCS about which discriminability might be measured.

The lower frame of Fig. 8 shows the means of the individual *S*s' standard deviations about their mean run lengths. Again least-squares linear fits provided good descriptions of the data, with both slopes being about 0.1 and the Y-intercepts being somewhat higher following nonreinforced trials. In the case of the standard deviation data, both between- and within-*S*s variability was somewhat more of a problem than had been the case with the means data. This appeared to be caused by a greater lack of long-term

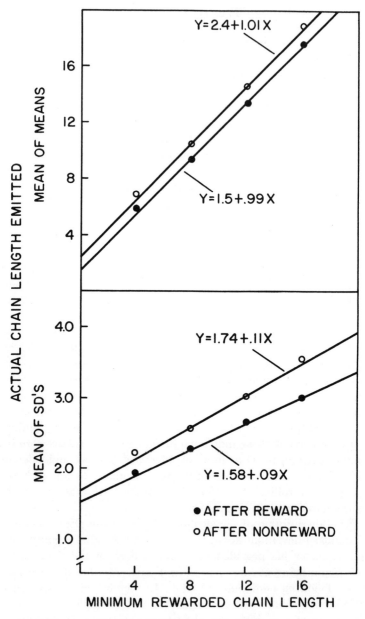

FIG. 8. Means and standard deviations of numbers of consecutive lever presses in Experiment Five as a function of the minimum number required for reinforcement, with punishment for short runs.

stability in the former. Nevertheless, the linear functions shown in the figure reasonably described the individual Ss.

Turning to the question of the applicability of this data to obtaining a discriminability function for accumulated RCSs, it may be proposed that this can be accomplished by examining the function relating the standard deviations of run lengths to their means. Since both the means and the standard deviations were linear functions of N, they were necessarily linear functions of each other. In the present case the desired functions were

$$Y = 1.48 + .10X$$

for trials following nonreinforcement and

$$Y = 1.44 + .09X$$

for trials following reinforcement. Viewing food-tray entry as a yes-no response to the discriminability of accumulated RCSs from those at a standard represented by the mean number of lever presses preceding a tray entry, the two functions just given may be considered to represent differential sensitivity to accumulated RCSs as a function of the magnitude of the standard. Following this logic, these functions would appear to typify the previously presented, second version of Weber's law, where Y is the differential threshold, X is the standard stimulus, the Y-intercept is a detecton threshold, and the slope is Weber's fraction. The similarity of these two functions also indicates that accuracy of differential responding to number of responses as a stimulus was not sensitive to whether the last trial was reinforced, although this variable had the obvious effects of increasing both the mean and the variance of the next run.

Several possible limitations on the present results should be discussed. First, some caution should be urged in extrapolation to other values of N. Subsequent to the experiment just reported, the same Ss were exposed to Ns of 24 and then 36. All the relations stated here for N in the range of 4 to 16 held at these additional values. Nevertheless, there is undoubtedly some value of N beyond which these relationships would deteriorate if for no other reason than a failure to maintain stable responding. Extrapolation to values of N below 4 is even more questionable, since investigation of such values is effectively precluded by the distortion and positive skew which would necessarily be introduced into the run-length distributions.

Another source of concern with the present experiment is the possibility that the run-length distributions may have been distorted by the greater frequency of presentation of the RCSs of smaller numbers of responses. Such considerations might suggest the application of a per-opportunities correction (Anger, 1956) to the run-length distributions. Present space does not allow a detailed critique of such an analysis. Suffice it to indicate that the uncorrected distributions obtained in the present study were, for whatever reasons, quite symmetric.

Experiment Six

The results of the last experiment suggested that an adequate method for obtaining a discriminability function for number of responses as a stimulus had been obtained and that Weber's law held for that dimension. In order to obtain such a technique, however, several aspects of the discrete-trials FR procedures used earlier were modified. The degree to which the present results may be generalized to the earlier procedures must thus be viewed with some caution until the effects of these modifications are understood.

One difference between the procedure of the last experiment and a discrete-trials FR chain was the lack of a distinctive exteroceptive stimulus change following completion of the requisite number of lever presses. This modification was certainly desirable in that it assured placement of R_T solely on the basis of RCSs. In terms of the present model for HBSs, the reintroduction of such an exteroceptive cue should simply decrease the over-all mean and variability of anticipatory R_T's. Fortunately this assumption may be easily tested. A related problem was the lack of absolute control over number of lever presses per trial with the current technique. This control is of course necessary, since number of lever presses has become the dependent variable. The importance of this factor might be investigated by examining the effects of extensive experience with an enforced number of lever presses on subsequent performance in the present paradigm.

Probably the most serious departure of the present procedure from that of a discrete-trials FR was in respect to the consequences of a premature food-tray entry. In the previous FR paradigms such an intrusion had no programmed consequences, but in the present procedure it produced a nonreinforced intertrial interval and reinitialization of the lever-pressing requirement. In order to assess the effects of this departure, a slight modification of the last experiment was done with 8 naïve rats. The procedures were identical except that a food-tray entry before N lever presses had no programmed consequences. Thus an intertrial interval and initialization of the lever-press sequence occurred only after S^R, which in turn followed the first tray entry subsequent to N lever presses.

The results of this experiment are depicted in Fig. 9. As can be seen, both the means and the standard deviations of the run-lengths distributions were again well fit by straight lines. The segregation of run lengths on the basis of whether the previous tray entry was reinforced had a rather different significance in the present experiment than in the last. In the present case all trials terminated with S^R, so the after-reinforcement functions refer to lever-pressing before the first tray entry of a trial, while the after-nonreinforcement functions refer to any lever-pressing runs subsequent to this first entry. The much lower slope of the means function after nonreinforcement was thus the result of Ss' executing an initial run which was linearly related to N, with the length of any subsequent runs being relatively independent of N. It should also be noted that even in the means function after reinforcement there was a progressively larger undershooting as the minimum response requirement increased. This cumulative error was not surprising in view of the removal of all programmed consequences of such errors.

Turning to the question of discriminability relations for the present data, the functions relating standard deviations of run lengths to their means were

$$Y = 1.10 + .21X$$

after reinforcement and

$$Y = -1.70 + 1.28X$$

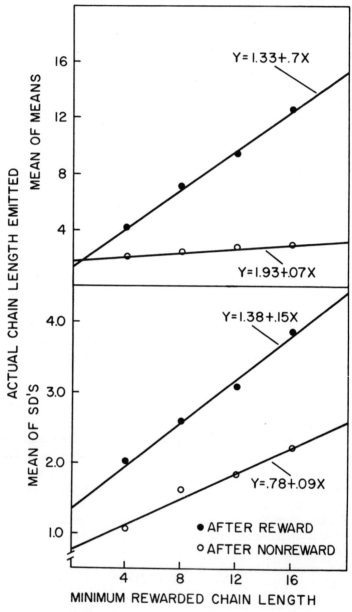

Fig. 9. Means and standard deviations of numbers of consecutive lever presses in Experiment Six as a function of the minimum number required for reinforcement, with no programmed consequences for short runs.

228

after nonreinforcement. Comparing the after-reinforcement function to those of the previous experiment, the apparently lower detection threshold and larger Weber fraction were undoubtedly the effects of removing punishment for premature tray entries. This should provide sufficient caution against interparadigm generalization of the Weber fractions provided by any of the present techniques. On the other hand, the fact that a linear relationship was again obtained, in spite of these parameter variations, suggests that the generality of Weber's law for the current stimulus dimension may be quite extensive.

Finally, the negative detection threshold and extremely insensitive Weber fraction for the after-nonreinforcement function is probably best interpreted as indicative of responding without regard for RCSs. That is to say that when premature tray entries had no programmed consequences, Ss executed an initial run of lever presses under the control of N and mediated by RCSs. If this run was not sufficiently long to produce S^R, then a series of very short runs was executed independently of N or RCSs, until S^R was obtained.

Conclusions

It seems reasonable to conclude that the results presented in this chapter clearly indicate the utility of a stimulus-oriented approach to the problems of behavioral chaining. More particularly, the present model, involving the postulation of a gradient of response-correlated stimuli functioning as conditioned reinforcements for homogeneous responding and discriminative stimuli for nonhomogeneous, terminal components of a behavior sequence, appears to provide a reasonable framework for the integration of a wide variety of phenomena from homogeneous behavior sequences. The clear demonstration of the applicability of Weber's law to the stimulus dimension of number of responses not only provides a basis for quantification of the present model but should also remove some of the stigma resulting from the alleged impossibility of measuring response-correlated stimuli by purely behavioral techniques. With the availability of the battery of techniques presented in this chapter, it is to be hoped that a number of additional questions

230   *Current Issues in Animal Learning*

concerning chained behavior might soon be answered. A complete list of such problems could not be provided here, but among them would be such issues as the integrity of behavioral chains in experimental extinction, and more precise identification of the nature of response-correlated stimuli by investigation of their modification by additional variables.

REFERENCES

Amsel, A. The role of frustrative nonreward in noncontinuous reward situations. *Psychol. Bull.*, 1958, **55**, 102–119.

Anger, D. The dependence of interresponse times upon the relative reinforcement of different interresponse times. *J. exp. anal. Behav.*, 1956, **52**, 145–161.

Collier, G., Knarr, F. A., & Marx, M. H. Some relations between the intensive properties of the consummatory response and reinforcement. *J. exp. Psychol.*, 1961, **62**, 484–495.

Crespi, L. P. Quantitative variation of incentive and performance in the white rat. *Amer. J. Psychol.*, 1942, **55**, 467–517.

Deaux, E. B. Measurement of anticipatory goal responding under different magnitudes of reward and magnitude shifts in instrumental runway conditioning. Unpublished doctoral dissertation, University of Texas, 1967.

Denny, M. R., Wells, Ruth H., & Maatsch, J. L. Resistance to extinction as a function of the discrimination habit established during fixed-ratio reinforcement. *J. exp. Psychol.*, 1957, **53**, 451–456.

DiLollo, V., & Walker, E. L. Speed and basal resistance level (BRL) in a segmented straight alley. *Psychol. Rec.*, 1964, **14**, 499–505.

Donahoe, J. W., Schulte, V. G., & Moulton, A. E. Stimulus control of approach behavior. *J. exp. Psychol.*, 1968, **78**, 21–30.

Drew, G. C. The speed of locomotion gradient and its relation to the goal gradient. *J. comp. Psychol.*, 1939, **27**, 333–372.

Ferster, C. B., & Skinner, B. F. *Schedules of reinforcement.* New York: Appleton-Century-Crofts, 1957.

Hull, C. L. The goal gradient hypothesis and maze learning. *Psychol. Rev.*, 1932, **39**, 25–43.

Hull, C. L. The rat's speed-of-locomotion gradient in the approach to food. *J. comp. Psychol.*, 1934, **17**, 393–422.

Hull, C. L. *Principles of behavior.* New York: Appleton-Century, 1943.

Hull, C. L. *A behavior system.* New Haven: Yale University Press, 1952.

Hurwitz, H. M. B. Some properties of behavior under fixed ratio and counting schedules. *British Journal of Psychology*, 1962, **53**, 167–173.

Kelleher, R. T. Chaining and conditioned reinforcement. In W. K. Honig (Ed.), *Operant behavior: Areas of research and applications.* New York: Appleton-Century-Crofts, 1966.

Keller, F. S., & Schoenfeld, W. N. *Principles of psychology.* New York: Appleton-Century-Crofts, 1950.

Knarr, F. A., & Collier, G. Taste and consummatory activity in amount and gradient of reinforcement functions. *J. exp. Psychol.*, 1962, **63**, 579–588.

Logan, F. A. *Incentive: How the conditions of reinforcement affect the performance of rats.* New Haven: Yale University Press, 1960.

Mechner, F. Probability relations within response sequences under ratio reinforcement. *J. exp. anal. Behav.*, 1958a, **2**, 109–121.

Mechner, F. Sequential dependencies of the length of consecutive response runs. *J. exp. anal. Behav.*, 1958b, **2**, 229–233.

Mechner, F., & Guevrekian, L. Effects of deprivation on counting and timing in rats. *J. exp. anal. Behav.*, 1962, **5**, 463–466.

Perin, C. T. The effect of delayed reinforcement upon the differentiation of bar responses in white rats. *J. exp. Psychol.*, 1943, **32**, 95–109.

Platt, J. R., Senkowski, P. C., & Mann, R. Discrimination, contrast and chaining: Effects of prior training without discriminanda and response-contingent delay at discriminandum presentation. *J. exp. Psychol.*, 1969, **82**, 38–45.

Rilling, M. E. Number of responses as a stimulus in fixed interval and fixed ratio schedules. *J. comp. physiol. Psychol.*, 1967, **63**, 60–65.

Rilling, M. E., & McDiarmid, C. G. Signal detection in fixed-ratio schedules. *Science*, 1965, **148**, 526–527.

Skinner, B. F. *The behavior of organisms.* New York: Appleton-Century, 1938.

Spence, K. W. The role of secondary reinforcement in delayed reward learning. *Psychol. Rev.*, 1947, **54**, 1–8.

Spence, K. W. The relation of response latency and speed to the intervening variables and N in S–R theory. *Psychol. Rev.*, 1954, **61**, 209–216.

Spence, K. W. *Behavior theory and conditioning.* New Haven: Yale University Press, 1956.

Weiss, R. F. Deprivation and reward magnitude effect on speed throughout the goal gradient. *J. exp. Psychol.*, 1960, **60**, 384–390.

Weiss, R. F. Response speed, amplitude, and resistance to extinction as joint functions of work and length of behavior chain. *J. exp. Psychol.*, 1961, **61**, 245–256.

Wist, E. R. Amount, delay, and position of delay of reinforcement as parameters of runway performance. *J. exp. Psychol.*, 1962, **63**, 160–166.

Stimulus Control Within Response Sequences[1]

JOHN W. DONAHOE

University of Kentucky[2]

The major focus of the research reported in this chapter is the identification of the sources of stimulation which control performance within response sequences. A response sequence is defined as a conditional relationship between a series of instrumental behaviors $(R_1, R_2, \ldots, R_i, \ldots, R_t)$ and reinforcement such that the terminal response, R_t, of the sequence is followed by reinforcement. In the learning laboratory common examples of such sequences are locomotor behavior in the runway and bar pressing in the operant chamber. So defined, the term *response sequence* is essentially descriptive in nature and contains no necessary implications regarding the antecedents of which R_i is a function. Within the context of stimulus-response theory the determination of the antecedents of R_i is equivalent to the specification of the stimuli which control R_i. A response is said to be controlled by a stimulus to the extent that variations in some attribute of that stimulus are accompanied by variations in the probability of the response. The greater the covariation of the response with the stimulus attribute, the greater

[1] Support for the conduct of the investigations reported herein was provided by grants MH 07332 and MH 10706 from the United States Public Health Service, National Institute of Mental Health. Support for the preparation of this manuscript was provided by the Faculty Research Committee, University of Kentucky. Although their individual efforts are acknowledged in the appropriate places in the text, I would like to express special appreciation to four of my former students —W. Raney Ellis III, James H. McCroskery, W. Kirk Richardson, and Vincent G. Schulte. Not only did they assist in the conduct of these experiments, but also many of these investigations represent a collaborative enterprise in the fullest sense of the term. I should also like to thank three of my present students— Jeremiah P. Collins, James V. Couch, and Alexander Weinstein—for aid in preparing the manuscript.
[2] Now at the University of Massachusetts.

is the degree of stimulus control. Among the subclasses of stimulus control which may be discerned is discriminative stimulus control. In discriminative control the covariation of the response with the stimulus attribute is established by their joint correlation with some property of a reinforcing stimulus, customarily its presence and absence (Brown & Jenkins, 1968).

RESEARCH GOALS

The specific purposes of the present research were to determine the sources of discriminative stimulus control within response sequences as a function of : (a) the correlation of external stimulation with behavior within the response sequence, and (b) the correlation of internal (response-produced) stimulation with behavior within the response sequence.

Assessment of External Control

Behavior within a response sequence may be accompanied by stimulation which arises from sources beyond the periphery of the organism and which makes contact with the organism by way of one or more of the exteroceptive systems. Attributes of such external stimulation may vary systematically with features of the response sequence (correlated external stimulation) or may be independent of the response sequence (uncorrelated external stimulation). For example, in a runway situation stimuli arising from the start box are not accompanied by reinforcing events, whereas stimuli arising from the goal box are accompanied by such events. The runway situation, therefore, permits the correlation of external stimulation with the delay of reinforcement following responses within the sequence. Where such a correlation exists, there coexists the possibility of discriminative control of responding within the sequence by external stimuli (external control) in that responding in the presence of some stimuli (e.g., goal-box stimuli) is followed by reinforcement, whereas responding in the presence of other stimuli (e.g., start-box stimuli) is followed by nonreinforcement. Consistent with the principle of discriminative stimulus control, response probability should increase as the difference between prevailing stimulation and stimulation present during reinforcement decreases. Reasoning of this general form has been used to account for the "goal gradient" (Arnold, 1947; Hull, 1932, 1934, 1952). Contrariwise, if the attributes of external stimulation are uncorrelated with reinforcement, then a necessary condition for the establishment of discriminative control is not met and behavior within the response chain should not be under external control.

Assessment of Internal Control

In addition to external sources of stimulation, stimuli arising from preceding responses may potentially be a source of control for subsequent responding within the response sequence. Again, consider the runway situation. The internal stimulus consequences of R_t are followed by reinforcement with shorter delay than are the stimulus consequences of R_i. Therefore, a necessary condition for the discriminative control of responding by response-produced stimuli (internal control) is met. However, whether the foregoing correlation of internal stimulation with reinforcement is a sufficient condition for discriminative control is an empirical question which is dependent upon the stimulus properties of the number of responses (or some transformation of their occurrence such as relative frequency or rate). In order to assess the role of internal control of behavior within response sequences, it must be possible to arrange for circumstances in which the correlation between internal stimulation and reinforcement may be manipulated. Like external control, responding controlled by internal stimuli should increase in frequency as the internal stimulus situation present during reinforcement is more closely approximated within the response sequence.

METHODOLOGICAL CONSIDERATIONS

Selection of an Experimental Procedure

Desirable properties of a procedure to be used for the analysis of the stimulus control of performance within response sequences would include the following: (a) Responses which comprise the sequence should be easily and directly measureable. (b) Responses should be functional units of behavior in the sense that their probabilities of occurrence are sensitive to the contingencies of reinforcement. (c) The procedures should permit the experimental manipulation of the correlation of external stimulation with reinforcement independent of other variables. (d) The procedures should permit the manipulation of the correlation of internal (response-produced) stimulation with reinforcement independent of other variables. On both a priori and empirical grounds, the operant situation conforms to these requirements more closely than does the runway situation.

Clearly, the detailed and accurate measurement of performance within the response sequence is a prerequisite for the identification of the sources of stimulus control. In the operant situation in which a discrete response is used, the precision with which the response is monitored is subject to purely technical limitations. The frequency of the response, its distribution in time (Mueller, 1950; Skinner, 1938), and its vigor (Herrick, 1963; Notterman, 1959) can all be reliably assessed. The index of performance in the runway, however, is typically the time or its reciprocal—speed in one or more of the segments of the runway. This measure is an integration over a series of locomotor responses whose potential differences in topography, distribution in time, and vigor within a segment are refractory to measurement. The importance of a detailed specification of the response is indicated by the finding that mean response rate as a measure of performance masks features of the temporal distribution of responding which are of crucial significance for the development of an adequate theoretical analysis of discriminative stimulus control (Blough, 1969; Crites et al., 1967; Migler, 1964; Migler & Millenson, 1969). Analyses of comparable molecularity in the runway have been precluded by measurement problems, although similar complexities do appear to arise (e.g., Cotton, 1953).

Because of the ability to monitor precisely the discrete response in the operant situation, it has been possible to evaluate the sensitivity of the response to the contingencies of reinforcement. The available evidence indicates that the distribution of the individual response in time is clearly affected by the operation of reinforcement and that the exact nature of the contingency does importantly determine the temporal distribution of responding, as had been suggested by Skinner (1938). The foregoing conclusion is supported both by those studies in which the probability of reinforcement for a given temporal distribution of responding is determined indirectly by the schedule of reinforcement (Anger, 1956; Ferster & Skinner, 1957; Morse, 1966; Williams, 1968) and by those studies in which differential reinforcement of responses within the distribution is determined directly by synthetic schedules (Blough, 1966; Shimp, 1966, 1967).

In order to investigate the control which external stimulation exerts over behavior within a response sequence, it is necessary that the experimenter be able to manipulate the correlation of the attributes of external stimuli with the operation of reinforcement. This can be readily accomplished in the operant situation by providing a stimulus whose attributes covary with some property of the schedule of reinforcement. Indeed, preliminary investigations (Ferster & Skinner, 1957) of the effects of external stimulation have been undertaken in which the stimulus attribute has been corrclated with either responses ("added counter," pp. 89–109) or time ("added clock," pp. 266–298). In the runway situation, however, the systematic experimental manipulation of external stimulation is rendered difficult by virtue of the fact that the locomotor response moves the organism through space, thereby permitting the behavior to exert considerable control over incident stimulation. To use Brunswik's term, an "artificial tying" (Brunswik, 1947) of external stimulation to behavior within the response sequence exists in the runway situation.

If the contribution of internal response-produced stimulation to performance within the response sequence is to be determined, it must similarly be possible to manipulate the correlation of these stimuli with reinforcement. In the operant situation, the correlation of responding with reinforcement may be varied by means of the rule, or schedule, of reinforcement, which states the necessary and sufficient conditions under which R_t is followed by reinforcement. For example, a fixed-ratio rule states that R_t produces reinforcement when $t = c$, where c is some fixed number of responses. The complexity of the rule and the nature of the terms in it (responses, time, stimuli, and various interactions of these) may be specified at the discretion of the experimenter, as limited by only technical considerations. In the runway, however, the rate at which responding occurs within the sequence is necessarily related to the delay in unconditioned reinforcement (food) or conditioned reinforcement (goal-box stimuli). Typically, the faster the oganism runs, the sooner is reinforcement forthcoming. While the sign of the correlation may be altered (e.g., Logan, 1960, 1961), the runway situation—because of its fixed length—permits only an approximately constant number of locomotor responses to be emitted before the goal box is reached. The "artificial tying" of response speed and external stimulation to reinforcement and to each other is a property of the runway as a procedure and not of locomotor behavior as a response system. With an activity wheel, a runway of variable length, the foregoing remarks do not apply, although the apparent nonindependence of successive locomotor responses does reduce their sensitivity to experimental manipulations (Knarr & Collier, 1962, p. 586; Williams, 1966).

Some Terminological Problems

Finally, before proceeding to a presentation of experimental work directed toward the identification of the sources of stimulus control of responding within behavior sequences, some comment should be made regarding certain terminological problems which arise when attempts are made to integrate the results obtained from laboratories which employ runway procedures and those which employ operant procedures. The words of Thorndike (1911), speaking of the then-current controversy between structuralism and behaviorism, reflect a portion of the motivation for the present attempt at clarification: "Worthy men have studied both, both are probably worthy of study" (p. 19).

The argument has been made that the operant and runway situations represent fundamentally different types of response systems which generate *heterogeneous* and *homogeneous* response sequences respectively (Spence, 1956, pp. 43–45). This conclusion is drawn following a characterization of the operant situation as one involving a series of dissimilar or heterogeneous responses (locomoting to the bar, raising the forepaws, pressing the bar, lowering to the food cup, seizing the food pellet, and, finally, consuming the pellet). The runway situation, on the other hand, is viewed as consisting of a series of similar, or homogeneous, responses (locomotor responses) which culminate in the consummatory response. Though the inference that the homogeneous sequence presents fewer problems for analysis than the heterogeneous sequence can itself be questioned on the grounds that response generalization is minimized in the latter type of sequence, the focus of the present discussion is that the heterogeneous-homogeneous distinction is only fortuitously associated with the bar-pressing and locomotor situations cited in the illustrations. A counterargument can be made, for example, that the levels of description used in the characterizations of the two situations are not comparable. Thus, one could with equal justification describe the operant situation as a homogeneous series of bar-pressing responses and the runway situation as a heterogeneous series of different leg movements. More constructive, and less polemical, is the observation that bar pressing as described in the illustration is reinforced on a continuous schedule of reinforcement, whereas locomotor responses in the runway illustration are reinforced on a ratio schedule. In short, the illustration confounds the two response systems with two different schedules of reinforcement. Such an analysis, therefore, identifies the reinforcement of locomotor responses in the runway with a ratio schedule of reinforcement of bar pressing in the operant chamber (Keller & Schoenfeld, 1950, pp. 93–94). Although doing so was inconsistent with his earlier treatment, in a later section of the same work Spence (1956) would appear to concur with the present analysis when he stated: "What these studies [those dealing with schedules of reinforcement] have demonstrated is that one can establish very long instrumental chains. Translated into the runway situation these types of studies are not nearly so dramatic as they appear in the context of the lever box, for what they have shown is that one can train a rat to take a great many steps, i.e., run a long way, to get a piece of food" (pp. 122–123).

Once the identification of runway behavior with a ratio schedule of reinforcement is made, however, a change is necessitated in the manner in which the term partial, or intermittent, reinforcement is used in runway and operant situations. A fixed-ratio schedule of reinforcement in the operant situation is no longer an intermittent, but a continuous, schedule of reinforcement. Similarly, only schedules in which reinforcement follows R_t with $p < 1$ should be termed partial reinforcement schedules (cf. Ferster & Skinner, 1957, pp. 67–71). Fortunately, a number of investigators share these terminological translations either implicitly or explicitly (e.g., Gonzalez, Bainbridge, & Bitterman, 1966; Porter & Hug, 1965; Weiss, 1961) and, increasingly, the adequacy of the translation is being evaluated on empirical grounds in the laboratory rather than on a priori grounds in unproductive disputation.

GENERAL STATEMENT OF METHODS

Contained in this section are a statement of the research strategy and a presentation of those aspects of the procedure which are common to the various experiments.

Research Strategy

In order to vary the correlation of external and internal (response-produced) stimulation with reinforcement, and thereby to assess the extent of external and internal control of performance within response sequences, the procedures described in Table 1 were employed. The rows and columns of Table 1 define the relationships of external and internal stimulation to delay of reinforcement, while the cells of the table contain appropriate operant procedures.

The condition in which both external and internal stimulation are correlated with reinforcement is accomplished through the use of a fixed-ratio (FR) schedule and an external stimulus some attribute of which (e.g., the intensity of a visual stimulus) changes monotonically as a function of responding. This condition, represented in the upper left portion of Table 1, is seen as a functional replication of the runway situation in that the relationship of both external and internal stimulation to reinforcement is, in principle, sufficient to provide for discriminative control by both external and internal

TABLE 1

EXPERIMENTAL PROCEDURES FOR THE STUDY OF THE EXTERNAL AND INTERNAL (RESPONSE-PRODUCED) STIMULUS CONTROL OF APPROACH BEHAVIOR

Relationship of External Stimulation to Delay of Reinforcement	Relationship of Internal Stimulation (Response-Produced) to Delay of Reinforcement			
	Correlated		Uncorrelated	
	Response Schedule	Stimulus Schedule	Response Schedule	Stimulus Schedule
Correlated	Fixed Ratio	Monotonic Change with Responding	Fixed Interval	Monotonic Change with Time
Uncorrelated	Fixed Ratio	Uncorrelated with Responding	Fixed Interval	Uncorrelated with Time

NOTE: The relationship of external and internal stimulation to delay of reinforcement is represented as either correlated or uncorrelated for convenience only. The various relationships may, of course, assume any value between zero (no correlation) and unity (perfect correlation) inclusive, through the use of variable response and stimulus schedules.

sources of stimulation. Whether behavior within the sequence is actually controlled by both sources of stimulation is, of course, an empirical matter. In the lower left cell of Table 1, internal stimuli remain correlated with reinforcement by means of a FR schedule, but external stimuli are no longer in the appropriate relationship to reinforcement to meet the necessary conditions for discriminative control.

In the two conditions described in the major right column of Table 1, a fixed-interval (FI) schedule of reinforcement is used to uncorrelate rate of responding with reinforcement. The rule operative in FI schedules has the property that the delay in reinforcement is independent of responding which occurs before the passage of the time interval specified by the particular FI schedule (Morse, 1966, p. 63). The first response after the passage of t-seconds is then reinforced. Thus, in principle, the essential conditions for internal control of behavior within the response sequence are not necessarily prescribed by the FI schedule. As was the case with the FR schedule, the relationship of external stimulation to reinforcement is varied to assess the contribution of external stimulus control to performance.

Subjects and Apparatus

Albino rats (Sprague-Dawley strain) were used in the majority of the investigations reported here. The animals were approximately 90 days old upon receipt by the laboratory. After 7 to 10 days of acclimatization, during which free-feeding weights were obtained, Ss were typically reduced to 80% of normal body weight and maintained at this level for the duration of the experiment. Some investigations were also conducted in which pigeons (White Carneau) were used. The birds were from 1 to 3 years of age and, after the determination of free-feeding weights, were also maintained at 80% of normal body weight throughout the experiment. All Ss were fed a measured ration 1 hour following the completion of each daily experimental session.

The operant chambers used for the experiments employing rats as Ss contained a retractable bar which served as a manipulandum and a 1/2-inch white pilot lamp located 2 1/2 inches above the bar, which served as the source of external stimulation. The intensity of the light could be varied in intensity from 3 to 20 ftc. in 10 equal logarithmic increments. A food cup located 1 inch to the side of the bar provided at the appropriate times a reinforcement consisting of a 45-milligram Noyes food pellet. Four identically constructed chambers were employed in most studies and the experimental conditions were balanced across chambers. Four commercially constructed operant chambers (Lehigh Valley Electronics) were used in the investigations employing pigeons as *S*s. Each chamber contained a 1-inch response key which served as the manipulandum and a food well through which *S* could receive 3-second access to mixed grain as reinforcement. Both the rat and pigeon chambers were located within sound-attenuating hulls which were ventilated by blowers and furnished with an 80-db. white noise which served as a masking stimulus. The experimental events were programmed by means of electromechanical and solid-state timing and switching circuits located in rooms adjacent to the experimental rooms. Responding was monitored by counters and cumulative recorders.

Measurement of Stimulus Control

During FR schedules in which the number of responses per trial is constant, the time was recorded in n successive fractions of the trial. Thus, if there were t responses per trial, each trial was divided into n fractions, each containing t/n responses. The time measures were converted to units of responses/minute by dividing the constant number of responses per fraction by the variable time required to complete that fraction of the sequence. During FI schedules in which the time per trial is constant, the number of responses in successive fractions of the trial was recorded. The responses occurring within the n fractions of each trial were converted to units of responses/minute by dividing the variable number of responses per fraction by the constant amount of time per fraction. Thus, the measure of performance within response sequences, both for sequences in which responding was correlated with reinforcement (FR schedules) and for sequences in which responding was uncorrelated with reinforcement (FI schedules) was the same—rate of responding in successive fractions of the sequence.

The shape of the function describing the relationship between rate of responding and successive fractions within the response sequence was used as the measure of stimulus control. Hereafter, this function is referred to as the approach gradient. The measure was selected consistent with the assumption that the response strength at any given fraction within the sequence is inversely related to the difference between the stimuli prevailing during that fraction and the external and internal stimulus conditions present when the terminal response of the sequence is reinforced. That is, response strength should be relatively high when the prevailing stimuli are similar to those stimuli present when the response is reinforced and relatively low when the prevailing stimuli are dissimilar to stimuli present when the response is reinforced. The foregoing is essentially a statement of the principle of stimulus generalization. With the correlation of responding with reinforcement held constant, the response strength within successive fractions of the sequence should increase more rapidly with a correlated than with an uncorrelated external stimulus to the extent that performance is under external control. Similarly, with the correlation of external stimuli with reinforcement held constant, differences in the shape of the approach gradients reflect internal control of performance. The data from the experiments which follow were evaluated by appropriate analysis of variance procedures.

EXTERNAL vs. INTERNAL CONTROL

Responding Uncorrelated with Reinforcement

The investigations described in this section deal with stimulus control within response sequences in which responding within the sequence is uncorrelated with reinforcement by means of a FI schedule. The procedures employed are those described in the major right column of Table 1.

Experiment One: Correlated vs. Uncorrelated External Stimulation

The purpose of the first experiment was to determine whether external stimuli control performance within response sequences in which responding is uncorrelated with reinforcement. Sixteen deprived albino rats, after being given two days of feeder training and two days of continuous reinforcement, were randomly assigned to two groups of 8 Ss each. Both groups received reinforcement on a FI 50-second schedule of reinforcement for 15 daily sessions of 20 FI trials per session. In this experiment the bar remained throughout the session in the chamber, which was completely darkened during the intertrial interval of 90-seconds duration. The group with a correlated external stimulus began each trial with a stimulus intensity of 3 ftc. and received ten equal logarithmic increments in intensity, to a maximum of 20 ftc. at the completion of the 50-second trial. The group with an uncorrelated external stimulus received a constant intensity of 20 ftc. throughout the trial.

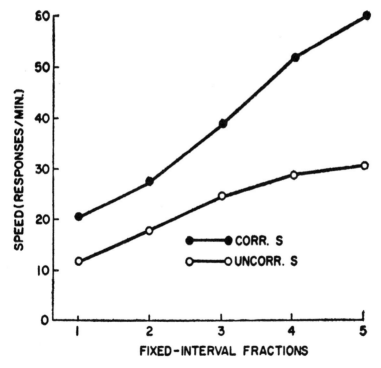

Fig. 1. Fixed-interval (FI 50-second) approach gradients as a function of the correlation of external stimulation with reinforcement. (From Donahoe, Schulte, & Moulton, 1968)

In this and all subsequent experiments the terminal light intensity persisted for 5 seconds after the terminal response of the sequence to ensure that the food pellet was consumed in the presence of the stimulus. The rate of responding was measured in five successive fractions of each FI response sequence.

Figure 1 depicts the mean response rate within the sequence for the correlated and uncorrelated stimulus conditions averaged over the last three days of training. The approach gradient obtained with the correlated external stimulus increased more rapidly than the gradient obtained with the uncorrelated external stimulus ($p < .01$). Thus, in a response sequence in which rate of responding within the sequence was uncorrelated with reinforcement, evidence for external stimulus control of performance was obtained. An additional finding was that the height of the gradient was greater with the correlated external stimulus ($p < .05$).

Experiment Two: Effects of Extended Training on External Control

In the preceding experiment, although the gradient associated with the correlated external stimulus increased more rapidly, the gradient associated with the uncorrelated stimulus also showed a positive slope. Therefore, while in principle the use of a FI schedule does not produce a correlation between rate of responding and reinforcement, in practice such a correlation does arise. The existence of a correlation between responding and reinforcement after exposure to a FI schedule has, of course, been known for some time (Skinner, 1938) and is referred to as the "FI scallop" (Ferster & Skinner, 1957). Though the mechanisms that generate the FI scallop are important objects of study in their own right (see Morse, 1966), the significance for the present inquiry is that the correlation of rate of responding with reinforcement provides a potential basis for the development of internal control within the response sequence. That is, after an extended exposure to a FI schedule in which low rates of responding are not followed by reinforcement and high rates of responding are followed by reinforcement, the stimulus consequences of responding are differentially associated with reinforcement and, consequently, the necessary conditions for the development of internal control are met.

The primary purpose of the present experiment was to determine if extended exposure to a FI schedule did, indeed, produce an approach gradient which was under internal stimulus control. In addition, the experiment was designed to investigate two other matters: (a) the role of nonreinforced responses during the dark intertrial interval in generating external stimulus control within the trial, and (b) the interrelationship between stimulus-intensity control, or dynamism, and discriminative stimulus control. With respect to the importance of intertrial responses for stimulus control, it can be argued that Ss in Experiment One were functionally exposed to FI 140-second trials (90 seconds in darkness followed by 50 seconds during which the light increased in intensity) instead of FI 60-second trials preceded by 90-second intertrial intervals. Accordingly, while external control was demonstrated, the origin of control could have been either the generalization of extinction effects from the dark intertrial interval into the trial or the generalization of acquisition effects from the terminal stimulus intensity of the trial to stimuli in earlier fractions of the trial. In order to determine which interpretation of the origin of external stimulus control was correct, the response bar was retracted during the dark intertrial interval of the present study, thereby eliminating the effects of intertrial responding as the origin of stimulus control within the trial.

Stimulus-intensity control—the correlation of response strength with stimulus intensity independent of the difference between the prevailing intensity and the intensity present during reinforcement —was assessed by employing two types of correlated external stimulus conditions. In one subgroup the correlated stimulus increased in intensity throughout the sequence; in the other subgroup the correlated stimulus decreased in intensity throughout the sequence. To the extent that stimulus-intensity control is a product of the same variables that underlie discriminative control, as is implied by the Perkins-Logan analysis of stimulus-intensity dynamism (Logan, 1954; Perkins, 1953), then both discriminative and stimulus-intensity control should covary in their occurrence.

Thirty-two deprived rats received feeder training and continuous reinforcement as in Experiment One and then were given 20 daily sessions of FI training. During Phase I of the experiment, each session consisted of 20 FI 60-second trials with a 60-second intertrial interval during which the response bar was retracted and the operant chamber darkened. Sixteen animals were given a correlated external stimulus which changed monotonically in 10 equal logarithmic increments from 3 to 20 ftc. For 8 of the *S*s in the correlated group the stimulus intensity increased during the trial; for the other 8 *S*s the stimulus intensity decreased. The remaining 16 *S*s received an uncorrelated external stimulus. Unlike the uncorrelated stimulus condition of the first experiment, in which the light intensity remained constant, the uncorrelated stimulus condition of the present experiment consisted of the same ten light intensities used in the correlated stimulus condition but given in random orders. All ten intensities appeared within each trial but the order varied

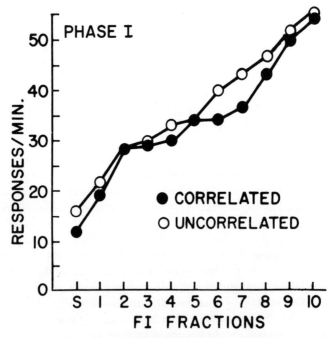

Fig. 2. Fixed-interval (FI 60-second) approach gradients during Phase II as a function of the correlation of external stimulation with reinforcement. Responding during the intertrial interval was prevented by retraction of the response bar.

from trial to trial, as determined by a 10 × 10 Latin square. This provided a superior control for the effects of the external stimulus, since both the correlated and the uncorrelated stimulus conditions were matched for stimulus intensity and stimulus change. The rate of responding was measured within ten successive fractions of each FI 60-second trial, and a measure of starting speed was also obtained. (Starting speed is the reciprocal of the latency of the first response transformed to units of responses/minute, to be comparable to the other measures of performance.)

The approach gradients obtained with the correlated and uncorrelated external stimulus conditions are shown in Fig. 2. These data were averaged over the last two days of training during Phase I. Unlike the gradients obtained in the first experiment, the present approach gradients did not differ as a function of the external stimulus correlation at this or any earlier stage of training. Accordingly, the external control previously obtained was a result of nonreinforced responding in the dark intertrial interval period. An examination of the increasing and decreasing intensity subgroups of the correlated stimulus condition also showed no effects of the stimulus intensity (dynamism).

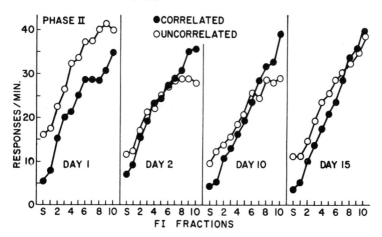

Fig. 3. Fixed-interval (FI 120-second) approach gradients during Phase II as a function of the correlation of external stimulation with reinforcement and days of training. The starting speed (S) and rate of responding during ten successive fractions of the response sequence are shown.

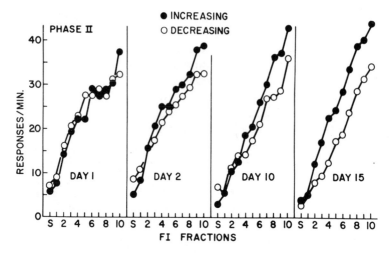

FIG. 4. Fixed-interval (FI 120-second) approach gradients during Phase II as a function of the direction of change in stimulus intensity for the correlated external stimulus condition.

In order to determine whether external control within the response sequence could be produced solely by responding during the sequence, the duration of the trial was increased to FI 120 seconds for all *S*s during Phase II. The external stimulus correlation remained as in Phase I. Increasing the duration of the FI trial was intended to permit sufficient nonreinforced responding during the initial fractions of the trial to produce discriminative control by the external stimulus. Figure 3 contains the approach gradients from days 1, 2, 10, and 15 of Phase II as a function of the external stimulus correlation. Now, in agreement with the results from the preceding experiment, the approach gradients with the correlated external stimulus were steeper than the gradients with the uncorrelated external stimulus ($p < .01$). That is, there was again evidence for external control of performance within response sequences in which rate of responding is uncorrelated with reinforcement. Note, however, that as training progressed the differences in the shapes of the approach gradients grew smaller so that, by the end of Phase II, the absolute magnitude of the effect of the external stimulus correlation was diminished. In Fig. 3 are shown the approach gradients for the increasing and decreasing stimulus-intensity subgroups of the correlated stimulus condition. The training days shown in Fig. 4 are the same as contained in Fig. 3. While the direction of change in stimulus intensity had no effect on the approach gradient during Phase I when discriminative control was absent, the shapes of the gradients were clearly affected during Phase II when discriminative control was present ($p < .01$). The effect of stimulus intensity was to increase response strength when the intensity was high and, generally, to decrease response strength when intensity was low. In contrast to discriminative control, stimulus-intensity control, or dynamism, became more pronounced as training progressed ($p < .01$).

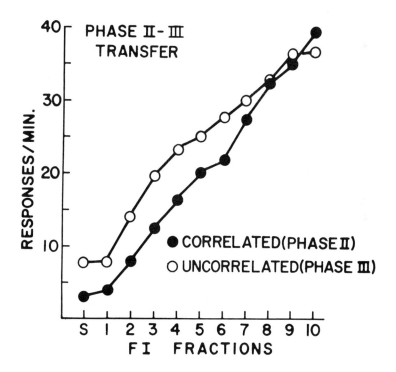

Fig. 5. Change in the FI 120-second approach gradient after transfer from correlated (Phase II) to uncorrelated (Phase III) external stimulus conditions.

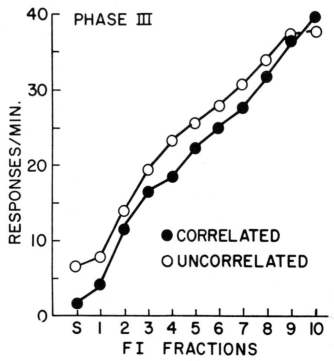

Fɪɢ. 6. Fixed-interval (FI 120-second) approach gradients during the final session of Phase III as a function of the correlation of external stimulation with reinforcement.

In order to determine whether external control of performance within the response sequence was present at the end of Phase II, one-half the Ss in the correlated stimulus condition were transferred to the uncorrelated stimulus condition during Phase III. One-half the Ss in the transfer test had received an increasing stimulus intensity during Phase II; the others had received a decreasing intensity during Phase II. Figure 5 contains the mean approach gradients from the last 10 trials of performance during the correlated stimulus condition and from the first 10 trials during the transfer to the uncorrelated stimulus condition. Evidence for external control was found in that the slope of the approach gradient was steeper with a correlated external stimulus than with an uncorrelated external stimulus ($p < .01$). The remaining 8 Ss in the correlated external stimulus condition continued to receive a correlated stimulus during ten additional days of training in Phase III. In Fig. 6, the approach gradient obtained from these *S*s on the last day of Phase III is compared with the gradient from those *S*s which continued to receive an uncorrelated external stimulus in Phase III. After 45 daily sessions (900 trials) of training, the shapes of the approach gradients no longer differed as a function of the correlation of external stimulation with reinforcement ($p > .05$), although there remained some tendency for the gradient from the correlated stimulus condition to be somewhat lower at the outset of the trial and higher at the termination of the trial.

Although no statistically reliable evidence of external control of performance was found during the final session of Phase III training,

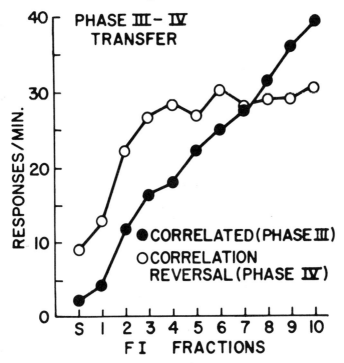

FIG. 7. Change in FI 120-second approach gradient after transfer from correlated external stimulation (Phase III) to a reversal of the correlation of external stimulation with reinforcement (Phase IV).

the possibility existed that the performance of the *S*s receiving the correlated and uncorrelated stimulus conditions was controlled by antecedents which were, in part at least, different. Accordingly, during Phase IV, the direction of the stimulus-intensity change was reversed within the correlated stimulus condition. If performance within the response sequence was solely under internal control, the shape of the approach gradient should have remained constant. If, on the other hand, performance was solely under external control, the slope of the approach gradient should have been reversed. That is, response strength should be highest at the beginning of the sequence and lowest at the end of the sequence. Figure 7 shows the outcome of reversing the correlation of external stimulation with reinforcement. The shape of the gradient was markedly affected ($p < .01$) but was a compromise between the expectation based upon exclusive control by internal stimuli and that based upon exclusive control by external stimuli.

Finally, it should be noted that in Experiment Two, in which responding during the intertrial interval was prevented by retraction of the response bar, no difference in the heights of the gradient were found as a function of the correlation of external stimulation with reinforcement. This finding was unlike that obtained in Experiment One, in which the height of the correlated gradient was above that of the uncorrelated gradient. However, because a randomly changing stimulus intensity was employed in the uncorrelated stimulus condition of Experiment Two rather than a constant stimulus as in Experiment One, the origin of the effect on gradient height remains unclear. Additional data bearing on this matter are presented in Experiment Four.

Based upon the findings from Experiments One and Two, the following conclusions may be drawn: (a) Performance during response sequences in which responding within the sequence is uncorrelated with reinforcement is controlled by correlated external stimuli (external control). (b) If no correlated external stimulus is provided, performance within the response sequence produces an approach gradient of positive slope (internal control). (c) With extended training, differences in the shapes of the approach gradients as a function of the correlation of external stimuli with reinforcement diminish, although residual external control may be shown by transfer tests. (d) Stimulus-intensity control, or dynamism, and discriminative stimulus control covary, with discrimination appearing to be a prerequisite for the differential effects of stimulus intensity on response strength.

Responding Correlated with Reinforcement

The investigations described in this section are concerned with the stimulus control of response sequences within which responding is correlated with reinforcement. As described in the left column of Table 1, FR schedules were employed with external stimulation being either correlated or uncorrelated with reinforcement.

Experiment Three: Correlated vs. Uncorrelated External Stimulation

The purpose of the present experiment was to determine if the shape of the approach gradient is a function of the correlation of external stimuli with reinforcement. After deprivation and pre-training, 16 Ss were given 10 daily sessions, each session consisting of 30 FR-20 trials separated by a 90-second intertrial interval during which the operant chamber was darkened. The response bars remained in the chambers throughout the session. For the 8 Ss receiving a correlated external stimulus, the light intensity increased in ten equal logarithmic increments from 3 to 20 ftc. within each FR trial. For the 8 Ss receiving an uncorrelated, external stimulus, the light intensity remained constant at 20 ftc. Responding was measured in four successive fractions of the response sequence.

The approach gradients obtained from the correlated and uncorrelated stimulus conditions averaged over the last three days of training are shown in Fig. 8. No evidence for external control of performance within the sequence was found in that the shapes of the gradients did not differ as a function of the external stimulus correlation ($p > .05$). Note, however, that the height of the correlated gradient was greater than that of the uncorrelated gradient ($p < .01$) as had been obtained in Experiment One, in which the response bar was also available during the intertrial interval. Note also that response rate in the present experiment, in which responding was correlated with reinforcement, was uniformly greater

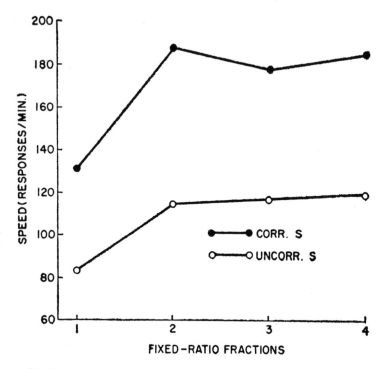

FIG. 8. Fixed-ratio (FR-20) approach gradients as a function of the correlation of external stimulation with reinforcement. (From Donahoe, Schulte, & Moulton, 1968)

than that obtained in Experiment One, in which responding was uncorrelated with reinforcement ($p < .01$).

In order to determine the generality of the failure to find external control within sequences in which responding is correlated with reinforcement, two additional control experiments were conducted. Ellis (1967) replicated Experiment Three but used auditory click frequency rather than visual intensity as the correlated stimulus attribute. No evidence of external stimulus control was obtained. Thus, the previous finding was not a function of the particular stimulus dimension used in Experiment Three. A second control experiment was run, in which the temporal duration of the response sequence was equated through the use of FI 20-second and FR-40 schedules (Donahoe, Schulte, & Moulton, 1968). With the duration

of the trial equated, external control was found when responding
was uncorrelated with reinforcement by way of the FI procedure
($p < .025$) and no external control was found when responding
was correlated with reinforcement using the FR procedure ($p >
.05$). Thus, differences in trial duration were not responsible for the
failure to find external control in Experiment Three.

*Experiment Four: Effect of the Length of the Response Sequence on Internal
Control*

The internal, correlated stimulus conditions prevailing throughout the approach sequence were manipulated by using two FR
sequences of different length (FR 20 and FR 40) within each of the
conditions of external stimulation. Increasing the length of the
sequence was designed to increase the difference between response-
produced stimuli at the beginning and end of the trial. To the extent
that FR approach behavior is under the control of internal stimuli,
the shape of the approach gradients should differ as a function of
the length of the sequence. To optimize internal control of behavior
within the FR sequence, the bar was retracted from the test chamber
between trials. Thus, unlike Experiments One and Three, in which
responding was permitted during the intertrial interval, each
response reduced within-sequence delay. Prevention of intertrial
responding also permitted an evaluation of the hypothesis that the
greater response speed found under correlated external stimulus
conditions in Experiments One and Three arose from nonreinforced
intertrial responses.

As in Experiment Three, a FR approach sequence was employed
and the external stimulus was either correlated or uncorrelated
with responding, Two correlated external stimulus conditions
were used, a stimulus whose intensity *increased* throughout the
approach sequence (Group I) and a stimulus whose intensity
decreased (Group D). Group D provided a control for the effects of
stimulus intensity independent of the correlation of intensity with
reinforcement. Two uncorrelated stimulus conditions were also
used. For one group the stimulus intensity remained *constant*
(Group C). For the second group the stimulus intensity varied
randomly within each approach sequence (Group R). Group R

provided a control for the effects of response-contingent, external stimulus change on approach behavior and also permitted an evaluation of the hypothesis that differences in response speed previously found between correlated and uncorrelated external stimulus conditions (Experiments One and Three) resulted from greater net intratrial generalization of extinction effects under constant stimulus conditions. If the hypothesis of differential intratrial generalization of extinction is valid, response speed in Group C should be less than in Group R.

Following deprivation and pretraining, the 64 Ss were randomly assigned to one of the eight treatment combinations generated by the four external stimulus conditions (I, D, C, and R) and two lengths of fixed-ratio schedule (FR 20 and FR 40). In Group I the intensity increased from 3 to 20 ftc. in ten equal logarithmic increments; in Group D the intensity decreased in the same manner from 20 to 3 ftc. In Group R the intensity changed so that all 10 stimulus intensities were present within each FR trial but the change was random. Across all Ss in Group R, the average intensity within each fraction of the fixed-ratio schedule was equal, for the intensities were selected according to a Latin-square principle. In Group C the stimulus remained at the geometric mean of the ten stimulus intensities, 7.8 ftc., throughout each trial. For all groups, therefore, the average intensity of the external stimulus was identical. Ss received 12 daily sessions, with each session consisting of 20 FR trials separated by a 60-second intertrial interval during which the response bar was retracted and the operant chamber was darkened. Response rate within ten successive fractions of the sequence and starting speed were measured.

Figure 9 depicts the effects of external stimulus correlation and FR length on the approach gradient averaged over the last three days of training. As in Experiment Three, there was no evidence of external control, since the shape of the gradients did not differ as a function of the correlation of external stimulation with reinforcement ($p > .05$). The effects of internal stimulation are shown by a comparison of the shapes of the gradients obtained with the two lengths of FR sequences. The shape of the gradients differed reliably ($p < .01$), with the steeper gradient being obtained with the FR-40 sequence length. Thus, the assumption that response sequences in

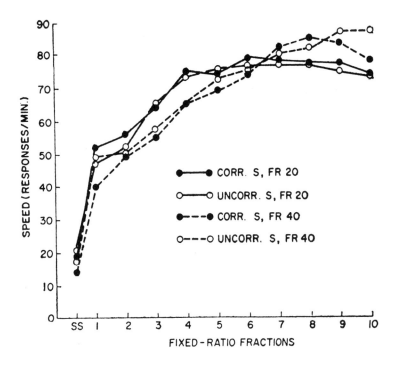

FIG. 9. Fixed-ratio (FR) approach gradients as a function of the correlation of external stimulation with reinforcement and the length of the response sequence. (From Donahoe, Schulte, & Moulton, 1968)

which responding is correlated with reinforcement are under internal control was supported. As in Experiment Two, the prevention of intertrial responding eliminated the differences in gradient height previously observed in Experiments One and Three. This finding is consistent with the interpretation that the locus of earlier differences in gradient height was nonreinforced intertrial responding. No support was obtained for the hypothesis that differences in gradient height were caused by differences in net generalized extinction effects, since the C and R subgroups within the correlated stimulus condition did not differ in response rate ($p > .05$).

Experiment Five: A Test of the Hypothesis that Behavior within Sequences in which Responding Is Correlated with Reinforcement Is Under Internal Control

Rather than being controlled by external stimulation, the findings in Experiment Four are consistent with the hypothesis that performance in response-correlated sequences is controlled by internal stimulation of a response-produced origin. According to this view, the stimulus complex in which the nth response occurs is presumed to differ somewhat from the stimulus complex in which previous responses occur, and if the organism is reinforced in the presence of the stimulus consequences of n responses and is non-reinforced in the presence of the stimulus consequences of fewer responses, then response-produced stimulation comes to serve as a discriminative stimulus because of its consistent differential relationship to reinforcement.

The purpose of the present experiment was to alter the consistent differential relationship of response-produced stimulation to reinforcement by employing an intertrial-interval procedure which reversed the correlation between rate of responding and reinforcement present during the trial. Within the intertrial interval, responding was made to produce a delay in the onset of the response-correlated FR trial. Consequently, the relationship of reinforcement to rate of responding between trials was inconsistent with the relationship within trials. If the analysis of the origin of the control of response-correlated approach chains by response-produced stimulation is correct, then the introduction of inconsistency should reduce the weighting given internal stimuli and permit the development of the control of responding by external stimulation. The experimental design permitted the investigation of two forms of stimulus control: (a) discriminative stimulus control and (b) stimulus-intensity control. Again, to the extent that stimulus-intensity control is a product of the same variables that underlie discriminative control (Logan, 1954; Perkins, 1953), then both forms of stimulus control should be simultaneously evident.

The 32 Ss were randomly assigned to one of the four treatment groups generated by the conditions of external stimulation. For Groups I and D the intensity of the stimulus light was correlated with reinforcement. In group I the intensity *increased* with responding from 3 to 20 ftc. In Group D the intensity *decreased* with responding from 20 to 3 ftc. For groups R and C the intensity of the stimulus light was uncorrelated with reinforcement. In Group R the same ten stimulus intensities used in Groups I and D were employed within each trial but the orders of presentation were *random*, as determined from a 10 × 10 Latin square. In Group C the stimulus intensity remained *constant* throughout the trial at 7.8 ftc., the geometric mean of the ten stimulus intensities. For all groups, therefore, the average intensity of the external stimulus was identical.

Following deprivation and pretraining, all Ss were given 18 daily sessions of training with a response-correlated approach sequence consisting of a FR schedule of 20 responses to one reinforcement (FR 20). Each session contained 20 FR-20 trials separated by intertrial intervals during which responding delayed the onset of the subsequent trial for t seconds. The value of t was gradually increased from 5 to 50 seconds to maintain the intertrial interval approximately constant at 60 seconds across all sessions. The measures of performance within the sequence were the rates of responding within ten successive fractions of the sequence and starting speed.

External control was assessed by a comparison of the gradients associated with the correlated and uncorrelated stimulus conditions. These gradients, averaged over the last three days of training, are shown in Fig. 10. With a correlated external stimulus the approach gradient gradually attained a maximum rate which was sustained for the remainder of the sequence. With an uncorrelated external stimulus the approach gradient increased more precipitously and then monotonically declined during the latter half of the sequence. These differences in gradient shape, shown in the upper portion of Fig. 10, were reliable ($p < .01$). Stimulus-intensity control was evaluated by a comparison of the shapes of the approach gradients obtained from Groups I and D within the correlated stimulus condition. As shown in the middle panel of Fig. 10, Group I achieved a maximum rate relatively late within the trial, whereas Group D achieved a maximum rate relatively early. Thus, each group displayed greatest response strength when stimulus intensity was high and less response strength when stimulus intensity was low. The differences in gradient shape were statistically significant

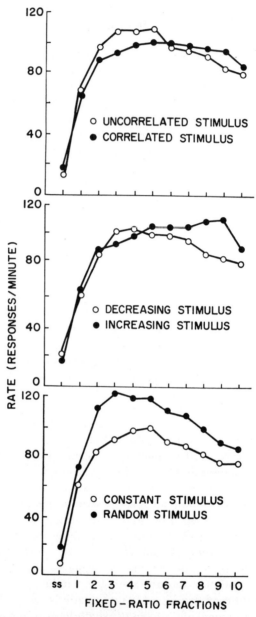

FIG. 10. Fixed-ratio (FR-20) approach gradients as a function of the correlation of external stimulation with reinforcement (upper panel), stimulus intensity (middle panel), and constant versus random uncorrelated external stimulation (lower panel). (From Donahoe & McCroskey, 1969)

($p < .025$) and provide evidence for stimulus-intensity control. Note that stimulus-intensity control was not found in Experiment Four, in which discriminative control was absent. The lower panel of Fig. 10 contains the approach gradients from Groups C and R. These gradients did not differ in shape or height ($p > .05$), although there was a tendency for response rates to be somewhat higher with the random, uncorrelated external stimulus.

Experiment Six: Direct Evidence for Discriminative Control Based upon Feedback from Responding

The results of experiments with response sequences in which responding within the sequence was correlated with reinforcement by means of the FR procedure are consistent with the hypothesis that such sequences are under internal control. Variations in the shape of the gradients as a function of the length of the sequence (Experiment Four) and as a function of inconsistency in the relationship of responding with reinforcement (Experiment Five) suggest that the stimulus consequences of responding are the origin of this internal control. Although there is a great deal of information from the response-differentiation literature (Notterman & Mintz, 1965) which strongly implicates response-produced stimuli in the control of subsequent responding, little direct evidence is available which would permit an examination of the discrimination and generalization of internal stimulus control.

Schulte (1969), in doctoral dissertation work conducted in our laboratory, sought to obtain such direct evidence. Subjects were exposed to a two-component, heterogeneous response sequence in an attempt to bring the second component (R_2) under the control of stimuli arising from the first (R_1). R_1 was a bar-pressing response, with the force required to operate the bar being varied. R_2 was a response of approaching and nosing open a door covering a food cup adjacent to the bar. For the discrimination groups, R_2 produced two 45-milligram pellets following an R_1+ response and nonreinforcement following an R_1- response. R_1+ and R_1- were presented in random alternation. For half the Ss in the discrimination condition, R_1+ was the depression of a 40-gram bar and R_1- was the depression of an 80-gram bar. For the remaining half of the discrimination Ss, the force required for $R_1 +$ and $R_1 -$ was reversed. In the discrimination groups, therefore, if R_2 was to come under stimulus control, the discrimination could only be mediated by means of the differential stimulus consequences of $R_1 +$ and $R_1 -$. Three control groups were run. One group received an R_1 of 40 grams followed by 50% random reinforcement of R_2; one group received an R_1 of 80 grams followed by 50% random reinforcement of R_2; and the final control group received a random alternation of R_1's of 40 and 80 grams, each R_1 followed by 50% random reinforcement of R_2. Six Ss served in each of the two discrimination and the three control groups.

Following deprivation and pretraining, all Ss received 30 daily sessions of discrimination training under the appropriate conditions. Each session consisted of 20 discrete trials of the R_1, R_2 sequence. At the completion of 30 sessions, all Ss were given a stimulus-generalization test along the dimension of the force required to execute R_1. The following values of R_1 were used: 20, 40, 60, 80, and 100 grams. The stimulus-generalization test was conducted in extinction for 5 consecutive sessions during which each value of R_1 was presented a total of 25 times. The dependent variable during both acquisition and generalization was the speed (reciprocal of latency) of approaching and opening the food cup (R_2) after executing a bar-pressing response (R_1).

Each S in the two discrimination groups acquired the discrimination ($.05 > p > .01$). That is, Ss rapidly opened the food-cup door after $R_1 +$ and slowly, if at all, opened it after $R_1 -$. No S in the three control groups responded differentially to the food-cup door preceding reinforced and nonreinforced trials. Therefore, the data from the discrimination phase of the experiment clearly indicated that response-produced stimulation arising from R_1 provided for the discriminative control of R_2. Direct evidence of internal control was found.

Figure 11 contains the mean generalization gradients obtained from the two discrimination groups and the three control groups. The dependent variable was the speed of approaching the food cup (R_2), expressed as a proportion of the total speed. Clearly, the discrimination groups approached the food cup more rapidly as the

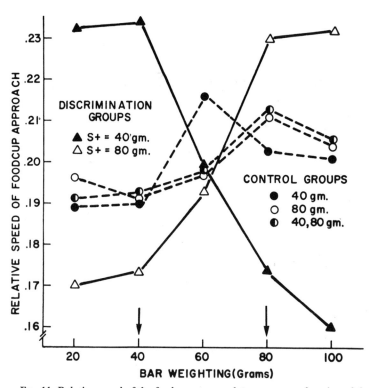

FIG. 11. Relative speed of the food-cup approach response as a function of the force required to operate the bar during generalization testing. (Adapted from Schulte, 1969)

similarity of the force required to execute R_1 more closely approximated R_1+ $(p < .01)$. Moreover, the generalization gradients associated with the group for which $R_1+ = 40$ grams and with the group for which $R_1+ = 80$ grams differed reliably in the expected manner $(p < .01)$. The speed of approach to the food cup for the control groups did not vary as a function of the force required to execute R_1 $(p > .05)$. Thus, generalization gradients along the dimension of response-produced stimuli were obtained which were comparable to those customarily found with exteroceptive stimuli (Hanson, 1959).

The findings from the preceding experiments dealing with the stimulus control of performance within response sequences in which responding was correlated with reinforcement may be summarized as follows: (a) The average rate of responding was greater within sequences in which responding was correlated with reinforcement than within sequences in which responding was uncorrelated with reinforcement. (b) Without the introduction of special procedures, performance within correlated response sequences was not controlled by external stimulation. (c) Based upon the changes in gradient shapes which were produced by manipulation of the length of the sequence (Experiment Four) or by inconsistency in the correlation of responding with reinforcement (Experiment Five), sequences in which responding was correlated with reinforcement were controlled by response-produced stimuli (internal control). (d) Differences in response-produced stimuli provided a sufficient condition for the discriminative control of subsequent responses (Experiment Six). (e) The occurrence of nonreinforced responses in the presence of stimuli dissimilar to those prevailing during the reinforcement of the response, whether such nonreinforced responses occurred during the intertrial interval (Experiment Three) or during the sequence (Experiments Four and Five), increased the rate of responding within the sequence, particularly in the terminal fractions of the sequence. (e) As in experiments dealing with sequences in which responding was uncorrelated with reinforcement, stimulus-intensity control, or dynamism, and discriminative control covaried in their presence and absence (Experiment Five).

DISCUSSION

The foregoing experiments had as their major purpose the determination of the sources of stimulation which control performance within a ubiquitous aspect of behavior, the response sequence. The findings indicate that sequences in which responding is correlated with reinforcement are under internal control and that sequences in which responding is uncorrelated with reinforcement are under external control initially and then become increasingly under internal control as training progresses. Thus, while a number of theorists have alluded to the potential importance of response-produced stimuli (Hull, 1952, p. 158; Spence, 1956, p. 135), the present experiments indicate that a heavy explanatory burden must be borne by stimuli of internal origin in future theoretical analyses of response sequences, especially those sequences in which responding is correlated with reinforcement.

Consistent with the preceding conclusion, experiments employing a locomotor response in the runway have failed to alter performance within the response sequence by the manipulation of runway–goal–box similarity (DiLollo, 1964; Gonzalez & Diamond, 1960; Hughes, David, & Grice, 1960). Similarly, recent work conducted in the operant situation indicates that when response-produced stimulation is differentially associated with reinforcement, as occurs with FR schedules and with extended training under FI schedules, internal stimuli are the dominant source of discriminative control (Rilling, 1967, 1968).

In the determination of stimulus control it is important, however, to distinguish between instances in which a number of stimuli are simultaneously correlated with reinforcement, as was the case in the present experiments, and instances in which the number of correlated stimuli are restricted. For example, in a series of experiments performed by Dews (1965, 1966a, 1966b), the FI scallop persisted in a situation in which the argument that behavior was controlled by response-produced stimuli would be difficult to maintain. The competence of the organism for the establishment of control by a wide range of stimulation exists. Those sources of stimulation which furnish the controlling stimuli in a specific situation are a function of such variables as the characteristics of the sequence, stimulus dominance, and, perhaps, selective attention mechanisms (Mackintosh, 1965; Sutherland, 1964; Trabasso & Bower, 1968). To assume otherwise is to commit oneself to the pursuit of folly (Watson, 1907). What the present experiments have shown is that one characteristic of the sequence—the correlation of responding with reinforcement—importantly determines whether external or internal sources of stimulation control behavior within the sequence.

The conditions necessary for the production of discriminative control, whether deriving from external or internal origins, and the phenomena associated with the development of discriminative control within response sequences appear to be consistent with results obtained from traditional procedures for the study of discrimination formation (e.g., Hanson, 1959). Typically, such experiments have found that the presentation in random order of one stimulus (S+) in which reinforcement is available and of a second stimulus (S−) in which reinforcement is unavailable produce a decrease in the rate of responding to S− and an elevation in the rate of responding to S+ relative to the response rate found when only S+ training is given. In keeping with the findings from the discrimination literature, nonreinforced responding during the intertrial interval elevated responding during the trial (Experiments One and Three) and nonreinforced responding within the trial lowered responding during the initial fractions of the trial and elevated responding during the terminal fractions of the trial (Experiments Two, Four, and Five). Theoretical analyses of the facilitation of responding to S+ as a consequence of nonreinforced responding to S− have attributed the facilitatory effect to the emotional, or aversive, consequences of nonreinforcement (Amsel, 1962; Terrace, 1966). The view that stimuli associated with nonreinforcement acquire aversive properties would suggest that response strength increases as the terminal stimuli of the controlling stimulus dimension are approached not only because those are the stimuli to which the response has been most strongly conditioned but also because responding provides escape from noxious stimulation.

While interpretations relating findings from the discrimination literature with findings from the discriminative control of performance within response sequences seem promising, their verisimilitude is weakened by a potentially important procedural difference between the two classes of experiments: in studies of discrimination formation, the stimuli are presented in a random or quasi-random order. In studies of discriminative control by correlated stimuli within response sequences, however, the stimuli are necessarily always presented in a fixed, monotonic order. Thus, the transitions among stimuli are invariant in studies of discriminative control within response sequences but are variable in studies of discrimination formation. The last two experiments in the chapter deal with the effects of stimulus transitions, or sequences, on the acquisition and generalization of stimulus control.

SEQUENTIAL EFFECTS IN STIMULUS CONTROL

As previously indicated, knowledge of the formation and generalization of stimulus control as assessed in the operant situation arises chiefly from procedures in which the stimulus events are presented in a random order. In the typical study of discrimination formation, S + and S − are successively presented in random order, with acquisition scheduled during S + and extinction scheduled during S −. In the typical study of the generalization of stimulus control following discrimination formation, a number of test stimuli are successively presented in random order, with extinction scheduled during all stimuli. The purpose of the following experiments was to examine the role, if any, of sequential effects in the genesis of phenomena associated with the acquisition and subsequent generalization of stimulus control.

Experiment Seven: Sequential Effects in the Acquisition of Stimulus

According to the conditioning-extinction theory of discrimination formation (Spence, 1937), acquisition in the presence of the positive stimulus (S +) and extinction in the presence of the negative stimulus (S −) are sufficient conditions for the development of a discrimination. In so far as the formation of a successive operant discrimination is concerned, conditioning-extinction theory has been shown to be incomplete in that one or two sessions of extinction in the presence of S − following acquisition in the presence of S + does not produce the typical postdiscrimination gradient (PDG) of stimulus generalization (Honig, Thomas, & Guttman, 1959). The typical PDG is characterized by: (a) a displacement of the mode of the PDG away from S − (peak shift), (b) an increase in the height of the PDG in the vicinity of the mode (contrast), and (c) an increase in the slope of the PDG on the S − side of the gradient (steepening) (Hanson, 1959). While the foregoing study demonstrates that a series of S + sessions followed by S − sessions on subsequent days is not a sufficient condition for the development of discriminative control, it fails to indicate what condition is sufficient.

The standard discrimination procedure involves the random alternation of S + and S −. That is, it consists of four types of sequences of two stimuli—S + S +, S + S −, S − S +, and S − S −.

The first and fourth sequences define simple acquisition and extinction and are not therefore the locus of stimulus control. Stimulus control must arise from either or both of the middle two sequences —S+S— and S−S+. Accordingly, a preliminary experiment was conducted (Donahoe, Ellis, & Risner, 1968) in which pigeons were first reinforced for responding to S+ alone and then were placed in either of two groups. In Group AE, Ss were given a number of S+ periods in which *acquisition* was scheduled followed by a number of S− periods in which *extinction* was scheduled. In Group EA, Ss were given a number of S − periods in which extinction was scheduled, followed by a number of S+ periods in which acquisition was scheduled. Thus, Group AE received one S+S− sequence each day, while Group EA received one S−S+ sequence each day. After a number of such training sessions, Ss were given a test of stimulus generalization. The differences in the PDGs as a function of the S+S− and S−S+ training procedures were of such a nature that Ellis elected to investigate the effects of the stimulus sequence on discrimination formation in his doctoral dissertation (Ellis, 1968). The methods and results of the Ellis experiment are reported below:

The purpose of the present experiment was to study the effects of various sequences of stimuli on the acquisition of stimulus control. Four experimental sequences were studied: S+S−, S−S+, S+S−S+, and S−S+S−. The first two sequences represent the ways in which two different stimuli may be ordered. Each of the last two sequences is composed of both basic sequences (S+S− and S−S+), but the order of the basic sequences is reversed. Thus, the S+S−S+ sequence consists of an S+S− sequence followed by an S−S+ sequence, whereas the S−S+S− sequence consists of an S−S+ sequence followed by an S+S− sequence. If only stimulus sequences of length two contribute to discrimination formation, then the S+S−S+ and S−S+S− sequences should not differentially affect performance, even though the S+S− and S−S+ sequences may have differential effects.

Forty-two pigeons tested in a one-key operant chamber served as Ss. The stimulus dimension of the discrimination was visual intensity. The following stimulus values were used: $S_1 = 2.25$, $S_2 = 3.56$, $S_3 = 5.64$, $S_4 = 8.94$, $S_5 = 14.17$, $S_6 = 22.46$, and $S_7 = 35.61$ ftc.

The various stimuli were separated by equal logarithmic increments.

After feeder and key-peck training, all Ss were given 10 daily sessions of variable-interval (VI) 60-second training for responding to $S+(S_4)$. Each session consisted of 30 60-second $S+$ periods separated by 5-second periods during which the test chamber was darkened. Each of the 42 Ss was then assigned to one of seven groups. Group C1 continued to receive only $S+$ and served as a control for the effects of continued training. Group C2 received $S+$ training but, in addition, received a session of $S-(S_6)$ before each generalization test. Group C2 therefore constitutes a partial replication of the Honig, Thomas, and Guttman experiment (1959). Group D received both $S+$ and $S-$ periods randomly presented within a session and replicated the conventional discrimination procedure. Group AE received $S+$ periods in which acquisition was scheduled followed by $S-$ periods in which extinction was scheduled during each session. Thus, Group AE received one $S+S-$ sequence each session. Group EA received $S-$ periods in which acquisition was scheduled followed by $S+$ periods in which extinction was scheduled during each session. Thus, Group EA received one $S-S+$ sequence each session. Group AEA received $S+$ periods followed by $S-$ periods followed by $S+$ periods during each session, that is, one $S+S-S+$ sequence per session. Group EAE received $S-$ periods followed by $S+$ periods followed by $S-$ periods during each session, that is, one $S-S+S-$ sequence per session. For all groups receiving $S+$ and $S-$ within a single session (Groups D, AE, EA, AEA, and EAE), the number of like sequences $(S+S+$ and $S-S-)$ was equated with 9 like sequences, being given each session.

A total of 14 daily sessions was administered according to the described conditions and then all groups except Group C1 were transferred for 12 sessions to the random orders of $S+$ and $S-$ used throughout training with Group D. Interpolated between the training sessions were occasional daily sessions in which a generalization test was given. Generalization testing occurred during sessions 12, 15, 20, 25, 34, 39, and 44. Thus, there were four generalization tests interpolated between sessions containing the special sequence training and three generalization tests interpolated between sessions during which all groups but Group C2 received $S+$ and $S-$ in a random order.

At the completion of VI training in S + alone, the mean rate of responding was 51 responses per minute and did not differ among the seven groups. The base-line rate (BR) for each S during VI training served as a reference point from which the relative rate of responding was computed for all remaining sessions by dividing the obtained rate (OR) in that session by BR. Thus, rates in excess of BR are shown by relative rates greater than 1.0; rates below BR are shown by relative rates less than 1.0.

The performance during acquisition sessions will be considered first, followed by a presentation of the results during generalization testing. Figure 12 depicts performance in the groups receiving the S + S −, S − S +, S + S − S +, and S − S + S − sequences. The data to the left of the vertical line were obtained while the special sequences were in effect. For all sequence groups (AE, EA, AEA, and EAE), the rate during S + increased and the rate during S − decreased as a function of training sessions ($p < .01$). The other group receiving S + and S − periods within a session was Group D, whose performance is shown in the lower panel of Fig. 13. Again, the S + and S − rates drew apart as a function of training sessions. An analysis of variance of the performance of all groups receiving S + and S − periods within the same session (D, AE, EA, AEA, and EAE) was conducted. The relative rates of responding during S + and S − diverged at different rates for the various groups ($p < .01$). Using the standard discrimination group (Group D) as a reference, the S + rate increased more slowly in the EA and AE groups, whereas the S − rate decreased more slowly in the AEA and EAE groups. All groups, however, showed evidence of behavioral contrast in that the rate during S + at the end of training was above the BR ($p < .01$). Moreover, as measured during the last three sessions of training with the special sequences (sessions 26, 27, and 28), the difference between the rates of responding during S + and S − was the same for all groups ($p > .05$). The difference between S + and S − rates was highly reliable ($p < .01$). Thus, on the basis of terminal acquisition performance for those groups receiving both S + and S − within a single session, it may be concluded that all groups were performing similarly.

The acquisition performance of groups C1 and C2 is shown in the upper panel of Fig. 13. The C1 group, which received only S +

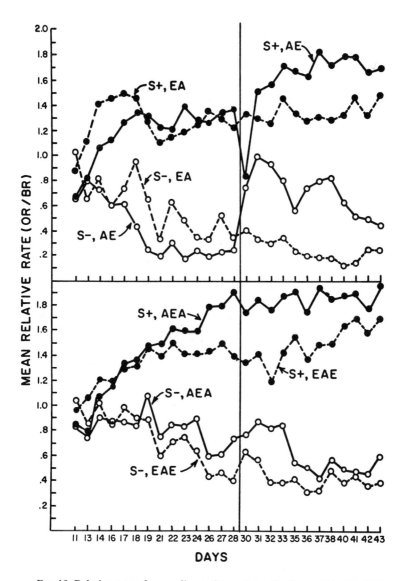

FIG. 12. Relative rates of responding to S+ and S− for Groups EA, AE, AEA, and EAE during the discrimination sessions. During sessions to the left of the vertical line, the special stimulus sequences were administered; during sessions to the right of the vertical line, the standard random sequences were administered. (From Ellis, 1968)

273

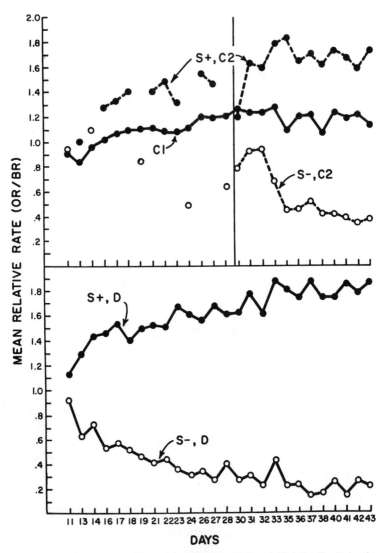

Fig. 13. Relative rates of responding to S+ and S− during the discrimination sessions. The upper panel depicts the performance of Groups C1 and C2. During sessions to the right of the vertical line, Group C2 was transferred to the standard random sequence. The lower panel depicts the performance of Group D, which received the standard random sequences throughout training. (From Ellis, 1968)

274

training, also responsed at a higher rate as sessions progressed, although the increase was less than that obtained with the other groups. The C2 group, which received one session of extinction in the presence of S− preceding each generalization session, displayed a greater increase in S+ rate and a decrease in S− rate as training progressed. The finding of behavioral contrast in group C2 in which extinction during S− was temporally separated from S+ training replicates a similar recent finding reported by Bloomfield (1967).

Consideration is now given to the performance of the various groups during the generalization tests interpolated between the acquisition sessions. Figure 14 contains the generalization gradients obtained after 1 (Test 1), 3 (Test 2), 7 (Test 3), and 10 sessions (Test 4) of acquisition training. The gradients in the left column of Fig. 14 are those which ultimately showed peak shift, contrast, and steepening. Note that all groups that displayed the hallmarks of the PDG (Groups D, EA, AEA, and EAE) contained the S−S+ sequence. Note further that those special sequence groups that contained an S+S− sequence in addition to the S−S+ sequence developed the PDG more slowly than Groups D and EA. The gradients in the right column of Fig. 14 are those which failed to show peak shift, contrast, and steepening. Note that all such groups (C1, C2, and AE) did not contain the S−S+ sequence and that contrast in the generalization test was absent in the C2 and AE groups, although contrast was present during acquisition. The failure of the C2 condition to produce a conventional PDG confirms the findings of Honig, Thomas, and Guttman (1959). Extinction during S−, whether it occurred during a separate session (Group C2) or only after S+ within the same session (Group AE), simply lowered the generalization gradient.

After 14 sessions of acquisition training with the special stimulus sequences, all groups except C1 were transferred to the random sequences used in Group D. If stimulus control of performance by S+ and S− had been established, the animals should have responded appropriately when S+ and S− were presented in a random sequence. That portion of Fig. 12 to the right of the vertical line depicts the response rates obtained with the AE, EA, AEA, and EAE groups when transferred to the random sequence. Groups

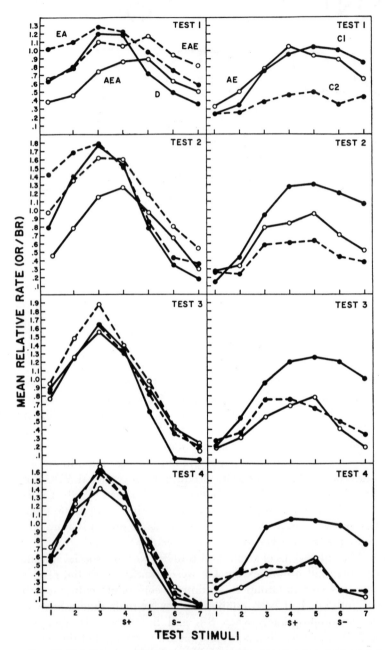

FIG. 14. Relative generalization gradients obtained during tests interpolated among discrimination sessions during which the special stimulus sequences were administered. (From Ellis, 1968)

EA, AEA, and EAE transferred to the random sequence with no disruption in the differential response rates to $S+$ and $S-$. Group AE showed no positive transfer whatsoever. The right-hand portion of Fig. 13 depicts the performance of the C2 group (upper panel) after transfer to the random sequence and the continuation of performance in the C1 (upper panel) and D groups. Group C2 also failed to transfer to the random sequence. A summary statistic, the $S+$ proportion, which expresses differential performance as a ratio of the responses during $S+$ to the total number of responses facilitates comparisons among the groups and is contained in Fig. 15. The $S+$ proportions for Groups C2, EA, AE, AEA, and EAE were derived from the 12 transfer sessions; the $S+$ proportions for Group D were derived from the first twelve days of training on the random sequence. Note that the groups that received the $S-S+$ sequence during acquisition (Groups EA, AEA, and EAE) made approximately 70% of their total responses during $S+$ on the first

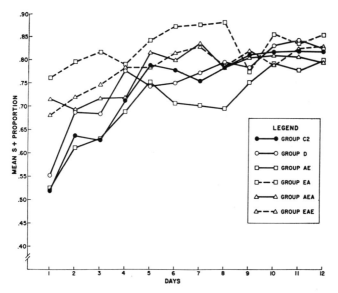

FIG. 15. Proportion of responses to $S+$ during the 12 sessions after transfer to the standard random sequences for Groups C2, AE, EA, AEA, and EAE and during the first 12 sessions of the standard random sequences for Group D. (From Ellis, 1968)

exposure to a random sequence, whereas the groups that did not receive the S − S + sequence during acquisition (Groups C2 and EA) made only approximately 50% of their total responses during S +. Furthermore, the acquisition of differential performance in the C2 and AE Groups after fourteen days of training with the special sequences did not differ from the initial acquisition of the discrimination by Group D.

The generalization tests given following 4 (Test 5), 8 (Test 6), and 12 sessions (Test 7) of transfer to the random sequence are shown in Fig. 16. The left column contains the generalization gradients from those groups which produced a normal PDG at the end of acquisition. As is evident, the D, EA, AEA, and EAE groups continued to yield a PDG which displayed peak shift, contrast, and steepening, although the absolute level of responding declined somewhat over the seven generalization tests. In the right column are shown the generalization gradients from those groups which failed to give a normal PDG during acquisition training. Following transfer to the random sequence, the C2 and AE groups displayed a normal PDG. The heights of the PDGs were comparable to those obtained in the other groups during earlier generalization tests. The C1 group which continued to receive only S + training maintained a relatively flat gradient, although the level of responding declined still further.

Discriminative control of responding, which is customarily identified with differential response strength during a random sequence of S + and S − and with the appearance of the PDG (peak shift, contrast, and steepening), occurred only when the S − S + sequence was present within a single session. The S − S + sequence is a sufficient condition for stimulus control because transfer to the random sequence and the PDG were produced by the EA group. The S − S + sequence is a necessary condition for stimulus control because neither transfer to the random sequence nor the PDG were produced by the AE group. Because of the similarity in the performance of the AEA and EAE groups which received S + S − S + and S − S + S − sequences, respectively, the order in which the transitions between stimuli occur does not appear critical. That is, a sequence involving more than two stimuli does not contribute substantially to discrimination performance beyond the

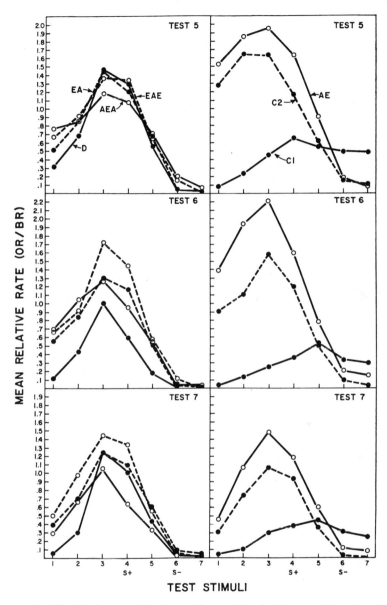

FIG. 16. Relative generalization gradients obtained during tests interpolated among discrimination sessions during which the standard random stimulus sequences were administered.

two-stimulus sequences which it contains. If anything, the acquisition of differential responding to S+ and S− and the PDG may be retarded by stimulus sequences other than S−S+ when the total number of stimulus sequences is small.

The results of the present experiment may appear to present some difficulties for those analyses that specify invariant relationships between behavioral contrast, peak shift, and discriminative control. It has been suggested, for example, that "a sufficient condition for the occurrence of the peak shift is a reduction in the rate of responding to one of two alternating discriminative stimuli" (Terrace, 1968, p. 739). This is clearly not the case, for both the C2 and AE groups showed a reduction in response strength to S− which was indistinguishable in magnitude from the reduction shown by those groups receiving the S−S+ sequence, but neither group demonstrated a peak shift during the generalization tests. Similarly, it has been suggested that "those training conditions that produce contrast also result in a peak shift" (Terrace, 1968, p. 729; Terrace, 1966). Contrast was produced in both Group C2 and Group AE, and yet no peak shift was shown during generalization testing. These discrepancies from expectations regarding the interrelationships among discrimination, contrast, and peak shift are more apparent than real, however, for ambiguity exists concerning the terms *contrast* and *discrimination*. The definition of contrast developed by Reynolds (1961) and shared by Terrace (1968) includes among its defining operations a change in the schedule of reinforcement during S− at the onset of discrimination training. In the present experiment, no schedule of reinforcement other than extinction was ever present during S−. Thus, responding during S− was the indirect result of generalization from S+ and not the direct result of a reinforcement history during S−. It should be noted, though, that the term contrast is not used consistently, for example, in its application in errorless discrimination experiments, in which the schedule of reinforcement during S− also does not change (Terrace, 1966, p. 321).

Consistent with frustration theory (Amsel, 1962) and with experimentation (e.g., Terrace, 1968, Experiment 1), changes in reinforcement density greatly affect contrast. The present experiment does indicate that an elevation in the rate during S+ (contrast) does not arise exclusively from the same antecedents as does heightening of the PDG, although the term contrast is sometimes used to refer to both phenomena. All groups exposed to S−, whether within or between sessions containing S+, showed an increase in S+ rate above group C1, although only those conditions containing the S−S+ sequence demonstrated a heightening of the PDG. The finding that increases in S+ rate can be produced both by extinction during S− over widely separated intervals (Group C2) and within the same session (Groups AE, EA, AEA, and EAE) may implicate the conditioned and unconditioned emotional responses, respectively, identified in frustration theory. The finding of "transient" contrast (Bloomfield, 1967; Nevin & Shettleworth, 1966) is also consistent with this dichotomy.

Ambiguity also exists regarding the operations that define discrimination. Clearly, the finding that the response rate in S+ is above the response rate in S− is not a sufficient condition for the inference of discriminative control by the stimulus dimension(s) of S+ and S−. The C2 and AE groups responded differentially to S+ and S− during acquisition and yet showed no positive transfer to the random sequence. If the dimensions upon which S+ and S− have nonzero projections were not controlling differential performance during acquisition, the question arises concerning what were the controlling stimuli. Jenkins (1965) has discussed the potentially significant role of the confounding of stimuli arising from the reinforcement operation with the to-be-discriminated stimuli, and additionally, research from other laboratories concerned with successive acquisition and extinction periods (e.g., Jensen & Cotton, 1960) may be relevant to this inquiry.

The finding that the crucial element in the formation of an operant discrimination is the S−S+ sequence cannot be readily rationalized by any theory known to the author. Relatively few theories are designed to accommodate sequential effects in any form, although elaborations of frustration theory (Amsel, 1962), after-effects theory (Capaldi, 1966), and certain mathematical models of learning (e.g., Bush & Mosteller, 1951; Gambino & Myers, 1967) may hold some promise. On an empirical level, however, the present results place no impediments in the path of using information from the discrimination situation to analyze stimulus control within response sequences, for the S − S + sequence is necessarily contained within all response sequences.

Experiment Eight: Sequential Effects in the Generalization of Stimulus

The purpose of this experiment was to evaluate the contribution of sequential factors to the generalization of discriminative stimulus control. To accomplish this goal, the postdiscrimination gradients (PDGs) were compared following single-stimulus (SS) and multiple-stimulus (MS) generalization test procedures (Donahoe, McCroskery, & Richardson, 1968). In the SS procedure each *S* is presented with only one test stimulus following discrimination training. The PDG, therefore, is a function relating estimates of response strength from independent groups at each value of the stimulus dimension. In the MS procedure each *S* is presented with all test stimuli following discrimination training. The PDG, with this procedure, is a function relating estimates of response strength, all of which are derived from the same group of *S*s. Because of the relatively rapid extinction of responding in many instrumental situations, the SS procedure was the most frequently used (e.g., Grice & Saltz, 1950) until the advent of Guttman's method (Guttman, 1956). In it acquisition training is given with a variable-interval (VI) schedule operative during the positive stimulus (S +), and resistance to extinction is sufficiently enhanced to permit the attainment of stable PDGs with the MS test procedure (e.g., Hanson, 1959).

Although the MS test procedure produces a stimulus-generalization gradient which may be displayed in a single *S*, it also permits the possible intrusion of effects associated with the fact that *S* is exposed to a succession of different test stimuli. Such sequence effects, if present, may affect the estimates of response strength for the various test stimuli and thereby complicate interpretations seeking to relate characteristics of the PDG to discrimination performance during acquisition. A number of investigators have appreciated these potential difficulties, and comparisons between SS and MS test procedures have been made, although only after nondiscriminated training to S +. Early work suggested that the two test procedures gave somewhat different results (Kalish & Haber,

1963), but later research indicated that, when appropriate experimental and analytical techniques were employed which controlled the steepening of the generalization gradient in extinction, the two procedures yielded approximately equivalent gradients (Hiss & Thomas, 1963; Thomas & Barker, 1964).

The present experiment investigated the comparability of generalization gradients obtained with SS and MS test procedures following *discrimination* training. A context model which leads to the expectation of differences in the generalization gradient after discrimination training to S +, but not after nondiscrimination training, is as follows: In a random series of test stimuli, a given stimulus (S_j) will sometimes be preceded by a stimulus (S_i) associated with greater response strength, $S_i > S_j$, and sometimes by a stimulus associated with less response strength, $S_i < S_j$. If differences in response strength arise in part from inhibitory processes generated during acquisition of the discrimination due to extinction in the negative stimulus $(S-)$—an assumption for which there is considerable support (Farthing & Hearst, 1968; Honig, Boneau, Burstein, & Pennypacker, 1963; Jenkins & Harrison, 1962; Weisman & Palmer, 1969)—then the sequence $S_i > S_j$ meets the necessary and sufficient conditions for negative induction and the sequence $S_i < S_j$ meets the conditions for positive induction according to Pavlov (1927). Thus, the context in which S_j appears during the assessment of the PDG should affect the response to S_j.

In the MS procedure, the response to S_j should be diminished when $S_i > S_j$ and should be augmented when $S_i < S_j$, relative to the response strength to S_j in the SS procedure. The simplest context model consistent with the above is $R'_j - R_j = f(R_j - R_i)$, where R'_j is the response strength to S_j in a MS test, and R_i and R_j are the response strengths to S_i and S_j, respectively, in an SS test. Although the concept of induction arose from work with classically conditioned responses, there is compelling evidence for the existence of induction effects with instrumental responses as well (e.g., Reynolds, 1961; Senf & Miller, 1967). The net effect of induction in a series of test stimuli symmetrically distributed about S + would be a displacement of the mode of the PDG away from S − (peak shift), an increase in the height of the PDG in the vicinity of the mode (contrast), and an increase in the slope of the PDG on the S− side of the gradient (steepening)—all of which characterize empirical PDGs.

Twenty-four pigeons were tested in operant chambers containing a single response key which could be transilluminated with white light at an intensity of 5.64, 8.94, or 22.46 ftc. Following feeder training and key-peck training, all Ss were given 10 daily sessions of VI training, the last 7 sessions of which were at a value of VI 60 seconds. During the VI training the intensity of the key was 8.94 ftc. After pretraining, all Ss were administered 8 sessions of discrimination training, using a successive procedure in which VI 60 seconds was in effect during S+ (8.94 ftc.), and extinction was in effect during S− (22.46 ftc.). Each discrimination session consisted of a quasi-random sequence of 21 30-second exposures to S+, and 21 30-second exposures to S−, with the stimulus periods separated by a 5-second period during which the chambers were darkened. After the initial 8 sessions of discrimination training, a series of sessions of generalization testing and discrimination training were given. In general each S received four cycles consisting of 4 sessions of discrimination training followed by a stimulus-generalization test. Two types of generalization tests were given: (a) a MS test in which a test stimulus (S_T), S+, and S− were presented in quasi-random order during a single session, and (b) an SS test in which either S_T, S+, or S− was presented for the entire session. The intensity of S_T was 5.64 ftc. In Group I (N = 6), Ss were given three MS tests (SG 1, SG 2, and SG 3) followed by an SS test with S− alone (SG 4). In Group II (N = 18), each S received three SS tests (SG 1, SG 2, and SG 3) followed by a MS test (SG 4). The SS tests in Group II were administered in accordance with a Latin-square plan which ensured that each S was exposed to each of the test stimuli during 1 session.

During discrimination training and generalization testing, the number of responses in each 30-second stimulus period were recorded.

Figure 17 contains the PDGs obtained from SG 1, SG 2, and SG 3, during which Group I received three MS tests and Group II received three SS tests. The dependent variable was the rate of responding during generalization testing expressed as a proportion of response rate to S+ during the preceding discrimination session.

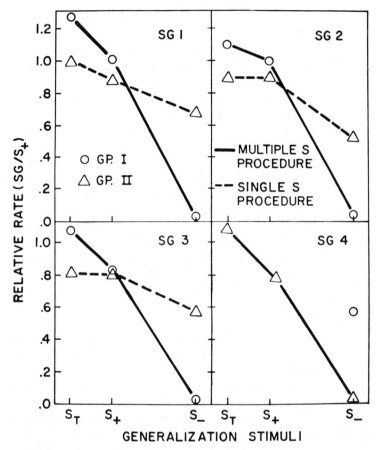

FIG. 17. Postdiscrimination gradients of stimulus generalization obtained with successive tests (SG 1, SG 2, SG 3, and SG 4), using multiple-stimulus and single-stimulus procedures.

All three generalization tests agree in showing that the MS test procedure produced a higher rate during S_T and a lower rate during $S-$ than the SS test procedure. Because statistical tests showed the absence of any effects of repeated generalization testing on the PDG, the SS and MS gradients could be directly compared without complication because, over the course of the three generalization tests, all *S*s in both groups had been exposed to all stimuli. In confirmation of the impression from Fig. 17 that the test procedure markedly affected the shape of the PDG, the interaction of test procedure with stimuli was highly significant ($p < .01$). Comparisons between the two PDGs revealed that the response rate during S_T was higher ($p < .025$) and the response rate during $S-$ was lower ($p < .01$) with the MS procedure than with the SS procedure. The response rates to $S+$ did not differ.

The result of switching the test procedure for Groups I and II during SG 4 is shown in the lower right panel of Fig. 17. Group I, which responded at an extremely low rate to $S-$ during SG 1, SG 2, and SG 3 when the MS procedure was used, showed a sharply increased rate to $S-$ when the SS procedure was instituted ($p < .01$) and did not differ from the rate to $S-$ shown by Group II during SS testing. Group II, which responded appreciably to $S-$ during SG 1, SG 2, and SG 3 when the SS procedure was used, showed a sharply decreased rate to $S-$ during SG 4 when a MS test was given ($p < .01$). Moreover, the shape of the PDG obtained from Group II with a MS test during SG 4 did not differ from the shape of the mean PDG obtained from Group I with MS testing during SG 1, SG 2, and SG 3.

According to the simple context model presented earlier, the response to S_j in a MS generalization test is altered only by differences in response strength associated with the immediately preceding stimulus, S_i. To assess the adequacy of the model in accounting for the sequential features of the data, the response rate in the presence of S_T, $S+$, and $S-$ was plotted as a function of S_i in Fig. 18. As expected, the response to S_j varied as a function of S_i ($p < .01$). Also, as anticipated, the response to S_j was greater when preceded by $S-$ than by S_T ($p < .01$). Although statistically reliable, the magnitude of these local context effects was not sufficient to account for the observed differences between the MS and SS gradients. Moreover, the gradient formed by connecting the points at which $S_i = S_j$ (see Fig. 17, dashed line) does not replicate the SS gradient as required by the model.

The present experiment clearly demonstrates that the PDG is highly dependent upon the procedure employed in generalization testing. The use of the MS test procedure produced a shift in the mode of the PDG away from $S-$, an increase in response strength

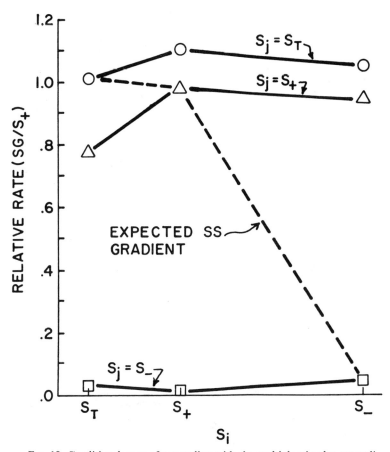

Fig. 18. Conditional rates of responding with the multiple-stimulus generalization test procedure. The strength of response to S_j is plotted as a function of the immediately preceding stimulus (S_i) in the generalization test.

in the vicinity of the mode, and a decrease in response strength in the vicinity of S−. Thus, the hallmarks of the PDG as distinguished from the gradient following nondiscriminated training to S+ are enhanced as a consequence of testing each S at all values of the test stimuli. This is not to say that the preceding three features of the PDG result solely from context effects which arise from within the MS procedure. Steepening of the PDG on the S− side of the gradient also occurred with the SS procedure, and the response to S_T was somewhat augmented when compared with gradients obtained from other research in the laboratory after nondiscriminated training to $S+$ (Ellis, 1968). Thus, steepening and peak shift with the MS test procedure appear to be a joint function of the summation of gradients of acquisition and extinction, as specified by Spence's theory (1937), and of context effects, as determined in the present experiment. However, the contrast effect in which the PDG is not contained within the gradient following nondiscrimination training to $S+$ does appear to be attributable solely to context effects. Not surprisingly, it has been the contrast effect obtained with MS testing which has been most refractory to incorporation within conditioning-extinction theory (Hanson, 1959).

The origin of the enhancement of postdiscrimination phenomena is, in part, the particular sequences of stimuli used in the generalization test. That is, in the stimulus sequence S_iS_j, the response to S_j was augmented when S_i was the occasion for a lower response rate. Because of the existence of context effects which arise from within the test period itself, attempts to derive one set of conditioning and extinction gradients about $S+$ and $S-$, respectively, which are simultaneously consistent with both discrimination and multiple-stimulus generalization performance, are foredoomed to failure. Similarly, attempts to predict the PDG obtained with MS generalization testing from the summation of gradients of acquisition and extinction obtained after orthogonal discrimination training may be expected to be only partially satisfactory in that PDG should be higher than predicted from the summation of gradients in the vicinity of the mode and lower than predicted in the vicinity of $S-$, because of context effects operating on the PDG. The errors of prediction in experiments of this type (Hearst, 1968; Marsh, 1968) have, in fact, been of the type indicated by the foregoing analysis.

As applied to the generalization of stimulus control within response sequences, the occurrence of context effects during generalization testing is consistent with the steeper approach gradients found with correlated stimulation. Since the stimulus dimension controlling responding within the approach sequence must neccssarily assume values which progressively approximate the value present during reinforcement, the context effect would act to elevate responding in the terminal fractions of the sequence.

SUMMARY AND CONCLUSIONS

A major finding of the present experiments is that the correlation of responding with delay of reinforcement determines whether external or internal sources of stimulation control performance within response sequences. When responding is uncorrelated with reinforcement by means of a FI schedule, external stimuli control performance; when responding is correlated with reinforcements by means of a FR schedule, internal (response-produced) stimuli control performance. Since performance within response sequences is frequently used in the measurement of discrimination learning (e.g., successive discrimination learning in the runway situation and multiple schedules in the operant situation), additional work is needed to determine whether differences in the sources of stimulus control within sequences interact with stimulus control between sequences.

A second major finding is that the sequences in which stimuli are presented have profound effects on the acquisition and generalization of stimulus control. In acquisition, the $S-S+$ stimulus sequence is the necessary and sufficient condition for the establishment of stimulus control using standard operant procedures. In generalization, sequential effects enhance peak shift and steepening of the postdiscrimination gradient and produce contrast. While these sequential effects are consistent with results obtained from the study of stimulus control within response sequences, their generality must be determined, for they have implications of a fundamental nature for the genesis of discriminative control.

REFERENCES

Amsel, A. Frustrative nonreward in partial reinforcement and discrimination learning: Some recent history and theoretical extension. *Psychol. Rev.*, 1962, **69**, 306–328.

Anger, D. The dependence of interresponse times upon the relative reinforcement of different interresponse times. *J. exp. Psychol.*, 1956, **52**, 145–161.

Arnold, W. J. Simple reaction chains and their integration. I. Homogenous chaining with terminal reinforcement. *J. comp. physiol. Psychol.*, 1947, **40**, 349–364.

Bloomfield, T. M. Some temporal properties of behavioral contrast. *J. exp. anal. Behav.*, 1967, **10**, 159–164.

Blough, D. S. The reinforcement of least-frequent interresponse times. *J. exp. anal. Behav.*, 1966, **9**, 581–591.

Blough, D. S. Generalization gradient shape and summation in steady-state tests. *J. exp. anal. Behav.*, 1969, **12**, 91–104.

Brown, P. L., & Jenkins, H. M. Autoshaping of the pigeon's keypeck. *J. exp. anal. Behav.*, 1968, **6**, 1–8.

Brunswik, E. *Systematic and representative design of psychological experiments*. Berkeley: University of California Press, 1947.

Bush, D. R., & Mosteller, F. A model for stimulus generalization and discrimination. *Psychol. Rev.*, 1951, **58**, 413–423.

Capaldi, E. J. Partial reinforcement: A hypothesis of sequential effects. *Psychol. Rev.*, 1966, **73**, 459–477.

Cotton, J. W. Running time as a function of amount of food deprivation. *J. exp. Psychol.*, 1953, **46**, 188–198.

Crites, R. J., Harris, R. T., Rosenquist, H., & Thomas, P. R. Response patterning during stimulus generalization in the rat. *J. exp. anal. Behav.*, 1967, **10**, 165–168.

Dews, P. B. The effect of multiple S^Δ periods on responding on a fixed-interval schedule. III. Effect of changes in pattern of interruptions, parameters, and stimuli. *J. exp. anal. Behav.*, 1965, **8**, 427–435.

Dews, P. B. The effect of multiple S^Δ periods on responding on a fixed-interval schedule. IV. Effect of continuous S^Δ with only short S^D probes. *J. exp. anal. Behav.*, 1966a, **9**, 147–151.

Dews, P. B. The effect of multiple S^Δ periods on a fixed-interval schedule. V. Effect of periods of complete darkness and of occasional omissions of food presentation. *J. exp. anal. Behav.*, 1966b, **9**, 573–578.

DiLollo, V. Runway performance in relation to runway-goal–box similarity and changes in incentive amount. *J. comp. physiol. Psychol.*, 1964, **58**, 327–329.

Donahoe, J. W., Ellis, W. R., III, & Risner, M. Effects of stimulus sequence on discrimination formation. Unpublished experiment, University of Kentucky, 1968.

Donahoe, J. W., & McCroskery, J. H. Stimulus control within response-correlated approach chains. *J. exp. Psychol.*, 1969, **80**, 512–516.

Donahoe, J. W., McCroskery, J. H., & Richardson, W. K. Effects of induction on the postdiscrimination gradient. Unpublished manuscript, University of Kentucky, 1968.

Donahoe, J. W., Schulte, V. G., & Moulton, A. E. Stimulus control of approach behavior. *J. exp. Psychol.*, 1968, **78**, 21–30.

Ellis, W. R., III. Effects of the correlation of auditory stimulation on approach behavior. Unpublished experiment, University of Kentucky, 1967.

Ellis, W. R., III. AE and EA transitions: Their role in stimulus discrimination and stimulus generalization. Unpublished doctoral dissertation, University of Kentucky, 1968.

Farthing, G. W., & Hearst, E. Generalization gradients of inhibition after different amounts of training. *J. exp. anal. Behav.*, 1968, **11**, 743–752.

Ferster, C. B., & Skinner, B. F. *Schedules of reinforcement.* New York: Appleton-Century-Crofts, 1957.

Gambino, B., & Myers, J. L. The role of event runs in probability learning. *Psychol. Rev.*, 1967, **74**, 410–419.

Gonzalez, R. C., Bainbridge, P., & Bitterman, M. E. Discrete-trials lever pressing in the rat as a function of pattern of reinforcement, effortfulness of response, and amount of reward. *J. comp. physiol. Psychol.*, 1966, **61**, 110–122.

Gonzalez, R. C., & Diamond, L. A test of Spence's theory of incentive motivation. *Amer. J. Psychol.*, 1960, **73**, 396–403.

Grice, G. R., & Saltz, E. The generalization of instrumental response to stimuli varying in the size dimension. *J. exp. Psychol.*, 1950, **40**, 702–708.

Guttman, N. The pigeon and the spectrum and other perplexities. *Psychol. Rep.*, 1956, **2**, 449–460.

Hanson, H. M. Effects of discrimination training on stimulus generalization. *J. exp. Psychol.*, 1959, **58**, 321–334.

Hearst, E. Discrimination learning as the summation of excitation and inhibition. *Science*, 1968, **162**, 1303–1306.

Herrick, R. M. Lever displacement during continuous reinforcement and during a discrimination. *J. comp. physiol. Psychol.*, 1963, **56**, 700–707.

Hiss, R. H., & Thomas, D. R. Stimulus generalization as a function of testing procedure and response measure. *J. exp. Psychol.*, 1963, **65**, 587–592.

Honig, W. K., Boneau, C. A., Burstein, K. R., & Pennypacker, H. S. Positive and negative generalization gradients obtained after equivalent training conditions. *J. comp. physiol. Psychol.*, 1963, **56**, 111–116.

Honig, W. K., Thomas, D. R., & Guttman, N. Differential effects of continuous extinction and discrimination training on the generalization gradient. *J. exp. Psychol.*, 1959, **58**, 145–152.

Hughes, D., David, J. D., & Grice, G. R. Goal box and alley similarity as a factor in latent extinction. *J. comp. physiol. Psychol.*, 1960, **53**, 612–614.

Hull, C. L. The goal-gradient hypothesis and maze learning. *Psychol. Rev.*, 1932, **39**, 25–43.

Hull, C. L. The rat's speed of locomotion gradient in the approach to food. *J. comp. Psychol.*, 1934, **17**, 393–422.

Hull, C. L. *A behavior system: An introduction to behavior theory concerning the individual organism.* New Haven: Yale University Press, 1952.

Jenkins, H. M. Measurement of stimulus control during discriminative operant conditioning. *Psychol. Rev.*, 1965, **64**, 365–376.

Jenkins, H. M., & Harrison, R. H. Generalization gradients of inhibition following auditory discrimination training. *J. exp. anal. Behav.*, 1962, **5**, 435–441.

Jensen, G. D., & Cotton, J. W. Successive acquisitions and extinctions as related to percentage of reinforcement. *J. exp. Psychol.*, 1960, **60**, 41–49.

292   *Current Issues in Animal Learning*

Kalish, H. I., & Haber, A. Generalization. I. Generalization gradients from single and multiple stimulus points. II. Generalization of inhibition. *J. exp. Psychol.*, 1963, **65**, 176–181.

Keller, F. S., & Schoenfeld, W. N. *Principles of psychology.* New York: Appleton-Century-Crofts, 1950.

Knarr, F. A., & Collier, G. Taste and consummatory activity in amount and gradient of reinforcement functions. *J. exp. Psychol.*, 1962, **63**, 579–588.

Logan, F. A. A note on stimulus intensity dynamism (V). *Psychol. Rev.*, 1954, **61**, 77–80.

Logan, F. A. *Incentive.* New Haven: Yale University Press, 1960.

Logan, F. A. Discrete-trials DRL (differential reinforcement of low rate). *J. exp. anal. Behav.*, 1961, **4**, 277–281.

Mackintosh, N. J. Selective attention in animal discrimination learning. *Psychol. Bull.*, 1965, **64**, 124–150.

Marsh, G. Prediction of post discrimination gradient from summation of gradients of excitation and inhibition. Paper presented at Psychonomic Society meeting, St. Louis, 1968.

Migler, B. Effects of averaging data during stimulus generalization. *J. exp. anal. Behav.*, 1964, **7**, 303–307.

Migler, B., & Millenson, J. K. Analysis of response rates during stimulus generalization. *J. exp. anal. Behav.*, 1969, **12**, 81–90.

Morse, W. H. Intermittent reinforcement. In W. K. Honig (Ed.), *Operant behavior: Areas of research and application.* New York: Appleton-Century-Crofts, 1966. Pp. 52–108.

Mueller, C. G. Theoretical relationships among some measures of conditioning. *Proceedings of the National Academy of Science, Washington*, 1950, **36**, 123–130.

Nevin, J. A., & Shettleworth, S. J. Analysis of contrast effects in multiple schedules. *J. exp. anal. Behav.*, 1966, **9**, 305–315.

Notterman, J. M. Force emission during bar pressing. *J. exp. Psychol.*, 1959, **58**, 341–347.

Notterman, J. M., & Mintz, D. E. *Dynamics of response.* New York: Wiley, 1965.

Pavlov, I. P. *Conditioned reflexes.* London: Oxford University Press, 1927.

Perkins, C. C., Jr. The relation between conditioned stimulus intensity and response strength. *J. exp. Psychol.*, 1953, **46**, 225–231.

Porter, J. J., & Hug, J. J. Effects of number and percentage of rewarded trials on the acquisition and extinction of lever pressing using a discrete-trial procedure. *J. exp. Psychol.*, 1965, **70**, 575–579.

Reynolds, G. S. Behavioral contrast. *J. exp. anal. Behav.*, 1961, **4**, 57–71.

Rilling, M. E. Number of responses as a stimulus in fixed-interval and fixed ratio behavior. *J. comp. physiol. Psychol.*, 1967, **63**, 60–65.

Rilling, M. Effects of timeout on a discrimination between fixed-ratio schedules. *J. exp. anal. Behav.*, 1968, **11**, 129–132.

Schulte, V. G. The discrimination of the stimulus consequences of responses differing in work requirement. Unpublished doctoral dissertation, University of Kentucky, 1969.

Senf, G. M., & Miller, N. E. Evidence for positive induction in discrimination learning. *J. comp. physiol. Psychol.*, 1967, **64**, 121–127.

Shimp, C. P. Probabilistically reinforced choice behavior in pigeons. *J. exp. anal. Behav.*, 1966, **9**, 443–455.

Shimp, C. P. The reinforcement of short interresponse times. *J. exp. anal. Behav.*, 1967, **10**, 425–434.

Skinner, B. F. *The behavior of organisms: An experimental analysis.* New York: Appleton-Century, 1938.

Spence, K. W. The differential response in animals to stimuli varying within a single dimension. *Psychol. Rev.*, 1937, **44**, 430–444.

Spence, K. W. *Behavior theory and conditioning.* New Haven: Yale University Press, 1956.

Sutherland, N. S. The learning of discriminations by animals. *Endeavor*, 1964, **23**, 140–152.

Terrace, H. S. Stimulus control. In W. K. Honig, (Ed.), *Operant behavior: Areas of research and application.* New York: Appleton-Century-Crofts, 1966.

Terrace, H. S. Discrimination learning, the peak shift, and behavioral contrast. *J. exp. anal. Behav.*, 1968, **11**, 727–741.

Thomas, D. R., & Barker, E. G. The effects of extinction and "central tendency" on stimulus generalization in pigeons. *Psychon. Sci.*, 1964, **1**, 119–120.

Thorndike, E. L. *Animal intelligence.* New York: Macmillian, 1911.

Trabasso, T., & Bower, G. H. *Attention in learning: Theory and research.* New York: Wiley, 1968.

Watson, J. B. Kinesthetic and organic sensations: Their role in the reactions of the white rat to the maze. *Psychol. Monographs*, 1907, **8**, No. 33.

Weisman, R. G., & Palmer, J. A. Factors influencing inhibitory stimulus control: Discrimination training and prior nondifferential reinforcement. *J. exp. anal. Behav.*, 1969, **12**, 229–237.

Weiss, R. F. Response speed, amplitude, and resistance to extinction as joint functions of work and length of behavior chain. *J. exp. Psychol.*, 1961, **61**, 245–256.

Williams, D. R. Relation between response amplitude and reinforcement. *J. exp. Psychol.*, 1966, **71**, 634–641.

Williams, D. R. The structure of response rate. *J. exp. anal. Behav.*, 1968, **11**, 251–258.

Determinants of Inhibitory Stimulus Control[1]

Ronald G. Weisman

Queen's University at Kingston

Some version of the concept of inhibition is generally included in theoretical analyses of discrimination learning (Pavlov, 1927; Spence, 1937; Hull, 1952). However, experimental analysis of the role of inhibitory factors in operant conditioning was not notably rapid. Slow progress may be attributed in part to the measurement problems alluded to in Skinner's (1938) critical discussion of Pavlovian conditioned inhibition. These measurement problems are best illustrated by example: suppose that an animal is found to be responding in the presence of one stimulus, say S_1, but not in the presence of another stimulus, say, S_2. Do these bare facts provide evidence of inhibitory control? Most investigators would agree that differential responding to S_1 and S_2 is not evidence that S_2 has become an inhibitory stimulus. The "summation" experiment, first suggested by Pavlov (1927), is purported to be a test of inhibitory control. In the summation experiment, S_2 is superimposed on S_1, with the typical result that excitatory and inhibitory "strengths" appear to summate to produce a lower rate of responding to the $S_1 + S_2$ compound than to S_1 alone. The operation of superimposing S_2 on S_1 must invariably change the stimulus complex away from that present at reinforcement during prior training. Thus, a decrement in responding to the $S_1 + S_2$ complex can implicate excitatory control by S_1 without

[1] Much of the author's work cited in this chapter was supported by the National Research Council of Canada (grant APA–182). The sole exception was an experiment conducted with David Premack while the author was an NIMH postdoctoral fellow.

labeling the decrement as inhibition. For example, even if S_1 and S_2 were each separately correlated with reinforcement, a decrement in responding to the $S_1 + S_2$ complex might still result. Apparently neither the absence of responding to $S_1 + S_2$ nor a decrement in responding to S_2 alone is sufficient evidence for the presence of inhibitory control. We seem to be faced with the problem with which we began. How do we distinguish between the presence of an inhibitory effect and the absence of an excitatory effect?

Excitatory and Inhibitory Stimulus Control

From the foregoing discussion, it might appear that the measurement of inhibitory control involves problems not encountered in the study of excitatory control. The presence of responding to S_1 defines excitatory control no more than the absence of responding in S_2 defines inhibitory control. Mainly as a result of work by Jenkins and Harrison (1960, 1962; Jenkins, 1965), the generalization test has become the "usual" method for identifying both excitatory and inhibitory stimulus control in operant discrimination learning. These investigators (1960) showed that while simple operant training in the presence of a 1,000-Hz. tone resulted in nearly equal responding to several tones, discrimination training between reinforcement in the presence of the 1,000-Hz. tone and nonreinforcement in the absence of any tone resulted in a peaked gradient about 1,000 Hz. The sloping profile of responding over variations across the stimulus dimension provided evidence for excitatory stimulus control.

The test for inhibitory stimulus control proceeds in much the same manner as that for excitatory stimulus control. The procedure has been to correlate reinforcement with a stimulus (S_1) in a different physical dimension than the stimulus correlated with extinction (S_2) in an operant discrimination. Later, during a postdiscrimination generalization test conducted in extinction, S_2, various other stimuli on the same dimension as S_2, and S_1 are presented. Stimuli on the same dimension as S_2 are presumably all at equal distance from S_1 in the sense that they are all on a dimension not varied during discrimination training.[2] Post-discrimination generalization tests on the S_2 dimension have usually yielded gradients in which variation of the stimulus has resulted in progressive increases in responding as the distance between the generalization stimulus and S_2 increased. Shallow inverted or U-shaped gradients about S_2 have been obtained in the dimension of tone frequency (Jenkins & Harrison, 1962), line orientation (Honig et al., 1963; Weisman & Palmer, 1969) and wave length (Terrace, 1966a). Thus the postdiscrimination test can be used to uncover the presence of inhibitory stimulus control much as it has been used to uncover the presence of excitatory stimulus control. Moreover, as Jenkins (1965) pointed out, the U-shaped gradient allows us to infer that the preceding training established S_2 as a signal for not responding, just as an excitatory gradient permits us to say that S_1 was previously established as a signal for responding.

[2] It is not yet clear how one demonstrates that all the stimuli on the S_2 dimension are at an equal distance from S_1. Tests of inhibitory control depend heavily on this assumption. If S_1 and S_2 are both in the dimension sampled during the test, then perhaps only a poorly scaled excitatory gradient was obtained. The line-orientation dimension, for example, comes in for this form of critical attention. If the bird only attends to a small area of the key, changes in the orientation of the line may only serve to increase or reduce the amount of this area covered by green or white light. This would place both S_1 and S_2 on the same dimension and, if true, would invalidate a large body of inhibitory stimulus-control literature. It is easy to think of objections to the above view. Most objections only nibble at the edges of the argument, that is, few birds always peck at the same spot on the key, excitatory and inhibitory gradients are not symmetrical, etc.

The real error in the one-dimension criticism is that it fails to predict the results of the postdiscrimination line-orientation test. Consider the following pair of experiments. In the first experiment birds are switched from *mult* VI 1-minute VI 1-minute to *mult* VI 1-minute VI 5-minute; in a second experiment birds are switched from *mult* VI 5-minute VI 5-minute to *mult* VI 1-minute VI 5-minute. Now, if a vertical line is S_1, correlated with the VI 1-minute schedule in both experiments, then fairly steep excitatory gradients will be observed in *both* experiments. Yet if the vertical line is S_2, correlated with the VI 5-minute schedule in both experiments, only the first experiment will yield inhibitory control. (The foregoing assumes that no line is projected on the key during the opposite stimulus component). No single-dimension account of the results of the first experiment can explain the results of the second experiment. Appeals to the reasonable nature of the view that no stimulus dimension can be orthogonal to another are to no avail. Even dimensions that are functionally orthogonal to S_1 over limited range can probably provide a test for inhibitory stimulus control over that range.

We shall concentrate mainly on the determinants of inhibitory stimulus control. However, two commonly observed by-products of operant discrimination learning, the peak shift and behavioral interactions in multiple schedules, are sometimes discussed in the context of inhibitory control. The next two sections of this chapter introduce these phenomena.

The Peak Shift

Sometimes the postdiscrimination test is in a dimension common to both S_1 and S_2. The finding has been a shift in the peak of the gradient from the stimulus correlated with reinforcement, S_1, away from the stimulus correlated with extinction, S_2 (Hanson, 1959). It has been suggested that the peak shift is a result of the formation of an underlying U-shaped gradient of inhibition about S_2 (Thomas & Williams, 1963; Terrace, 1966b). Hearst's (1968) manipulation of empirically derived gradients is an interesting extension of this view. But it is not necessary to subscribe to the rather cumbersome hypothesis that the peak shift is the result of the algebraic summation of excitatory and inhibitory gradients just because it is likely that both the peak shift and inhibitory stimulus control are the result of some form of operant inhibitory control. For the present at least, we should follow Jenkins's (1965) advice to pursue the two phenomena independently.

Interactions in Multiple Schedules

Although a low rate of responding in the presence of one of two alternating discriminative stimuli does not necessarily implicate an inhibitory process, much useful information can be gleaned from rate functions obtained during discrimination training. Reynolds (1961) noted that in the course of discrimination training on a multiple schedule of reinforcement, the rate of responding to S_1 may change as a result of a change in the schedule correlated with S_2. He suggested a classificatory scheme that simplified the discussion of interactions in a multiple schedule. If the rate of response to S_1 increases, the interaction is positive; if the rate decreases, the interaction is negative. If the change in the rate of responding to S_1 is toward the rate of responding to S_2, the interaction is called *induction;* if the change is in a direction opposite the rate prevailing in S_2 the change is called *behavioral contrast.* A frequently observed interaction is positive behavioral contrast. When S_1 is correlated with variable-interval (VI) reinforcement and S_2 is correlated with extinction (EXT), the rate of responding to S_1 often increases dramatically (Reynolds, 1961; Terrace, 1963a). It was of course following *mult* VI EXT discrimination training that inhibitory stimulus control and the peak shift were first obtained (Jenkins & Harrison, 1962; Hanson, 1959).

DISCRIMINATION TRAINING

The peak shift, inhibitory stimulus control, and behavioral contrast are sometimes grouped together as symptoms of inhibitory or aversive control arising from at least some forms of operant discrimination learning. This view will be discussed at length in a later section. In the meantime, it is worthwhile to ask whether simple extinction is sufficient to produce inhibitory control or whether interspersed reinforcement and extinction is an important antecedent of the phenomena. Honig, Thomas, and Guttman (1959) showed that reinforcement in the presence of one wave length followed by separate (simple) extinction to an adjacent wave length did not result in a shift in the peak of the postdiscrimination gradient. Weisman and Palmer (1969) found only flat line orientation gradients after reinforcement and extinction at a vertical line and no evidence of behavioral contrast to a blank key presented during nondifferential reinforcement and again during the test. Moreover, the duration of discrimination training has been shown to be an important determinant of the amount of inhibitory control (Farthing & Hearst, 1968). Apparently, some aspect of discrimination training is a necessary antecedent of these phenomena.

REDUCTION IN THE RATE OF RESPONDING TO A DISCRIMINATIVE STIMULUS

Terrace (1966b) has pointed out that inhibitory stimulus control, the peak shift, and behavioral contrast can be related. The three phenomena may be the result of a form of operant discrimination learning dependent on inhibitory or aversive control by S_2. More explicitly, Terrace (1968) has proposed a reduction in response rate to S_2, rather than any reduction in reinforcement frequency, as the determinant of inhibitory control. The origin of Terrace's hypothesis seems to lie in a series of experiments concerned with "errorless" discrimination (1963a, 1963b, 1964, 1966a). In this work Terrace has shown that: (a) under certain circumstances birds can learn a discrimination between a stimulus correlated with reinforcement, S_1, and another stimulus, S_2, correlated with nonreinforcement with few, if any, errors (responses to S_2); (b) that typical, that is, "errorful" discrimination is disrupted by injections of Chlorpromazine and Imipromine, but errorless discrimination is not affected by either drug; and (c) contrast, the peak shift, and inhibitory stimulus control are seen after errorful, but not after errorless, discrimination learning. Terrace implicated responding rather than reinforcement because both errorless and errorful discriminations correlate nonreinforcement with S_2, but only errorful discrimination correlates extinction, a reduction in the rate of responding, with S_2. This analysis may prove accurate even if other, as yet unspecified, differences between errrorful and errorless discrimination learning are uncovered.

The present discussion has proceeded as if the only possible multiple-schedule discrimination was between stimuli correlated with VI schedules and stimuli correlated with extinction. In fact any combination of schedules of reinforcement, each correlated with a discriminative stimulus, may be presented in a multiple schedule (Ferster & Skinner, 1957). In the following discussion the schedule correlated with S_1 is almost always VI 1-minute reinforcement. The frequencies of reinforcement and of electric shock, as well as the rate of responding, correlated with S_2, were manipulated by variations in the schedules of reinforcement and punishment presented during S_2.

Although the peak shift was first investigated using *mult* VI EXT schedules, the phenomenon does not appear to be dependent on the alternation of reinforcement and extinction. Guttman (1959) obtained a peak shift following *mult* VI 1-minute VI 5-minute training. Terrace (1968) found that both postdiscrimination peak shift and behavioral contrast appeared to be dependent on a reduction in the rate of responding to S_2. He produced a reliable reduction in response rate by preceding *mult* VI 1-minute VI 5-minute discrimination with *mult* VI 1-minute VI 1-minute nondifferential reinforcement. If discrimination training was preceded by *mult* VI 5-minute VI 5-minute nondifferential reinforcement *and* did not reduce responding to S_2, then no peak shift was observed.

Is the peak shift a symptom of inhibitory control, when schedules of positive reinforcement are correlated with both S_1 and S_2? Weisman (1969b) investigated inhibitory stimulus control following discrimination training similar to that administered by Terrace (1968). He required a discrimination between a white vertical line and its absence, on a green surround, whereas Terrace used wavelength stimuli. Inhibitory stimulus control and behavioral contrast followed a reduction in responding to S_2 in Weisman's experiment.

In the preceding work, inhibitory stimulus control followed a reduction in response rate and reinforcement frequency. Weisman (1969a, 1969b) has studied multiple-schedule discriminations that did not result in any change in the frequency of reinforcement correlated with S_2. The schedules correlated with S_2 in this work differentially reinforced the nonoccurrence of pecking. If responses preceded for a specified time by the nonoccurrence of responding are reinforced, and nonreinforced responses postpone reinforcement, the schedule is termed the differential reinforcement of low rate (DRL). If the specified time period must terminate without a response, and *any* response postpones reinforcement, the schedule is termed the differential reinforcement of other behavior (DRO). In one experiment (Weisman, 1969b) birds were shifted from *mult* VI 1-minute VI 1-minute to VI 1-minute DRL. The frequency of reinforcement was held constant by manipulation of the duration of the DRL requirement. In a second experiment (Weisman, 1969a) birds were shifted to *mult* VI 1-minute DRO, but the experiment was in other ways like the DRL discrimination. Both multiple schedules generated behavioral contrast and inhibitory stimulus control, even though the frequency of reinforcement correlated with S_2 was unchanged from prior nondifferential reinforcement and was nearly identical to that correlated with S_1. These results indicate that a reduction in the relative rate of reinforcement, correlated with a discriminative stimulus, is not a necessary antecedent of inhibitory stimulus control or behavioral contrast. Instead, both phenomena may be the result of a reduction in the rate of responding to a discriminative stimulus. These data, and those of Terrace (1968) for a peak shift following *mult* VI 1-minute DRL, are in line with Terrace's (1966b) hypothesis that a stimulus (S_2) correlated with a reduction in the rate of responding becomes a "functional $S-$."

CONTINGENCY BETWEEN RESPONDING AND REINFORCEMENT

The case for Terrace's (1968) hypothesis linking a reduction in the rate of responding correlated with S_2 and the symptoms of inhibitory and aversive control has been presented. Clearly the results of a substantial number of experiments are in line with the hypothesis.

However, not all the operations that reduce the response rate to S_2 result in inhibitory stimulus control. Nevin (1968) has already reported a possible boundary condition. He increased the rate of reinforcement correlated with S_2 during *mult* VI 3-minute DRO training. Postdiscrimination gradients obtained from this condition were flat, and induction rather than contrast occurred in S_1. Thus Nevin's results are an exception to Terrace's rule relating inhibitory stimulus control to a reduction in the rate of responding to S_2.

Nevin's results might be caused by some special features of his experiment (cf. Weisman, 1969a), or they might be part of a more general class of negations of Terrace's rule. The present section deals with the latter alternative. Suppose only a subset of all possible procedures for reducing the rate of responding to S_2 produces behavioral contrast and inhibitory stimulus control. Consider two effective procedures for generating a rate reduction in S_2: (a) Increasing the correlation in time between responding and nonreinforcement. This subset would include extinction, DRL, and a shift from a VI 1-minute to a VI 5-minute schedule. (b) Increasing the correlation in time between not responding and reinforcement. The only "pure" example of this subset that comes to mind is the response-dependent variable-time schedule (VT) in which reinforcements are delivered independently of responding and, thus, often after a period of nonresponding. Rescorla and Skucy (1969) showed that responding can reach a very low stable rate under VT.[3] The DRO schedules used by Weisman (1969a) and Nevin (1968) differed in the degree to which they correlated nonreinforcement with responding and reinforcement with not responding. Weisman (1969a) held equal the frequency of reinforcement for responding to S_1 and for not responding to S_2, but markedly reduced the correlation in time between responding and reinforcement in S_2. Nevin's (1968) *mult* VI DRO schedules tended to increase the frequency of reinforcement for not responding, while only moderately reducing the correlation in time between responding and reinforcement in S_2.

Consider the following possible exception to Terrace's rule. After nondifferential reinforcement (*mult* VI 1-minute VI 1-minute), birds are switched to a multiple schedule in which VT 1-minute is correlated with a vertical line on a green surround, S_2, and VI 1-minute is correlated with the green surround alone, S_1. The rate of responding to S_2 would be reduced as the contingencies correlated with S_1 and S_2 interacted with responding. Would the *mult* VI 1-minute VT 1-minute schedule yield behavioral contrast and inhibitory stimulus control? Terrace's rule suggests that both phenomena would be obtained. The present hypothesis makes a different prediction. Since the shift from VI to VT increases the correlation between the nonoccurrence of responding and reinforcement but does not appear to affect the correlation between responding and nonreinforcement, neither behavioral contrast nor inhibitory stimulus control would be expected. The hypothesis specifically indicts an increase in the correlation between responding and nonreinforcement as an important antecedent of both phenomena.

BEHAVIORAL INTERACTIONS IN THE POSTDISCRIMINATION GRADIENT

Behavioral contrast precedes the observation of inhibitory stimulus control and the peak shift. Terrace (1966b) once suggested

[3] The VT schedule used by Rescorla and Skucy (1969) reduced responding to a lower rate than the fixed-time schedule used by Skinner (1938) in a similar experiment. FT following regular FI would maximize the correlation in time of reinforcement and responding and thus prolong responding when compared to the change from regular VI to VT, where more uniform response rates would prevail.

that contrast may itself be a determinant of the post discrimination gradient. Other aspects of the interaction between the components in multiple schedules may also be relevant. Perhaps it was an oversight to view the generalization test as quite separate from the discrimination training it followed. For example, positive behavioral contrast can be observed in the generalization data of birds that showed a similar interaction during discrimination training (Weisman & Palmer, 1969). Other interactions, for example, negative contrast and induction, observed during discrimination learning (Reynolds, 1961; Catania & Gill, 1964; Nevin & Shettleworth, 1965) may be "buried" in the immense number of sequential stimulus patterns presented during the typical postdiscrimination generalization test.

Donahoe, McCroskery, and Richardson (1968)[4] trained birds to discriminate between two stimuli on the brightness dimension using a *mult* VI 1-minute EXT schedule. Later, they obtained gradients based on testing at three points in the brightness dimension; some birds had a three-stimulus test, others were tested at only one brightness value at a time. Gradients constructed from the data of birds tested the latter way were much flatter than those obtained from birds tested at all three values simultaneously. Only birds that received the three-stimulus test showed clear evidence of a peak shift. The investigators chose to interpret their finding as evidence for "contextual effects" (in Reynold's terms, behavioral interactions) in the postdiscrimination gradient. One drawback in their design was the necessity of alternating discrimination and generalization sessions in order to obtain three single-stimulus tests. Multiple testing can affect the shape of the post discrimination gradient (Terrace, 1966c).

There is another, perhaps simpler, method for extracting the interactions between stimuli presented during a generalization test. An example from preliminary work conducted in this author's laboratory will illustrate the procedure. Discrimination training (*mult* VI 1-minute EXT) was followed by a generalization test in extinction but using only three stimuli: a blank green surround (S_1), a vertical white line on a green surround (S_2), and another

[4] A description of this work is given as Experiment Eight in Donahoe's chapter in this volume.

line orientation (S_g). The test was arranged so that each stimulus preceded itself and each of the other two stimuli an equal number of times and in a randomized sequence of the three stimuli taken two at a time. Behavioral interactions were observed in the data obtained from some of the birds. That is, when both S_2 and S_g were preceded by S_2 these birds responded about equally to each, but when both S_2 and S_g were preceded by either S_1 or S_g the birds responded much less to S_2. However, only about half the birds showed this interaction pattern, yet all the birds tested showed an inhibitory effect (less responding to S_2 than to S_g). Apparently a behavioral interaction model of inhibitory stimulus control will have to be based on more than interactions occurring during the generalization test.

EMOTIONAL AND AVERSIVE CORRELATES OF NONREINFORCEMENT

It is well known that Skinner (1938) rejected Pavlov's formulation of conditioned inhibition. Skinner's redefinition of inhibition as a subset of conditioned emotional reactions is not often cited. "Failure to reinforce a response is one of the operations depressing reflex strength through an emotion change, and there is little or no distinction to be drawn between inhibition and one kind of emotion" (Skinner, 1938, p. 233). In fact, gross emotional responses to a stimulus correlated with extinction have been observed (Terrace, 1966b).

An equivalence between the emotional effects of the nonreinforcement of responding and the punishment of responding has been suggested (Terrace, 1968). Nonreinforcement and shock correlated with responding in the presence of a discriminative stimulus can have the following effects: (a) a reduction in the rate of responding to stimulus, (b) behavioral contrast (Brethower & Reynolds, 1962; Terrace, 1968), (c) postdiscrimination peak shift (Terrace, 1968), (d) a U-shaped gradient of responding, that is, inhibitory stimulus control (Honig, 1966; Weisman & Palmer, 1969), and (e) elicited aggression (Azrin, Hutchinson, & Hake, 1966). Apparently, at least some of the procedures for the delivery of electric shock and extinction have functionally equivalent effects on discrimination learning. Further evidence of this sort was presented by Grusec (1968). He showed that the addition of electric shock to a previously established errorless discrimination resulted in a peak shift in the postdiscrimination gradient. Electric shock also increased the peak shift obtained with a procedure that involved errors. It would appear that the effects of electric shock and extinction combine in the direction predicted by Terrace's (1963a) hypothesis.

That hypothesis would also predict that a stimulus correlated with extinction, S_2, would function as a conditioned aversive stimulus. For example, does the termination of S_2 generate escape behavior, and would a contingency between responding and the presentation of S_2 reduce the future probability of a response? The answers to these questions are not so easy to obtain as might first appear. If response-contingent termination of S_2 has the effect of reinstating the discriminative stimulus for reinforcement, then conditioned reinforcement rather than escape might well account for the result. Similarly, a reduction in the rate of responding resulting from a contingency between responding and the presentation of S_2 correlated with nonreinforcement does not necessarily demonstrate that S_2 is a conditioned punisher. The implication is that the acquisition of a response that increases the frequency of food reinforcement would not seem to require further explanation.

Rilling, Ahlskog, and Askew (1968) trained birds to escape S_2 by darkening the operant chamber. The escape response occurred only infrequently during the discriminative stimulus for VI 30-second reinforcement. However, considerable escape responding occurred during S_2. Weisman and Premack (1966) examined the punishment function of S_2. After *mult* VI 5-minute EXT discrimination was established, responses emitted during the stimulus correlated with reinforcement produced brief presentation of S_2. The rate of responding, measured in the absence of S_2, was reduced by a factor of two. Other stimuli in the same dimension as S_2 reduced responding less than S_2, that is, a gradient of conditioned punishment was obtained. It is worth noting that the magnitude of the escape and punishment effects described above is not so great as that observed when S_2 was correlated with electric shock (Hake & Azrin, 1965).

Neither escape responding nor punishment are permanent

features of discrimination training involving nonreinforcement. Behavioral contrast and the peak shift are also much reduced as a result of extended discrimination training (Terrace, 1966c). The effect of extended discrimination training on inhibitory stimulus control is not known. A flat gradient might be obtained after extended training in which the emotional effects of nonreinforcement dissipate. It may be the case that the emotional reaction to nonreinforcement and not nonreinforcement per se is the critical determinant of aversive and inhibitory control (Terrace, 1966b).

REFERENCES

Azrin, N. H., Hutchinson, R. R., & Hake, D. F. Extinction-induced aggression. *J. exp. anal. Behav.*, 1966, **9**, 191–204.

Brethower, D. M., & Reynolds, G. S. A facilitative effect of punishment on unpunished behavior. *J. exp. anal. Behav.*, 1962, **5**, 191–199.

Catania, A. C., & Gill, C. A. Inhibition and behavioral contrast. *Psychon. Sci.*, 1964, **1**, 257–258.

Donahoe, J. W., McCroskery, J. H., & Richardson, W. K. Effects of induction on the post-discrimination gradient. Paper presented at Psychonomic Society meeting, St. Louis, 1968.

Farthing, G. W., & Hearst, E. Generalization gradients of inhibition after differential amounts of training. *J. exp. anal. Behav.*, 1968, **11**, 743–752.

Ferster, C. B., & Skinner, B. F. *Schedules of reinforcement.* New York: Appleton-Century-Crofts, 1957.

Grusec, T. The peak shift in stimulus generalization: Equivalent effect in errors and non-contingent shock. *J. exp. anal. Behav.*, 1968, **11**, 239–249.

Guttman, N. Generalization gradients around stimuli associated with different reinforcement schedules. *J. exp. Psychol.*, 1959, **58**, 335–340.

Hake, D. F., & Azrin, N. H. Conditioned punishment. *J. exp. anal. Behav.*, 1965, **8**, 279–293.

Hanson, H. M. Effects of discrimination training on stimulus generalization. *J. exp. Psychol.*, 1959, **58**, 321–334.

Hearst, E. Discrimination learning as the summation of excitation and inhibition. *Science*, 1968, **162**, 1303–1306.

Honig, W. K. The role of discrimination training in the generalization of punishment. *J. exp. anal. Behav.*, 1966, **9**, 377–384.

Honig, W. K., Boneau, C. A., Burstein, K. P., & Pennypacker, H. S. Positive and negative generalization gradients obtained after equivalent training conditions. *J. comp. physiol. Psychol.*, 1963, **56**, 111–116.

Honig, W. K., Thomas, D. R., & Guttman, N. Differential effects of continuous extinction and discrimination training on the generalization gradient. *J. exp. Psychol.*, 1959, **58**, 145–152.

308 *Current Issues in Animal Learning*

Hull, C. L. *A behavior system.* New Haven: Yale University Press, 1952.
Jenkins, H. M. Generalization gradients and the concept of inhibition. In D. I. Mostofsky (Ed.), *Stimulus generalization.* Stanford, California: Stanford University Press, 1965. Pp. 55–61.
Jenkins, H. M., & Harrison, R. H. Effect of discrimination training on auditory generalization. *J. exp. Psychol.*, 1960, **59**, 246–253.
Jenkins, H. M., & Harrison, R. H. Generalization gradients of inhibition following auditory discrimination learning. *J. exp. anal. Behav.*, 1962, **5**, 435–441.
Nevin, J. A. Differential reinforcement and stimulus control of not responding. *J. exp. anal. Behav.*, 1968, **11**, 715–726.
Nevin, J. A., & Shettleworth, Sara. An analysis of contrast effects in multiple schedules. *J. exp. anal. Behav.*, 1966, **9**, 305–315.
Pavlov, I. P. *Conditioned reflexes.* London: Oxford University Press, 1927.
Rescorla, R. A., & Skucy, J. C. Effect of response-independent reinforcers during extinction. *J. comp. physiol. Psychol.*, 1969, **67**, 376–380.
Reynolds, G. S. Behavioral contrast. *J. exp. anal. Behav.*, 1961, **4**, 57–71.
Rilling, M. E., Ahlskog, J. E., & Askew, H. R. Aversive effects of discrimination. *Amer. Psychologist*, 1968, **23**, 647.
Skinner, B. F. *The behavior of organisms.* New York: Appleton-Century-Crofts, 1938.
Spence, K. W. The differential response in animals to stimuli varying within a single dimension. *Psychol. Rev.*, 1937, **44**, 430–444.
Terrace, H. S. Discrimination learning with and without "errors." *J. exp. anal. Behav.*, 1963a, **6**, 1–27.
Terrace, H. S. Errorless discrimination learning in the pigeon: Effects of chloropromazine and imipramine. *Science*, 1963b, **140**, 318–319.
Terrace, H. S. Wavelength generalization after discrimination learning with and without errors. *Science*, 1964, **144**, 78–80.
Terrace, H. S. Discrimination learning and inhibition. *Science*, 1966a, **154**, 1677–1680.
Terrace, H. S. Stimulus control. In W. K. Honig (Ed.), *Operant behavior: Areas of research and application.* New York: Appleton-Century-Crofts, 1966b. Pp. 271–344.
Terrace, H. S. Behavioral contrast and the peak shift: Effects of extended discrimination training. *J. exp. anal. Behav.*, 1966c, **9**, 613–617.
Terrace, H. S. Discrimination learning, the peak shift, and behavioral contrast. *J. exp. anal. Behav.*, 1968, **11**, 727–741.
Thomas, D. R. & Williams, J. L. A further study of stimulus generalization following three-stimulus discrimination training. *J. exp. anal. Behav.*, 1963, **6**, 171–176.
Weisman, R. G. Some determinants of the post-discrimination gradient of inhibition. Paper presented at Eastern Psychological Association meeting, Philadelphia, 1969a.
Weisman, R. G. Some determinants of inhibitory stimulus control. *J. exp. anal. Behav.*, 1969b, **12**, 443–450.

Weisman, R. G., & Palmer, J. A. Factors influencing inhibitory stimulus control: Discrimination training and prior non-differential reinforcement. *J. exp. anal. Behav.*, 1969, **12**, 229–237.

Weisman, R. G., & Premack, D. Generalization gradients of conditioned punishment and reinforcement determined by the relative probability of reinforcement. Paper presented at Psychonomic Society meeting, St. Louis, 1966.

Stimulus Selection, Attention, and Related Matters[1]

David R. Thomas

University of Colorado

In theorizing about such divergent phenomena as perception and concept formation in humans and discrimination learning in lower animals it has become common practice to consider the "information processing capacity" or "channel capacity" (cf. Broadbent, 1958) of the organism. Assuming a physical limit to the amount of information which a particular nervous system can process or transmit at a given point in time, it has been proposed that some mechanism must operate to filter the input to select for transmission or storage those stimulus events most likely to be of significance to the organism. This selective mechanism may operate on the basis of instructions, past experience, an innate hierarchy of stimulus significance determined at conception, etc. (cf. Baron, 1965; Gilbert, 1969; and others).

It has also been proposed that discrimination learning is a two-stage process. First, the subject must learn which attribute or attributes of the stimuli are relevant for the solution of the problem, and only later are specific response tendencies, such as turn right or bar press, attached to or associated with particular stimulus values. For instance, for rats to learn to discriminate between horizontal and vertical white bars on a black field in a jumping stand, they must first learn that orientation is the relevant cue and later learn, for example, to jump toward horizontal and away from

[1] This research was supported by research grant NIH–HD–03486 from the National Institute of Health. Many students have participated in this project, but the contributions of Joseph Lyons, Frederick Freeman, Richard W. Switalski, John G. Svinicki, Marilla D. Svinicki, D. E. Scott Burr, and Kenneth O. Eck are particularly noteworthy.

311

vertical. To accomplish this, responses to position, brightness, etc., must first be eliminated.

Notions such as the above are freely expressed in the writings of Lawrence (1950), Mackintosh (1965a), Sutherland (1964), Trabasso and Bower (1968), and others. In one version of selective attention theory, that of Sutherland and Mackintosh, the selective mechanism is labeled a "stimulus analyzer" and a set of rules is proposed which governs the operation of the analyzers. Specifically, it is assumed that behavior controlled by an environmental cue is mediated by the operation of the appropriate stimulus analyzer so that if that analyzer is not "switched in" the cue will be ineffective either in eliciting a previously learned response or in acquiring control over new response tendencies. Actually, as might be expected, this is an oversimplification, and more recent statements of analyzer theory (cf. Mackintosh, 1965a) have acknowledged that the state of an analyzer is not all or none. In other words, more than one analyzer can be simultaneously switched in, some more strongly than others. The more strongly an analyzer is switched in, the more strongly will the relevant environmental cues be associated with subsequent behavior. However, because of physical limitations of the organism, the more strongly one analyzer is switched in, the less strongly others will be switched in. How strongly an analyzer is switched in is presumed to depend on the validity of its outputs, that is, "on differences in its outputs being consistently associated with the subsequent occurrence of events of importance to the animal" (Sutherland, 1964, p. 57).

An organism may be said to be "selectively attending" to that dimension for which the appropriate stimulus analyzer (e.g., that for wave length, brightness, etc.) is (most strongly) switched in. Evidence of such attention may be inferred from correct performance in a transfer test, a sloping generalization gradient when the dimension in question is varied, etc.

The fact that not all potential stimuli which impinge upon an organism's receptors are equally likely to gain control over that organism's behavior has been acknowledged since the time of William James (1890). It seems obvious that organisms differ in the salience attributed to different cues as a function of individual and species differences in sensory capacity, the momentary state of the organism, past experience with the cue in question, stimulus intensity, the spatial orientation of the subject, and so on. In addition, if two or more cues are available for the solution of a particular problem the subject may favor the easiest one, that is, it may select that dimension along which the stimulus events differ most discriminably. It is also clear that more than one stimulus can simultaneously gain some control over the subject's behavior, though not necessarily to the same degree. Furthermore, pretraining has been shown to influence which aspects of a complex stimulus subsequently gain more control over behavior, perhaps by making certain cues or dimensions "distinctive" (cf. Lawrence, 1950). These basic facts of stimulus selection are not in dispute. What we do wish to question is the contention of some selective attention theorists that stimuli "compete" for attention or control over behavior, so that the more attention paid to one stimulus aspect or attribute, the less necessarily is paid to others. Explicit statements of this "inverse hypothesis" are numerous. Sutherland and Mackintosh (1964, p. 529) asserted that "in a discrimination situation containing two cues, the more an individual learns about one cue, the less it will learn about the other." This prediction is explicitly made in several additional papers by the same authors.

In a review of various meanings of the term *attention,* vom Saal (1967, p. 13) stated: "The fourth meaning of attention reserves it for situations where increased control by one stimulus dimension is found to be accompanied by decreased control by a second stimulus dimension. Such a relation will be termed a trading relation."

Switalski, Lyons, and Thomas (1966, p. 665) proposed "the assumption that the controlling influence of all (internal and external) stimuli is of fixed extent, following the analogy of a pie. Thus the greater the number of controlling stimuli and the greater their influence, the lesser the degree of control available to other stimuli, i.e., the smaller their share of the pie."

The inverse hypothesis is so commonly assumed by selective attention theorists that it is appropriate to point out that it does not necessarily follow from the postulation of a stimulus selection mechanism or from a fixed channel capacity. In their pie analogy Switalski, Lyons, and Thomas (1966) did not acknowledge the implicit assumption that the *whole pie* is allocated to different stimuli, so that an enlarged share for one necessarily means a reduced share for another. If part of the pie were unassigned, a larger share for one stimulus might not be available at the cost of a smaller share for another; indeed both shares might increase concurrently. To say that part of the pie is unassigned is simply to say that the subject is working below his capacity to transmit and process information. In view of the substantial complexity of the stimuli which animals have proved capable of discriminating, it seems quite justifiable to make such as assumption for the simple situations in which an animal is required to discriminate between two wave lengths, two tones, etc., as typically employed in our laboratory. Other theorists, such as Bower and Trabasso (1963) and Broadbent (1961), have also suggested that the inverse hypothesis may only apply in complex or demanding experimental situations.

An additional implicit assumption of Switalski, Lyons, and Thomas (1966) was that the size of the pie is fixed. Although this might be true of a particular point in time, it seems reasonable to speculate that the (attentional) pie might increase over time as a consequence of such things as maturation or learning experiences. In particular, we have made the argument elsewhere (cf. Thomas, 1969; Eck, Noel, and Thomas, 1969) that discrimination training enhances the capacity of the organism to attend to stimulus dimensions other than the one involved in such training. The evidence which led to this conclusion will be reviewed later in this chapter.

An updated version of the pie hypothesis would contend: (a) that certain training experiences can increase the degree of control gained by several aspects of a complex stimulus, and (b) that at a given point in time there will be an inverse relationship between the degree of control gained by different stimulus dimensions only when the information-processing capacity of the subject is being "strained." As pointed out previously, there is now substantial evidence in support of point (a), but the evidence relevant to point (b) remains to be obtained.

In this chapter we shall describe a program of research designed to investigate the relationship between the degree of control acquired by two dimensions of a complex training stimulus. In particular, we have attempted on most occasions to test the hypothesis that increases in stimulus control by one dimension are associated with decreases in control by another dimension. Studies performed in other laboratories which have tested the same hypothesis often will be discussed, particularly as they relate to our own work. Our definition of the problem as involving the measurement of stimulus control along a given dimension precludes consideration of many examples of stimulus selection which are not relevant to the inverse hypothesis as we have defined it. One example thus precluded is the finding by Egger and Miller (1962) that of two stimuli which invariably precede food delivery, the first, or informative, stimulus will gain conditioned reinforcing value, while the second, redundant, stimulus will not. Another example is the related finding by Kamin (1969) in a CER situation that if rats learn to suppress responding in the presence of a noise, and later a light is added to the noise, they will not learn to suppress in the presence of the light, although they would have if not for the prior training with the noise. In this situation, as in the preceding one, no measure of stimulus control by any attribute of the light other than its presence-absence is taken. For our purposes, this is an important limitation. A high rate of responding in the presence of a particular dimensional stimulus (e.g. a wave length) is not sufficient evidence of control by the wave-length dimension, since equally high rates may be emitted in the presence of all wave lengths. By the same token, a low rate may signify stimulus control of an inhibitory tendency if higher rates are emitted to generalization test stimuli. Attention may be just as legitimately inferred from inhibitory gradients as from excitatory ones (cf. Jenkins, 1965).

In our work, to achieve generality, several different species of subjects, training and test conditions, measures of attention or stimulus control, etc., were used. It is probably fair to say at the outset that our results generally contradict predictions based on the inverse hypothesis. Often particular reference is made to stimulus analyzer theory because this is a particularly explicit statement of the selective attention position, but for the most part the comments could refer equally well to several other related theories. A discussion of the relationship of these findings to those of others and their significance for a general theory of attention will conclude the chapter.

It may be useful in describing the experiments performed in our laboratories to first discuss aspects of rationale and procedure common to most of them. Except where otherwise noted, the experiments have used pigeons as subjects and have utilized operant conditioning techniques. The birds are trained to peck a key illuminated by a particular stimulus, say a light of 550 mμ. After several days of variable interval reinforcement for responding to this stimulus, a generalization test is performed (in extinction) in which the subjects are exposed to a random sequence of short exposures (e.g., 30 seconds) of a wide range of test stimuli (in this case, wave lengths), including the original. A measure of rate of responding typically reveals the highest response rate to the training stimulus value and a progressively decreasing rate to stimuli increasingly removed from this value. This decremental generalization gradient provides a measure of stimulus control: the steeper the gradient, the greater the control. It may also be used to infer that the subject attended to that aspect of the training stimulus which is manipulated to produce the gradient, and the steeper the gradient, the greater the degree of attention that may be inferred. If the bird had not attended to the wave-length of the training stimulus, it would necessarily respond randomly and nondifferentially to test stimuli which differ only along the wave-length dimension.

In the example given, the birds were trained with a stimulus, in this case a particular wave length, and then tested for generalization along one dimension (wave length) of that stimulus. Of course, it would be equally plausible to test along other dimensions of the stimulus (e.g., brightness, saturation), in order to infer whether the birds had attended to those aspects of the training stimulus.

Typically, individual *S*s' generalization gradients are plotted in two ways: (1) in terms of total responses made to each of the test stimuli, that is, absolute gradients, and (2) in terms of the percentage of total responses emitted to each generalization test stimulus, that is, relative gradients. This latter procedure permits the obtaining of a group-average gradient to which each subject contributes equally and which is therefore more stable and more representative of individual performance than is an average based on absolute gradients. Newman and Grice (1965) have pointed out that different conclusions may result from comparisons of absolute or relative gradients. This is certainly mathematically correct, but it happens only very rarely. We typically prefer relative gradients for the reasons cited above. In none of the studies to be described were group differences in absolute gradients in a direction other than that observed in the comparison of relative gradients.

Most of the generalization studies carried out in our laboratory have employed some sort of discrimination training before the administration of the generalization test. Switalski, Lyons, and Thomas (1966) have provided a useful nomenclature for describing the relationship between discrimination training and subsequent generalization testing. In "intradimensional" training, the positive and negative stimuli are on the same dimension (e.g., wave length), which is the dimension then explored in generalization testing. With interdimensional training, the positive (or negative) stimulus lies along the generalization test dimension, but the other stimulus is either the absence of the first or is on a dimension orthogonal to the test dimension. An example would be a 1,000-cps. tone as S+, silence as S−, and generalization tested along the dimension of frequency (pitch). In "extradimensional" training, the positive and negative stimuli lie on the same dimension, but generalization testing is subsequently carried out along another dimension, which was either present but constant in original training or was introduced later. An example would be discrimination training between two colors at equal brightness and subsequent testing along the brightness dimension.

It seems obvious that one way to call attention to a particular aspect of a training stimulus is to make that aspect relevant to the well-being of the organism. The literature abounds with studies which, following Hanson (1959) have found that discrimination training between two wave lengths sharpens the subsequently obtained wave-length gradient. Riccio, Urda, and Thomas (1966) observed quite flat but reliably decremental generalization gradients by manipulating the angle of the floor on which the pigeons had been standing during reinforced training. Discrimination training between two different floor inclinations sharpened the gradient markedly, however (see Fig. 1). Similar effects have been observed

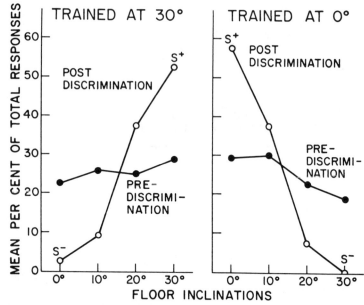

FIG. 1. An example of the effects of intradimensional discrimination training on stimulus generalization. Two groups of pigeons were given single-stimulus training with the floor fixed (at 0° or 30°) and then were given (pre-discrimination) generalization tests. Following discrimination training, a (post-discrimination) generalization test revealed a dramatic sharpening of stimulus control by floor inclination. (From Riccio, Urda, & Thomas, 1966)

along such stimulus dimensions as line angle, brightness, loudness, and pitch.

The results of intradimensional discrimination training referred to above are entirely consistent with an attentional interpretation. The degree to which a given analyzer (say for wave length) is switched in is assumed to vary with the validity, or significance, of its outputs. Unfortunately, the findings are also consistent with (a) common sense, and (b) opposed theoretical orientations, such as that of Spence (1936, 1937). Indeed, the algebraic summation of gradients of excitation and inhibition postulated by Spence to result from intradimensional discrimination training clearly leads to the prediction of a sharpened generalization gradient.

It is appropriate at this point, therefore, to consider when invoking a concept like attention is useful and therefore scientifically justifiable. Attention has sometimes (cf. Terrace, 1966) been identified with individual or group differences in stimulus control after a comparable training experience. Honig (1969a) has suggested (and we agree) that it may be more fruitful to limit the use of the concept to situations in which it can be shown that, following acquisition of a response to a dimensional stimulus (for instance, a particular wave length), stimulus control by that dimension varies systematically with experimental manipulations independent of that acquisition. The identification of attention with manipulable stimulus control suggests that either increases or decreases in stimulus control may be attributed to an attentional process and/or that there may be more than one kind of attentional process. Both of these points will be further discussed in the context of the experimental studies to which they are relevant.

One experimental situation particularly appropriate for studying attentional effects, as we have defined them, involves what Switalski, Lyons, and Thomas (1966) have called "inter-dimensional" training. Such a procedure was employed in the experiment by Jenkins and Harrison (1960) referred to earlier. As indicated, single-stimulus training with one tone frequency led to essentially no control of responding by the frequency dimension. A training condition which produced such control was a discrimination between a particular tone (S+) and silence (S−). Note that silence is off of and orthogonal to the dimension of tonal frequency.

In our laboratory we have performed several experiments with a monochromatic light as one stimulus and a vertical white line on a black surround as the other. Whereas silence and tone provide a test dimension (frequency) orthogonal to the nondimensional stimulus, with our procedure we can vary two dimensions, wave length and line angle, each independent of the other. Our first experiment with these stimuli (Switalski, Lyons, & Thomas, 1966) did not take advantage of the dimensionality of both stimuli, but subsequent studies have. The experiment did, however, produce data which seem to warrant an attentional interpretation. In this study we observed that the degree of control exercised by the wave-length dimension (reflected in the steepness of a generalization gradient along this dimension) is a function of the consequences of responding to a nonwave-length stimulus (a white vertical line on a black surround) which was programmed to alternate randomly with the reinforced wave-length stimulus. In this study, a wave-length generalization gradient was first obtained from each of two groups of pigeons following single-stimulus training. After this, Group 1 was given additional training in which responding to the line and the color were equally reinforced ("interdimensional non-differential training"), and a second generalization test revealed a gradient significantly flattened relative to the single-stimulus control condition. For Group 2, following their first generalization test, only responding to the color was reinforced ("interdimensional discrimination training") and relative to their control condition the wave-length generalization gradient of this group was significantly steepened. The steepening of generalization by interdimensional discrimination training had previously been shown by Jenkins and Harrison (1960) for the tonal frequency dimension. In the Switalski *et al.* study the finding was somewhat equivocal because even under unaltered training conditions a second generalization test (in extinction) typically yields a steeper gradient than the first. It should be remembered, however, that Jenkins and Harrison (1960) obtained the same result without a prior test.

To provide additional information about this point, Lyons (1968) subsequently replicated our finding without administering a generalization test before the administration of discrimination training. Lyons ran three groups of pigeons in his experiment. One group responded to 555 mμ for VI reinforcement but was extinguished for responding to the vertical line. A second group learned the same discrimination but with a modification of Terrace's (1963) procedure allowing no responses to the line by blacking it out when a bird apparently was about to peck at it. A third (control) group was "yoked" to the second, so that whenever a member of Group 2 was reinforced or blacked out (for attempting to respond to the line) its yoked (control) partner was also. The stimulus on the key was always 555 mμ for this control group.

All three of the groups were tested for wave-length general-ization. The discrimination trained group (with errors) produced the steepest gradient, the control group produced the flattest, and the errorless group was intermediate between the two. Even the errorless gradient was reliably steeper than the control, causing Lyons to question Terrace's contention that an errorless S− stimulus is essentially neutral. If it were neutral, presumably alternating it with S+ in training would not have affected the gradient obtained around S+.

The results of Switalski, Lyons, and Thomas (1966) have also been replicated by Lyons and Thomas (1967) in a within-subjects design. A group of nine pigeons was first trained to respond to a 555-mμ stimulus for variable interval reinforcement and then was tested for wave-length generalization. Next the Ss were given 16 days of discrimination training with one-minute periods of 555 mμ (VI reinforced) alternated with one-minute periods of the white vertical line (extinguished), and this treatment was followed by a second generalization test. Then the birds were given 12 successive days of training in which both the 555-mμ and the vertical-line stimuli were equally reinforced, followed by another generalization test.

On the day following the third test, the nine Ss were returned to the discrimination training condition for 16 more days, the last followed immediately by a fourth generalization test like the preceding three. On the next day the conditions were alternated again, and the Ss underwent the first of 12 consecutive days of nondifferential training, the last followed by another generalization test, and so on. Aside from the original single-stimulus condition and the discrimination training condition which followed it, each bird was exposed to six alternations from discrimination to nondifferential training or vice versa.

In this experiment every subject showed a steepened gradient following discrimination training and a flattened gradient following nondifferential training, with not a single deviation from this pattern. These results are shown in Fig. 2.

There can be no question, then, that interdimensional discrimination training steepens generalization gradients (along the positive stimulus dimension), and there would seem to be no reason for a straightforward conditioning-extinction theory (e.g., that of Spence) to predict that it would. This finding, plus the demonstration that nondifferential training flattens generalization gradients, led Switalski, Lyons, and Thomas (1966) to propose their pie

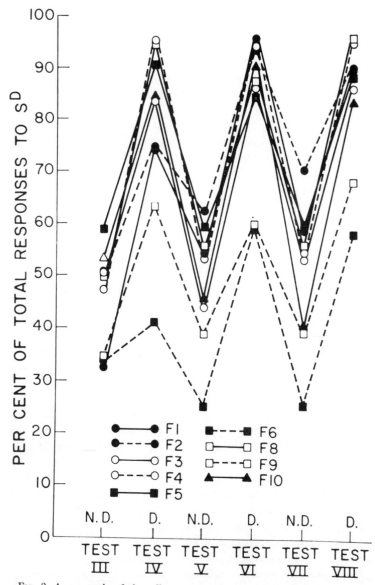

Fig. 2. An example of the effects of interdimensional training on stimulus generalization. For each bird the value plotted is the percentage of total responses given to 555 mµ during the wave-length generalization test; the higher this value, the steeper the gradient. Under the nondifferential (ND) training condition, responses to 555 mµ and to a white vertical line on a black surround were equally reinforced; under the discrimination training (D) condition, only the wave-length value accompanied reinforcement. (From Lyons & Thomas, 1967)

hypothesis. Their argument was simply that with nondifferential training both stimuli come to control responding, thus less control is available to each. Following discrimination training, presumably only one of the two training stimuli exercises control, thus more is available to that one.

The pie hypothesis seemed consistent also with the results of two experiments dealing with the effects of reinforcement schedule on exteroceptive stimulus control. Hearst, Koresko, and Poppen (1964) had shown that DRL schedules produce flatter (angularity) generalization gradients than do VI schedules, and Thomas and Switalski (1966) had shown that a VR schedule produces flatter (wave-length) gradients than does a VI schedule matched for reinforcement frequency and interreinforcement time. The suggestion had been made by Hearst *et al.* that when a reinforcement contingency emphasizes temporal discriminations or proprioceptive feedback from prior behavior, the control exercised by exteroceptive stimuli will consequently be reduced. The results of the Thomas and Switalski (1966) experiment were consistent with this suggestion and led the authors to propose: "Quite conceivably what we have observed in this study is an instance of a much more general phenomenon, i.e., whenever two stimuli of either internal or external origin both become cues for a learned response the degree of control exercised by either is thereby reduced" (Thomas & Switalski, 1966, p. 240). This statement is clearly a precursor to the pie hypothesis.

Suggested modifications designed to bring the pie hypothesis more in line with current knowledge have already been offered. Another point which needs to be made is that the number of controlling stimuli which is relevant in predicting the amount of stimulus control is the number which controls the emission of the response, that is, the excitatory stimuli. It has frequently been shown (Honig *et al.*, 1965; Jenkins & Harrison, 1962; Lyons, 1969; Terrace, 1966; Weisman, 1969; and others) that the negative stimulus in interdimensional discrimination training comes to exert inhibitory control over the response, as demonstrated by the existence of an inverted (U-shaped) gradient of generalization with its minimum at the S− value. Thus interdimensional discrimination training does not reduce the total number of controlling stimuli (by one), but it does reduce the number of excitatory stimuli.

Whether the steepening of generalization gradients by inter-dimensional discrimination training is consistent with stimulus analyzer theory is open to some question. The question reduces to what constitutes different outputs of a given analyzer. Surely green and blue qualify as different outputs of a wave-length (color) analyzer, but do green and nongreen (i.e., a white vertical line on a black surround)? At a common-sense level the comparison of these two stimuli would not necessarily call attention to the wave length of the monochromatic stimulus, since the two stimuli differed also in such things as presence-absence of the line and brightness. Although the wave-length analyzer might be more strongly switched in as a result of interdimensional training, so might the brightness analyzer, the line-angle (orientation) analyzer, and others. Perhaps one could appeal to Baron's (1965) notion of a stimulus-attending hierarchy and argue that wave length is a particularly salient cue for a pigeon, and thus it would be this analyzer which would be strengthened rather than the others. In contemplating what an analyzer does or does not do, it is easy to lose sight of the fact that an analyzer is a fiction, a hypothetical construct which may be assumed to operate in any way whatever if it aids in the prediction of behavior.

In speculating as to why interdimensional discrimination training should steepen gradients of generalization, whereas inter-dimensional nondifferential training flattens them, another, entirely different hypothesis has presented itself. Certainly dis-crimination training results in the subjects' attaching different response tendencies to different stimuli. In addition, however, suppose that such training had a more general effect, that is, that the animal learned the validity of external stimuli as signifying events or contingencies of significance for the welfare of the organism. In this way the benefits of discrimination training would not be specific to the dimension or dimensions varied in training but might generalize to other aspects of the training stimulus as well. By the same token, nondifferential training might serve to teach the animal the insignificance of external stimuli and/or the futility of behaving differentially in their presence, and this learning might generalize to stimuli not involved in the initial training. There is indeed evidence in the literature that under some circumstances animals can learn the futility of their behavior, a phenomenon called "conditioned helplessness" (cf. Seligman, Maier, & Solomon, 1969).

The results of the Switalski, Lyons, and Thomas (1966) experiment are as consistent with the hypothesis that discrimination training leads to a heightened "general attentiveness" as they are with a selective-attention interpretation. To choose between these alternative interpretations, it is essential to employ an experimental situation in which the two viewpoints would make opposed predictions. Incidental learning and, in particular, generalization testing following "extradimensional discrimination training" provide such a situation.

An early experiment relevant to the selective- versus general-attention controversy was performed by Reinhold and Perkins (1955). These investigators gave rats discrimination training, using floor texture, rough or smooth, as the relevant dimension. One brightness of cue card at the end of the runway was present under both S+ and S− conditions. Two control groups were also run. One was given the same number of S+ presentations, with the S− never presented; the second also received only S+ presentations but was reinforced intermittently to control for lack of reinforcement during S− periods for the experimental group. Response strength was tested to the positive training stimulus (cue card) and to a novel stimulus which differed in brightness from the training condition. The S+ floor texture was held constant during the test. A generalization decrement was found for all three groups, but the decrement was significantly greater for the experimental group. Thus discrimination training along one dimension steepened the gradient along another dimension as well.

Honig (1969b) used an "extradimensional" procedure in which the test dimension was not present during discrimination training. For one group of pigeons, discrimination training was given between two colors, white and pink. A second group was given "pseudo-discrimination" training with the same two stimuli. For both groups, the total number of reinforced periods was the same, and they occurred in the same temporal sequence. For the true discrimination (TD) group, reinforcement was always correlated with one stimulus, extinction with the other. For the pseudo-discrimination (PD) group, reinforcement was randomly and equally associated with both stimuli. In Honig's experiment a third group was only presented the $S+$, with blackout periods replacing $S-$ presentations. Typically, no responding occurred during blackouts, and extinction was in effect.

When a TD subject met criterion it was switched, along with a PD and a control S with the same amount of training, to the next (single-stimulus) stage of the experiment. The training stimulus in this stage was three black vertical lines on a white surround. Several days of VI single-stimulus training were followed by a generalization test in extinction, along the angularity dimension. Honig found that the TD group yielded the steepest gradient and the PD group the flattest, with the control group intermediate between the two. These results are entirely comparable to those obtained with interdimensional training by Switalski, Lyons, and Thomas (1966), despite the fact that in the Honig experiment the TD and PD training was temporally separated from, or preceded, the acquisition of control over responding by the test dimension.

The results of the Honig (1969b) experiment and the Reinhold and Perkins (1955) experiment seem unequivocally contradictory to stimulus analyzer theory. That theory would necessarily predict that Honig's TD training would strengthen the color analyzer, so that in subsequent single-stimulus training the S would attend more strongly to the color of the stimulus (more than following PD training), thus learning less about the line angle. This would be reflected in a flatter angularity generalization gradient following TD training, a finding directly opposite that obtained.

Similarly, analyzer theory would predict that Reinhold and Perkins's (1955) rats in the experimental group would attend additionally to the floor texture and thus learn less about the brightness of the cue card, whereas the opposite was found to be the case. The fact that discrimination training transferred positively across stimulus modalities in the Reinhold and Perkins experiment is particularly significant with regard to the specification of a mechanism to account for the transfer. Where transfer is from one visual dimension to another, (peripheral) observing responses (cf. Wyckoff, 1952) are an obvious candidate. Looking carefully at the key to observe the color of the light projected through it would certainly help the animal to notice the line later placed on the key. This argument loses some of its power because the pigeon necessarily looks where it pecks, but even if we ignore this, the argument breaks down when, as in the case of Reinhold & Perkins, we obtain crossmodal positive transfer. How could attending to tactual stimulation from the floor texture facilitate reception of brightness cues at the end of the maze? Instead, a central attentional mechanism seems required. Reinhold and Perkins suggested one, proposing that discrimination training produces a "set-to-discriminate," akin to a learning set, which is reflected in a sharpened generalization gradient along an "irrelevant" dimension. The kinship of this notion to our concept of general attentiveness should be obvious to the reader.

The Honig and the Reinhold and Perkins experiments seemed quite convincing to us, but we felt that the extradimensional training situation provided so clear-cut a test of alternative theoretical positions regarding the nature of attention that it would be fruitful to explore it further. Before discussing this additional work, it may be useful at this point to discuss the advantages of the extradimensional design for the study of attentional effects. Our chief concern in this research has been to determine the relationship between stimulus control along two dimensions, the training dimension and the test dimension, in order to test the inverse hypothesis. In *inter*dimensional training it is impossible to specify a single training dimension, since S+ and S− may differ in many ways. In *extra*dimensional training, the training dimension is clearly specified and furthermore the effects of discrimination and nondifferential training on the training dimension are well known. Discrimination training sharpens control, nondifferential training weakens it (cf. Kalish & Guttman, 1957, 1959). Thus with the extradimensional design there would be two possible findings consistent with the selective attention inverse hypothesis: (1) discrimination training on Dimension 1 flattens gradients on Dimension 2, and (2) nondifferential training on Dimension 1 sharpens gradients on Dimension 2. Note that a general attentiveness position predicts the opposite outcome, that is, the same effects, sharpening or flattening, on both training and test dimensions. Note also that this is what Reinhold and Perkins (1955) and Honig (1969b) found.

We have recently reported a series of five related extradimensional experiments (Thomas, Freeman, Svinicki, Burr, & Lyons, 1970). The first experiment was essentially a replication of the Honig study. One group of pigeons (TD) was trained to discriminate between two (successively presented) wave lengths, whereas a second group (PD) was given nondifferential reinforcement with the same two wave-length values. In the second stage, all birds received single-stimulus training with a vertical white line superimposed on the previously reinforced (for the TD group) wave length. Subsequent generalization testing (in extinction) with various line angles, now on a black background, yielded significantly steeper relative generalization gradients for the members of the TD group.

Experiment 2 was designed to determine whether the obtained positive transfer depended upon a particular (dominance?) relationship of the two stimulus dimensions involved. The TD birds were trained to discriminate between two different line angles (on a black surround), were then given single-stimulus training with the positive line angle superimposed on a particular wave length, and finally were tested for wave-length generalization (with the line removed). Again, TD training produced a sharper gradient than did comparable PD training.

Having replicated the major Honig finding in Experiments 1 and 2, we decided to return to the Reinhold and Perkins one-stage paradigm but with the increased control and precision afforded by the operant techniques which we, and Honig, had used. In Experiment 3, pigeons were trained to discriminate between two wave lengths, with a vertical white line superimposed on each. A second group received PD training with the same two stimuli. Again the TD birds subsequently gave sharper angularity generalization gradients, as shown in Fig. 3.

Like Experiment 2, Experiment 4 was designed to determine whether the same positive transfer effect can be observed in both directions. It can! In Experiment 4 the training dimension was angularity and the test dimension was wave length, but again TD training produced the sharper gradient.

In Experiment 5 we replicated the crossmodal aspect of the Reinhold and Perkins experiment in what was, by far, the most

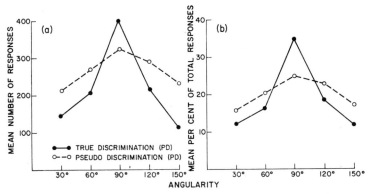

Fig. 3. An example of the effects of extradimensional training on stimulus generalization. Both groups of pigeons were exposed to randomly alternating presentations of 555 mμ and 538 mμ, each with a vertical white line superimposed. For the PD group both values were equally reinforced; for the TD group, only 555 mμ accompanied reinforcement. Subsequent generalization testing revealed a sharper angularity gradient for the TD group, whether plotted in absolute (a) or in relative (b) terms. (From Experiment 3 in Thomas, Freeman, Svinicki, Burr, & Lyons, 1969)

elaborate study in the series. A TD group of pigeons was trained to discriminate between two different angles of floor tilt while a green light continuously illuminated the response key. A single-stimulus control group was matched to the TD birds in the sense that the birds were run in pairs; the control bird experienced only the positive floor tilt, but it received the same number and patterning of reinforcements as its partner. A PD group received nondifferential training with the same two floor tilts, and a second single-stimulus control group was matched to the PD group.

As in all the preceding experiments, TD training produced reliably sharper (wave-length) generalization gradients than did PD training. The TD gradient was reliably sharper than its single-stimulus control; the PD gradient was insignificantly flatter than its single-stimulus control. As expected, the two control gradients did not differ.

In Experiments 1–4 in the Thomas, Freeman, Svinicki, Burr, and Lyons (1970) series, when generalization testing was carried out along one dimension, for instance, wave length, the other (training) dimension, in this case angularity, was removed from the test stimuli. This was done deliberately in an attempt to distinguish between attention (i.e., cue selection during training) and cue utilization during testing as factors influencing the slope of generalization gradients. It is vital that this distinction be made, and several selective attention studies have produced ambiguous results because of a failure to do so.

The point is simply this: when a generalization test reveals a sloping generalization gradient along a given dimension, for example, wave length, it is appropriate to conclude that the subject attended to that aspect of the training stimulus. Assuming that testing conditions are held constant, when one training condition leads to a steeper gradient than another (excepting, of course, intradimensional discrimination training), it can be inferred that under the former condition the animal paid more attention to the relevant stimulus attribute than under the latter. When generalization testing fails to reveal a sloping gradient, however, this does not necessarily mean that the subject did not attend at all to the stimulus dimension in question. Conditions of the test itself also influence the slope of generalization gradients and may prevent the occurrence of a sloping gradient, when under other test conditions, attention to a particular dimension is clearly in evidence. An example of such an error occurred in a study reported by Newman and Baron (1965). One group of pigeons in this study was given single-stimulus training to respond to a compound stimulus, a white vertical line on a green surround. After 10 days of variable interval training, the birds were tested for generalization, in extinction, with five different angles of the line presented in random order, each on the green surround. The angles used were vertical and 22.5° and 45° on either side of vertical.

Newman and Baron found no gradient of generalization under this condition but rather obtained approximately equal responding to all stimuli tested. They explained this finding in terms of a hypothesized hierarchy of attending to different attributes of the stimulus. Presumably color is higher in the pigeons' attending hierarchy than is angularity, and therefore the *S*s attended to the former to the complete exclusion of the latter.

Freeman and Thomas (1967) questioned this conclusion on two bases. Following single-stimulus training, angularity gradients tend to be quite flat. Newman and Baron tested over a relatively restricted range (90°) in comparison with other angularity generalization studies. Quite possibly a decremental gradient would have appeared if generalization testing had covered a greater range.

More importantly we were concerned about the possible role of the green background during the test for angularity generalization. It seemed possible that if color were dominant over angularity, the presence of the positive color during testing might have dominated the Ss' behavior, causing them not to utilize what they had learned about the vertical line during training. To test these speculations

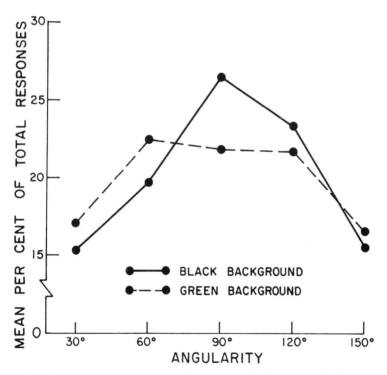

FIG. 4. An example of a masking effect in generalization testing. Both groups received single-stimulus training with a vertical white line on a 555-mμ surround. The relative angularity generalization gradient when tested without the 555-mμ background was significantly steeper than when tested with it. (From Freeman & Thomas, 1967)

we trained many birds as Newman and Baron had done and then tested them over a somewhat increased angularity range (120°) in two different ways, with the green background and without it. In the no-background condition, the lines appeared against a black surround.

The results of this experiment, as shown in Fig. 4, revealed a relatively flat but reliably decremental gradient with the green background and a reliably steeper one with the black background. Thus Newman and Baron were incorrect in concluding that the S did not attend to the angle of the line under their single-stimulus training condition.

The findings of the Freeman and Thomas (1967) experiment have recently been replicated in our laboratory in a within-subjects design by Marilla D. Svinicki, who trained 10 birds with the same line-on-green stimulus used by Newman and Baron (1965) and Freeman and Thomas (1967). In generalization testing, each bird was exposed alternately to a series of five angles on the green surround, then the same five angles (in different random order) on black, then on green, then on black, etc., until each S had been tested for six series under each condition. Thus for each bird a gradient could be plotted for both background conditions and a within-S comparison of gradient slopes made. Eight of the birds yielded steeper gradients under the black background condition, and the mean (relative) generalization gradients obtained under the two conditions differed reliably in slope.

This finding has also been reported in a study by Newman and Benefield (1968) in which pigeons pecked at a blank key and received food on a variable interval schedule, with each feeding preceded by a short exposure of a white vertical line on a green surround. Subsequently the birds were tested for generalization with various angles of line continuously present on the pecking key, with a green background in one group or a black background in the other. Again the black background condition produced the sharper gradient.

In the Freeman and Thomas, the Svinicki, and the Newman and Benefield studies, the presence of a monochromatic background did not prevent the appearance of an angularity gradient, but it did have a significant, though usually small, flattening effect.

Although there have been some unsuccessful attempts to replicate this finding (e.g., Baron & Bresnahan, 1969), it is clear that a masking of stimulus control by a dominant dimension can occur and should be considered before inferring attention, or the lack of it, from the slope of generalization gradients. A particularly striking example of such a masking effect was reported in a crossmodal experiment with rats as subjects by Thomas, Burr, and Eck (1970) and will be described later in this chapter.

It would be premature to conclude on the basis of the above evidence that the most powerful test of stimulus control by a particular dimension necessarily involves the presentation of values from that dimension in isolation. If the level of responding maintained by such stimuli is extremely low, differential responding to them may be impossible to demonstrate reliably. This occurred in a study reported by Farthing and Hearst (1970). Pigeons were trained to respond to a white vertical line on a blue surround and then each bird was tested in two ways, with "elements"—green, blue, horizontal (on black), and vertical (on black)—or "compounds"—green horizontal, blue horizontal, green vertical, and blue vertical. Responding tended to be more controlled by color than by line tilt. Furthermore, only compound trials proved sensitive enough to reveal consistent differential control within the weaker, the line-tilt, dimension. The near-zero response output to horizontal and vertical lines when presented alone (as elements) could have led to the erroneous conclusion that the birds had not attended at all to the line-tilt dimension during training. Thus rather than a masking effect by one dimension over another, in this experiment a multiplicative effect was found, with the effect of the weak dimension increased by combination with the strong dimension. Although the specifics of the Farthing and Hearst result are the opposite of those of the "masking" studies, the lesson to be learned from their experiment is the same. The failure to obtain a sloping generalization gradient under one particular test condition may only *suggest* that S has not attended to that aspect of the training stimulus, since an alteration in the conditions of testing may reveal differential responding which was otherwise latent. Thus the distinction between attention and cue utilization (during the stimulus-control test) remains a valid and significant one.

All the extradimensional discrimination training studies described above produced evidence contradictory to a selective-attention (inverse-hypothesis) prediction. The logic of those experiments seems straightforward enough: if attention to one dimension of a complex stimulus is increased (by appropriate discrimination training), attention to other stimulus dimensions must suffer. The suggestion was made earlier in the chapter, however, that discrimination training may increase the size of the (attentional) "pie," that is, increase the capacity of the subject to attend to more than one dimension of the stimulus. If this were so, then within *S*s the inverse relationship between gradient slopes predicted by selective attention theory might still be attained. This would be so if those subjects which showed the most steepening along the training dimension showed the least steepening along the test dimension and vice versa. The extradimensional discrimination training studies were not carried out in a manner which would permit a test of this hypothesis, since no test for generalization was ever carried out along the training dimension. Logically the question of the relationship between the slopes of gradients measured along two dimensions of a training stimulus can be answered without first giving the animal discrimination training. Thomas, Burr, and Svinicki (1969) reported an experiment in which 20 pigeons were given single-stimulus variable-interval training with a white vertical line on a green surround and then were tested for generalization along both wave-length and angularity dimensions. During presentations of the wave lengths, the line was removed; correspondingly, the lines appeared against a black background. Stimuli from the two dimensions were alternated (i.e., a color, a line, a color, etc.) throughout testing. Thus, for each bird a gradient was obtained along the two dimensions. The measure of generalization slope used was simply the percentage of total responses within each test dimension that was given to the peak, or maximum, value within that dimension. A Pearson Product Moment correlation coefficient, computed using the two peak percentage values obtained from each bird, was significantly different from zero, and contrary to selective attention prediction, *in the positive direction*. Thus, in agreement with the extradimensional discrimination training studies, this experiment also suggests that attention is *general* rather than *selective* and that subjects who pay more attention to color also pay more attention to line angle.

In a recent paper Wagner, Logan, Haberlandt, and Price (1968) reported an extradimensional (crossmodal) study which seems to support the selective attention position. Three different experiments produced entirely comparable results, so only one of them need be considered in detail here. In Experiment 1, rats in one group were trained to discriminate between two tone-plus-light compounds in which the tones differed in frequency but the light was the same. A second group experienced the same two stimuli but were equally reinforced (and extinguished) for responding to both. Wagner *et al.* called these conditions correlated and uncorrelated, and as the reader will note that they correspond exactly to what we, following Honig, have called true discrimination and pseudodiscrimination. The purpose of the experiment was to measure the degree of control over responding acquired by the incidental cue, the light. Whereas we have used generalization slope for this purpose, Wagner *et al.* simply measured response probability in the presence of the light when presented alone. They found that the PD (uncorrelated) group responded reliably more than the TD (correlated) group and then concluded that the cue value of the light (in the TD group) was reduced by the presence of a more valid cue, the tone. This interpretation is, of course, entirely consistent with selective attention theory, although it should be pointed out that this is not the interpretation which Wagner *et al.* prefer.

The finding of less responding to the incidental cue following TD training was replicated in two other experiments and in each case was highly reliable. Although this finding seems consistent with selective attention theory, a logical argument can be made that it is not. The problem, in part, is determining what constitutes an acceptable basis for inferring attention to a particular stimulus (dimension). We have contended that differential responding to values taken from the dimension in question (i.e., a sloping generalization gradient) is an essential condition for inferring attention to that dimension. Note that during the test Wagner *et al.* manipulated no aspect of the light (brightness, duration, etc.); thus no measure of stimulus control by any feature of the light was taken. Had one been obtained, the investigators might have reached a very different conclusion. They might have found, for example, that TD animals respond more selectively than PD animals when different light intensities are introduced in testing.

A case can also be made that the data obtained by Wagner *et al.* are consistent with the general attentiveness position outlined earlier. That position states that discrimination training leads to an increased tendency to respond differentially to all stimulus change, not just to the one dimension along which the training stimuli may differ. Both the TD and the PD rats in the Wagner *et al.* experiment were trained to respond to a compound (light plus tone) stimulus. The light-alone thus constitutes a generalized stimulus. Because TD rats are more discriminating animals, they would be expected to respond less to any generalized stimulus than do PD animals, which have, in effect, been taught to ignore stimulus differences. This interpretation of the Wagner *et al.* finding is illustrated in Fig. 5.

If this interpretation is correct, then the results of the Wagner *et al.* experiment are consistent with those of the extradimensional discrimination training studies with pigeons reviewed earlier. Several experiments recently performed in our laboratory and reported by Thomas, Burr, and Eck (1970) suggest that this is indeed the case. Our initial plan was to attempt to replicate the Wagner *et al.* finding, with certain minor modifications of procedure designed to increase the comparability of the study to our earlier work with pigeons. One major change was the inclusion of a second light test value at a brightness different from the first in order to obtain a two-point generalization gradient along the irrelevant (light-intensity) dimension. In the first experiment the rats in Group 1 were given TD training involving one tone-plus-light compound (T_1L_1) which signified (variable-interval) reinforcement, and another (T_2L_1) which signified extinction.

The second (PD) group received the same stimulus sequence, but reinforcement accompanied each of the stimuli half of the time. For half the subjects T_1 was 2,500 cps., for half it was 4,000. L_1 was always the same (bright) value. The two stimuli were presented successively in random order during 1-minute periods. For each TD rat a paired PD partner was run at the same time and with the same stimulus sequence but different reinforcement contingency.

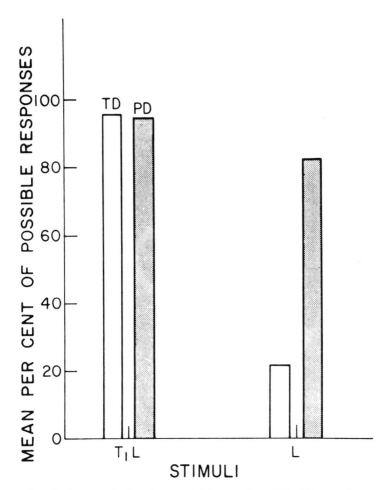

Fig. 5. A generalization decrement interpretation of the Wagner, Logan, Haberlandt, and Price finding. In the TD group, reinforcement was "correlated" with tonal frequency; in the PD group ("uncorrelated"), it was not. T_1L is the S+ training stimulus (for the TD group); L is the light value presented alone. (Data plotted from Table 2 in Wagner, Logan, Haberlandt, & Price, 1968)

The subjects were trained 1 hour per day until the TD rat met a predetermined criterion (ten S+ responses to each S− response), at which time that subject and its paired PD partner were tested.

Testing was in extinction but was preceded by a 20-minute reinforced warm-up period under the usual training conditions. The test consisted of seven randomized series of 1-minute presentations of the compounds T_1L_1, T_1L_2, T_2L_1, T_2L_2, and L_1 and L_2 presented in the absence of any tone.

During the test, the TD group maintained a good discrimination, responding about ten times as much to T_1 (when paired with either light) as to T_2. The PD group responded equally to both tones, and for neither group did the light value make a difference. Thus, for example, T_1 paired with the training light value, T_1L_1, produced no more responses than did the T_1L_2 combination. When the lights were presented alone, responding again was equivalent for both values. In agreement with the Wagner *et al.* finding, the TD group responded significantly less to the two lights than did the PD group. Thus, the Wagner *et al.* finding was replicated, despite the substantial procedural differences between the two experiments.

What was most puzzling about Experiment 1 was, not the successful replication of Wagner's result, but rather the lack of differential responding to the two light values. In a pilot study performed as a class project, rats trained in a similar manner and tested with only the two light intensities showed a substantial generalization decrement. Since the major procedural difference between the pilot study and the subsequent one was the inclusion of the tone values in the test, the hypothesis was suggested that the tones had masked the control over responding which the light had acquired in training. The second experiment was designed to test this hypothesis. In Experiment 2 no warm-up preceded the test, which was administered 24 hours after the TD subject reached criterion. Group 1 received the same test series as was used in the first experiment, and Group 2 was tested on the light values only, all tones being omitted. A less rigorous criterion, five S+ responses for each S− response, was also employed in Experiment 2. The results of this experiment are presented in Figs. 6 and 7.

As Fig. 6 indicates, the results from Group 1, which received the light and tone test, again confirmed the Wagner *et al.* findings and were comparable to those obtained in the first experiment. The TD subjects maintained the tone discrimination regardless of which

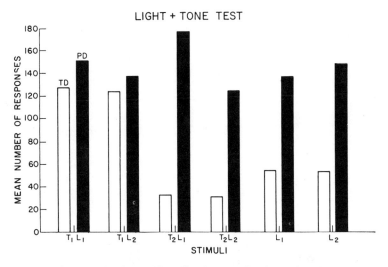

FIG. 6. An example of a masking effect in generalization testing. The presence of tones during the test inhibited differential responding to the two brightness values. See details in text. (From Thomas, Burr, & Eck, 1969)

light was present, while the PD animals responded approximately equally to all four compounds. Responses to the lights alone were significantly less for the TD than for the PD animals, but responses to L_1 and L_2 were not significantly different. The results of the light-only test were quite different. As shown in Fig. 7, the absolute response differences between the TD and PD subjects were again present; however, the data also revealed a clear generalization decrement. The absolute magnitude of the decrement was greater, though not significantly so, for the TD group. We computed for each subject the percentage of total responses given to each of the light values and then the mean of these individual percentages. The two-point relative generalization gradient was significantly steeper for the TD subjects than for the PD subjects. In fact, in terms of percentage of total responses to L_1, there was no overlap between the TD and PD groups; that is, every TD subject gave a higher proportion of responses to L_1 than did any PD subject.

Thus the results of the Thomas, Burr, and Eck (1970) study are entirely consistent with the general attentiveness interpretation of

LIGHT ONLY TEST

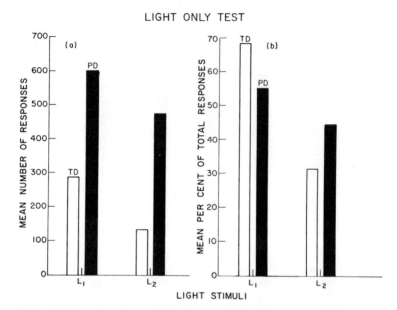

FIG. 7. The unmasking of stimulus control by light intensity. When tones were omitted from the generalization test, a significant decrement appeared with the change in brightness. The decrement was somewhat larger for the TD group in the absolute plot (a) and strikingly, and significantly, larger in the relative plot (b). (From Thomas, Burr and Eck, 1969)

the Wagner *et al.* experiment and with the results of the pigeon experiments conducted earlier, as far as the steepening of generalization by extradimensional discrimination training is concerned. On the other hand, there do seem to be important species differences, for example in the degree to which one stimulus dimension or modality can mask another. In our pigeon work, where training was on color and the test was on angularity, the color was removed from the key during testing in order to get a clearer picture of the extent to which the angle had gained control over behavior. We observed masking effects, as evidenced by a flattening of the gradient, by representing the training dimension during the test, although these effects were quite small. With rats, apparently the masking of brightness by tone is *total* and greater than anything we have ever observed with pigeons. Perhaps this is because both color and line angle are visual dimensions and the pigeon is such a "visual organism." On the other hand, it may be that because the albino rat is such a nonvisual organism, it was possible for the tone to mask brightness completely. Suffice it to say that this is a most striking example of the validity of maintaining the distinction between attention and cue utilization in drawing inferences from generalization test results.

If, as postulated, discrimination training heightens attentiveness to all stimuli (or stimulus differences), then it should facilitate the acquisition of a subsequent discrimination independent of the first. "Discrimination learning sets," as first observed by Harlow (1949), may involve such a general attentiveness factor. Reinhold and Perkins (1955) specifically noted the apparent relationship between what they called a "set-to-discriminate" and the learning-set phenomenon. They did not point out, however, the many obvious differences between their extradimensional procedure (and that used in our subsequent studies) and the one used in the typical learning-set experiment. We have used lower animals rather than primates, successive discrimination training rather than simultaneous; and substantial training on a single problem rather than a little training on a great many. It remained to be determined, therefore, whether the learning-set analogy was a valid one, and we have performed several experiments which now suggest that it is. The first of these was reported by Eck, Noel, and Thomas (1969). The design of this experiment, which is somewhat complex, is schematically represented in Fig. 8.

Four groups of pigeons were given variable interval training to respond to a vertical (90°) white line in Stage I of the experiment. For two of these groups, TD and no-line control, a 60° line was alternately presented and responses to it were extinguished; a third group, PD, was equally reinforced for responding to both lines; and a fourth group, single-stimulus control, experienced only the vertical. In Stage II all groups were trained to discriminate between two successively presented wave lengths, 555 and 538 mµ, with a white vertical line superimposed on each except in the case of the no-line control. The TD and no-line control groups mastered the wave-length discrimination equally rapidly and significantly more rapidly than the PD and single-stimulus control groups, which

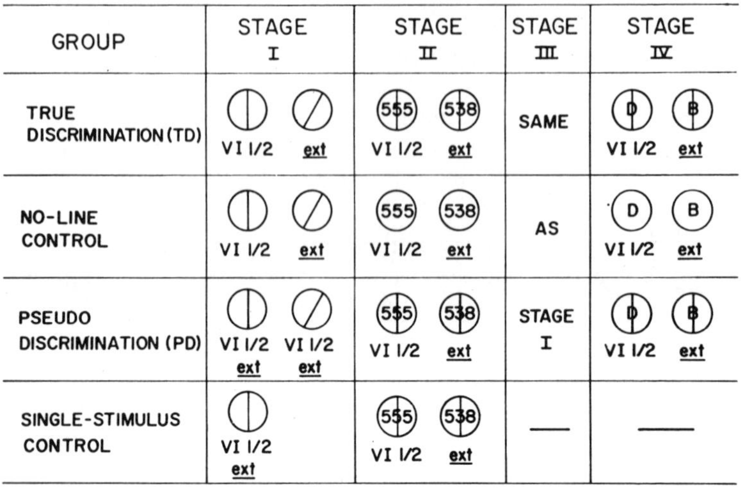

342   *Current Issues in Animal Learning*

GROUP	STAGE I	STAGE II	STAGE III	STAGE IV
TRUE DISCRIMINATION (TD)	⊕ ⊘ VI 1/2 ext	(555) (538) VI 1/2 ext	SAME	⊕ ⊕ VI 1/2 ext
NO-LINE CONTROL	⊕ ⊘ VI 1/2 ext	(555) (538) VI 1/2 ext	AS	D B VI 1/2 ext
PSEUDO DISCRIMINATION (PD)	⊕ ⊘ VI 1/2 VI 1/2 ext ext	(555) (538) VI 1/2 ext	STAGE I	⊕ ⊕ VI 1/2 ext
SINGLE-STIMULUS CONTROL	⊕ VI 1/2 ext	(555) (538) VI 1/2 ext	—	—

Fig. 8. A schematic representation of the conditions of the Eck, Noel, and Thomas (1969) experiment.

did not differ. Thus, as predicted, discrimination training did facilitate the acquisition of a subsequent discrimination independent of the first (see Fig. 9a).

A secondary purpose of the Eck, Noel, and Thomas experiment was to test the selective attention hypothesis that the more the subject attends to one aspect of a complex stimulus, the less it necessarily attends to others. The white vertical line was super-imposed on the two wave lengths (except for the no-line control group) in the expectation that the TD birds, having learned to respond to the vertical line in Stage I, would continue to attend to this stimulus in Stage II to the detriment of their wave-length discrimination performance. This simply did not occur. The failure of the PD group to perform worse than the single-stimulus control is somewhat inconsistent with the generalization test results previously reported, although the sharpening of gradients by TD training has typically been a larger and more reliable effect than the flattening of gradients by PD training.

At the completion of Stage II in the Eck, Noel, and Thomas experiment, it was decided to retrain the birds under the original condition (Stage III) and then to compare them in the acquisition

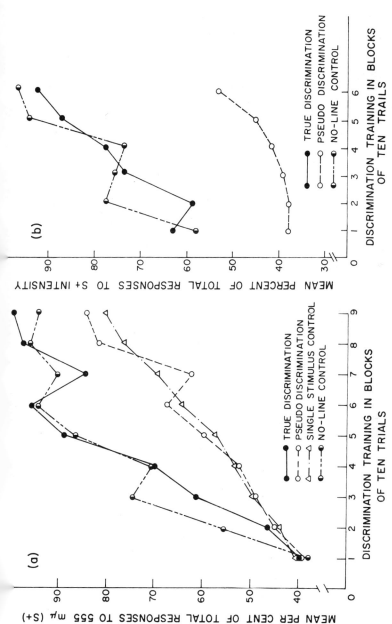

Fig. 9. Discrimination learning as a function of prior discrimination and nondifferential training. See text for details. (From Eck, Noel & Thomas, 1969)

343

of another novel discrimination, between two different brightnesses of white light. The single-stimulus control group was dropped from the experiment, but the other three groups were continued. In Stage IV the birds learned a brightness discrimination in which, for TD and PD groups only, the vertical line was superimposed on both values. Again the TD and no-line control groups performed equally and were significantly superior to the PD group (see Fig. 9b).

Eck and Thomas (1970) have recently reported a replication of these findings, regarding only the differences between the TD and PD groups, in an experiment in which the line angle superimposed on the wave lengths and brightnesses was the previously negative 60°. In this case response rate to the two wave lengths and brightnesses was initially suppressed in the TD group, but relative responding to the two stimuli was not affected. Again the TD group mastered both discriminations, wave length and brightness, significantly faster than the PD group.

All the research described thus far has produced results consistent with the proposition that discrimination training produces a "state" of general attentiveness so that the animal is increasingly sensitive to stimulus differences in addition to those relevant to the acquisition of the original discrimination. Furthermore, none of the research has supported the contention that the more the subject attends to one stimulus dimension, the less it attends to others. It is appropriate, therefore, to consider studies which are purported to confirm this inverse hypothesis.

An experiment by Newman and Baron (1965) was previously discussed in the context of distinguishing between attention, or cue selection during learning, and cue utilization during testing. It may be recalled that one group in that experiment received single-stimulus training with a vertical line-on-green stimulus and later revealed no stimulus control by line angle when tested with a green background. Another group was trained with the same stimulus as S+ and a homogeneous green key as S−. A third group had the same S+ but a homogeneous red key as S−. Only the group with the blank green S− showed stimulus control by line angle. A selective attention interpretation would be that when S+ and S− differed along the color dimension, control by color was increased and therefore control by line (angle) was reduced. When S+ and

S — were the same (green) color, control by color was presumably reduced, leading to an increase of control by line angle. Reasonable as this analysis seems, it is not supported by any data. For example, in the red S — group, although we may assume that color gained control by virtue of the discrimination training, there is no evidence that line angle lost any control, since it exerted no control in the single-stimulus group either. By the same token, although it is clear that the green S — group showed enhanced control by line angle, there is no evidence that it showed reduced control by color, since no appropriate measure was taken. Furthermore, the enhanced control by angularity may be subject to a cue utilization rather than an attentional interpretation. The use of green in both S + and S — stimuli may have reduced the degree to which the green background masked control by line angle during generalization testing rather than affecting the amount of attention paid to the line during training. For all these reasons, the Newman and Baron (1965) experiment does not provide strong support for the inverse hypothesis.

Evidence apparently consistent with the inverse hypothesis has been reported by Miles and Jenkins (1965). In this research the compound stimuli to be discriminated consisted of a tone and a bright key light as S +, and the absence of the tone and a light as S —. In one group the S — light intensity was the same as for S +, in another group the S — intensity was zero (dark), and in other groups intermediate brightnesses were used. The birds were subsequently tested for generalization to four light values, with and without the tone being present. The finding of particular interest here is the extent to which the tone came to control behavior, that is, the degree to which responding (summed across all light values) was higher with tone present than with tone absent. As might be expected, when the same light value appeared in S + and S —, the light exerted the least control (i.e., the flattest gradient) and the tone exerted a great deal. In general, as the difference between the training-light values increased, the control acquired by the tone decreased, a finding which Miles and Jenkins labeled "overshadowing." However, the results did not unequivocally support the inverse hypothesis. The condition which produced the least control by tone, the dark S — condition, also produced relatively little control by light intensity. Also, despite the fact that the light was irrelevant for the TL_1-L_1 group, considerable control over responding was, surprisingly, developed by light intensity in this group. If Miles and Jenkins had tested a light-only single-stimulus group, they might well have found a much flatter light-intensity gradient. If so, they would have been forced to conclude that tone-presence versus tone-absence discrimination sharpened the brightness gradient, a finding not at all in keeping with the inverse hypothesis. Although in a general way Miles and Jenkins found an inverse relationship between stimulus control by the two test dimensions, they presented no evidence that an increase in control by tone was accompanied by *reduction* in control by light intensity. There was no (single-stimulus) control condition from which such a reduction might be measured. Quite possibly what Miles and Jenkins observed was a differential increase in stimulus control by the two dimensions, a finding not incompatible with the general attentiveness position, as it has been proposed here. Another limitation of the study, from our viewpoint, was Miles and Jenkins's failure to vary any aspect of the tone (other than presence-absence) in testing for stimulus control by tone. In our discussion we have referred to the "dimension" of the tone. Presence and absence are certainly values along an intensity dimension, but it would have been instructive if Miles and Jenkins had provided a measure of control by some qualitative aspect of the tone, for example, frequency or pitch.

In the Miles and Jenkins (1965) study on overshadowing, training began with the compound stimuli, and stimulus selection thus occurred in the course of the compound-stimulus training. An alternative procedure, which has been more frequently employed, involves the "blocking" of the acquisition of stimulus control by a cue which is introduced after learning on the basis of a different cue has already taken place. In blocking experiments, stimulus control by one element or dimension is prevented or reduced by the preliminary training carried out with the other.

It should be noted that the Honig (1969b) experiment and Experiments 1 and 2 in the Thomas, Freeman, Svinicki, Burr, and Lyons (1970) series employed a blocking design. In those (extradimensional) studies, discrimination was initially trained along one dimension, then responding to the second (test) dimension was acquired in single-stimulus training. Rather than reducing the acquisition of control by the second dimension, in these experiments the ("irrelevant") pretraining enhanced it.

Often in Stage II the blocking design involves a second discrimination problem rather than single-stimulus training. With this procedure two values of the test dimension accompany the two values of the training dimension. An example of this procedure is seen in an experiment by Mackintosh (1965b). In his experiment three groups of rats were run, but only two of them need concern us here. Both of these groups learned a simultaneous discrimination between, for instance, a horizontal black bar (S+) and a vertical white one (S−). One of the groups had been pretrained on a successive brightness discrimination—jump right to two black squares, left to two white ones. The hypothesis was that this pretrained group would attend particularly to brightness and would therefore learn less about orientation in the subsequent phase of the experiment than would the control Ss. To test this hypothesis, Stage II training was continued in a third stage, but with interspersed orientation- and brightness-transfer tests. In agreement with the prediction, the (brightness) pretrained rats scored lower than the controls in the orientation-transfer tests, a finding in support of the inverse hypothesis. Mackintosh also reported the results of the brightness-transfer tests, although he did not discuss them. Surprisingly the (brightness) pretrained group also scored lower, though probably not significantly, in the brightness-transfer test. Thus the group which learned less about orientation did not learn more about brightness, although the inverse hypothesis demands that it should have. Ironically, therefore, the inclusion of a brightness–transfer-test measure weakened the impact of this experiment as support for the selective attention position.

Still another experiment by Mackintosh (1965c) has been offered as support of the inverse hypothesis. In this extraordinarily complicated experiment, rats were pretrained to attend to one stimulus dimension, orientation or color; then were given single-stimulus training with a particular value, for instance, a white vertical bar; and then were tested for generalization along the two dimensions of the training stimulus. A control group received only single-stimulus training before generalization testing. It was predicted that rats pretrained on one of the two dimensions and then tested for generalization along that same dimension, would have steeper gradients than the controls. Of more concern to us here is the prediction that rats which were pretrained on color and subsequently tested on orientation would show flatter gradients than the controls. Note that this is the very opposite of what has been found in a large number of extradimensional training experiments, as described previously in this chapter.

Mackintosh did succeed in obtaining results which were consistent with his predictions, but his findings can be questioned on several grounds. The first is his idiosyncratic procedure for obtaining generalization gradients. Some rats were trained to approach the previous training stimulus, say a white vertical bar, and to avoid, for example, a novel white horizontal bar. Others were trained to approach the novel stimulus and to avoid the familiar one, that is, to perform a discrimination reversal. The degree to which the non-reversal problem was easier than the reversal problem defined the slope of the generalization gradient, in terms of either percentage of correct responses or trials to extinction. The assumption was made that the more the subject has learned about a particular value of the training stimulus, the easier it would be to continue to respond to this value and the more difficult it would be to perform a reversal. It is odd that Mackintosh would take such a position since he has personally reported several experiments (cf. Mackintosh, 1962, 1963, 1965d, etc.) showing an "overtraining reversal effect," that is, that more training, and thus presumably more learning, may facilitate rather than impede reversal learning. The relationship between amount learned about a stimulus and ease of reversal learning is doubtlessly so complicated that it seems highly questionable to infer the former from the latter!

Still another reason for concern about the Mackintosh experiment is the fact that single-stimulus training did not lead to any generalization gradient at all initially (certainly an atypical result), and furthermore even with the trials to criterion measure, no significant gradient of orientation was ever found for the single-stimulus group. The flattening of the irrelevant pretraining group's gradient (relative to that of the single-stimulus control group) was thus not evident initially and only developed over the course of testing for generalization. This suggests that factors other than the difference in the Stage I pretraining condition may have been responsible for the generalization slope differences which developed during Stage III. In the extradimensional discrimination training studies we have performed, generalization slope differences between TD and PD groups were typically immediately present at the start of generalization testing.

Another blocking experiment was recently reported by vom Saal and Jenkins (1968). Their procedure differed from that used by Mackintosh in that one task, successive discrimination, rather than two tasks, first successive and then simultaneous discrimination, was used. In this procedure, a discrimination is trained in Stage I, and in Stage II the cues from the second dimension are added redundantly to the Stage I cues. Following pretraining with a white key, an experimental group of pigeons was trained to discriminate between red and green. Then, in Stage II a tone of 1,000 cps. was added to the presentation of the red key, and a white noise accompanied the green. Other (control) groups had either single-stimulus or no (color) pretraining before the red + tone versus green + noise discrimination. When tested for discrimination between tone and noise in the presence of a neutral (white) key, it was determined that the pretrained animals showed less auditory-stimulus control than did the various control groups. Thus a blocking effect did occur. Additional analysis of the data, however, revealed several findings inconsistent with the inverse hypothesis. For example, although the single-stimulus control group in this experiment showed the highest auditory control of all groups, it did not show less visual control than the other groups.

Although blocking is predictable from a selective attention viewpoint, alternative interpretations of the phenomenon are also possible. One of these, suggested by vom Saal and Jenkins, emphasizes the significance of the number of unreinforced responses to S− produced by different training conditions. Terrace (1966) has reviewed a great many studies which suggest that S− responding may contribute significantly to the establishment of stimulus control. Presumably, the more S− responding, the more control developed. In the vom Saal and Jenkins experiment, the discrimination group, having learned in Stage I not to respond when the

key was green, continued to make very few S— responses in Stage
II. This lack of responding in the presence of the negative auditory
stimulus (noise) might have been the reason that this group acquired
so little control by tone-noise in Stage II. In the Mackintosh (1965b)
incidental-cue–learning experiment, the pretrained group also
made fewer errors in Stage II; thus the same explanation might
apply there.

Vom Saal (1967) has criticized the Mackintosh experiment on
still another basis. With regard to reduced learning about the
redundant cue in Stage II, he writes: "Some factor might work to
reduce the control acquired by both cues—training a prior successive discrimination, for example, might very well cause slower
learning about *any* cue in a subsequent simultaneous discrimination.
If this occurred, we might find very little increase in control by the
first cue in the Discrimination Group as compared with the Control
Group. The facilitative effect of acquired distinctiveness in the
Discrimination Group would be reduced or entirely cancelled out
by the overall disruption effect of having received prior successive
discrimination training. This same disruptive effect might cause the
Discrimination Group to learn significantly *less* about the second
cue." (vom Saal, 1967, p. 117.)

The results of the Mackintosh (1965a) experiment are consistent
with vom Saal's interpretation. As we have already pointed out, the
(brightness) pretrained Ss actually showed, probably nonsignifi-
cantly, less control by brightness than did the control group. The
results of still another experiment (Sutherland & Holgate, 1966)
which showed less learning about a cue made incidental by prior
training are subject to the same criticism.

It is important to point out that these incidental cue experiments
do typically show more learning about the primary cue than about
the incidental cue. There is no doubt that pretraining can determine which aspects of a subsequently presented stimulus compound
gain greatest control over behavior (cf. Johnson & Cumming,
1968; Lawrence, 1950; etc.). "Acquired distinctiveness" by one
cue, however, logically need not come at the cost of attention to
other cues. It is this inverse hypothesis which has concerned us
throughout this chapter, and we are now in a position to conclude
that the evidence against if far outweighs that in its favor.

At the beginning of this chapter it was pointed out that it is unquestionably true that not all stimuli or stimulus dimensions gain equal control over the behavior which they accompany. Many factors determine the selection of one cue over another, including a host of experimental manipulations, some of which have been discussed here. Much of the research we have reviewed has demonstrated attentional effects, as we have defined them, that is, systematic variations in stimulus control produced by experimental manipulations not involving the stimulus dimension in question. The one finding most often encountered has been that discrimination training, within or across dimensions, also enhances the sensitivity of the subject to stimulus change along dimensions and modalities not involved in the original training. In a wide range of experiments involving different species, different tests of attention, different training procedures, etc., strong evidence for general attentiveness has been obtained. Support for the inverse hypothesis, on the other hand, has been conspicuous by its absence. Although such phenomena as overshadowing and blocking, which are predictable from the inverse hypothesis, have occasionally been observed, often the same experiments have either produced data inconsistent with the inverse hypothesis or have suggested alternative interpretations of the basic phenomena. We can safely conclude that the inverse hypothesis, which is an integral part of stimulus analyzer theory and several other selective attention formulations, is *not* descriptive of a basic law of animal discrimination learning. An experimental design which will produce data which consistently support the inverse hypothesis has yet to be discovered. Mackintosh and Honig (1969) have recently suggested that a blocking design involving a second discrimination problem in Stage II may be necessary to somehow engage a selective mechanism. Since the bulk of the contradictory evidence comes from studies in which only one value of the test dimension was used in training, their suggestion merits serious consideration. The difficulty of the Stage II discrimination may also have to be considered. The possibility remains (as mentioned earlier in connection with the pie hypothesis) that support for the inverse hypothesis will come from situations in which the animals' capacity to attend is strained.

The emphasis in our laboratory has been on testing the reliability and the generality of the general attentiveness effect rather than on seeking conditions under which the opposite phenomenon is attained. This effort is continuing, and current research in our laboratory involves some additional Stage I manipulations, including simultaneous rather than successive discrimination learning, and errorless training procedures as well as standard ones.

The inverse hypothesis has so frequently found support in the human literature on selective attention (cf. Egeth, 1967) that it may be fruitful, in closing, to speculate as to why the animal literature has been less hospitable to it. Surely the capacity to process information in homo sapiens cannot be lower than it is in rats, pigeons, and other "lower" species. Two very different categories of experiments with human subjects seem to have provided support for the inverse hypothesis. One involves a concept-formation task in which two or more stimulus attributes are relevant, but redundant, in providing a solution. In this situation, studied extensively by Trabasso and Bower (1968), some subjects learn about both dimensions but others learn about one dimension to the exclusion of the other. When this happens it is often accompanied by a verbal report of a conscious strategy employed by the subject. Thus the stimulus selection which occurs is not an automatic or natural consequence of the limitations of the subject but rather is a product of a conscious decision concerning how to most efficiently solve a complex problem. It has been claimed that rats also are capable of employing such strategies (cf. Krechevsky, 1938), but this remains a controversial matter.

The second category of experiments favorable to the inverse hypothesis includes those which make real demands on the perceptual capacity of the subject. Egeth (1967) has reviewed the evidence for selective attention in humans derived from four different perceptual situations—recognition of tachistoscopically presented materials, listening to one of several simultaneous auditory messages, speeded classification of multidimensional objects, and searching through complex visual fields. Typically the subjects are instructed to attend selectively, and efficient performance of the task demands that they do so. Even if we grant the highly questionable assumption that pretraining with one stimulus dimension in an animal study is equivalent to instructing a human to utilize that dimension exclusively, it is still typically the case that in animal discrimination learning there is time to attend, perhaps alternately, to several dimensions of the training stimuli and there is little or no penalty for doing so. To the contrary, if the human subject should be inclined to ignore the instructions to be selective, he would soon learn that successful performance in the experimental task prohibits his doing so.

It would seem that the greater conceptual capacity of humans and the task demands of the situations commonly studied with human subjects both account for the selectivity which seems so typical of human perception and yet is so rare in animal discrimination learning. Quite possibly some experimental situations will be more likely than others to induce hypothesis testing or some such problem-solving strategy in lower animals. A more obvious approach, however, would be to design for animals experimental tasks more similar to those used in the human perceptual research. There seems little doubt that under comparably demanding circumstances, evidence for the inverse hypothesis in the behavior of subhuman animals would be readily forthcoming.

REFERENCES

Baron, M. R. The stimulus, stimulus control, and stimulus generalization. In D. I. Mostofsky (Ed.), *Stimulus generalization*. Stanford, California: Stanford University Press, 1965.

Baron, M. R., & Bresnahan, E. L. Cue utilization vs attention: Effects of chromatic surround upon generalization along the angularity dimension in pigeons. Paper presented at Midwestern Psychological Association meetings, Chicago, 1969.

Bower, G., & Trabasso, T. Reversals prior to solution in concept identification. *J. exp. Psychol.*, 1963, **66**, 409–418.

Broadbent, D. E. *Perception and communication*. New York: Pergamon Press, 1958.

Broadbent, D. E. Human perception and animal learning. In W. H. Thorpe & O. L. Zangwill (Eds.), *Current problems in animal behavior*. Cambridge: Cambridge University Press, 1961.

Eck, K. O., Noel, R. C., & Thomas, D. R. Discrimination learning as a function of prior discrimination and nondifferential training. *J. exp. Psychol.*, 1969, **82**, 156–162.

Eck, K. O., & Thomas, D. R. Discrimination learning as a function of prior discrimination and nondifferential training: A replication. *J. exp. Psychol.*, 1970, in press.

Egeth, H. Selective attention. *Psychol. Bull.*, 1967, **67**, 41–57.

Egger, M. D., & Miller, N. E. Secondary reinforcement in rats as a function of the information value and reliability of the stimulus. *J. exp. Psychol.*, 1962, **64**, 97–104.

Farthing, G. W., & Hearst, E. Attention in the pigeon: Testing with compounds or elements. *Learning and motivation*, 1969, in press.

Freeman, F., & Thomas, D. R. Attention *vs* cue utilization in generalization testing. Paper delivered at Midwestern Psychological Association meeting, Chicago, 1967.

Gilbert, R. M. Discrimination learning? In R. M. Gilbert & N. S. Sutherland (Eds.), *Animal discrimination learning*. London: Academic Press, 1969.

Hanson, H. M. Effects of discrimination training on stimulus generalization. *J. exp. Psychol.*, 1959, **58**, 321–334.

Harlow, H. F. The formation of learning sets. *Psychol. Rev.*, 1949, **56**, 51–65.

Hearst, E., Koresko, M. B., & Poppen, R. Stimulus generalization and the response reinforcement contingency. *J. exp. anal. Behav.*, 1964, **7**, 369–380.

Honig, W. K. Attention and the modulation of stimulus control. In D. I. Mostofsky (Ed.), *Attention: Contemporary Studies and Analyses*. New York: Appleton-Century-Crofts, 1969a.

Honig, W. K. Attentional factors governing the slope of the generalization gradient. In R. M. Gilbert & N. S. Sutherland (Eds.), *Animal discrimination learning*. London: Academic Press, 1969b.

Honig, W. K., Boneau, C. A., Burstein, K. R., & Pennypacker, H. S. Positive and negative generalization gradients obtained after equivalent training conditions. *J. comp. physiol. Psychol.*, 1963, **56**, 111–116.

James, W. *The principles of psychology*. Vol. 1. New York: Holt, 1890.

Jenkins, H. M. Generalization gradients and the concept of inhibition. In D. I. Mostofsky (Ed.), *Stimulus generalization*. Stanford, California: Stanford University Press, 1965.

Jenkins, H. M., & Harrison, R. H. Effect of discrimination training on auditory generalization. *J. exp. Psychol.*, 1960, **59**, 246–253.

Jenkins, H. M., & Harrison, R. H. Generalization gradients of inhibition following auditory discrimination learning. *J. exp. anal. Behav.*, 1962, **5**, 435–441.

Johnson, D. F., & Cumming, W. W. Some determiners of attention. *J. exp. anal. Behav.*, 1968, **11**, 157–166.

Kalish, H. I., & Guttman, N. Stimulus generalization after equal training on two stimuli. *J. exp. Psychol.*, 1957, **53**, 139–144.

Kalish, H. I., & Guttman, N. Stimulus generalization after training on three stimuli: A test of the summation hypothesis. *J. exp. Psychol.*, 1959, **57**, 268–272.

Kamin, L. J. Predictability, surprise, attention, and conditioning. In B. A. Campbell & R. M. Church (Eds.), *Punishment and aversive behavior*. New York: Appleton-Century-Crofts, 1969.

Krechevsky, I. A study of the continuity of the problem-solving process. *Psychol. Rev.*, 1938, **45**, 107–133.

Lawrence, D. H. Acquired distinctiveness of cues. II. Selective association in a constant stimulus situation. *J. exp. Psychol.*, 1950, **40**, 175–188.

Lyons, J. Stimulus generalization as a function of interdimensional discrimination training with and without errors. Unpublished doctoral dissertation, Kent State University, 1968.

Lyons, J. Stimulus generalization as a function of discrimination learning with and without errors. *Science*, 1969, **163**, 490–491.

Lyons, J., & Thomas, D. R. Effects of interdimensional training on stimulus generalization. II. Within-subjects design. *J. exp. Psychol.*, 1967, **75**, 572–574.

Mackintosh, N. J. The effects of overtraining on a reversal and a nonreversal shift. *J. comp. physiol. Psychol.*, 1962, **55**, 555–559.

Mackintosh, N. J. The effect of irrelevant cues on reversal learning in the rat. *Brit. J. Psychol.*, 1963, **54**, 127–134.

Mackintosh, N. J. Selective attention in animal discrimination learning. *Psychol. Bull.*, 1965a, **64**, 124–150.

Mackintosh, N. J. Incidental cue learning in rats. *Quart. J. exp. Psychol.* 1965b, **17**, 292–300.

Mackintosh, N. J. The effect of attention on the slope of generalization gradients. *Brit. J. Psychol.*, 1965c, **56**, 87–93.

Mackintosh, N. J. Overtraining, reversal, and extinction in rats and chicks. *J. comp. physiol. Psychol.*, 1965d, **59**, 31–36.

Mackintosh, N. J., & Honig, W. K. "Blocking" and attentional "enhancement" in the pigeon. Paper presented at Eastern Psychological Association meeting, Philadelphia, 1969.

Miles, C. G., & Jenkins, H. M. Overshadowing and blocking in discriminative operant conditioning. Paper presented at Psychonomic Society meeting, Niagara Falls, 1965.

Newman, F. L., & Baron, M. R. Stimulus generalization along the dimension of angularity: A comparison of training procedures. *J. comp. physiol. Psychol.*, 1965, **60**, 59–63.

Newman, F. L., & Benefield, R. L. Stimulus control, cue utilization and attention: Effects of discrimination training. *J. comp. physiol. Psychol.*, 1968, **66**, 101–104.

Newman, J. R., & Grice, G. R. Stimulus generalization as a function of drive level, and the relation between two measures of response strength. *J. exp. Psychol.*, 1965, **69**, 357–362.

Reinhold, D. B., & Perkins, C. C., Jr. Stimulus generalization following different methods of training. *J. exp. Psychol.*, 1955, **49**, 423–427.

Riccio, D. C., Urda, M., & Thomas, D. R. Stimulus control in pigeons based on proprioceptive stimuli from floor inclination. *Science*, 1966, **153**, 434–436.

Saal, W. vom. Blocking the acquisition of stimulus control in operant discrimination learning. Unpublished master's thesis, McMaster University, 1967.

Saal, W. vom, & Jenkins, H. M. Blocking the acquisition of stimulus control in operant discrimination learning. Paper presented at Eastern Psychological Association meeting, Washington, D.C., 1968.

Seligman, M. E., Maier, S. F., & Solomon, R. L. Unpredictable and uncontrollable events. In F. R. Brush (Ed.), *Aversive conditioning and learning*. London: Academic Press, 1969.

Spence, K. W. The nature of discrimination learning in animals. *Psychol. Rev.*, 1936, **43**, 427–449.

Spence, K. W. The differential response in animals to stimuli varying within a single dimension. *Psychol. Rev.*, 1937, **44**, 430–444.

Sutherland, N. S. The learning of discrimination by animals. *Endeavor*, 1964, **23**, 148–152.

Sutherland, N. S., & Holgate, V. Two-cue discrimination learning in rats. *J. comp. physiol. Psychol.*, 1966, **61**, 198–207.

Sutherland, N. S., & Mackintosh, N. J. Discrimination learning: Non-additivity of cues. *Nature*, 1964, **201**, 528–530.

Switalski, R. W., Lyons, J., & Thomas, D. R. Effects of interdimensional training on stimulus generalization. *J. exp. Psychol.*, 1966, **72**, 661–666.

Terrace, H. S. Discrimination training with and without errors. *J. exp. anal. Behav.*, 1963, **6**, 1–27.

Terrace H. S. Stimulus control. In W. K. Honig (Ed.), *Operant behavior: Areas of research and application.* New York: Appleton-Century-Crofts, 1966.

Thomas, D. R. The use of operant conditioning techniques to investigate perceptual processes in animals. In R. M. Gilbert & N. S. Sutherland (Eds.), *Animal discrimination learning.* London: Academic Press, 1969.

Thomas, D. R., Burr, D. E. S., & Eck, K. O. Stimulus selection in animal discrimination learning: An alternative interpretation. *J. exp. Psychol.*, 1970, in press.

Thomas, D. R., Burr, D. E. S., & Svinicki, M. D. Evidence for a positive relationship between degree of control acquired by two dimensions of a complex stimulus. *Nature*, 1969, in press.

Thomas, D. R., Freeman, F., Svinicki, J. G., Burr, D. E. S., & Lyons, J. The effects of extra-dimensional training on stimulus generalization. *J. exp. Psychol.*, 1970, **83**, monograph pp. 1–21.

Thomas, D. R., & Switalski, R. W. Comparison of stimulus generalization following variable-ratio and variable-interval training. *J. exp. Psychol.*, 1966, **71**, 236–240.

Trabasso, T., & Bower, G. H. *Attention in learning: Theory and research.* New York: Wiley, 1968.

Wagner, A. R., Logan, F. A., Haberlandt, K., & Price, T. Stimulus selection in animal discrimination learning. *J. exp. Psychol.*, 1968, **76**, 171–180.

Weisman, R. G. Some determinants of inhibitory stimulus control. *J. exp. anal. Behav.*, 1969, **12**, 443–450.

Wyckoff, L. B., Jr. The role of observing response in discrimination learning. Part I. *Psychol. Rev.*, 1952, **59**, 431–442.

An Analysis of the Role of Reward and Reward Magnitude in Instrumental Learning[1]

E. J. Capaldi

Purdue University

The experimental data reported here provide additional information concerning how reward magnitude controls instrumental behavior. The present research was designed within the framework of a sequential approach to reward magnitude (Capaldi, 1966, 1967). The underlying assumptions of this approach differ considerably from those which have been entertained within a variety of other contexts (see Capaldi & Lynch, 1967). In particular, the sequential conceptualization of reward magnitude differs critically from that which has been developing roughly since 1950 within what may be called the Hull-Spence tradition (e.g., Amsel, 1958, 1962; Hull, 1952; Spence, 1956). The sequential approach recommends a strong reinforcement principle as opposed to contiguity, internal stimulus change as opposed to motivational-emotional change and, of course, a sequential orientation as opposed to a nonsequential one. The experimental data reported here, although most favorable to the sequential approach, are unfavorable, and extremely so, to the contiguity-motivational models embedded in a variety of current nonsequential theories.

[1] This research was supported in part by National Institute of Child and Health Development grant HD 00949–06. The writer wishes to express his appreciation for the invaluable assistance of Elizabeth D. Capaldi, Robert Godbout, Kenneth Kassover, and David Ziff in the preparation of this report.

The present research is also relevant to a second category of issues (effects of intertrial interval and others) which are themselves not directly related to reward magnitude. These came under investigation here because, as will be seen, current conceptions of reward magnitude cannot be tested without taking cognizance of this second category. It should be indicated that recent developments in the reward magnitude area render it particularly ripe for the sort of hypothesis-testing research reported here. This is most fortunate because within almost any approach to learning "the reward magnitude assumption set" is central, in the sense of being involved in almost any deduction entertained by the theory. Thus the implications of confirming or disconfirming the reward magnitude assumption set are, for any theory of learning, general rather than specific.[2]

MAGNITUDE OF "PARTIAL REWARD":
THEORETICAL ALTERNATIVES

Hulse (1958) and later Wagner (1961), employing irregular reward schedules and a 24-hour intertrial interval (ITI), reported that the group which received large reward showed greater resistance to extinction (R to E) than the group which received small reward. This result has been characterized by Amsel (1962) and Lawrence and Festinger (1962) as indicating that R to E increases as magnitude of "partial reward" (MPR) increases. They assume, first of all, that R to E is an increasing function of the frustration or dissonance which is generated on nonrewarded trials. Frustration or dissonance is an increasing function of expectation (or r_g), which is itself an increasing function of magnitude of reward, hence the deduction R to E f MPR.

[2] Many hypotheses are contained, to a greater or lesser extent, within the nonsequential-contiguity-motivational framework, and to deal with all of them here, much less with their shades of emphasis, would entirely confuse matters. Primarily, comments will be directed at two representatives of these traditions, the frustration hypothesis (Amsel, 1958; Spence, 1960) as the representative of the Hull-Spence S–R approach, and the dissonance hypothesis (Lawrence & Festinger, 1962) as the representative of the cognitive approach. It should be noted that an earlier Hull (1943) was less contained within the contiguity-motivational-nonsequential tradition than the later Hull (1952). Our remarks here are, of course, directed mainly at the later Hull.

According to the sequential hypothesis (e.g., Capaldi, 1966, 1967), no relationship whatever exists between R to E and MPR. Rather, R to E is increased only if a large reward trial follows a nonrewarded trial. That is, R to E is an increasing function of the magnitude of reward contained in the transition from nonrewarded trials to rewarded trials (N–R transition). Speaking sequentially, the Hulse-Wagner investigations are seen as having confounded two distinct variables—total magnitude of reward, which is a nonsequential variable, and reward magnitude contained in the N–R transition, which is a sequential variable.

These variables have been unconfounded in several ways in more recent investigations (Capaldi & Lynch, 1968; Capaldi & Minkoff, in press; Leonard, 1969). In the Leonard study, for example, there were three daily trials, and reward could be large (L) or small (S) or absent (N). A group trained each day SNL showed considerably more R to E than a group trained LNS. Note that these groups received the same "total reward magnitude," but Group SNL received larger reward in the N–R transition than Group LNS. An even more damaging result from the theoretical standpoint of frustration and dissonance was that, despite having received over-all smaller reward magnitude, Group SNL showed greater R to E than a group trained LNL. This indicates, speaking sequentially, that the larger the reward magnitude contained in the transition from rewarded trials to nonrewarded trials (R–N transition), the *less* the R to E (see Capaldi, 1967). However, it is clear that neither Amsel nor Lawrence and Festinger nor their many followers would accept the results of the more recent reward magnitude studies as particularly destructive of their frameworks. Why this is so will be shown below.

Varied Magnitude of Reward: Related Theoretical Issues

Lawrence and Festinger (1962), and possibly Amsel (1962), have argued that nonreward which can be anticipated is not really nonrewarding (dissonance producing or frustrating). According to Lawrence and Festinger, regular reward schedules of the type employed by Leonard (or Capaldi and associates) allow the animal to anticipate nonreward. Accordingly, such studies have more to do with anticipation than with magnitude of partial reward.[3]

Amsel (1967) has suggested that there may be two types of partial reinforcement effect (PRE). Though the massed trial PRE may possibly be regulated by sequential variables and processes, the spaced trial PRE is certainly regulated by frustration. Since the recent reward magnitude studies employed relatively massed trials (longest ITI = 15 minutes in Capaldi & Minkoff), they cannot be taken as disconfirming frustration. This view is not nearly so innocuous as it may perhaps sound. Recognize that our general view of instrumental learning has been strongly influenced historically by our view of the PRE, and rightly so. Amsel's massed versus spaced trial distinction, then, ultimately may involve a two-process account of instrumental learning generally.

Distinctions of the sort described above have been the rule in partial reward. Hull (1952), for example, saw the PRE as a massed trial phenomenon only, regulated by what we now call sequential processes. This view allowed Hull (1952) to develop a major theoretical position without attending to the complexities raised by the PRE, relegating the PRE and its implications to a terminal note at the end of a chapter. Recently, Gonzalez and Bitterman (1969) appear to have returned more or less to a Hullian position. According to them, only the massed trial PRE which is regulated by sequential processes is real, the spaced trial PRE being apparent and regulated by contrast. Black and Spence (1965), like Amsel (1967), identified two sorts of PRE, on a different basis, however. The PRE obtained following a very small number of training trials (too few a number in their view to allow frustration to develop) is regulated by sequential processes. The more extended trial PRE, however, is regulated by frustration.

There are at least two ways to view these distinctions. They may be viewed as proper, as demanded by the available experimental information; or they may be viewed, as we view them, as devices (not intentional ones, of course) which protect particular theoretical statements from the implications of obstreperous data.

---

[3] The absence of a protest here might be interpreted as indicating that we view the Lawrence and Festinger analysis as valid. We do not. Nor do we view as valid subsequent similar analyses to be considered here.

As we view them, the distinctions have served, and presently serve, to introduce profoundly conservative influences into our theorizing and to delay or inhibit the development of the sort of general theory which is at present so badly needed. One aim of the research which follows is to illustrate the illusory quality of the many distinctions which have been proposed, and thereby to facilitate a more general approach to learning phenomena.

EXPERIMENT ONE: MAGNITUDE OF "PARTIAL REWARD" AT 24-HOUR ITI

If one imagined an experimental finding that would do the maximum damage to the greatest number of the distinctions just reviewed, it would take the following form. The finding would demonstrate that the same variable known to regulate the PRE under massed trials also does so under spaced trials. Moreover, the variable in question would be a sequential one; the ITI would be 24 hours, no less; and the schedule of reward would be irregular rather than regular. Fortunately, by employing reward magnitude in a "partial reward" schedule, it is possible to design an experiment which simultaneously meets all these conditions, while at the same time being relevant to various current conceptions of reward magnitude. Four groups of Ss were trained in a runway at one trial each day, receiving either large (L) reward, small (S) reward, or nonreward (N), according to the irregular reward schedule shown in Table 1.

TABLE 1
REWARD SCHEDULES OF EXPERIMENT 1

Groups	Trials																					
	1	2	3	4	5	6	7	8	9	10	11	12	13	14	15	16	17	18	19	20	21	22
LNL	L	L	L	N	N	N	L	N	N	L	N	N	N	L	L	L	L	L	N	N	L	L
SNS	S	S	S	N	N	N	S	N	N	S	N	N	N	S	S	S	S	S	N	N	S	S
SNL	S	S	S	N	N	N	L	N	N	L	N	N	N	L	S	S	S	L	N	N	L	L
LNS	L	L	L	N	N	N	S	N	N	S	N	N	N	S	S	L	L	L	N	N	S	S

Groups LNL and SNS correspond to the sorts of groups employed by Hulse and Wagner; that is, total magnitude of reward and reward magnitude contained in the N–R transition are confounded. Note that all groups have four N–R transitions. Groups SNL and LNS allow a test of the hypothesis that differences in the

Hulse-Wagner situation were unrelated to total reward magnitude per se and were regulated, in fact, by magnitude of reward contained in the N–R·transition, that is, N–L versus N–S. Note that over a period of days, Groups SNL and LNS receive the same magnitude of reward. However, Group SNL, like Group LNL (which receives over-all greater reward magnitude), receives N–L transitions, while Group LNS, like Group SNS (which receives over-all lesser reward magnitude), receives N–S transitions. The N–R transitions hypothesis suggests, then, that Groups LNL and SNL will not differ from each other and will show greater R to E than Groups LNS and SNS, which also will not differ from each other. (We exclude here consideration of L–N transitions.) These findings would correspond closely to those obtained using massed trials and regular schedules, thus indicating that similar variables regulate R to E when trials are spaced and the reward schedule is irregular. The total reward magnitude hypothesis suggests, on the other hand, that Group LNL should show greater R to E than Groups LNS and SNL, which should not differ from each other, and that Group SNS should show the least R to E. This finding, or one approximating it, would differ substantially from the massed trial–regular schedule sort of finding, and thus would offer support for many of the distinctions previously considered (ITI and so on), as well as the frustration-dissonance conceptualization of reward magnitude.

Methods

The 36 male rats, obtained from the Holtzman Company, Madison, Wisconsin, were about 90 days old upon arrival at the laboratory. The Ss were randomly divided into four groups of 9 Ss each.

The straight-alley runways employed in the three investigations reported here were of identical dimensions. Each was 82 inches long and 4 inches wide, and was enclosed by 9-inch high sides, covered with hinged 1/2-inch hardware cloth. Each was constructed of wood and painted a mid-gray. There were three basic sections: start, 14 inches; middle or run, 52 inches; and goal, 16 inches. When a 10-inch start treadle was depressed by the rat, whose front paws were always placed on the treadle's extreme forward edge, a .01-second clock started. This clock stopped and a second started when S broke an infrared beam 4 inches from the treadle's tip (start time). Interrupting the second beam, 52 inches from the first, stopped the second clock (run time) and started a third clock. A third infrared beam was located 12 inches from the second beam and 2 inches from the front edge of a brass $2 \times 4\,1/4 \times 1\,1/2$–inch food cup, covered by a tightly fitting, automatically controlled, sliding metal lid operated by an electric motor. Interrupting it stopped the third and last clock (goal time) and opened the lid covering the food cup. When S broke the third beam, a brass guillotine door 12 inches from the alley's distal end was lowered manually. The elapsed time on the three clocks was summed and is termed *total*.

Upon arrival at the laboratory the rats were housed in group cages and given free access to food and water for 5 days. On the sixth day (Day 1 of pretraining) all Ss were placed in individual cages and restricted to a 12-gram per day maintenance diet of Wayne Lab Blox with ad lib water. All animals were handled daily during pretraining and were habituated to the unbaited apparatus in groups of 4 for 5 minutes on Days 7 and 9. On Days 7 through 10 of pretraining, each rat received ten .045-gram Noyes pellets in the home cage.

The 22 days of acquisition training, administered to each group on the basis of the schedules shown in Table 1, began after the tenth day of pretraining. There was one trial per day in acquisition and extinction (26 days). Reward magnitude was either large (L), twenty-two .045-gram Noyes pellets, or small (S), two pellets. S was never removed from the goal box until all pellets had been consumed, and then was removed immediately. On all nonrewarded (N) trials S was confined to the goal box for 30 seconds.

The Ss were run in squads of 4, 1 S from each group in each squad. The within-squad running order was varied daily. On all trials the S was placed in the apparatus as described above and was given 60 seconds to traverse each alley section. If S failed in this, it was assigned a time score of 60 seconds for that alley section and all not yet traversed alley sections, and was picked up and placed in the goal box. Following a trial the animal was returned to the home cage, where 15 minutes later it received the 12-gram daily ration, minus the amount eaten in the apparatus. An additional feature of the experimental conditions employed here, the relevance of which will become clear when Experiment 3 is considered, should be noted. The number of transitions from large reward trials to nonrewarded trials (L–N transitions, see Table 1) were, of course, none in Group SNS, two in Group LNS, three in Group SNL (plus one L–S transition), and four in Group LNL.

Results

In the terminal stages of acquisition the three groups which received large reward magnitude trials ran rapidly and differed from each other only negligibly. The small magnitude group, SNS, however, was considerably slower than the remaining groups, except in the goal section, where differences tended to be smaller. On the last day of acquisition, for example, employing total speeds, differences between the groups were highly significant ($F = 10.18$, $df = 3/32, p < .001$), but the differences were exclusively occasioned by the slower running of Group SNS relative to the remaining three groups. Because of the acquisition differences, the speed scores were transformed into rate measures, as recommended by Anderson (1963). Employed as the estimate of the acquisition asymptote were the speeds on the last 6 days of acquisition and the first day of extinction, while the extinction asymptote was taken to be the reciprocal of 60 seconds in each alley section and 180 seconds in total.

The rate measures for total for each of the four groups on each day of extinction are shown in Fig. 1. As can be seen, Groups LNL and SNL differed from each other only negligibly and showed greater R to E than Groups LNS and SNS. Also, the rate measures for Group LNS tended to fall below those of Group SNS from about Trial 10 onward. The lesser R to E of Group LNS, relative to Group SNS, was largest in the run section, where it approached but did not reach significance, and reflects differences in acquisition asymptote. On the basis of the speed scores themselves, Groups SNS and LNS were quite comparable following the initial extinction trials.

A simple analysis of variance, employing the rate measures over

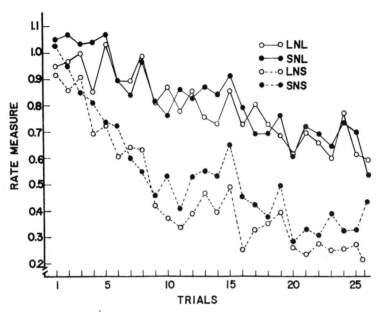

Fig. 1. Rate of extinction in each of the four groups on each trial of extinction in total.

all the extinction trials, indicated that differences for totals were significant ($F = 11.87$, $df = 3/32$, $p < .001$), as they were in the run and goal section but not the start section. A subsequent Duncan's range test indicated that neither in total nor in any alley section did Group LNL differ from Group SNL. Similarly, Groups SNS and LNS failed to differ, except as previously mentioned in the run section, where differences approached but did not reach significance ($.05 < p < .10$). In total and run and goal, but not start, Groups LNL and SNL differed significantly from Groups SNS and LNS ($p < .01$).

Discussion: Experiment One

The following matters are clear. The findings of Experiment 1 correspond to those expected by the N–R transition hypothesis. On the other hand, the findings of Experiment 1 appear to do serious injury to the reward magnitude hypothesis proposed by frustration and dissonance. Too, the findings of Experiment 1 are those obtained in partial reward magnitude investigations when trials are massed and regular rather than, as here, spaced and irregular. All available magnitude findings, then—massed versus spaced trial, regular versus irregular schedule—even including those of Hulse and Wagner, are consistent with a single and simple generalization, that R to E is independent of MPR and is an increasing function of magnitude of reward contained in the N–R transition. The findings of Experiment 1, then, reduce the wide distinction made between regular and irregular reward schedules by Lawrence and Festinger, but also suggest that the massed and spaced trial PRE, rather than being regulated by different variables and processes (Amsel, 1967; Gonzalez & Bitterman, 1969), is regulated by the same variables and processes, these variables and processes being of a sequential character.

Why, according to the sequential hypothesis, is R to E an increasing function of the reward magnitude contained in the N–R transition? Assume that nonreward produces a distinctive stimulus (S^N). Assume further that this stimulus occurs on the subsequent trial. If the subsequent trial is a rewarded one, S^N is conditioned to the approach reaction (S^N–R_A). The strength of this conditioning is considered to be stronger the larger the reward magnitude; that is, the hard reinforcement principle is adopted that conditioning occurs only on rewarded trials and the strength of this conditioning is greater the greater the reward magnitude (see Capaldi, 1966; Capaldi & Lynch, 1967). The strength of the connection S^N–R_A, then, is stronger for groups experiencing N–L transitions than for groups experiencing N–S transitions. The S^N–R_A connection is the mechanism of the PRE. This is because in extinction (successive nonrewarded trials) S^N occurs. Since S^N has acquired in acquisition a greater capacity to evoke R_A under N–L than under N–S transitions, it is clear that R to E should increase as magnitude of reward in the N–R transition increases.

How and why is S^N present on subsequent trials? One conceivable way is for S^N to persist. This is the so-called aftereffect conception (c.g., Sheffield, 1949). The present results unequivocally militate against such a view. For one thing, it is obviously absurd to think of a stimulus as persisting for 24 hours. For another, the

current issues in animal learning

A Colloquium

James H. Reynierse, Editor

university of nebraska press
lincoln

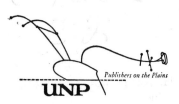

Publishers on the Plains
UNP

Copyright © 1970 by the University of Nebraska Press
International Standard Book Number 0–8032–0744–1
Library of Congress Catalog Card Number 78–98389
Manufactured in the United States of America

Contents

Contents

Preface

The University of Nebraska was established on 15 February 1869 at the first regular session of the state legislature of the then-new state of Nebraska. This volume was organized in recognition of that event and the University of Nebraska Centennial. The 12 papers included were originally presented during the 1968–69 centennial year as a part of an expanded centennial colloquium series sponsored by the psychology department of the university and financed by a training grant from the National Institute of Mental Health and grants from the University of Nebraska Research Council.

Twenty years after the university was established, psychology became a prominent topic at Nebraska. In 1889, Dr. Harry Kirke Wolfe joined what was then a small instructional staff as Lecturer in Philosophy. Although he was the only instructor in that subject and was responsible for teaching the entire philosophy and psychology curriculum, the growth of psychology was immediate and rapid. University of Nebraska catalogs for the years before 1889 list only a single course in general psychology; but with Wolfe's arrival the curriculum was immediately expanded to three courses, including experimental psychology with laboratory. Indeed, Wolfe, after obtaining the Ph.D. under Wundt at Leipzig in 1886, had returned to Nebraska, where he had taken an A.B. degree in 1880, and organized the seventh psychology laboratory in an American academic institution (Garvey, 1929). The original laboratory was primarily instructional but was expanded to include original research the following year (Wolfe, 1890). Wolfe's own research interests were in psychophysics, although he apparently was not a prolific investigator. As a teacher, however, he left a permanent mark upon psychology. Edwin R. Guthrie and Madison Bentley indicated that Wolfe was their main influence, and Walter B. Pillsbury acknowledged Wolfe, along with Titchener, as a principal teacher (Boring & Boring, 1948). Each of the three men had been influenced by Wolfe as undergraduates at Nebraska. For his leadership in promoting psychology as a laboratory science and for his unusual influence as a teacher, this volume is dedicated to the memory of Harry Kirke Wolfe.

Selection of animal learning as the central integrating theme of this book was not arbitrary. Rather, it identifies one of the current research interest areas of a significant number of Nebraska faculty members and students. Collectively the contributions represent a broad spectrum of strategies and tactics. The range of specific problems is selective and obviously not exhaustive, although an attempt was made to include a diversity of empirical and theoretical approaches.

In behalf of the Department of Psychology, I would like to express appreciation to each of the participants who visited it during the past year. For myself, I would like to thank David Levine, chairman of the department, for his encouragement and support of this project. Finally, for myself and in behalf of the visiting speakers, I would like to thank Ruben Ardila, Gus Lumia, James Miller, Gaylon Oswalt, Arnold Powell, Corky Rieder, and Linda Soukup for their superior efforts as an informal welcoming committee.

JAMES H. REYNIERSE

REFERENCES

Boring, E. G., & Boring, M. D. Masters and pupils among American psychologists. *Amer. J. Psychol.*, 1948, **61**, 527–534.

Garvey, C. R. List of American psychological laboratories. *Psychol. Bull.*, 1929, **26**, 652–660.

Wolfe, H. K. Psychology at the University of Nebraska. *Amer. J. Psychol.*, 1890, **3**, 276–277.

Polythetic Biopsychology: An Alternative to Behaviorism

DONALD D. JENSEN

Indiana University[1]

The biological study of animal behavior has had an enormous influence upon the development of American psychology. Out of controversy regarding animal consciousness came a point of view which was introduced into psychology by John B. Watson in 1912; this point of view, *behaviorism*, has become the dominant and virtually unquestioned metatheory of contemporary psychology. Current research and textbooks, with rare exceptions, accede to the dicta that psychology is the science of behavior and that psychological concepts are to be defined in terms of observable behaviors.

If advances in psychological theory and method made during the last half century are to be attributed to behaviorism, so also must certain conceptual deficiencies characteristic of this period. Deficiencies of behavioristic psychology are herein discussed, and an alternative point of view, which developed from more recent controversies regarding animal behavior, is offered. This alternative, *polythetic biopsychology*, employs definitional procedures of numerical taxonomy to clarify the meaning of psychological concepts.

THE ORIGINS OF WATSONIAN BEHAVIORISM

The biological origins of behaviorism are not commonly appreciated. John B. Watson is normally described as the founder of behaviorism, with scant attention being directed to the personal and direct interactions which occurred between him and H. S. Jennings (1868–1947), an American biologist whose views antedated

---

[1] Now at the University of Nebraska.

Watson's and were clearly behavioristic. Consideration of this matter is desirable to make understandable certain characteristics of Watsonian behaviorism.[2]

Jennings, a leader in American biology during the first half of this century, went to the University of Michigan for his undergraduate training (1890–93) and a year of graduate study and to Harvard to finish his graduate training (A.M., 1895; Ph.D., 1896). His thesis was a descriptive study of the development of rotifers, but he meanwhile acquired from C. B. Davenport an enthusiasm for the experimental methods which were just then spreading among biologists. In 1897, Jennings received a traveling fellowship and spent a year in Europe, in Jena with Verworn and at the Naples biological station, where he began a decade-long program concerning the behavior of lower organisms. This work continued through several temporary positions and culminated in two books, *Contributions to the Study of the Behavior of Lower Organisms* (1904) and *Behavior of the Lower Organisms* (1906). Jennings left the University of Pennsylvania in 1906 and went to Johns Hopkins University, where he remained until his retirement in 1938. While Jennings was completing his work on behavior, Mendel's laws of inheritance were being rediscovered. Soon after arriving at Johns Hopkins, Jennings began the study of inheritance in protozoa, and he continued to work and write about genetics and problems of general biology for the rest of his life. Although for a time he taught laboratory courses in the behavior of lower organisms, even this stopped after S. O. Mast joined the faculty in 1911.

Jennings's work on behavior can be seen as a continuation of the evolutionary study of mind that began with Darwin and occupied such early workers as Romanes, Lubbock, and Preyer. These men had the principal aim of demonstrating that various mental functions had evolved, just as had man's physical organs. The question of where sensations, perceptions, memory, consciousness, etc., first arose in the phylogenetic series was primary for these workers. Meanwhile others (Verworn, Jacques Loeb) were concerned with explaining animal behavior in terms of physiochemical influences and without use of anthropomorphic, psychic, or mentalistic

[2] See Jensen (1962) for a fuller but similar discussion of the relationship between the men.

terms, that is, those which refer to human subjective experience. Loeb modeled his explanations on Sachs's theory of tropisms of plants, in which stimulus-directed movement occurs until bilaterally symmetrical stimulation results. Jennings accepted the objective, experimental *modus operandi* of Verworn and Loeb but denied the general utility of the tropism theory, with its emphasis on external stimuli. He emphasized the complexity and variability of behavior in lower organisms and the importance of internal factors as determinants of behavior.

Jennings stopped active work with behavior about 1908, well before the behavioristic views of Watson appeared. The question of how Jennings influenced the behavioristic movement in American psychology then arises. To answer that question we must consider the reaction his work evoked from certain other workers.

His books received criticism from two quarters, from the defenders of Loeb's tropism theory and from the psychologists who were offended by Jennings's language and methodology. Jennings's reply to the first group of critics, who felt his attack on Loeb's doctrines was a retreat from objectivism, is of interest because it effectively states his basic approach and his relation to the still-earlier work of Loeb.

> Certain authors seem to identify the "tropism theory" with the view that the behavior of organisms is to be explained by objective, experimentally determinable factors. They feel that an attack on the "tropism theory" is an attack on this view; this comes forth notably in the criticisms made by Loeb and Torrey, and it is evident in the attitude of some other writers.
>
> There is, so far as I can see, nothing in the facts and relations which I have brought out that in any way opposes the principle that behavior is to be explained by objective, experimentally determinable factors—or indeed that bears in any way on the question. I have simply assumed throughout that it *is* to be explained in that way, and I do not see how experimental investigations can proceed on any other basis. Beginning my work in 1896, when the movement led by Loeb against the use of psychic concepts in explaining objective phenomena was in full swing, I considered that battle fought and won; I have, therefore, ever since proceeded, without discussion or ado of any sort, on that basis. Everyone must recognize the tremendous service done by Loeb in championing through thick and thin the necessity for the use

of objective, experimental factors in the analysis of behavior. No convinced experimentalist, knowing the previous history of the subject, can reread, as I have just done, Loeb's early work on behavior without being filled with admiration for the clear-cut enunciation, defense, and application of the principles on which valuable experimental work has rested since that time, and on which it must continue to rest.

Any differences of opinion between Loeb and myself are then matters of detail; they concern merely the results of the application of the agreed principles of investigation. It has seemed to me that some of the experimentalists have rested content with superficial explanations; that they do not realize the complexity of the problems with which they were dealing. This has been the history of most applications of experiment to biology; the more thorough the work, the deeper are the problems seen to be.

Thus I have not hesitated to bring forth facts tending to show the inadequacy of the physio-chemical factors thus far set forth, and doubtless some have suspected that this was done with the concealed purpose of discrediting the general adequacy of such factors. This is a complete mistake; I did not till lately realize even the existence of such a suspicion. Complete confidence in the experimental method removes anxiety as to the effect of criticizing the details of its application. My objections are only to the adequacy of particular factors; they are based on experimental grounds, and the difficulties they raise are to be resolved only by experimental study. There is a vast difference between holding that behavior is fundamentally explicable on experimental grounds, and holding that we have already so explained it.

In a recent paper Loeb has intimated that even if the behavior of the organisms under consideration were as complex as that of man, the same objective and experimental methods must be used in analyzing it. To this I fully agree, and the behavior of man is of course no more to be excepted from this treatment than is that of any other organism. (Jennings, 1908, pp. 708–709)

One of the reasons why Jennings received criticism from the followers of Loeb was that he used concepts which applied to human behavior (trial and error, perception, choice, etc.) in describing the behavior of lower organisms. Jennings continually emphasized, however, that he referred only to the "objective manifestations" of these concepts, that is, to the verifiable behavior to which the concepts refer and not to the subjective experiences of man. It is the clear enunciation of the idea that psychological concepts must be

defined in terms of objectively observable, verifiable behavior that
marks Jennings as a behaviorist.

Somewhat different criticisms came from the psychological
quarter. In the *Psychological Bulletin* the reviewer spiced his comments
with ridicule while attacking the suggestion of continuity between
the behavior of lower animals and of man. The use of introspective
evidence by the reviewer also contrasts with behavioristic practice,
as does the emphasis of the reviewer on the concept of consciousness:

> Unfortunately, Jennings, while not a psychologist, has nevertheless
> in this volume wandered off into the green pastures of the psychologist
> (and has even nibbled at the stubble of the philosopher)! He was not
> content to allow his experimental facts to stand as facts, but must needs
> raise the question which stands (needlessly) as the bête noir of the
> student of behavior. Are the lower organisms conscious? Or, to phrase
> it from the objective standpoint, "Do there exist in the lower organisms
> objective phenomena of a character similar to those which we find in
> the behavior of man?" Jennings gives an affirmative answer: "So
> far as the objective evidence goes, there is no difference in kind, but a
> *complete continuity between the behavior of lower and of higher organisms*"
> (italics added). Jennings then goes on to say that "no statement
> concerning consciousness in animals is open to verification or refutation
> by observation and experiment. . . . All that experiment and observa-
> tion can do is to show us whether the behavior of lower organisms is
> objectively similar to the behavior that in man is accompanied by con-
> sciousness. If this question is answered in the affirmative, as the facts
> seem to require . . . then it may perhaps be said that objective investi-
> gation is as favorable to the view of the general distribution of con-
> sciousness as it could well be." It is at this point that we must raise the
> question which is fundamental to our science. Have we any other
> criterion than that of behavior for assuming that our neighbor is
> conscious? And do we not determine this by the complexity of his
> reactions (including language under behavior)? Complexity in con-
> scious content is always accompanied by complexity in adjustment.
> This idea is the basal one in functional psychology. If my monkey's
> adjustments were as complex as those of my human subject in the
> laboratory, I would have the same reason for drawing the conclusion
> as regards a like complexity in the mental processes of the two. Nor
> would my opinion "then be largely dominated by general philosophical
> considerations drawn from other fields." My inferences would alike
> in the two cases be based upon observed *facts* of behavior. Jennings

has not shown, nor has anyone else shown that the behavior of lower organisms is objectively similar to that in man. To make the reviewer's position clear, Jennings's statements concerning the presence of perception in lower organisms may be cited. "When we say an animal *perceives* something, or shows a perception of something, we base this statement upon the observation that it reacts in some way to this thing. On the same basis, we could make the statement that amoeba perceives all classes of stimuli which we ourselves perceive, save sound (which is, however, essentially one form of mechanical stimulation). Perception as judged from our subjective experiences means much more; how much of this may be present in animals outside of ourselves we cannot know." The flaws in Jennings's psychology are surely patent to every student of experimental psychology. Is simple reaction to a stimulus the only *objective manifestation* of perceptual behavior in man? Certainly not! There are hundreds of others beside the overt movement of the voluntary muscles which can be directly observed, such as eye movement, convergence, accommodation, changes in respiration, circulation, changes in tonus of musculature, etc., and still others which can be inferred, as concerted reaction between different cortical systems; cortical "retention" of the modifications of past stimuli, etc. It is the task of the experimental psychologist to refine upon and to add to this list of objective manifestations of the perceptual act. So far as we know, some such complexity in adjustment is *necessary to every perceptual act*. If we may be allowed to call introspection in at this point, we find that it everywhere supports our contention that where you have complexity in content you likewise have complexity in adjustment; if subjectively to the human "experiencer" there is more than simple reaction towards a stimulus in a perception, objectively there is more too. If Jennings would show that the adjustments of the amoeba to a sensory stimulation were as complex *from the objective or behavior standpoint* as our own adjustments to a like stimulus, we would not only be willing to grant him that his amoeba *perceives* but also we would be forced to make the assumption for the very same cogent reasons that we assume our fellow man perceives.

The same lack of psychological analysis is to be found in Jennings' assertion that lower organisms behave as though they consciously discriminate, and that they react as though they had representations. From the standpoint of the contribution of facts, the book is exceedingly valuable. That portion of the book dealing with the analysis of behavior has a somewhat dubious value because of its vagueness and complexity, and its constant allusions to pleasure and pain and to other psychical

*S*s are fed in the home cage between trials. What should persist, then, if anything, is the aftereffect of reward, S^R, not that of nonreward, or S^N. If S^N does not persist, what does it do? Previously we have said (e.g., Capaldi, 1967) that S^N is reinstated. That is, when the *S* is returned to the learning situation, S^N appears. Now r_g is said to be evoked or elicited, and S^N is said to be reinstated. Reinstatement contrasts with elicitation in at least two ways. The appearance of S^N is not related to a learning process. Thus, it is no more difficult to obtain S^N (or S^R) following a single nonreward than following 100 nonrewards. Further, the appearance of S^N is not necessarily tied to a response intermediary. In contrast, the stimuli s_g or s_f depend upon the elicitation of the response intermediaries r_g or r_f, respectively. Clearly, then, S^N is the product of a memory process, while r_g involves a learning process. The appearance or reinstatement of S^N depends upon two minimal conditions: (1) prior nonreward and (2) presentation of the external stimuli which accompanied prior nonreward.

It is clear from the above that if nonreward occurs in the external stimulus context x and x is re-presented, S^N will be reinstated. It is also clear that if we present not x but y, a totally different stimulus context (e.g., the home cage), then S^N will not be reinstated (see in this connection Capaldi & Spivey [1963]). However, let us say that we present a stimulus similar to x but not x itself, for example, x'. This describes the usual discrimination learning situation, that is, black and white discriminanda are not totally dissimilar. Under these circumstances, portions of S^N will be reinstated. Discrimination learning has been treated to some extent elsewhere (Capaldi, in press).

EXPERIMENT TWO: VARIED MAGNITUDE OF REWARD

Sometimes experiments designed within the sequential framework employ reward schedules which are entirely regular. For example, an animal may receive two different reward magnitudes each day, large (L) and small (S) in the fixed order LS. As we have seen, because of the element of regularity, some investigators, for example, Lawrence and Festinger (1962), do not find such experiments entirely convincing. Experiment 2 employs a simple experimental technique designed to meet such objections. On some of the days the animal is trained, for example, LS. However, on other days the animal is trained LL. The purpose of the technique is to prevent the animal from learning that large reward on trial 1 is always followed by small reward on trial 2 (LS and LL). The significance of this technique may be appreciated by reviewing current available information in the area of varied magnitude of reward.[4]

If rats are given varied magnitude of reward at a 24-hour ITI according to an irregular schedule, for example, SSSLLSL, etc., R to E is increased (Logan, 1960; Logan, Beier, & Kincaid, 1956). According to the sequential hypothesis (e.g., Capaldi, 1967), R to E is increased by varied magnitude of reward because of transitions from S trials to L trials (S–L transitions). The gross similarity between S–L transitions and N–R transitions is, of course, too obvious to go unnoticed, although a complete understanding of the relationship between the two would require a broad theoretical discussion, one which is at this point inappropriate. In any event, not only the sequential hypothesis but perhaps any hypothesis which can explain the PRE would also be capable of explaining the varied magnitude effect when irregular schedules are employed. Clearly a more subtle and determinate experimental situation must be identified if we are to choose between available theoretical alternatives.

Regular schedules supply such a situation. The chief advantage of regular schedules is that one can observe the effects of a particular kind of transition in isolation from other kinds of transitions. An irregular schedule of varied magnitude of reward, as can be seen above, contains all four types of major transitions—S–L, L–S, S–S, and L–L. Leonard, in an ingenious experiment employing two trials a day according to fixed repeating or regular schedules, observed the effects of each kind of transition in isolation. Each day four groups were trained either SL (trial 1 small reward,

---

[4] The technique appropriately described as employing regular schedules "within days" but irregular schedules "over days" was first utilized by Capaldi and Minkoff (in press), who described its implications in somewhat different terms than employed here. Capaldi and Minkoff reported that R to E increased as magnitude of reward in the N–R transition increased and as a variable, to be described later (Experiment 3), called N–length increased.

trial 2 large reward), LS, SS, or LL. Within a sequential context Leonard's experimental design is called a "decomposition design" because it attempts to decompose a complex irregular schedule into what, from a sequential point of view, are its simple and fundamental analytic units or constitutent elements. Leonard's results in terms of R to E from greatest to least were SL, SS, LL, and LS, an ordering consistent with sequential principles (e.g., Capaldi, 1967; Leonard, 1969). Other experiments (Marx & Edwards, 1966; Marx, Tombaugh, Cole, & Dougherty, 1963), employing more than two daily reward magnitudes, have shown that an ascending series of reward magnitudes (from S to L through graded steps) produced greater R to E than a descending series of reward magnitudes (from L to S), a finding consistent with that of Leonard. Perhaps, then, varied magnitude of reward per se does not increase R to E. Perhaps varied magnitude of reward increases R to E only when the several magnitudes occur in a particular order or sequence, from smaller to larger.

Hypotheses such as frustration and dissonance which not only cannot predict such order or sequential effects but find them most inimical to their theoretical assumptions would regard the above conclusion as objectionable. They might assume, for example, that it is easier to anticipate small reward, and thus not experience frustration or dissonance, when reward magnitudes descend (LS) than when they ascend (SL). According to these views, then, varied magnitude of reward per se does increase R to E, *provided that discrimination or anticipation is prevented*. It would follow from this line of argument that if discrimination were prevented, descending magnitudes would in fact produce increased R to E. That is, in the absence of such discrimination, the small reward trials would produce frustration or dissonance, and R to E would be increased. On the other hand, however, if discrimination were prevented and a descending group showed no increase in R to E relative to a consistently rewarded control group, it would increase our confidence that the locus of the varied magnitude effect is the S–L transition. Furthermore, under the conditions described, the absence of increased R to E in the descending, or LS, group would be totally inexplicable within the context of the frustration or dissonance hypotheses, inasmuch as it must be presumed that such a group would experience frustration or dissonance on the small reward trials. Experiment 2 employed three groups, trained at two trials each day. On 10 of the 15 acquisition days the groups were trained either SL, LS, or LL. On the remaining 5 days all groups were trained LL. Inasmuch as the LL training should forestall or perhaps entirely preclude the formation of a discrimination, it might be expected on the basis of frustration-dissonance that Group LS would show greater R to E than would Group LL and R to E, perhaps as great as that of Group SL.

Methods

The 36 male rats, also purchased from the Holtzman Company, were about 90 days old upon arrival at the laboratory.

The runway employed was of the same dimensions as in Experiment 1. A trial was begun as in Experiment 1.

Upon arrival at the laboratory the rats were housed in group cages and given free access to food and water for 5 days. On the sixth day all Ss were placed in individual cages and restricted to a 12-gram-per-day maintenance diet of Wayne Lab Blox with ad lib water. All animals were handled daily during pretraining and were habituated to the unbaited apparatus in groups of 4 for 5 minutes on both Days 12 and 14. On Days 12 through 15 each rat received ten .045-gram Noyes pellets in the home cage.

On the sixteenth day after their arrival in the laboratory, the 36 Ss were randomly assigned to three groups of 12 Ss each: Group SL, Group LS, and Group LL. On each of the 15 acquisition days there were two daily trials, reward being either large (L), twenty .045-gram Noyes pellets, or small (S), two pellets. On Days 4, 5, 8, 12, and 13 of acquisition all Ss received large reward (LL) on both acquisition trials. On the remaining 10 days of acquisition, Group SL received S on trial 1 (T_1) and L on trial 2 (T_2), while Group LS received L on T_1 and S on T_2 and Group LL received L on T_1 and T_2.

There were twelve squads of 3 Ss, each squad consisting of 1 S from each group. The running order of Ss within a squad was randomized daily. For three of the squads (A squads) acquisition training began on the sixteenth day after arrival in the laboratory, for three more squads (B squads) on the seventeenth day, and so on. The A squads were run later in the day than the B squads, and so on, to ensure that in both acquisition and extinction all *S*s would be run at the same time each day. Following the last day of acquisition training, there were twelve extinction trials, all administered on the next day. The *S*s were confined to the goal box for 30 seconds on nonrewarded trials. If a rat failed to leave a particular alley section within 60 seconds, it was picked up and placed in the goal box, a time of 60 seconds being recorded for all untraversed sections. The ITI in acquisition ranged from 2 to 7 minutes, depending upon reward condition (L or S) and stage of training. In extinction the ITI ranged between 2 and 8 minutes, depending upon stage of training. The 12-gram daily diet minus the amount fed in the apparatus was given to *S* in the home cage 10 to 15 minutes after the last trial of each day.

Results

Differences between Groups SL, LS, and LL were not significant for total speed employing the last 3 days of acquisition ($F < 1$). An analysis was also performed in the case of each group, comparing T_1 speeds versus T_2 speeds as a check on discrimination. The T_1 versus T_2 speeds were compared in each group, employing the last 3 days of acquisition and the last day of acquisition (total of six comparisons). None of these differences approached significance, most yielding $F < 1$. Close inspection of individual *S* data, as opposed to the more general group analyses described above, also provided no consistent basis for inferring that discrimination between T_1 and T_2 occurred in either the SL or LS group. For every SL animal that was somewhat to considerably slower on T_1 than on T_2 on the last day of acquisition, there was an LL animal which performed in a more or less similar fashion. The same was true for the LS group; an LS animal running somewhat more slowly on T_2 than on T_1 could be matched with a corresponding LL animal. If one employed as still another yardstick for inferring discrimination the number of *S*s which ran differently on T_1 and T_2 in Groups SL and LS, however small the differences, the conclusion would be, if anything, that Group SL discriminated better than Group LS. On the last day of acquisition 9 of the 12 animals in Group SL were slower on T_1 than on T_2 (most of the differences, of course, were very small), but in Group LS only 5 of the 12 animals were slower on T_2 than on T_1 (most differences likewise being very small). The acquisition data, then, supply no basis for assuming that discrimination between T_1 and T_2 occurred either in Group SL or Group LS, although, perhaps, 1 or possibly 2 animals in each of these groups may have acquired some tendency to discriminate.

Figure 2 shows the extinction speeds for total for each of the three groups on each trial of extinction. The data shown in Fig. 2 could hardly be more straightforward: Group SL showed increased R to E, and Group LS showed no tendency toward greater R to E

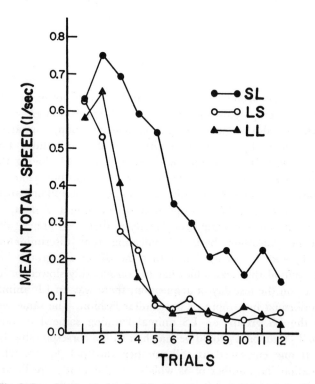

Fig. 2. Running speed of each of the three groups on each trial of extinction in total.

than Group LL. An analysis of the data shown in Fig. 2 indicated that the differences were highly significant for total ($F = 16.80$, $df = \frac{2}{33}$, $p < .001$), as were the differences in all alley sections.

Discussion: Experiment Two

That a varied magnitude group trained SL showed greater R to E than a consistently rewarded control group or LL is not difficult to understand in terms of either frustration or dissonance; indeed this result is expected. What is totally inexplicable within these frameworks, however, is that Group LS showed no tendency whatever toward increased R to E, much less showing R to E as great as that of Group SL. The finding for Group LS is unexplainable within the frustration-dissonance context because the experimental conditions made discrimination in this group unlikely, a conjecture supported by close examination of the acquisition data. Thus on small-reward trials Group LS should have experienced some frustration or dissonance and therefore should have demonstrated at least some increase in R to E. It showed none whatever, being no more resistant to extinction than Group LL. Even granting that Group LS experienced frustration or dissonance on small-reward trials, it therefore must be concluded that frustration or dissonance is not per se a sufficient condition for increasing R to E. The failure of these hypotheses to deal with the results of Experiment 2 cannot reasonably be considered as an isolated or discrete failure. First, as was shown earlier, the S–L transitions hypothesis is consistent with the total body of varied magnitude data, regular or irregular schedules, long or short ITI. Secondly, S–L transitions are obviously related to N–R transitions, and, as was shown, the N–R transitions hypothesis is consistent with the total body of partial reward magnitude data and the available body of reward schedule data as well (e.g., Capaldi, 1966). To view the frustration-dissonance failure to deal with the results of Experiment 2 as an isolated case would be, then, to ignore the implications of a truly impressive body of experimental data which has been accumulating for years, for example, see Grosslight, Hall, and Murnin, 1953.

Let us see why within the sequential framework S–L transitions are regarded as the locus of the varied magnitude effect. Under

S–L transitions, the stimulus produced by small reward or S^S occurs on the subsequent trial and is conditioned to the approach reaction (R_A) by means of large reward. Under L–S transitions, S^L is conditioned on the subsequent trial to R_A by means of small reward. First of all, then, the association $S^S–R_A$ in Group SL is stronger than the association $S^L–R_A$ in Group LS—S^S is conditioned by means of large as opposed to small reward. Secondly, the stimulus occurring in extinction or S^N is considered more similar to the stimulus S^S than to the stimulus S^L (Capaldi, 1967). Thus for two reasons, greater associative strength and similarity, S^N will receive more generalized associative strength from S^S than from S^L. In extinction, therefore, S^N will have a stronger capacity to evoke R_A when S–L transitions have occurred than when L–S transitions have occurred. In contrasting Group SL with Group LL, it is evident that S^S will be as strongly conditioned to R_A as will S^L. However, since S^N is more similar to S^S than to S^L, R to E will be greater in Group SL than in Group LL.

We complicate this simple picture somewhat when we include L–L transitions along with the S–L or L–S transitions, as in Experiment 2. Mainly, Group SL learns $S^L–R_A$ as well as $S^S–R_A$, and Group LS has S^L conditioned by large reward as well as by small reward. While this should serve perhaps to increase R to E in both groups (as opposed to either S–L or L–S transitions alone), it is still predicted within sequential theory that Group SL should show greater R to E than Group LS. That is, even under these conditions S^N is supplied greater generalized associative strength by S^S than by S^L (similarity). It should be noted that in Leonard's investigation, Group LS showed less R to E than Group LL, as predicted by sequential theory. This is predicted because, although S^L is conditioned to R_A in both groups, it is less strongly conditioned in Group LS than in Group LL (smaller reward magnitude). In the present experiment, R to E was as great in Group LS as in Group LL. It is perhaps clear from the sequential analysis that a reduction of differences between Group LS and Group LL should have occurred in Experiment 2. This is because in Experiment 2 on occasion Group LS had S^L conditioned to R_A by means of large reward, rather than, as in Leonard's investigation, only by means of small reward.

Experiment Three

Experiment 3 employed rather more complex sequential principles than the earlier experiments considered here, and we ask the reader who may not be entirely familiar with such principles to bear with us. The major purpose of Experiment 3 is to show, in a convincing manner, that incorporating large reward in a partial reward schedule may under some conditions reduce R to E, and severely so. Other purposes, more exploratory in character, will become clear as we go along. Let us take Leonard's (1969) investigation as our point of departure. Recall that Leonard, employing entirely regular schedules at three trials per day, found that a group trained SNL showed greater R to E than a group trained LNL. In sequential terms, both groups received the same magnitude of reward in the N–R transition (N–L) but different magnitudes of reward in the R–N transition (S–N versus L–N). Leonard also reported that a group trained SNS showed greater R to E than a group trained LNS. One interpretation of these findings is that the greater the reward magnitude in the R–N transition, the *less* the R to E. These findings, as Leonard observed, are diametrically opposed to the frustration-dissonance conceptualization of the reward magnitude variable, inasmuch as these hypotheses suggest that R to E is an increasing function of magnitude of partial reward. However, in what is by now a familiar story, Leonard's results were obtained employing massed trials and entirely regular schedules of reward, and thus would be rejected by both frustration and dissonance as tests of those hypotheses. One purpose of Experiment 3 was to determine the effects of magnitude of reward contained in the R–N transition when trials were spaced (minimum ITI = 20 minutes) and the reward schedule was irregular. However, the schedules employed in Experiment 3 were constructed with other purposes in mind, and thus the schedules were irregular only in the sense that they could not be learned by the rat. In order to understand these purposes, an example framed in terms of external stimuli rather than internal stimuli will prove useful.

Assume that an animal is rewarded in both a black alley and a white alley. Then R_A, the approach reaction, will come under the control of two different stimuli, S^B and S^W. Further, if the number of trials to black and white is equated and the reward magnitude in both alleys is the same, then, all else equal, the strength of the connections S^B–R_A and S^W–R_A will be the same. A similar analysis may be applied in connection with internal stimuli, for example, S^N. First, as has been made clear in other places (e.g., Capaldi, 1966), if a rewarded trial is preceded by three nonrewarded trials (NNNR), R to E will be greater than if only one nonrewarded trial precedes the rewarded trial (NR). This variable is called N-length by Capaldi (1964) and run-length by Gonzalez and Bitterman (1964). Assume that what happens over a series of nonrewarded trials is that S^N is progressively altered or modified. Represent the stimulus occasioned by a single nonreward as S^{N_1}, and that occasioned by three successive nonrewards as S^{N_3}. It can be seen that if one animal experiences NR we will have S^{N_1}–R_A and if another animal experiences NNNR we will have S^{N_3}–R_A. If, however, the same animal is trained NRNNNR, then it will learn S^{N_1}–R_A *and* S^{N_3}–R_A; that is, two somewhat different internal stimuli will acquire the capacity to evoke R_A (as in the black and white example). And, while the stimuli are different (say as different as black and white alleys), the capacity of each to evoke R_A is the same because S^{N_1} and S^{N_3} have been conditioned equally often by the same reward magnitude. But suppose we follow N by small reward and NNN by large reward (N S N N N L). Now the stimuli are not merely different, but S^{N_1} has a weaker capacity to evoke R_A (conditioned by means of S) than has S^{N_3} (conditioned by means of L).

Or suppose we do the opposite (N L N N N S). Now the connection S^{N_1}–R_A is stronger than the connection S^{N_3}–R_A, or the opposite of the case shown above.

There were four groups in the present study. This was arranged by preceding each of the schedules shown above either by LL or by SS. Both of the initial daily trials were rewarded (ie., LL or SS) in order to prevent the *S* from learning that reward was always followed by nonreward, i.e., to prevent discrimination.

In relation to the groups shown above, consider two sequential principles. First, R to E is a decreasing function of magnitude of reward contained in the R–N transition. Second, the longer the

N-length and the greater the capacity of the stimulus associated with the long N-length, for example, S^{N_2}, to evoke R_A, the greater will be R to E. Consider now two of the four groups shown above. In terms of the principles stated, the most resistant group should be SSNSNNNL—it has small reward in both of the R–N transitions and the long N-length (S^{N_3}) followed by large reward. The least resistant group should be LLNLNNNS. It has large reward in both of the R–N transitions, and S^{N_3} is conditioned to R_A only by means of small reward. Note, however, that the group trained LLNLNNNS experiences over-all larger magnitude of reward than the group trained SSNSNNNL (three daily L trials versus only one daily L trial) and thus would be expected within the frustration-dissonance framework to be the more resistant to extinction.

Methods

The 36 male rats, purchased from the Holtzman Company, were about 90 days old on arrival at the laboratory. They were randomly assigned to four groups of 9 Ss each.

The runway employed was of the same dimensions as in Experiments 1 and 2. A trial was begun as in those experiments.

The 20 Ss in the first replication (the 16 Ss in the second replication were at all points 5 days behind the first) were placed on deprivation about 3 weeks after arriving in the laboratory (12 grams per day.) On Days 10–13 after deprivation began, each S was handled for about 5 minutes and fed ten .045-gram pellets in the home cage, in addition to the daily diet. On Day 14 each S was given 10 minutes of alley exploration, the goal box being unbaited. On Days 15 and 16 each S was given a goal-box placement with two pellets reward. On Day 19 experimental training began.

All Ss received 9 days of acquisition training at eight trials each day, followed by 8 days of extinction training at eight trials each day. In acquisition and extinction, the Ss in a replication were run in rotation, no 2 Ss from the same group being run consecutively, the running order of Ss being varied daily, and the ITI never being allowed to fall below 20 minutes (often being longer). Large reward (L) consisted of eighteen pellets, small reward (S) of two pellets; on all nonrewarded (N) trials S was confined to the goal box for 30 seconds. On rewarded trials S was removed from the goal box immediately after having consumed the pellets.

The groups are designated on the basis of trial 1 reward magnitude (T_1, L, or S) and what is arbitrarily called T_2 reward magnitude, the reward magnitude given following the N-length of three. Thus Group SL was trained each day in acquisition, SSNSNNNL; Group SS, SSNLNNNS; Group LL, LLNSNNNL; and Group LS, LLNLNNNS. In extinction the S was allowed 60 seconds in each alley section. If S did not leave the start section within 180 seconds, it was placed in the goal box and a score of 60 seconds was assigned in each section; the S had 120 seconds to leave the run section and 60 seconds to leave the goal section.

Results

Differences in acquisition, particularly late acquisition, among the four groups were small and inconsequential; all groups ran equally fast. For example, an analysis of speeds on the last day of acquisition yielded $F < 1$ in each alley section and in total. Performance of the four groups on each of the days of extinction for the total measure is shown in Fig. 3. It can be seen that the groups were ordered from greatest to least R to E—SL, SS, LL, and LS—an ordering which was obtained in each alley section. An analysis employing the speeds shown in Fig. 3 indicated that large reward on T_1 significantly decreased R to E ($F = 10.61$, $df = 1/32$, $p < .005$) and that though large reward on T_2 increased R to E, this increase was not significant ($F = 1.03$).

Discussion: Experiment Three

The most indigestible result of Experiment 3 from a frustration-dissonance standpoint was that large reward on T_1 decreased R to E. Thus, the results of Experiment 3, obtained under conditions of fair spacing between trials (20 minutes) and schedules too irregular to be learned (at least they were not learned), support the results of Leonard, obtained under conditions of massed trials and regular

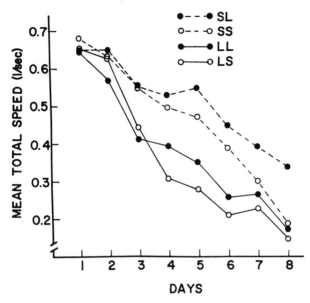

Fig. 3. Running speed of each of the four groups on each day of extinction in total.

schedules, which showed also that decreased R to E was associated with greater reward magnitude in the R–N transition.[5]

Within a sequential context, the role of reward magnitude in a so-called schedule of partial reinforcement is at least twofold. If large reward precedes nonreward (R–N transitions) it decreases R to E, and if large reward follows nonreward (N–R transitions) it increases R to E. Since a group trained (generally speaking) LNL shows greater R to E than a group trained SNS (e.g., Capaldi & Lynch, 1968; Leonard, 1969; Wagner, 1961; Experiment 1), it must obviously be assumed that the increasing effect on R to E of N–L transitions (relative to N–S transitions) exceeds the decreasing effect on R to E of L–N transitions (relative to S–N transitions).

---

[5] Recall that there was some tendency in Experiment 1 for Group LNS to show less R to E than Group SNS (two versus zero L–N transitions). The role of L–N transitions at a 24-hour ITI, rather than the 20-minute ITI employed in Experiment 3, is in need of further study—Experiment 1 was obviously not designed to assess this role.

It should be clear, then, that the greater R to E of LNL training relative to SNS training is the resultant or outcome of at least two interacting factors, one decreasing (R–N) and one increasing (N–R). By the same reasoning, it is also clear that the greater R to E of a so-called partial reward group, for example, RNR, relative to a consistently rewarded group, for example, RRR, is also the product or outcome of the same interacting factors—again the increasing effect on R to E of the N–R transition must considerably outweigh the decreasing effect on R to E of the R–N transition, or else there would not be any so-called PRE.

The sequential explanation of the decreasing effect on R to E of R–N transitions is as follows. Transitions of the R–N type generate inhibition. If the transition is L–N, S^L takes on inhibition and if the transition is S–N, S^S takes on inhibition. In R–N transitions, S^L takes on more inhibition than S^S—inhibition is greater the greater the reduction in reward magnitude. Inhibition generalizes from S^L (or S^S) to S^{N_1}, S^{N_2}, etc., the stimuli controlling the response in extinction. More inhibition generalizes to S^N from S^L than from S^S, thus L–N transitions more greatly weaken the capacity of S^N to evoke the reaction than do S–N transitions. Consequently, R to E is reduced more by L–N transitions than by S–N transitions.

The failure in Experiment 3 of groups receiving large reward following three N trials (SL and LL) to be significantly more resistant to extinction than groups receiving large reward following a single N trial (SS and LS) is, from a sequential viewpoint, disappointing (T_2 effects). However, the differences were in the proper direction: Group SL showed greater R to E than its control, Group SS; and Group LL showed greater R to E than its control, Group LS. Presumably, then, the sort of differences sought here might be obtained employing longer N-lengths, that is, longer than three. Of course, significant differences as a function of N-length and reward magnitude have been obtained previously under more simple experimental conditions than were employed here (Capaldi & Minkoff, in press).

One result of Experiment 3 which is rather surprising from a sequential viewpoint is that Group SS showed somewhat greater R to E than Group LL. Both groups, of course, had the same number of L–N transitions. However, Group LL had large reward following three nonrewards rather than one nonreward as did Group SS. If anything, then, on the basis of the analysis provided above, Group LL should have shown somewhat greater R to E than Group SS, or the opposite of what occurred. An intriguing possibility suggests itself as the cause of this discrepancy from sequential expectations. The L–N transition in Group SS consisted of only one prior large reward (SSNLNNNS), and the L–N transition of Group LL consisted of two prior large rewards (LLNSNNNL). Possibly, then, the greater the number of large rewards immediately preceding the nonreward, the greater the inhibition which is generated, and thus the less the R to E. There are other possibilities, but at present the one mentioned seems most plausible. It should be indicated that if the present assumption is correct, it would explain why the T_2 effects failed to achieve statistical significance here. It suggests too that when constructing a reward schedule, careful attention must be given to the possible effects of every trial contained in the schedule.

GENERAL DISCUSSION

General Comments

The construction of adequate theory demands as a first indispensable step the isolation of the experimental variables associated with the phenomena to be explained. The present results suggest that in the case of reward magnitude the specific variables are sequential in character. Of course, much evidence consistent with a sequential viewpoint on the effects of N–R or R–N transitions or other topics covered in this paper was previously available (e.g., Capaldi, 1966; 1967). The experimental information provided here, however, is particularly critical for several reasons. First, the particular sequential effects isolated here were demonstrated at long ITIs, supplementing and extending previous results of a similar kind reported under shorter ITIs. Thus the present results are not favorable either to the view that there is a massed trial PRE but not a spaced trial PRE (e.g., Gonzalez & Bitterman, 1969; Hull, 1952), or to the view that there are two different kinds of PRE, one for massed trials, the other for spaced trials (e.g., Amsel, 1967). Moreover, various sequential effects were demonstrated here under several different kinds of experimental conditions which effectively precluded the formation of a discrimination. Accordingly, the results reported here effectively dispose of the objection that sequential effects are artifacts of discrimination or anticipation (e.g., Lawrence & Festinger, 1962). It should not be overlooked that the experimental results reported here failed to confirm the reward magnitude conceptualizations offered by frustration and by dissonance, or more generally by the nonsequential-contiguity-motivational tradition. Rather, they support the views (e.g., Capaldi, 1966) that reward is necessary for learning, that the larger the reward magnitude the greater the learning, and that the reinforcement principle operates within a sequential context.

Recently Bitterman (1969), surveying the comparative data, fish and so on, has come to the conclusion expressed above, namely, that the comparative literature supports a strong principle of reinforcement. However, Bitterman also observed that because under consistent reward a small magnitude of reward produces greater R to E than a large magnitude of reward (in Bitterman's view the opposite is predicted by a hard principle of reinforcement), an anticipatory, or r_g, process must be assumed in the rat. Within a sequential context, at least, Bitterman's observation is not compelling. Consistent large and consistent small reward are conceptualized within sequential theory in terms of L–L and S–S transitions, respectively. It has been shown within sequential theory that S–S transitions should produce greater R to E than L–L transitions (e.g., Capaldi, 1967; Leonard, 1969). Clearly, then, anticipation or r_g is not necessary to an explanation of consistent reward effects. Furthermore, by employing the same sequential principles as are applied to S–S and L–L transitions, it is possible to explain available varied magnitude of reward data (i.e., SL versus LS, etc.), something which has not been accomplished within an anticipatory or r_g framework. Thus not only is anticipation, or r_g, not necessary to understanding consistent reward data, it is, within a more general context which includes varied reward data, not even feasible. In any event, specific interpretations of the results reported here have already been described. It would be profitable at this point to put these explanations in a broader context, examining their more general implications. This procedure should not only help to clarify differences between sequential theory and the more traditional, better understood nonsequential approach, but it should help as well to dispel various misconceptions which exist in connection with sequential theory.

Sequential Theory: An Acquisition Analysis

Extinction differences were predicted here by entertaining specific assumptions about what was learned in acquisition. As one example, in Experiment 2 it was assumed that while Group SL learned S^S–R_A (as well as S^L–R_A), Groups LS and LL learned S^L–R_A. In this connection, it should be noted that many consider that the sequential hypothesis is primarily an extinction theory. The error of this view is perhaps obvious. Within a sequential context the extinction measure provides the basis for inferring what the animal learned during the acquisition phase. It is simply not possible within a sequential context to entertain any prediction whatever about extinction without first identifying and specifying in reasonably precise terms what was learned in acquisition. If there is any point of difference with other hypotheses on this score, it is that extinction provides, at this time, a better measure for determining what was learned in acquisition than the relatively insensitive acquisition measure itself. As a matter of fact, the implications of sequential theory for acquisition constitute in effect what may be its most unique point of application, its major difference from nonsequential theories. A primary assumption of the sequential approach is that what the organism learns in acquisition is determined by the specific sequence in which trials are experienced. Sequence, then, is not merely a variable such as, for example, "drive," but rather sequence provides the framework within which the learning analysis is begun or undertaken and from which it proceeds. Put bluntly, organisms which experience different trial sequences literally learn different things, for example, associations, cognitions, and so on. This view, which cannot be overemphasized, follows directly from the proposition that different reward events, for instance, large reward, small reward, nonreward etc., have associated with them different and distinctive internal stimuli, such as S^L, S^S, S^N, etc. This being so, it is inescapable that the specific sequence in which reward events are experienced will determine what is learned. This view contrasts markedly, for example, with the nonsequential dissonance view that all animals which have received the same number of nonrewards (regardless of sequence) will show the same R to E because all have the same amount of dissonance reduction, that is, all have learned the same things.

Sequential vs. Nonsequential Theory: The Gap

What the suggestions of some investigators (e.g., Amsel, 1967; Black & Spence, 1965; Logan, 1968) amount to is that, in one way or another, it is possible for sequential and nonsequential theory to exist side by side, perhaps even to weave the two into a single over-all account of learning. Ultimately that may prove to be a proper view. However, the propositions described above, understood as we understand them, suggest that a wide gap exists between sequential and nonsequential theory, that the two are, not merely somewhat different, bur rather fundamentally incompatible. In our view, it is literally impossible, inconceivable, for the sequential theorist to employ the same language to describe learning as does the nonsequential theorist, much less to think about learning as he does, or to approach and design research as he does. From a sequential viewpoint the language, principles, and actual research of the nonsequential theorist at best are distantly related to the theoretical problems at hand and at worst are, with reference to those theoretical problems, actually misleading. These propositions can best be illustrated in terms of the research and issues dealt with in this paper; however, a too narrow identification of these propositions with the present research should be avoided by the reader.

First, the nonsequential theorist is apt to think and talk in terms of some entity called partial reward (or varied magnitude of reward, or discrimination learning, or negative contrast effects, etc.). No such category or categories exist or can exist (except as a complex compound) for the sequential theorist. He thinks rather in terms of transitions, R–N, N–R, R–R, etc., with partial reward being compounded out of the several transitions. Secondly, the nonsequential theorist is apt to think in terms of R to E as being increased by partial reward, or the negative contrast effect as being reduced by partial reward and so on (see Capaldi & Ziff, in press). The sequential theorist, on his part, thinks of partial reward, if he thinks of it at all, as having a variety of effects, for example, R–N transitions decrease R to E, N–R transitions increase R to E, and so on. From this standpoint, as previously indicated, a PRE occurs because the increasing effect on R to E of N–R transitions exceeds the decreasing effect on R to E of R–N transitions, the resultant or outcome being a PRE. Thirdly, a nonsequential theorist appears to think that what happens under one schedule of partial reward, usually an irregular one, will also happen under another schedule of partial reward. Witness such statements as partial reward increases R to E, or partial reward reduces the negative contrast effect, and so on. Obviously, the sequential theorist does not and could not generalize on the basis of some undifferentiated compound called partial reward. The sequential theorist generalizes on the basis of transitions. Generalization aside, in many cases it is difficult or impossible to determine even what variable produced the experimental findings which are reported by the nonsequential theorist. For example, the task of relating the Hulse-Wagner finding to magnitude of reward contained in the N–R transition required considerable experimental and conceptual effort, inasmuch as the experimental conditions employed in these investigations were such that a variety of factors interacted, sometimes in antagonistic ways. In this connection, if one will take the trouble to examine a nonsequential investigation through the eyes of a sequential theorist, he will at least recognize why the experiment seems, in the sequential context, to be highly uncontrolled. Plainer words are required to describe the actual situation. The truth of the matter is that when a nonsequential investigation is viewed within a sequential context, one literally sees, not a well-controlled laboratory study, but rather an irrelevant, misleading, concatenated task of possibly consummate complexity, differentiated from real-life learning situations, such as learning in the classroom, only to a degree. That is why, typically, it is so difficult, at least initially, to understand a nonsequential investigation from the standpoint of sequential theory. Many may think that this difficulty of understanding is related to the relatively underdeveloped form of sequential theory. To some extent that is true; the sequential approach is only at the beginning stages of its development. But that is not the whole story. A substantial part of the story is certainly that the nonsequential theorist, starting from inappropriate assumptions, produces an experimental design which is, in a real sense, uninterpretable, which contains variables which must be unconfounded before it can be made inteptable. More specifically, the sequential theorist would not ask how magnitude of partial reward affects R to E but rather how magnitude of reward contained in the N–R transition affects R to E. The question asked as a sequential theorist would ask it eliminates from the outset the experimental contamination produced by R–N, R–R, and N–N transitions.

The nonsequential theorist, on his part, perceives the typical sequential investigation as artificial and overly structured to the point of allowing irrelevant factors (e.g., anticipation or discrimination) to intrude. The reason for the differing perceptions of sequential and nonsequential theorists is, of course, obvious. The two views employ different and probably fundamentally incompatible units of theoretical analysis; thus they begin by asking different questions. The nonsequential theorist thinks of numbers of trials, rewarded and nonrewarded, and combinations of these which regulate the growth of particular processes, for example, r_g. The sequential theorist, having different units of theoretical analysis, the transitions, directs his attention to trial-to-trial events. He does so because animals experiencing different trial sequences will literally learn different things. In effect, the transitions are elementary analytic units, the constituent elements which comprise more complex learning situations. The sequential theorist is interested, and necessarily so, in the effects of these elements singly and in combination.

However artificial or highly structured the experiments reported here may seem to the nonsequential theorist, they are but distantly related to the sorts of experiments which seem most appropriate in a sequential context. The present experiments are, in a word, not structured enough to satisfy a sequential theorist. Such experiments as were performed here were done mainly to make contact with the more orthodox body of nonsequential theory. Experiment 1 is a good case in point. It should not be seen, even remotely, as a definitive experimental attempt to determine the effects of N–L versus N–S transitions. Experiment 1, of course, provided information about this point—information which is probably all right as far as it goes. How far it goes, however, is problematical. At this time, Experiment 1 (and the other studies reported here) are probably best construed as providing information concerning the effects of N–L versus N–S transitions when these have occurred in the context of other transitions, that is, under condtions which at this time must be regarded as complex. What the effects of the other transitions may have been on the N–L and N–S transitions is indeterminate at the moment. For example, Experiment 1 may have concealed certain effects that N–L and N–S transitions may have under other circumstances. Or N–L and N–S transitions may have the effects ascribed to them in Experiment 1 only when accompanied by the other transitions. There are, of course, other alternatives. These observations imply that we need to determine the effects of the transitions under a wide variety of circumstances. After many determinations of the sort described have occurred, we may find it profitable and feasible to specify in greater detail what occurs in connection with certain currently employed complex tasks. Among them we would include irregular reward schedules, irregular presentation of S$^+$ and S$^-$ in discrimination tasks, and so on. The idea here, of course, is the rather simple one that analysis must precede synthesis, and analysis within sequential theory proceeds from the framework of the transitions.

REFERENCES

Amsel, A. The role of frustrative nonreward in noncontinuous reward situations. *Psychol. Bull.*, 1958, **55**, 102–119.

Amsel, A. Frustrative nonreward in partial reinforcement and discrimination learning: Some recent history and a theoretical extension. *Psychol. Rev.*, 1962, **69**, 306–328.

Amsel, A. Partial reinforcement effects on vigor and persistence. In K. W. Spence & J. T. Spence (Eds.), *The psychology of learning and motivation: Advances in research and theory.* Vol. 1. New York: Academic Press, 1967. Pp. 1–65.

Anderson, N. Comparison of different populations: Resistance to extinction and transfer. *Psychol. Rev.*, 1963, **70**, 162–179.

Bitterman, M. E. Thorndike and the problem of animal intelligence. *Amer. Psychologist*, 1969, **24**, 444–453.

Black, R. W., & Spence, K. W. Effects of intertrial reinforcement on resistance to extinction following extended training. *J. exp. Psychol.*, 1965, **70**, 559–563.

Capaldi, E. J. Effect of N-length, number of different N-lengths and number of reinforcements on resistance to extinction. *J. exp. Psychol.*, 1964, **68**, 230–239.

Capaldi, E. J. Partial reinforcement: A hypothesis of sequential effects. *Psychol. Rev.*, 1966, **73**, 459–477.

Capaldi, E. J. A sequential hypothesis of instrumental learning. In K. W. Spence & J. T. Spence (Eds.), *The psychology of learning and motivation: Advances in research and theory*. Vol. 1. New York: Academic Press, 1967. Pp. 67–156.

Capaldi, E. J. Memory and learning: A sequential viewpoint. In W. Honig & N. Mackintosh (Eds.), *Dalhousie symposium on animal memory*. In press.

Capaldi, E. J., & Lynch, D. Repeated shifts in reward magnitude: Evidence in favor of an associational and absolute (noncontextual) interpretation. *J. exp. Psychol.*, 1967, **75**, 226–235.

Capaldi, E. J., & Lynch, A. D. Magnitude of partial reward and resistance to extinction: Effect of N–R transitions. *J. comp. physiol. Psychol.*, 1968, **65**, 179–181.

Capaldi, E. J., & Minkoff, R. Influence of order of occurrence of nonreward and large and small reward on acquisition and extinction. *J. exp. Psychol.*, in press.

Capaldi, E. J., & Spivey, J. E. Effect of goal-box similarity on the aftereffect of nonreinforcement and resistance to extinction. *J. exp. Psychol*, 1963, **66**, 461–465.

Capaldi, E. J., & Ziff, D. R. Effect of schedule of partial reward on the negative contrast effect. *J. comp. physiol. Psychol.*, in press.

Gonzalez, R. C., & Bitterman, M. E. Resistance to extinction in the rat as a function of percentage and distribution of reinforcement. *J. comp. physiol. Psychol.*, 1964, **58**, 258–263.

Gonzalez, R. C., & Bitterman, M. E. Spaced-trials partial reinforcement effect as a function of contrast. *J. comp. physiol. Psychol.*, 1969, **67**, 94–103.

Grosslight, J. H., Hall, J. R., & Murnin, J. Patterning effects in partial reinforcement. *J. exp. Psychol.*, 1953, **46**, 103–106.

Hull, C. L. *Principles of behavior*. New York: Appleton, 1943.

Hull, C. L. *A behavior system*. New Haven: Yale University Press, 1952.

Hulse, S. H. Amount and percentage of reinforcement and duration of goal confinement in conditioning and extinction. *J. exp. Psychol.*, 1958, **56**, 48–57.

Lawrence, D. H., & Festinger, L. *Deterrents and reinforcement*. Stanford, California: Stanford University Press, 1962.

Leonard, D. W. Amount and sequence of reward in partial and continuous reinforcement. *J. comp. physiol. Psychol.*, 1969, **67**, 204–211.

Logan, F. A. *Incentive*. New Haven: Yale University Press, 1960.

Logan, F. A. Incentive theory and changes in reward. In K. W. Spence & J. T. Spence (Eds.), *The psychology of learning and motivation: Advances in research and theory*. Vol. 2. New York: Academic Press, 1968. Pp. 1–30.

Logan, F. A., Beier, E. M., & Kincaid, W. D. Extinction following partial and varied reinforcement. *J. exp. Psychol.*, 1956, **52**, 65–70.

Marx, M. H., & Edwards, D. C. Speed of nonreinforced running response following increasing and decreasing orders of sucrose concentrations. *J. exp. Psychol.*, 1966, **71**, 160–161.

Marx, M. H., Tombaugh, J. W., Cole, C., & Dougherty, D. Persistence of non-reinforced responding as a function of the direction of a prior ordered incentive shift. *J. exp. Psychol.*, 1963, **66**, 542–546.

Sheffield, V. F. Extinction as a function of partial reinforcement and distribution of practice. *J. exp. Psychol.*, 1949, **39**, 511–526.

Spence, K. W. *Behavior theory and conditioning.* New Haven: Yale University Press, 1956.

Spence, K. W. *Behavior theory and learning.* Englewood Cliffs, New Jersey: Prentice-Hall, 1960.

Wagner, A. R. Effects of amount and percentage of reinforcement and number of acquisition trials on conditioning and extinction. *J. exp. Psychol.*, 1961, **62**, 234–242.

Index